ENVIRONMENTAL LAW
AND SUSTAINABILITY

宝库山精选：环境保护法律与可持续性

Digital editions
Environmental Law and Sustainability is available through most major e-book and database services (please check with them for pricing).

For information, contact:
Berkshire Publishing Group LLC
122 Castle Street
Great Barrington, Massachusetts 01230-1506 USA
www.berkshirepublishing.com
Printed in the United States of America

Library of Congress Cataloging-in-Publication Data

Environmental law and sustainability / editors, Klaus Bosselmann, Daniel S. Fogel, J.B. Ruhl.
    pages cm.—(Berkshire essentials)
   Includes bibliographical references and index.
   ISBN 978-1-61472-991-4 (pbk. : alk. paper)—ISBN 978-1-61472-951-8 (ebook)
   1. Environmental law, International. 2. Sustainable development—Law and legislation. I. Bosselmann, Klaus. II. Fogel, Daniel S. III. Ruhl, J. B.
   K3583.E58 2013
   344.04'6,—dc23   2013039151

BERKSHIRE 宝库山

Essentials

ENVIRONMENTAL LAW
AND SUSTAINABILITY

宝库山精选：环境保护法律与可持续性

Editors Klaus Bosselmann, Daniel S. Fogel, J.B. Ruhl, *et al.*

Ш BERKSHIRE
A global point of reference

About *Environmental Law and Sustainability*

Environmental Law and Sustainability, a Berkshire Essential, introduces environmental regulations and agreements from around the world, with a focus on those with the most potential for international impact. This concise handbook, designed for use in classrooms at the high school and college level, also compares legal systems between nations such as the United States and Canada; Australia and New Zealand; and India, Pakistan, and China, allowing readers to see how environmental laws are enacted—and enforced—differently around the globe. Other topics include biotechnology and nanotechnology legislation, and the "polluter pays" principle, a key aspect of international environmental policy.

THE **BERKSHIRE** *Essentials* SERIES

Berkshire Sustainability Essentials, distilled from the *Berkshire Encyclopedia of Sustainability*, take a global approach to environmental law, energy, business strategies and management, industrial ecology, and religion, among other topics.

- Religion and Sustainability
- Business Strategies and Management for Sustainability
- Energy Resources and Sustainability
- Energy Industries and Sustainability
- Ecosystem Services for Sustainability
- Environmental Law and Sustainability
- Finance and Investment for Sustainability
- Industrial Ecology and Sustainability

Distilled for
the classroom
from Berkshire's
award-winning
encyclopedias

BERKSHIRE ESSENTIALS from the *Berkshire Encyclopedia of China* and the *Berkshire Encyclopedia of World History, 2nd Edition* also available.

Contents

About Berkshire Essentials

For more than a decade, Berkshire Publishing has collaborated with a worldwide network of scholars and editors to produce award-winning academic resources on popular subjects for a discerning audience. The "Berkshire Essentials" series are collections of concentrated content, inspired by requests from teachers, curriculum planners, and professors who praise the encyclopedic approach of Berkshire's reference works, but who still crave single volumes for course use.

Each Essentials series draws from Berkshire publications on a big topic—world history, Chinese studies, and environmental sustainability, for instance—to provide thematic volumes that can be purchased alone, in any combination, or as a set. Teachers will find the insightful articles indispensable for stimulating classroom discussion or independent study. Students, professionals, and general readers all will find the articles invaluable when exploring a line of research or an abiding interest.

These affordable books are available in paperback as well as ebook formats for convenient reading on mobile devices.

Editors, Editorial Advisory Board, and Production Staff

Editors

The following people served as Editors for the sources of these articles (all from the *Berkshire Encyclopedia of Sustainability*):

From Volume 1, *The Spirit of Sustainability:* Willis Jenkins, General Editor, *Yale University;* Whitney Bauman, *Florida International University*

From Volume 2, *The Business of Sustainability:* Chris Laszlo, General Editor, *Case Western Reserve University;* Karen Christensen, *Berkshire Publishing Group;* Daniel S. Fogel, *Wake Forest University;* Gernot Wagner, Environmental Defense Fund; Peter Whitehouse, *Case Western Reserve University*

From Volume 3, *The Law and Politics of Sustainability:* Klaus Bosselmann, *University of Auckland,* Daniel S. Fogel, *Wake Forest University,* J.B. Ruhl, *Vanderbilt University Law School*

From Volume 4, *Natural Resources and Sustainability:* Daniel E. Vasey, General Editor, *Divine Word College,* Sarah E. Fredericks, *University of North Texas,* Lei Shen, *Chinese Academy of Sciences,* Shirley Thompson, *University of Manitoba*

Editorial Advisory Board

Ray Anderson, *Interface, Inc.;* Lester Brown, *Earth Policy Institute;* Robert Costanza, *University of Vermont;* Luis Gomez-Echeverri, *United Nations Development Programme;* John Elkington, *SustainAbility;* Daniel Kammen, *University of California, Berkeley;* Ashok Khosla, *International Union for Conservation of Nature;* and Christine Loh, *Civic Exchange, Hong Kong*

Production Staff

Project Coordinator
Bill Siever

Copy Editors
Linda Aspen-Baxter
Mary Bagg
Kathy Brock

Carolyn Haley
Barbara Resch
Elma Sanders
Chris Yurko

Editorial Assistants
Echo Bergquist

David Gagne
Ellie Johnston

Designer
Anna Myers

Introduction—Environmental Law and Sustainability

Many nations have enacted and strengthened regulations to protect the environment since the 1960s, and numerous international environmental treaties have also been adopted. The realities of economics are often part of these laws; many are subject to cost-benefit analysis and enforced with financial programs (such as cap and trade) and taxes.

While sustainability has been criticized as vague or ambiguous, it has nevertheless become "an established principle of international law" and is on the verge of "general acceptance as a norm of customary international law" (Gillroy 2006, 13). The concept of sustainability is also widely invoked as a touchstone of environmental laws adopted by individual nations.

Interpretations of Sustainability Affecting Law and Policy

The classic articulation of sustainable development appears in the 1987 Report of the World Commission on Environment and Development (commonly referred to as the Brundtland Report): "meeting the needs of the present without compromising the ability of future generations to meet their own needs." In June 1992, international negotiations through the United Nations Environment Programme (UNEP) resulted in the Rio Declaration and elaborated on this definition. The Rio Declaration recognized the "integral and interdependent nature of the Earth, our home" and articulated twenty-seven principles to advance economic development, environmental protection, and respect for human rights, all under the rubric of sustainable development. At the core of sustainability is the principle of intergenerational equity, a duty to preserve or enhance resources that may be necessary for

future generations of humans while providing adequately for those living in the present. Also of central importance is the principle of intragenerational equity, a duty to ensure justice among communities and nations in the present generation. The Rio Declaration interpreted this duty to include special solicitude for the economic needs and environmental concerns of developing nations (UNEP 1992, Principle 6) and recognition of the environmental and cultural claims of indigenous peoples (Principle 22). Ecocentrists, who believe species or ecosystems have value in their own right, have also argued for recognition of interspecies equity as a principle of sustainability, but that principle has found limited acceptance in public debate and legislation (Bosselman 2006). Other Rio Declaration principles of special relevance to environmental law include: citizen participation, including "access to judicial and administrative proceedings" (Principle 10); the "precautionary approach" (Principle 15); the use of economic instruments in environmental protection (Principle 16); and the "polluter-pays" principle (Principle 16).

There remain basic disagreements about the obligations associated with sustainability as affecting environmental law and policy (Revesz and Livermore 2008). The international-law scholar Edith Brown Weiss argues that the present generation has a duty to pass along the natural (and cultural) environment in as good condition as we found it (Weiss 1989). We also have a duty to preserve the diversity of the resource base. Renewable resources— plants, animals, soil, water and air—should be used sustainably; nonrenewable resources should be conserved by using them more efficiently and, where they are depleted or destroyed, by providing substitutes for them for use by future generations.

The economist Robert Solow argues for a less restrictive interpretation: our obligation is only "to conduct ourselves so that we leave to the future the option or the capacity to be as well off as we are" (2000, 132). This obligation is measured in terms "generalized capacity to create well-being, not any particular thing or any particular natural resource" (Solow 2000, 133). Solow acknowledges that we might choose to preserve certain resources—for example, a species or a landscape—because of their intrinsic value to us, but generally we are free to consume natural resources as long as we replace them with resources of equal or greater value, such as manufacturing capacity or technological knowledge. Solow endorses environmental protection as one way to advance this notion of sustainability, but not at the expense of other forms of investment that would offer greater capacity for future well-being. Contemporary environmental law embodies elements of both these constructions of sustainability.

Modern Environmental and Natural Resource Law

From the late 1960s and on into the twenty-first century, the United States and other nations have enacted or strengthened regulatory laws to assess the environmental impacts of government decisions, control air and water pollution, address sites contaminated by toxic waste, and manage introduction of toxic substances and materials into the environment from pesticides and other products. During this same period, many nations also enacted or strengthened laws to protect natural resources such as species, wetlands, forests, and fisheries. Important international treaties addressing transnational or global environmental issues were concluded during the same period, including the Montreal Protocol (depletion of the ozone layer), the Basel Convention (transboundary movement of hazardous waste), the Ramsar Convention (wetlands and waterfowl), CITES (Convention on International Trade in Endangered Species of Wild Fauna and Flora), the Biodiversity Convention (biodiversity conservation and sustainable use), and UNCLOS (United Nations Convention on the Law of the Sea). In the last two decades, the international community has taken initial steps to deal with global climate change with the UN Framework Convention on Climate Change and the Kyoto Protocol, which entered into force in 2005 and includes the first binding commitments for reduction of greenhouse gas emissions by developed nations.

Much of the national and international environmental law of the last four decades embodies the polluter-pays principle, the idea, as the Rio Declaration states, that "the polluter should, in principle, bear the cost of pollution" (UNEP 1992, Principle 16).

Most environmental laws impose restrictions on emissions, discharges, or other environmental intrusions by actors such as corporations, government entities, or individuals, which must shoulder the cost of meeting those restrictions. Some impose liability for damages on agents of environmental harm; an example is the United States' Comprehensive Environmental Response, Compensation, and Liability Act, which makes parties liable for the costs of cleaning up environmental contamination attributable to them. Pollution taxes are another form of polluter-pays provision to the extent that the tax reflects the costs of pollution imposed on others. These polluter-pays provisions advance the Rio principles by forcing firms and individuals to internalize the costs of environmental damage. But some governmental programs use subsidies to advance environmental goals, effectively paying the polluter not to pollute. An example is provisions of the US Farm Bill that pay farmers to reduce polluted runoff into lakes and rivers.

In the first wave of environmental law in the 1960s and 1970s, the favored approach was prescriptive: regulators specified a control technology or assigned a permissible level of pollution for each source. The level of pollution permitted might be based on the expected performance of an available control technology or on a desired environmental outcome, such as avoiding harm to fish habitat. This approach is often characterized as "command and control," because it includes both a prescriptive "command" to each source and the threat of civil or criminal enforcement ("control") if the command is not met. In part because of the limited compliance options it offers sources, commentators have criticized command-and-control regulation as inefficient and have advanced market-based alternatives such as "cap and trade" or pollution taxes (Ackerman and Stewart 1985).

Cap and trade has recently gained prominence in environmental law as an alternative approach to command and control and appears to be emerging as the instrument of choice to address global climate change. Under cap-and-trade programs, lawmakers set a cap on permissible emissions for a region or nation (or the globe in the case of climate change). Emission allowances are issued in the amount of the cap and may be freely traded among regulated sources; all sources must hold allowances at least equal to their emissions. Emitters for whom emissions reductions are relatively cheap can be expected to undertake reductions rather than buy allowances, and emitters for whom the reverse is true can be expected to

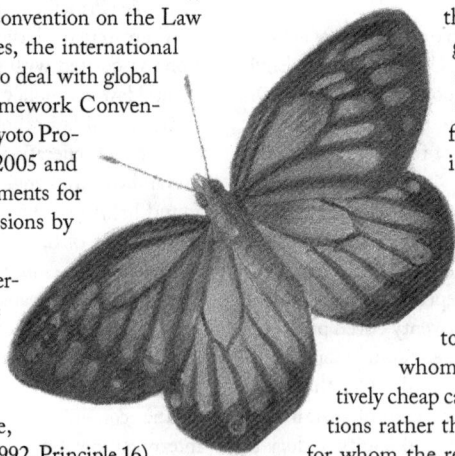

buy allowances rather than make reductions. The predicted result is that the trading of allowances will produce the most cost-effective allocation of reductions consistent with achieving the desired emission reduction goal. The Rio Declaration endorses the use of economic instruments of this sort, although some commentators have criticized cap and trade as undermining the polluter-pays principle by allowing polluters to purchase allowances (sometimes pejoratively referred to as "licenses to pollute") to meet their obligations (Kelman 1981b).

In the United States, the first national scale application of environmental cap and trade was the regime for reduction of sulfur dioxide emissions from power plants under the 1990 Clean Air Act Amendments; it is widely considered to have been successful in substantially reducing sulfur dioxide emissions at much lower cost than initially projected. The US Environmental Protection Agency (EPA) has extended the cap-and-trade approach to other air pollutants, such as nitrogen oxide and fine particulate matter, as well as to water discharges. Cap and trade is emerging as the instrument of choice to address global climate change both at the national and international level, although the alternative of emission taxes continues to have advocates. The Kyoto Protocol allows trading of greenhouse gas emissions allowances among the developed nations that are parties to the agreement (Article 17) and also provides for the creation of marketable emissions allowances by developing nations that are not parties (Article 12). The European Union Emissions Trading Scheme (EU ETS), established under the Kyoto Protocol, is the world's largest cap-and-trade system (Stavins 2007). Domestic legislation on climate change in the United States also appears likely to adopt a cap-and-trade approach.

There is vigorous dispute over the role of cost-benefit analysis in setting environmental law goals. Economists such as Solow argue that the policy touchstone should be welfare maximization with no special preference for the preservation of existing natural resources or levels of environmental quality. Resources are presumed to be fungible (Solow 1993). In making policy choices, the costs and benefits of options for government regulation or other protective measures are quantified and monetized to the extent possible, and this analysis is used to determine an optimal level of environmental protection where the marginal benefits of protection equal or exceed the marginal costs. Although few US environmental laws expressly base their regulatory goals on cost-benefit justification, a long-standing executive order requires that all major regulatory actions by federal agencies be accompanied by cost-benefit analyses reviewable by the Office of Management and Budget (OMB 2007). The European Union, according to Article 174(3) of the European Community Treaty, also requires consideration of benefits and costs in adopting new regulations, although it has placed less institutional emphasis on such analyses

There are numerous criticisms of cost-benefit analysis as a method for setting environmental and other public law goals, including the argument that placing prices on nonmarket goods, such as a human life or a wilderness, is immoral commodification. Critics also argue that features of cost-benefit analysis as it has been practiced in the United States result in systematic under-regulation. But in their book *Retaking Rationality* Richard Revesz and Michael Livermore (2008) contend that by correcting eight fallacies in current practice, the cost-benefit approach can provide a neutral way of systematically assessing alternative environmental goals.

Another approach to setting environmental goals is the precautionary principle, recognized by the international community in the Rio Declaration and also by Europe in the European Community Treaty. It is far less prominent in US policy deliberations. The Rio Declaration states a version of the principle: in the face of potentially serious or irreversible environmental harms, "lack of full scientific certainty shall not be used as a reason for postponing cost-effective measures to prevent environmental degradation" (UNEP 1992, Principle 15). Although the precautionary principle is not exclusive of other principles, such as consideration of costs and benefits, it is generally understood to give more weight to avoiding environmental risks than cost-benefit analysis (Fogel 2003). A recent comparative study of US and European environmental regulations, however, indicates that European regulations (presumably more influenced by the precautionary principle) and US regulations do not differ significantly in their stringency and show signs of convergence over time (Wiener 2003).

Citizen participation is a procedural principle often associated with sustainable practice. The Rio Declaration defines it to include access to information held by public authorities and also "access to judicial and administrative proceedings, including redress and remedy" (UNEP 1992, Principle 10). The 1996 United Nations Convention to Combat Desertification was the first global environmental legal instrument to require that decisions be made with the participation of those affected. (Holtz 1996, Article 3). The transnational North American Agreement on Environmental Cooperation allows citizens to file submissions claiming that a party nation is failing to enforce its environmental law (NAAEC 1993, Article 14). In the United States, major environmental laws authorize "any person" to pursue a judicial action against the government for failing to carry out its mandates under the laws or against others for violating restrictions imposed by the laws.

Jonathan Z. CANNON
University of Virginia School of Law

FURTHER READING

Ackerman, Bruce A., & Stewart, Richard B. (1985, May). Reforming environmental law. *Stanford Law Review, 37*(5), 1333–1365.

Ackerman, Frank, & Heinzerling, Lisa. (2004). *Priceless: On knowing the price of everything and the value of nothing.* New York: The New Press.

Bosselman, Klaus. (2006). Ecological justice and law. In Benjamin J. Richardson & Stepan Wood (Eds.), *Environmental law for sustainability* (pp. 129–164). Oxford, UK: Hart Publishing.

Consolidated Version of the Treaty Establishing the European Community. (2006). *Official Journal of the European Union.* (C321E) 37. Retrieved August 6, 2009 from http://eur-lex.europa.eu/LexUriServ/LexUriServ.do?uri=OJ:C:2006:321E:0001:0331:EN:PDF

Gillroy, John Martin. (2006). Adjudication norms, dispute settlement regimes and international tribunals: The status of environmental sustainability in international jurisprudence. *Stanford Journal of International Law, 42*(1), 1–52.

Holtz, Uwe. (1996). *United Nations Convention to Combat Desertification (UNCCD) and its political dimension.* Retrieved September 24, 2008, from http://www.unccd.int/parliament/data/bginfo/PDUNCCD(eng).pdf

Kelman, Steven. (1981a, January-February). Cost-benefit analysis: An ethical critique. *Journal on Government and Society Regulation, 5,* 33–40.

Kelman, Steven. (1981b). *What price incentives?: Economists and the environment.* Boston: Auburn House.

Kyoto Protocol to the United Nations Framework Convention on Climate Change. (1998). Retrieved September 24, 2008, from http://unfccc.int/kyoto_protocol/items/2830.php

North American Agreement on Environmental Cooperation (NAAEC). (1993). Retrieved April 20, 2009, from http://www.cec.org/pubs_info_resources/law_treat_agree/naaec/index.cfm?varlan=english

Office of Management and Budget (OMB). (2007, January 18). Executive Order 12866 of September 30, 1993, as amended by E.O. 13258 of February 26, 2002 and E.O. 13422 of January 18, 2007: Regulatory planning and review. Retrieved September 24, 2008, from http://64.233.169.104/search?q=cache:XPW6yuHjeocJ:www.whitehouse.gov/omb/inforeg/eo12866/eo12866_amended_01-

Report of the World Commission on Environment and Development. (1987, December 11). Retrieved September 24, 2008, from http://www.un.org/documents/ga/res/42/ares42-187.htm

Revesz, Richard L., & Livermore, Michael. (2008). *Retaking rationality: How cost-benefit can better protect the environment and our health.* New York: Oxford University Press.

Richardson, Benjamin J., & Wood, Stepan. (2006). Environmental law for sustainability. In Benjamin J. Richardson & Stepan Wood (Eds.), *Environmental law for sustainability* (pp. 1–18). Oxford, UK: Hart Publishing.

Solow, Robert M. (2000). Sustainability: An economist's perspective. In Robert N. Stavins (Ed.), *Economics of the environment: Selected readings* (4th ed., pp.131–138). New York: Norton.

Stavins, Robert. (2007, October). *A US cap-and-trade system to address climate change* (Discussion paper 2007-13). Washington, DC: The Brookings Institution. Retrieved September 24, 2008, from http://belfercenter.ksg.harvard.edu/files/rwp_07_052_stavins.pdf

United Nations Environment Programme (UNEP). (1992). *Rio declaration on environment and development.* Retrieved September 24, 2008, from http://www.unep.org/Documents.Multilingual/Default.asp?DocumentID=78&ArticleID=1163

Weiss, Edith Brown. (1989). *In fairness to future generations: International law, common patrimony, and intergenerational equity.* Ardsley, NY: Transnational Publishers.

Wiener, Jonathan B. (2003). Whose precaution after all? A comment on the comparison and evolution of risk regulatory systems. *Duke Journal of Comparative and International Law, 13,* 207–262. Retrieved April 20, 2009, from http://www.nicholas.duke.edu/solutions/documents/whose_precaution_after_all.pdf

Though barely out of its infancy, the science of conservation biology is taking its first steps toward a comprehension of biodiversity. It is able to identify species that are indicators or keystones for an entire ecosystem. . . . It can offer a crude measure for the overall health of the earth. For when the natural variety of species in a habitat declines, it is highly likely that the associated condition of the land, air, water, and food chain in that location is also declining. The necessity of a healthy environment, therefore, is helplessly intertwined with the importance of natural species diversity. Only life possesses both the ability and the liability to reflect fundamental environmental change. This is why biodiversity law will inevitably become the central tenet of environmental law.

WILLIAM J. SNAPE

Source: William J. Snape. (Ed.). (1996). *Biodiversity and the Law,* p. xxi. Washington, DC: Island Press.

Biotechnology Legislation

The way in which the international community governs biotechnology will significantly influence whether it achieves its great potential for contributing to sustainable development. Currently, sustainability principles are explicitly incorporated in only a few of the international regulations that are applicable to biotechnology. Provisions in some of the other regulations are broadly compatible with sustainability principles, but such provisions are poorly implemented.

Science and technology are essential contributors to sustainable development efforts: "It is not an exaggeration to assert that without science there can be no sustainable development" (UN Commission on Sustainable Development 1995, Point 7). Science and technology have the potential to substantially contribute to the development of environmentally sound technologies, improved health and food security, adapted agricultural inputs and practices, better resource management, and many other issues of sustainability. Biotechnology, as defined by the UN General Assembly (2003), is "a collection of techniques or processes that employ organisms or their units to develop useful products or services." Biotechnology is a key field with respect to the issues of sustainability. The way it is governed internationally has implications for sustainability—either facilitating or impeding it—because governance influences the pace and direction of scientific advances as well as who can access and benefit from them.

At the international level, biotechnology legislation consists of a range of international regulations, including voluntary standards, guidelines and codes, and legally binding treaties. While their legal status varies, all of these types of rules are used by states to govern their behavior.

The international rules that apply to biotechnology mainly address areas where major applications and impacts of biotechnology coincide with a high degree of international interdependence, such that individual state action is insufficient to effectively address an issue of common concern (e.g., protection of the environment). Several areas of governance meet this definition including arms control, drugs control, environmental protection, health and disease control, social and ethical impacts of human genetics, and trade. These areas overlap and interconnect in their coverage of biotechnology, and within these areas at least thirty-seven relevant regulations are identifiable.

Brief History and Key Framing Documents

The importance of science and technology to sustainability has been recognized internationally for nearly forty years. Their role is repeatedly emphasized in key international documents on environment and development and on sustainable development, including the 1972 Stockholm Declaration of the United Nations Conference on the Human Environment, Our Common Future: Report of the World Commission on Environment and Development, the 1992 Rio Declaration on Environment and Development, Agenda 21, and the Malmö Ministerial Declaration.

International biotechnology legislation has developed largely by default rather than by design. The applicable regulations do not share a common developmental history. Their adoption dates range from 1925 to 2008, which means they were adopted in different historical contexts, some prior to both the major scientific advances of the biotechnology revolution (e.g., the development of genetic engineering, genome sequencing techniques) and the international articulations of sustainability. Principles of sustainability, however, have been deliberately incorporated into some of the regulations developed since 1992.

Science, Technology, and Sustainability

The international community has recognized the importance of science and technology to sustainability efforts. As stated by the UN Commission on Sustainable Development (1995): "The new forces of modern science and technology, if harnessed properly . . . offer immense possibilities for solving many of the complicated problems that are currently impeding economic, social and environmentally sound and sustainable development." Continuing to promote technological and scientific advances in all countries is a necessity in the twenty-first century.

The international community's work on sustainable development emphasizes both the potential contributions of science and technology to sustainability and the threat posed by some advances if they are inappropriately managed. Science and technology can provide the basis for the development of environmentally sound technologies as well as the adaptation of currently damaging products and processes. They can also contribute to more equitable development and reduction of the gaps between developed and developing countries through capacity building for endogenous research and development, adaptation of technologies to the needs of developing countries, and diffusion of scientific knowledge and technology transfer.

Biotechnology is highlighted as a particularly important field in regard to sustainable development, with great benefits envisioned, but also with concern expressed about risks if not handled appropriately. This can be seen, for example, in Chapter 16 of Agenda 21, "Environmentally sound management of biotechnology"; in the Convention on Biological Diversity, adopted at the same international conference in 1992; and in the Malmö Ministerial Declaration of 2000: "The potential of the new economy to contribute to sustainable development should be further pursued, particularly in the areas of information technology, biology and biotechnology."

International Biotechnology Regulation

The full range of thirty-seven international regulations relevant to the applications and impacts of biotechnology can be found at www.genomics-gateway.net. These regulations are found in the following governance areas:

- *Arms control.* Here, rules that aim to prevent deliberate misuse of biology for hostile purposes are relevant, and cover advances in biotechnology, genetics, and genomics; prominent among these rules is the Biological Weapons Convention.

- *Drugs control.* Biotechnology can be used in the production of novel drugs (e.g., to produce advanced pain relieving drugs), but these may also be diverted to illicit channels, and biotechnology may be misused for the production of illicit drugs and for doping in sport. Trade in narcotic drugs and psychotropic substances is covered by three conventions overseen by the UN Office on Drugs and Crime, International Narcotics Control Board, and Commission on Narcotic Drugs. The World Anti-Doping Association governs sporting organizations through its World Anti-Doping Code, while governmental support for the code is provided by the International Convention Against Doping in Sport.

- *Environmental protection.* Biotechnology carries potential benefit for conservation of biological diversity (biodiversity), yet it also carries great risks if managed inappropriately. These issues are covered by the Convention on Biological Diversity (also known as the Convention on Biodiversity) and its Cartagena Protocol on Biosafety.

- *Health and disease control.* There are international rules concerning plant, animal, and human health that have relevance to the area of biotechnology because there are potential risks to health as well as benefits through improved diagnosis, treatment, and tracking of disease. Rules of the World Health Organization (WHO) cover human health, animal health is governed by the Office International des Epizooties, and plant health forms part of the work of the Food and Agriculture Organization (FAO). Some rules of the Codex Alimentarius Commission (a joint Commission of the WHO and FAO) apply to foods derived from or produced using genetically modified plants, animals, or microorganisms.

- *Social and ethical impacts of human genetics.* Biotechnological advances bring greater knowledge and understanding of human genetics. Alongside the benefits this brings (e.g., for the treatment of disease), human genetics is also perceived as potentially threatening to human dignity and human rights, and declarations have been developed to guide the use of these technologies within the United Nations Educational, Scientific and Cultural Organization (UNESCO) and the UN General Assembly.

- *Trade.* Products of biotechnology are traded internationally, and relevant to their control are rules on quality and health standards as well as technical regulations (overseen by the World Trade Organization); rules on intellectual property rights (covered by the World Trade Organization, World Intellectual Property Organization, and Union for the Protection of New Varieties of Plants); and rules on access to and use of genetic resources (overseen by the Convention on Biological Diversity Secretariat and the Food and Agriculture Organization).

While these rules are all applicable to biotechnology, they were not designed with this purpose in mind, and they generally apply as part of broader objectives. The rules were developed largely in separation from one another, at different times, and for different purposes. It is not surprising, therefore, to find that there are substantial differences in the extent to which they reflect principles of sustainability.

Sustainability in Biotechnology Legislation

Five of the thirty-seven international regulations applicable to biotechnology explicitly incorporate principles of sustainability:

- *The Convention on Biological Diversity (CBD)*. This was adopted alongside the Rio Declaration and Agenda 21 at the 1992 UN Conference on Environment and Development. Conserving biodiversity is an important part of sustainable development, and the CBD specifically addresses this. Biotechnology is covered in Articles 8(g), 16, and 19 and is included in all the convention's references to technology. It is viewed both as a useful tool that can assist in conservation and sustainability and as a potential threat to biodiversity, making reference, for example, to the need to manage risks associated with living modified organisms.
- *The Cartagena Protocol on Biosafety*. This protocol to the Convention on Biological Diversity was adopted in 2000 to address the potential risks to biodiversity from transboundary movements of living modified organisms. It utilizes principles of sustainable development, particularly the precautionary approach and the need for environmental risk assessment. Similar to the CBD, it recognizes both benefits and risks associated with biotechnology.
- *Bonn Guidelines on Access to Genetic Resources and the Fair and Equitable Sharing of the Benefits Arising out of their Utilization*. Maintaining diversity of genetic resources is a key aspect of biodiversity conservation. The Bonn Guidelines were adopted by the CBD's Conference of the Parties in 2002 to assist implementation of the convention's provisions on access to and benefit sharing from the use of genetic resources. Its objectives are compatible with a sustainability approach and include conservation and sustainable use of biodiversity, capacity building, poverty alleviation, and the realization of food security.
- *The International Treaty on Plant Genetic Resources for Food and Agriculture (ITPGR)*. Adopted in 2001 by the Food and Agriculture Organization, the ITPGR has similar aims to the Bonn Guidelines, but includes a strong emphasis on food security and sustainable agriculture. The ITPGR explicitly recognizes the role of biotechnology in the use of plant genetic resources for crop genetic improvement. It also recognizes the importance of scientific and technical capacity building for the fulfillment of its objectives.
- *The Universal Declaration on Bioethics and Human Rights (UDBEHR)*. This is one of three UNESCO declarations that focus on the human rights dimension of advances in genetics. The UDBEHR specifically addresses sustainability issues relating to human genetics. Three of its aims are: "to promote equitable access to medical, scientific and technological developments . . . ; to safeguard and promote the interests of present and future generations; . . . [and] to underline the importance of biodiversity and its conservation as a common concern of humankind" (UDBEHR 2005, Article 2).

In addition, a further twelve of the biotechnology regulations contain provisions on fulfilling capacity-building needs, which are compatible with sustainable development of biotechnology because they could assist in building relevant scientific, technological, and institutional capacities.

These provisions, however, are insufficiently implemented, which reflects a lack of political will by states to fulfill their commitments to sustainability. This was most recently noted by the UN secretary-general in his 2010 report on progress toward achieving the Millennium Development Goals:

> The shortfalls in progress towards the Millennium Development Goals are not because they are unreachable or because the time is too short, but rather because of unmet commitments, inadequate resources, lack of focus and accountability, and insufficient interest in sustainable development. (UNGA 2010, 31)

Relationship of International Rules to National Legislation

National legislation implementing international rules is necessary in most states for international rules to have effect. This means that many of the international rules relevant to biotechnology, particularly those that are legally binding treaties, have corresponding legislation at the national or regional level. Similar to the international landscape, national biotechnology legislation tends to consist of a variety of different rules, and responsibility for their development and implementation is usually dispersed across several government ministries or departments. For example, regulation of genetically modified organisms (GMOs) tends to be divided between departments for agriculture, environment, health, science, and trade. To illustrate, the European Union has separate rules on the contained use of GMOs, the deliberate release of GMOs, traceability and labeling of GMOs, transboundary movements of GMOs, genetically modified food and feed, the safety of workers handling biological agents, and the legal protection of biotechnology innovations (European Commission 2005). Responsibility for these rules falls upon its Directorates General for Agriculture and Rural Development; Enterprise and Industry; Environment; Health and Consumers; and Trade. Some national and regional biotechnology legislation reflects or incorporates principles of sustainability.

New Developments

Biotechnology legislation is not static, and there are several ongoing processes that are shaping or adding to the existing rules, some of which have particular relevance to sustainability issues. One example is the negotiation of an international regime on access and benefit sharing by the Convention on Biological Diversity's Conference of the Parties. This will promote the sustainable use of genetic resources and is likely to contain clauses relating to science and technology, including biotechnology.

Outlook: Room for Improvement

The way in which the applications and impacts of biotechnology are governed internationally influences the degree to which this key area of science and technology can contribute to sustainable development. It is not only the rules in the environmental area that are pertinent to this; there are significant interactions and overlaps (and also tensions and imbalances) with the other areas of regulation discussed. Sustainable management of biotechnology therefore requires coordination between the rules and institutions in all these areas.

In general, international commitments to sustainability are poorly fulfilled. There remains an acute lack of scientific and technological capacity in many developing countries, and barriers to accessing knowledge and innovation persist. Most research and development (R&D) remains concentrated on the interests of developed nations rather than on the needs of the many. Developed countries are home to approximately 18 percent of the world's population, but account for 76 percent of global R&D expenditure. In contrast, least developed countries, home to 12 percent of the world's population, only account for 0.1 percent of R&D spending (UNESCO Institute of Statistics 2009).

The lack of fulfillment of commitments to sustainability is a broad problem, not one specific to biotechnology. There is, however, much room for improvement in the implementation and strengthening of sustainability principles in the international governance of biotechnology.

Catherine RHODES
University of Manchester

See also in the *Berkshire Encyclopedia of Sustainability* Chemicals Legislation and Policy; Convention on Biological Diversity; Development, Sustainable—Overview of Laws and Commissions; Genetically Modified Organisms Legislation; International Law; Nanotechnology Legislation; Precautionary Principle

FURTHER READINGS

Commission on Science and Technology for Development (CSTD). (1997). *An assault on poverty: Basic human needs, science and technology.* Geneva: UNCTAD.

Convention on Biological Diversity Secretariat. (1992). Convention on Biological Diversity, with annexes. Retrieved September 2, 2010, from http://www.cbd.int/convention/convention.shtml

Convention on Biological Diversity Secretariat. (2000). Cartagena Protocol on Biosafety to the Convention on Biological Diversity, text and annexes. Retrieved September 2, 2010, from http://bch.cbd.int/protocol/text/

Convention on Biological Diversity Secretariat. (2002). Bonn guidelines on access to genetic resources and the fair and equitable sharing of the benefits arising out of their utilization. Retrieved October 11, 2010, from http://www.cbd.int/doc/publications/cbd-bonn-gdls-en.pdf

Convention on Biological Diversity Secretariat. (n.d.). Negotiations of the international regime on access and benefit-sharing (ABS). Retrieved September 2, 2010, from http://www.cbd.int/abs/ir

Department of Trade and Industry/LGC Ltd. (2004). *UK biotechnology regulatory atlas.* Retrieved October 4, 2010, from http://webarchive.nationalarchives.gov.uk/+/http://www.dti.gov.uk/ibioatlas/index.html

European Commission. (2005). Users guide to European regulation in biotechnology. Retrieved October 5, 2010, from http://ec.europa.eu/enterprise/sectors/biotechnology/files/docs/user_guide_biotech_en.pdf

Food and Agriculture Organization of the United Nations (FAO). (2001). International treaty on plant genetic resources for food and agriculture. Retrieved September 2, 2010, from http://www.plant-treaty.org/texts_en.htm

Genomics Gateway. (2009). Homepage. Retrieved September 15, 2010, from http://genomics-gateway.net

Rhodes, Catherine. (2010). *International governance of biotechnology: Needs, problems and potential.* London: Bloomsbury Academic.

UN Commission on Sustainable Development (CSD). (1995). Report of the secretary-general: Science for sustainable development. Retrieved September 2, 2010, from http://www.un.org/esa/dsd/csd/csd_csd03.shtml

UN Commission on Sustainable Development (CSD). (1997a). Report of the secretary-general: Environmentally sound management of biotechnology. Retrieved September 2, 2010, from http://www.un.org/esa/dsd/csd/csd_csd05.shtml

UN Commission on Sustainable Development (CSD). (1997b). Report of the secretary-general: Environmentally sound management of biotechnology, addendum. Retrieved September 2, 2010, from http://daccess-dds-ny.un.org/doc/UNDOC/GEN/N97/015/65/PDF/N9701565.pdf?OpenElement

UN Conference on Environment and Development (UNCED). (1992a). Agenda 21. Retrieved September 1, 2010, from http://www.un.org/esa/dsd/agenda21/res_agenda21_00.shtml

UN Conference on Environment and Development (UNCED). (1992b). Rio Declaration on Environment and Development. Retrieved September 1, 2010, from http://www.unep.org/Documents.Multilingual/Default.asp?documentid=78&articleid=1163

UN Conference on the Human Environment (UNCHE). (1972). Stockholm Declaration of the United Nations Conference on the Human Environment. Retrieved September 1, 2010, from http://www.unep.org/Documents.Multilingual/Default.asp?documentID=97&ArticleID=1503&l=en

UN Environment Programme (UNEP). (2000). Malmö Ministerial Declaration of the first Global Ministerial Environment Forum (GMEF). Retrieved August 31, 2010, from http://www.unep.org/malmo/malmo_ministerial.htm

UN Educational, Scientific and Cultural Organization (UNESCO). (2005). Universal Declaration on Bioethics and Human Rights. Retrieved October 12, 2010, from http://www.unesco.org/new/en/social-and-human-sciences/themes/bioethics/bioethics-and-human-rights/

UNESCO Institute of Statistics. (2009, May). Regional totals for R&D expenditure (GERD) and researchers, 2002 and 2007. Retrieved October 5, 2010, from http://stats.uis.unesco.org/unesco/tableviewer/document.aspx?FileId=252

UN General Assembly (UNGA). (2003). Document A/58/76. Report of the secretary-general: Impact of new biotechnologies with particular attention to sustainable development including food security, health and economic productivity. Retrieved August 16, 2010, from http://unctad.org/en/docs/a58d76_en.pdf

UN General Assembly (UNGA). (2010, February). Report of the secretary-general: Keeping the promise: A forward looking review to promote an agreed action agenda to achieve the millennium development goals by 2015. Retrieved October 5, 2010, from http://www.un.org/ga/search/view_doc.asp?symbol=A/64/665

World Commission on Environment and Development. (1987). *Our common future: Report of the World Commission on Environment and Development.* Oxford, UK: Oxford University Press.

YinLing, Liu. (2007, December). Regulating transgenic technology in China: Law, regulation and public policy. Retrieved October 4, 2010, from http://www.genomicsnetwork.ac.uk/media/10%20Liu.ppt

Cap-and-Trade Legislation

One approach to controlling greenhouse gas emissions, "cap-and-trade" places caps, or limits, on allowable emissions (set by the government) but permits participating facilities to buy and sell, or trade, "allowances" on the open market. The most prominent example in US law is the acid rain control program in the 1990 Clean Air Act Amendments. Cap-and-trade legislation is now being promoted to help mitigate global climate change.

Cap-and-trade legislation is intended to directly reduce emissions of a particular pollutant into the environment. The trading feature of this legislation is attractive to economists and others because it can significantly reduce costs. Cap-and-trade programs are a prominent feature of existing and proposed climate change mitigation efforts.

Acid Rain Control

The most prominent example of cap-and-trade legislation in the United States is the acid rain control subtitle in the Clean Air Act Amendments of 1990. This legislation, which reduced sulfur dioxide emissions at a fraction of the projected cost, has been used to support the use of cap-and-trade provisions in international and national climate change programs.

The Clean Air Act was adopted originally in 1970 and has resulted in significant reductions in a variety of pollutants, including particulates, nitrogen oxides, and lead. The primary focus of the Clean Air Act is to ensure that the level of these pollutants in the ambient or outdoor air does not exceed a level that is "requisite to protect public health." Once pollutants fall to the ground or onto the water, they are not of concern under this part of the Clean Air Act. The problem, of course, is that sulfur dioxide and other pollutants settling onto the ground or surface waters acidify

these environments, impair fish and insect life, and damage soil, forest, and crop productivity. The cap-and-trade provisions in the subsequent 1990 amendments were intended to reduce the total amount of sulfur dioxide that is emitted or loaded into the environment (not just the atmospheric concentration of that pollutant). And they were expected to do that as cheaply as possible.

The 1990 amendments required coal-fired electric-generating plants in the Midwest and Northeast to reduce their sulfur dioxide emissions by roughly 50 percent between 1990 and 2000. (A coal-fired power plant burns coal to generate electricity.) The legislation did that by setting a cap on overall emissions for 2000 that was roughly half the 1990 level. This cap was translated into corresponding caps for individual facilities.

Electric-generating facilities were not required by law to meet their cap—their mandatory lower level of emissions—in any particular way. They could install conventional air pollution controls, "wash" coal (removing impurities) before burning to reduce sulfur dioxide emissions, switch to less sulfur-intensive fuels (for example, from coal to natural gas), install a more efficient boiler, encourage energy savings by their customers, or do something else. The choice was entirely up to the operators of these facilities, and the US Congress expected that they would choose the cheapest means to do so.

In addition to these options, they could trade, or buy and sell, allowances. (An allowance is permission to emit, for instance, one ton of sulfur dioxide in a calendar year.) A basic premise of the legislation is that the costs of sulfur dioxide control—measured in dollars per ton of avoided emissions—vary from plant to plant. Thus some facilities may be able to reduce their emissions for fewer dollars per ton than other plants, and they may be able to do so even while reducing their emissions below the required cap. Under the 1990 amendments, the plant with the lower control costs can sell its excess emissions—in the form of allowances—to the plant with higher control costs.

Consider two plants, A and B, both of which have a cap that is 100 tons below current levels. Control costs at plant A are $30 per ton, and control costs at plant B are $70 per ton. Without trading, costs to meet the cap would be $3,000 for plant A and $7,000 for plant B, for a total of $10,000. With trading, plant A could reduce its emissions by 200 tons, and plant B could buy the "excess" reduction of 100 tons (in the form of 100 allowances) for a lot less than $7,000. (In a well-functioning market, competitive pressure will drive down the cost of allowances.) Thus plant A offsets some of its costs by selling allowances, and plant B is able to comply for a lower cost than it would otherwise pay. While cap-and-trade programs are often called trading programs, there would be no need or incentive to trade without the cap.

The 1990 amendments have worked as intended. Costs have been less than half of what was expected, and emissions were reduced more than required. During this same period, US gross domestic product and electricity generation also increased. According to a 2009 article by the Environmental Defense Fund, the program "has demonstrated that environmental protections need not compete with economic well-being."

Kyoto Protocol

In 1992, the United States became the fourth country in the world to ratify the United Nations Framework Convention on Climate Change (UNFCCC), which establishes an international legal structure to address climate change but does not establish any binding or numerical emission limits. When the parties began negotiating a protocol (a separate agreement under the convention) to set binding emission limits, the United States used its experience under the Clean Air Act to advocate trading mechanisms as a way of reducing costs. When this protocol was finalized in 1997 in Kyoto, Japan, it required developed countries to reduce their greenhouse gas emissions by 5 percent from 1990 levels by 2012. The required level of emissions reductions varied by country; the United States would have been obliged to reduce its emissions by 7 percent from 1990 levels, and western European countries (including the European Union) were required to reduce their emissions by 8 percent.

The protocol is in effect; it has been ratified by all developed countries except (ironically) the United States. (In 2001, President George W. Bush expressly repudiated the Kyoto Protocol "because it exempts 80 percent of the world, including major population centers such as China and India, from compliance, and would cause serious harm to the US economy.")

The Kyoto Protocol also contains several different emissions trading provisions to decrease the costs of those reductions. The Kyoto Protocol allows emissions trading between developed countries. As a result, these parties can take advantage of cost differences that exist between them (Article 17). The protocol also allows another form of emissions trading between developed countries, known as "joint implementation." Under joint implementation (Article 6), a developed country enters an agreement with another developed country to carry out an emissions reduction project in that other country and counts those reductions toward its own obligations. The protocol also created the clean development mechanism (CDM), an innovative kind of trading program (Article 12). The CDM allows developed countries to receive credit toward their required reductions for any reductions based on projects undertaken in *developing* countries. The twin purposes of the CDM are to assist developing countries "in achieving sustainable development" and to help developed countries meet their emissions reduction requirements. The CDM is particularly attractive because of the great difference between costs in developed and developing countries. One consequence of the Kyoto Protocol is the European Union's development and implementation of an emissions trading system.

The use of trading mechanisms in an international setting has raised a number of implementation and methodology issues:

- For both joint implementation and the clean development mechanism, the emissions reductions from the project must be "additional to any that would occur in the absence of the certified project activity" (Article 12.5(c)). It has often been hard in practice to determine that. As a consequence, credit may be given for reductions that would have occurred anyway.
- For many projects, such as carbon dioxide reductions that are achieved through forestry, it is difficult to directly determine the exact reductions that are being achieved. Reductions are calculated based on models and projections, which may or may not be reasonably accurate. By contrast, the power plants subject to trading in the United States are subject to continuous emissions monitoring, so it is relatively easy to determine the actual reductions being achieved.
- The US legal system contains a great many mechanisms assuring the integrity and enforceability of legal agreements, including the regulatory system on which they are based. In many developing countries, legal systems are less well developed and corruption is widespread. In consequence, it may be harder to enforce agreements

for reductions or guarantee the integrity of reductions claimed to be achieved in those countries.

At the end of 2009, international negotiations were being conducted for a successor agreement (or agreements) to the Kyoto Protocol. A successor agreement is needed because the compliance period for the Kyoto Protocol ends in 2012, and there is no international agreement for emissions reduction after that. One possibility is a second cap-and-trade agreement built on Kyoto that requires further reductions in greenhouse gas emissions.

European Union Emissions Trading System

The European Union has established the world's first international trading system for carbon dioxide emissions—the European Union Emissions Trading System (EU ETS). The system was established to help EU Member States comply with their Kyoto Protocol commitments. The EU ETS is set up to operate in three phases, or "trading periods." The first period, a trial period, ran from 2005 to 2007. Its purpose was not to meet Kyoto targets but to gain experience with emissions trading. The second period continues from 2008 to 2012, which coincides with the Kyoto Protocol. The third period will extend from 2013 to 2020.

Within the EU, the system raises several important implementation questions. One is whether the EU or member states will allocate allowances. Under the EU ETS, member states allocate allowances in the first and second periods, while the EU will do so in the third period. Another issue is whether allowances are allocated for free or auctioned. While the bulk of allowances are now allocated for free, there is a movement toward greater use of auctioning. Still another question is whether enforcement is done by the EU or member states. Although the system is EU-wide, enforcement is undertaken by member states. According to the European Environmental Agency (EEA), EU emissions in 2008 declined for the fourth consecutive year. If planned and existing measures are fully implemented, and member states take advantage of the clean development mechanism and other provisions of the Kyoto Protocol, the EEA projects that the EU will overachieve the 8 percent reduction target set in the Kyoto Protocol.

US Regional Initiatives

Ten northeastern and mid-Atlantic states participate in the Regional Greenhouse Gas Initiative (RGGI), which has developed a model rule to establish a cap-and-trade program for electric utilities. The ten states are: Connecticut, Delaware, Maine, New Hampshire, New Jersey, New York, Vermont, Massachusetts, Rhode Island, and Maryland.

The overall environmental goal for RGGI is for each state to adopt a carbon dioxide trading program for emissions from fossil fuel–fired electricity-generating units having a rated capacity equal to or greater than 25 megawatts. These states together have negotiated a model rule that is being used, in each state, as the basis for the program. Power plants are an attractive starting point because they have already experienced the sulfur dioxide trading program under the Clean Air Act. Emissions reductions are to occur from 2015 to 2018, at a rate of 2.5 percent annually for each of the four years. By 2018, each state's base annual emissions budget is to be 10 percent below its initial budget.

Similarly, the Western Climate Initiative (WCI) involves a regional emissions cap for multiple economic sectors and a cap-and-trade system. The WCI is comprised of seven western States (Arizona, California, New Mexico, Montana, Oregon, Utah, and Washington) and four Canadian provinces (British Columbia, Manitoba, Ontario, and Quebec). The goal of the WCI is to reduce greenhouse gas emissions by 15 percent from 2005 levels by 2020.

Proposed US Legislation

As of January 2010, comprehensive climate change legislation, based on cap-and-trade, is nearing passage in Congress. On 26 June 2009, the House of Representatives passed the American Clean Energy and Security Act (H.R. 2454). On 5 November 2009, the Senate Environment and Public Works Committee approved a somewhat similar bill, Clean Energy Jobs and American Power Act (S. 1733).

The heart of both bills is a cap-and-trade program for greenhouse gas emissions. The House bill would require the United States to reduce its greenhouse gas emissions by 83 percent from 2005 levels by 2050 (which equates to a 69 percent cut from 1990 emissions levels by 2050).

Both bills would create a cap-and-trade program for "covered entities." The term includes all electric power plants as well as factories and other facilities that produce 25,000 tons of carbon dioxide or carbon dioxide equivalent (gases such as methane and nitrous oxide). These facilities are responsible for about 85 percent of US greenhouse gas emissions.

These reduction requirements create an emissions cap or limit for covered facilities, and the level of this cap declines over time. Covered facilities can meet this cap more or

less as they see fit—for example, by becoming more energy efficient, switching to a less carbon-intensive fuel (from coal to natural gas), or using more renewable energy. Another option for covered facilities is trading, or purchasing emissions allowances. Like sulfur dioxide controls under the Clean Air Act, some facilities will be able to reduce their greenhouse gas emissions on a per-ton basis more cheaply than others. Those that do can trade or sell their "excess" reductions—in the form of allowances that are equal to one ton of carbon dioxide or carbon dioxide equivalent—to facilities where control costs are greater.

A cap-and-trade system such as that contained in these bills should lead to a price on carbon that would have ripple effects throughout an economy. (Though politically less likely, a carbon tax would have the same effect.) The price would be reflected in the market price for allowances. According to conventional economic wisdom, the economic pressure created by a cap-and-trade program should lead to less use of fossil fuels, greater use of less-carbon intensive fuels, and other changes that would result in lower greenhouse gas emissions.

The House and Senate bills contain a great many other provisions, to be sure. Many of these are directed at making sure that the emissions trading market is transparent, reliable, and functions smoothly. Others are directed at ensuring that the price of allowances doesn't get so high that the program becomes unaffordable for many facilities. Some provisions allow covered facilities to purchase "offset allowances" in the United States, primarily from foresters and farmers, to meet their emissions caps. Offset allowances are allowances generated by non-covered facilities in the form of reduced greenhouse gas emissions or increased carbon sequestration or storage. The bills would also establish a system of national emissions reporting.

For climate change legislation, cap-and-trade provisions raise the following issues:

- How to allocate allowances. Under the Clean Air Act, allowances are allocated for free. Under RGGI, many states are auctioning some or all of the allowances. Utilities prefer free distribution of greenhouse gas allowances because, they say, it reduces their costs. It may also make it easier to pass the legislation. The argument for auctioning, by contrast, is based on the idea that the government shouldn't give away something of value, and that it should not give an economic advantage to existing companies.

- Distribution of proceeds from the sale of allowances. To the extent allowances are sold rather than given away, the government could use or distribute the money for a variety of purposes—including fostering energy efficiency, retraining workers who are adversely affected, and research and development. Alternatively, some or all of the proceeds could be distributed to individual taxpayers as a kind of rebate, either on a one-time or continuing basis.

- How to treat existing regional initiatives such as RGGI and WCI. While there is understandable interest in using federal legislation to create a national cap-and-trade system, many believe that federal legislation should accommodate the time and investments already made in those programs.

- The extent to which cap-and-trade measures need to be supplemented with other rules. Because of market imperfections, the economic pressure caused by a cap-and-trade program will not always have the desired result. According to the economist Robert Stavins (2007), consumers often do not purchase products that are more energy efficient because they undervalue the economic savings of those products. In addition, the person with the ability to achieve greater energy efficiency (for example, the landlord) is frequently not the person who pays the energy bills (typically the tenant). The incentive, in other words, writes Stavins, is not directed at the person with the ability to make decisions that will reduce greenhouse gas emissions. Beyond that, he says, the price signal provided by a cap-and-trade or tax program is not likely to lead to sufficient investment in the variety of different research and development activities needed to mitigate climate change. Finally, while a cap-and-trade program can surely reduce the costs of emissions control, it is less likely to lead to more immediate environmental, social, and economic co-benefits than a performance standard of equivalent stringency. According to David Driesen, an author and professor of law, experience under the Kyoto Protocol shows that buyers of emissions allowances are primarily interested in reducing their costs, not in fostering or capturing the other benefits that may come from a use of a particular policy or measure (Driesen 2008). These limitations in a stand-alone cap-and-trade program strengthen the case for energy-efficiency policies, for measures that would drive greater levels of private investment, and for programs that would generate substantial economic, social, and environmental benefits in addition to greenhouse gas reductions.

These issues are addressed, to some degree, in two manners. First, other federal laws already indirectly address greenhouse gas emissions in ways that would complement

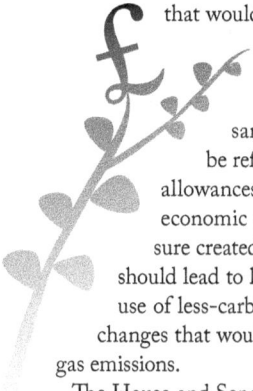

federal cap-and-trade legislation. The Energy Independence and Security Act of 2007, for example, requires automobiles and light trucks (including sport-utility vehicles) to achieve a combined standard for model year 2020 of at least thirty-five miles per gallon. Second, while the comprehensive climate change bills before Congress include cap-and-trade provisions, they also include a great many other provisions, some of which address these issues. The House bill, for instance, would establish a national energy efficiency program for buildings, would strengthen existing requirements for energy efficient lighting and appliances, and would foster energy efficiency in transportation and at industrial facilities. Still it is not clear whether such provisions would overcome the limitations of cap and trade.

Beyond these issues, there is a lingering question about whether a carbon tax would be a better approach. Cap-and-trade legislation would achieve a definite reduction because of the cap. By contrast, the emissions reduction effect of a tax is difficult to determine in advance. On the other hand, a tax is more economically efficient because it would apply to all sources of greenhouse gas emissions, rather than just those identified in the legislation itself. The comparative cost of the two programs would depend on their design details—how allowances are allocated and similar issues. A 2008 survey of economists by the General Accountability Office found that eleven favored cap and trade while seven favored a tax.

Implications

Cap-and-trade legislation has made it possible to achieve greater reductions of many pollutants, for a lower cost, than was previously thought possible. While it is understood to be a market mechanism for improving environmental quality, it is important to recognize that an old-fashioned "command-and-control" rule—capping emissions from each covered facility—provides the impetus for trading. Cap-and-trade legislation is thus best understood as a blend of traditional regulation with market-based regulation. It is an effective and indispensable tool in the quest for sustainable development.

John C. DERNBACH
Widener University Law School

See also in the *Berkshire Encyclopedia of Sustainability* Automobile Industry; Airline Industry; Climate Change Disclosure; Development, Sustainable; Energy Efficiency; Energy Industries (*assorted articles*); True Cost Economics

FURTHER READING

Dernbach, John C., & Kakade, Seema. (2008). Climate change law: An introduction. *Energy Law Journal, 29*(1), 12–14.

Driesen, David M. (2008). Sustainable development and market liberalism's shotgun wedding: Emissions trading under the Kyoto Protocol. *Indiana Law Journal, 83*(21), 52–57.

Environmental Defense Fund. (2008). The cap and trade success story. Retrieved July 5, 2009, from http://www.edf.org/page.cfm?tagID=1085

Environmental Protection Agency. (1990). Clean Air Act: Title IV—acid deposition control. Retrieved July 5, 2009, from http://www.epa.gov/air/caa/title4.html

European Environment Agency. (2009). *Greenhouse gas emission trends and projections in Europe 2009: Tracking progress towards Kyoto targets.* Retrieved December 31, 2009, from http://www.eea.europa.eu/publications/eea_report_2009_9

Faure, Michael, & Peeters, Marjan (Eds.). (2008). *Climate change and European emissions trading: Lessons for theory and practice.* Northampton, MA: Edward Elgar.

Government Accountability Office. (2008, May). *Climate change: Expert opinion on the economics of policy options to address climate change.* Retrieved July 5, 2009, from http://www.gao.gov/new.items/d08605.pdf

Stavins, Robert N. (2007). *Proposal for a US cap-and-trade system to address global climate change: A sensible and practical approach to reduce greenhouse gas emissions.* Retrieved July 5, 2009, from http://ksghome.harvard.edu/~rstavins/Papers/Stavins_Hamilton_Working_Paper_on_Cap-and-Trade.pdf

United Nations Framework Convention on Climate Change (UNFCCC). (1997). Essential background. Retrieved July 16, 2009, from http://unfccc.int/essential_background/items/2877.php

US Senate Committee on Environment & Public Works. (2008). Lieberman-Warner Climate Security Act of 2008. Retrieved July 5, 2009, from http://epw.senate.gov/public/index.cfm?FuseAction=Files.View&FileStore_id=aaf57ba9-ee98-4204-882a-1de307ecdb4d.

Yacobucci, Brent D.; Ramseur, Jonathan L.; & Parker, Larry. (2009). *Climate change: Comparison of the cap-and-trade provisions in H.R. 2454 and S. 1733.* Retrieved December 31, 2009, from http://assets.opencrs.com/rpts/R40896_20091105.pdf

Chemicals Legislation and Policy

In the past, criteria for "good" chemical properties were focused on qualities such as chemical stability and biological activity; environmental criteria were neglected, leading to the disastrous and widespread use of harmful chlorofluorocarbons (CFCs), the pesticide DDT, mercury, asbestos, and more. Since they are now used everywhere, chemicals' benefits and risks must be assessed, and their use should be regulated to avoid repeating past mistakes.

Global chemical policy is a young and dynamic area of international environmental policy. Over the last several decades, several chemicals-related international conventions, protocols, and amendments to existing instruments have been negotiated and have entered into force both at the regional and the global level. Moreover, with the United Nations' Strategic Approach to International Chemicals Management (SAICM), an institutional and political framework has been developed that promotes an integrated and comprehensive approach to chemicals management. In 2006, the first Intergovernmental Conference of Chemicals Management (ICCM 1) adopted SAICM in Dubai, which finally launched a process to strengthen institutional cooperation, coordination, and synergies between the different relevant institutions and processes at the global level, in particular between the Basel, Stockholm, and Rotterdam Conventions. The chemicals and waste regime (waste being an unfortunate side effect of the production and use of chemicals, but one that can be partially mitigated with proper management) has taken the lead in strengthening international environmental governance, not only addressing new challenges, but also developing new approaches for effective policy making and implementation. Thus, the chemicals and waste regime seems to be one of the most successful—if not the most successful—areas of international environmental policy.

Global Use of Chemicals

There are four main drivers for the use of chemicals on our planet: the increase of the global population; the higher standard of living (e.g., number of cars, electronics, etc.), the price of chemicals (dependent on availability); and chemical properties such as stability and inertness of construction materials or biological activity of pharmaceuticals. There is a win-win situation between the scarcity of a chemical and its sustainable use: scarcity increases the price. Therefore, in theory, rarer chemicals are used more carefully and in a more efficient way, which is good for the environment.

Environmental Governance and Monitoring

Chemicals can be found in gaseous, liquid, or solid states. On the molecular level, atoms of one or several elements can form molecules (e.g., water), polymers (e.g., plastic or proteins), salts (e.g., sodium chloride), metals, or metal alloys. The oldest classification of chemicals distinguishes between organic chemicals, which contain carbon, and inorganic chemicals. The legal classification distinguishes between substances, mixtures, and articles. Their regulation is grouped into industrial chemicals, biocides, pesticides, and pharmaceuticals. Chemicals are mainly synthesized from oil, but there are also "natural" chemicals extracted from plants.

Governance of chemicals follows a three-step cycle (personal communication with Bruno Oberle, director of the Swiss Federal Office for the Environment):

- **Step 1: Observation.** There is a need to observe the environment and to define certain parameters for

15

monitoring chemicals in order to get a sound basis of information.
- **Step 2: Regulation.** Regulation can be national, regional, or global. It also covers voluntary agreements.
- **Step 3: Evaluation.** The regulatory measures need to be evaluated. According to the results of the evaluation, the measures have to be amended, as appropriate.

After step 3, the cycle starts again beginning with step 1.

Observation and Monitoring Chemical Use

Monitoring chemicals is as old as chemistry itself; it helps the leaders to make the right management decisions. Monitoring is done by academia, industry, provincial, or federal governments. International organizations such as the European Environment Agency in Copenhagen and the secretariat of the Stockholm Convention in Geneva collect monitoring data. In a study, the geographical limit of the analysis has to be defined: it can be the whole world, a continent, a geographical region, a country, a city, or a single company. Only well-defined data allows the comparison between countries and a serious analysis of the situation. Important tools in that respect are the Chemical Abstract Service (CAS) numbers, "customs numbers" assigned by the World Customs Organization (WCO) that are used by customs authorities to identify dangerous chemicals, and the recommendations developed by multilateral environmental agreements (MEAs) such as the Stockholm Convention on Persistent Organic Pollutants (POPs).

Monitoring of chemicals can be done by four methods:

1. **Sales data** from production, market placement, and export
2. **Emission data** from point or diffuse sources, as depicted in pollutant release and transfer registers (PRTRs)
3. **Immission data** (the reception of material, such as pollutants, by the environment) measured by concentrations in air, water, and soil
4. **Substance flow analysis** through data on chemicals in defined compartments (production, import, export, use, waste disposal, water, air, soil, biota) including storage depots

In addition, impact data about the effect of chemicals on health and the environment are also needed.

High Production Volume Chemicals (HPVCs)

Since it is impossible to study all thirty thousand chemicals in commerce, it is necessary to set priorities. But it is difficult to prioritize when human toxicity and ecotoxicity are unknown. Therefore, the Organisation for Economic Co-operation and Development (OECD) decided on a pragmatic approach, prioritizing "high volume of production" (also known as high production volume, or HPV) chemicals, which it defines as "those chemicals which are produced at levels greater than 1,000 tonnes per year in at least one member country/region" (OECD 2004). The OECD Council decided in 1990 that member countries (mainly European nations but also Japan, South Korea, the United States, Canada, and several other developed nations) shall cooperatively investigate HPVCs in order to identify those which are potentially hazardous to the environment and/or to the health of workers and the general public. The most recent HPVC list was published by the OECD in 2004.

Properties other than HPV are also important, such as hazard potential. Laws such as REACH (Registration, Evaluation, Authorisation, and Restriction of Chemical Substances Directive)—a European Community regulation on chemicals and their safe use that came into force in 2007—study the most hazardous chemicals first. Most chemicals used within the European Union (EU) must be investigated and registered; marketing and selling unregistered substances is illegal. REACH provisions will be phased in over eleven years (European Commission–Environment 2010). With REACH, the EU has introduced a new principle: "No data, no market."

The OECD also developed a global portal to information on chemical safety, directories, and databases on chemicals (OECD 2010a). The global chemical industry, through the International Council of Chemical Associations (ICCA), launched a global High Production Volume (HPV) Chemicals Initiative in 1998 to speed up the process.

High Diversity of Chemicals

Due to the enormous biodiversity of nature and the fantasy of chemists, the number of chemicals has increased rapidly in the last fifty years, which is documented by the large numbers of chemicals found in the registry of the Chemical Abstracts Service (CAS), a division of the American Chemical Society. The CAS registry covers substances identified in the scientific literature from 1957 to the present, with additional substances going back to the early 1900s. It contains more than 55 million organic and inorganic substances. Approximately twelve thousand new substances are added each day (CAS 2010). Out of these many millions of chemicals, thirty thousand are in commerce.

Emerging Issues

There are two fundamentally different kinds of emerging issues that trigger the attention of policy makers: substances and policy-related topics. Thus, the term *emerging issue* can relate to substances that come to the public's attention, not only "new" chemicals, but also well-known chemicals that have been used for several decades (e.g., the very persistent polychlorinated biphenyls or PCBs, which were used for transformer oil and electronic capacitors). Secondly, *emerging issues* can also relate to new policy approaches and new policy instruments to address the challenges posed by chemicals. Examples of such new international policies are public–private partnerships, integrated approaches, or the institutional synergy process. All these new emerging issues will strongly shape the future international chemicals regime.

Substances-Related Emerging Issues

An issue can arise either because a chemical is only recently invented (such as the carbon nanotube) or because an old chemical comes to public attention again after being recently monitored in the environment. The leaking of PCBs into a river from a waste disposal facility near Freiburg, Switzerland, is just one example of an issue that involves "old" chemicals (Schmid et al. 2010). In this case, electronic waste containing capacitors with PCBs was stored in a landfill directly at a riverside. After thirty years the electronic waste in the landfill decomposed slowly; the PCB leaked into the river and poisoned the river sediment and the fish population near this landfill. The cantonal authorities banned the PCB-containing fish from the market, and the subject of PCBs emerged again in the newspapers and in the minds of citizens and politicians.

There are also several categories of substances that are considered "emerging issues."

Heavy metals

The challenges posed by heavy metals are not new or emerging: they are well-known. The recognition that the problems posed by heavy metals are not merely local but have a significant global dimension and therefore require an internationally coordinated response, however, is rather new. While specific international rules exist—mainly at the regional level or with regard to specific areas such as maritime pollution or transportation of hazardous goods—so far no horizontal environmental agreement has been developed addressing heavy metals. Thus, at the World Summit on Sustainable Development (WSSD) in 2002, the international community decided to "promote the reduction of the risks posed by heavy metals that are harmful to human health and the environment" (UNDESA 2002).

Mercury

It is well established today that the significant and globally adverse impacts from mercury require international action to reduce the risks to human health and the environment: based on Norway and Switzerland's initiatives and the work of an open-ended governmental working group, the United Nations Environment Programme (UNEP) Governing Council decided at its twenty-fifth session in 2009 to launch negotiations for a legally binding instrument on mercury (Governing Council 2009). The new convention on mercury is supposed to take a "comprehensive and suitable approach to mercury" that includes provisions to reduce the supply of mercury, the demand for mercury in products and processes, international trade in mercury, and atmospheric emissions of mercury. It should also address mercury-containing waste and contaminated sites; increase knowledge and information; specify arrangements for capacity building and technical and financial assistance; and address compliance. Switzerland and the other supporters of a mercury convention have always argued that a legally binding approach would not compete with or replace voluntary measures, such as those undertaken within UNEP's Mercury Partnership Programme; rather, a formal agreement could provide a strong and committed framework to complement and support such voluntary approaches. It can be expected that the mercury convention will further encourage such voluntary initiatives. Negotiations for the new convention are expected to conclude in 2013.

Nanotechnology

Nanoparticles are very small particles, sized between 1 and 100 nanometers. (The relationship [diameter] between a nanoparticle and an apple is the same as that between an apple and the Earth.) Nanoparticles may exhibit size-related properties that differ significantly from those observed in fine particles or bulk materials. First-generation products are already on the market in manufactured goods such as paints and coatings, cosmetics, medical appliances and diagnostics tools, clothing, household appliances, food packaging, plastics, and fuel catalysts. More sophisticated products such as pharmaceuticals and applications in energy storage and production are under development (SAICM 2009). In considering the commercial introduction of manufactured nanomaterials to achieve potential environmental benefits, countries should also give due consideration to potential health hazards or the environmental implications of the use of nanomaterials during their whole lifecycle. This includes the potential effects of production of the nanoscale materials, as well as the disposition of nanomaterials that may, for example, require new programs of recyclers or cause new concerns for disposal.

In 2006, the OECD established a Working Party on Manufactured Nanomaterials (WPMN) as a subsidiary body of its Chemicals Committee. As of 2010, the following areas are covered by the work plan of the WPMN (OECD 2010c):

- development of an OECD database on human health and environmental safety (EHS) research
- EHS research strategies on manufactured nanomaterials (including occupational health and safety)
- safety testing (and test guidelines) of a representative set of manufactured nanomaterials
- cooperation on voluntary schemes and regulatory programs
- cooperation on risk assessment
- the role of alternative methods in nano toxicology
- exposure measurement and mitigation

In addition, in 2007 the OECD's Committee for Scientific and Technological Policy established a Working Party on Nanotechnology (WPN) (OECD 2010b).

The International Organization for Standardization (ISO), a private global organization introducing all sorts of standards, has established Technical Committee 229 on Nanotechnologies with the following four working groups: terminology and nomenclature; measurement and characterization; health, safety, and environmental aspects of nanotechnologies; and material specifications (ISO 2010).

At the sixth session of the Intergovernmental Forum on Chemical Safety (IFCS) in 2008, Forum VI unanimously adopted the Dakar Statement, which consists of twenty-one nano recommendations for further actions (IFCS 2008). At SAICM ICCM 2 (2009) the conference agreed to refer the nano issue to the contact group established to discuss emerging policy issues and to add it to the agenda of ICCM 3 in 2012. The United Nations Institute for Training and Research (UNITAR) and the SAICM secretariat (with the support of Switzerland) launched a series of regional workshops to enhance information and provide capacity building on risk assessment and risk management of nanotechnology, based on the work of the OECD.

Emerging Organic Chemicals

Most of the emerging organic chemicals are halogenated (meaning a chemical compound that contains halogen atoms), such as the hormonally active endocrine disruptors (EDs) and perfluorinated compounds (PFCs). EDs are hormonally active chemicals that change the natural cycles of hormonal reactions. Typical examples of EDs are brominated flame retardants (BFRs) in plastic materials, certain UV filters in sunscreens, phthalates in plastic drinking bottles, as well as the "old" persistent organic pollutants (POPs) dioxin, PCB, and a metabolite of DDT. Some of these are regulated in the Stockholm Convention on Persistent Organic Pollutants.

Emerging Policy Approaches

The development of international chemicals and waste policy has not only involved addressing new and emerging challenges as described above; it has also been stimulated by the emergence of new policies. It is worth highlighting three new policy developments that will probably strongly shape the further evolution of the international chemicals and waste regime: the increasing involvement of non-state actors in policy development and implementation; the shift from specific toward integrated policy approaches; and effort to increase efficiency and effectivity through synergy, coordination, and cooperation within the international chemicals and waste regime.

Involvement of Non-State Actors

Since the 1990s, private actors such as industry, environmental nongovernmental organizations, and academia have become increasingly important in the area of international chemicals and waste management. Examples are the International Council of Chemical Associations (ICCA) for their contribution to the HPVC program, the International Pesticide Network (IPEN) for its policy work on pesticides, or the American Chemical Society (ACS) for the classification of chemicals. Thus non-state actors are fulfilling increasingly important roles as engines of international chemicals policy making, setting agendas for international policy processes and development, providing knowledge and scientific information, monitoring implementation, and lobbying state actors; they are also involved in partnership initiatives with governments, as well as the development of voluntary standards, and implementation of environment and development programs. Three areas of private actor involvement merit specific attention: (a) as participants in the development of new policies by governments, (b) as partners in public–private partnerships, and (c) as actors who directly develop and implement sound chemicals management policies.

Integrated Policy Approaches

While traditional international chemical policy has long addressed the challenges posed by chemicals by looking at the risks posed by a specific chemical in specific circumstances, over time the recognition has emerged that chemicals policy, in order to be effective and efficient, has to take a broader and a more integrated approach. Moving toward more integrated policies reflects not only a better understanding of chemicals and their interaction with each other and with the environment; it also reflects the general evolution of environmental policy and law from isolated ad hoc approaches toward comprehensive approaches that take into consideration the broader context of a specific challenge and reflect the complex interdependencies in the natural environment. By looking at chemicals throughout their entire life span and not only at the very moment when they become a risk to human health and the environment, the lifecycle—or "cradle to cradle" or "cradle to grave"—assessment (LCA) is the broadest reflection of such an integrated approach to chemicals policy making. LCA is applied in the concept of "chemicals leasing" developed by the United Nations Industrial Development Organization (UNIDO) and the Austrian Ministry for the Environment. In chemicals leasing, for example, a company sells colors for manufacturing cars not per kilogram but per surface area (square meters) of colored car surface. With this concept the color company does not need to sell the highest quantity of color material as possible, because profits are tied to the function of the chemical (in this case the color) rather than the volume of the chemical.

Such an integrated approach to chemicals management includes the Strategic Approach to International Chemicals Management (SAICM) developed by different UN organizations under the lead of UNEP and adopted in 2006 in Dubai. The UN Institute for Training and Research (UNITAR) is specialized in implementing SAICM. The Chemicals and Waste Management Programme (CWM) of UNITAR supports activities to protect human health and the environment from hazardous chemicals, while ensuring sustainable industrial development and facilitating the trade of chemicals. Project activities take place within the framework of implementing international agreements, such as SAICM, the Stockholm Convention, the Rotterdam Convention, and the Globally Harmonised System for Classification and Labelling of Chemicals (GHS).

Synergy, Coordination, and Cooperation

The evolution from ad hoc solutions toward integrated policy responses is also reflected at the institutional level. The international chemicals and waste regime has suffered from an ad hoc approach that has developed new institutions and instruments for each new problem that has been identified. Today there is broad recognition of a need for enhanced coordination and cooperation and a more coherent institutional framework and integrated structures.

Switzerland has promoted the goal to improve coordination among and effectiveness of multilateral environmental agreements (MEAs) since the beginning of this century and launched the concept of clustering the chemicals-related MEAs as an important tool to enhance synergies, linkages, coordination, and cooperation. This initiative has led to a process of not only co-locating the three main chemicals and waste conventions—Stockholm, Rotterdam, and Basel—in Geneva, but it has also led to the establishment of integrated secretariat structures and a joint head for all three convention secretariats, a process that will continue and further deepen.

The Future

This overview of emerging issues—both substances and policy approaches—in global chemicals policy reveals the impressively dynamic and innovative character of the international chemicals and waste regime. It has been able to address new challenges, and it has developed and adopted new approaches for effective policy making and implementation. The international chemicals and waste regime seems to be able to respond to emerging issues and new challenges both by launching new conventions, furthering voluntary approaches, developing a comprehensive strategic framework, and by developing new policy approaches such as strengthened non-state actor involvement, more integrated lifecycle approaches, and improved synergies for the traditionally fragmented conventions approach.

In the past, criteria for "good" properties were focused on the efficacy of chemicals to achieve specific objectives. Environmental criteria were neglected, which created threats to the environment and high expenses to correct damages. It is important not to repeat the mistakes with newly emerging chemicals. The list of emerging challenges still requires policy attention. Thereby, the three-step cycle of environmental governance (observation, regulation by MEAs, and evaluation) will remain a promising approach.

At the same time, the international chemicals and waste regime has to remain dynamic as well and able to respond to new issues. The future international chemicals and waste regime should provide a comprehensive, coherent, effective, and efficient framework that is "future proof," that is, able to respond to new challenges in a rapid and efficient manner. Most importantly, such a framework should make full benefit of the synergetic approach that is currently developed between and within the Basel, Rotterdam, and Stockholm Conventions.

With its process of enhancing effectivity and efficiency by strengthening institutional and political coordination, cooperation, and synergies, the global chemicals regime has even taken the lead in the broader efforts of strengthening international environmental governance. But enhancing synergies retrospectively—that is, bringing institutions and processes together after having been developed and finalized as independent frameworks—is complicated and resource intensive. Moreover, addressing each specific new emerging issue in an ad hoc manner with separate full-fledged institutions is inefficient. Therefore, it is hoped that policy makers and technocrats will realize that new frameworks should be open and dynamic to address also-emerging issues that require future policy response. It would not be efficient to develop a new legally binding instrument for each substance. Mercury is only one of several heavy metals and chemicals of global concern that will require international cooperation for the protection of human health and the environment. Therefore, a new convention on mercury should also be able to provide a future home for other heavy metals of global concern. If successful, enhancing institutional synergies will not only help to further strengthen sound chemicals-management efforts all over the world but will also strongly impact future policy development in the broader international context.

Georg KARLAGANIS
United Nations Institute for Training and Research (UNITAR)

Franz Xaver PEREZ
Ambassador, Federal Office for the Environment, Switzerland

See also in the *Berkshire Encyclopedia of Sustainability* Bhopal Disaster; Biotechnology Legislation; Convention on Persistent Organic Pollutants; Love Canal; Montreal Protocol on Substances that Deplete the Ozone Layer; Nanotechnology Legislation; Precautionary Principle; Registration, Evaluation, Authorisation, and Restriction of Chemicals; Restriction of Hazardous Substances Directive; Waste Shipment Law

FURTHER READINGS

Chemical Abstracts Service (CAS). (2010). CAS registry and CAS registry numbers. Retrieved October 4, 2010, from http://www.cas.org/expertise/cascontent/registry/regsys.html

European Commission–Environment. (2010). REACH: What is REACH?. Retrieved October 4, 2010, from http://ec.europa.eu/environment/chemicals/reach/reach_intro.htm

Governing Council of the United Nations Environment Programme (UNEP). (2009). Chemicals management, including mercury (16–20 February 2009) UNEP/GC.25/5/Add.2.

Intergovernmental Forum on Chemical Safety (IFCS). (2008). Forum VI: Dakar statement on manufactured nanomaterials. Retrieved October 5, 2010, from http://www.who.int/ifcs/documents/forums/forum6/report/en/index.html

International Council of Chemical Associations (ICCA). (2010). Global initiative on high production volume (HPV) chemicals. Retrieved October 4, 2010, from http://www.cefic.org/activities/hse/mgt/hpv/hpvinit.htm

International Organization for Standardization (ISO). (2010). Technical Committee 229: Nanotechnologies. Retrieved October 5, 2010, from http://www.iso.org/iso/iso_technical_committee?commid=381983

Organisation for Economic Cooperation and Development (OECD) Environment Directorate. (2004). The 2004 OECD list of high production volume chemicals. Retrieved October 19, 2010, from http://www.oecd.org/dataoecd/55/38/33883530.pdf

Organisation for Economic Cooperation and Development (OECD). (2010a). Environment directorate: Chemical safety, directories and databases on chemicals. Retrieved October 4, 2010, from http://www.oecd.org/linklist/0,3435,en_2649_34365_2734144_1_1_1_1,00.html

Organisation for Economic Cooperation and Development (OECD). (2010b). Science and technology policy: Nanotechnology. Retrieved October 5, 2010, from http://www.oecd.org/sti/nano

Organisation for Economic Cooperation and Development (OECD). (2010c). Working party on manufactured nanomaterials (WPMN). Retrieved October 5, 2010, from http://www.oecd.org/env/nanosafety

Schmid, Peter, et al. (2010). *Polychlorierte biphenyle (PCB) in Gewässern der Schweiz. Daten zur Belastung von Fischen und Gewässern mit PCB und Dioxinen, Situationsbeurteilung* (Umwelt-Wissen Nr. 1002). Bern, Switzerland: Bundesamt für Umwelt.

Scientific Committee on Emerging and Newly Identified Health Risks (SCENIHR). (2009, January 19). *Risk assessment of products of nanotechnologies.* Brussels, Belgium: European Commission Health & Consumer Directorate-General.

SGCI Chemie Pharma Schweiz. (2010). The Swiss chemical and pharmaceutical industry. Retrieved October 4, 2010, from http://www.sgci.ch/plugin/template/sgci/390/10393?selected_language=en and from http://www.sgci.ch/plugin/template/sgci/158/45503/---/Auss enhandel+Chemie+und+Pharma+2009+%28DE%29+%28Internet+Artikel+%28SGCI+Exporter%29%29

Strategic Approach to International Chemicals Management (SAICM). (2009, March 25). Background information in relation to the emerging policy issues of nanotechnology and manufactured nanomaterials (25 March 2009) SAICM/ICCM.2/INF/34. Retrieved December 1, 2010, from http://www.saicm.org/documents/iccm/ICCM2/meeting%20documents/ICCM2%2010%20emerging%20issues%20E.pdf

United Nations Department of Economic and Social Affairs (UNDESA), Division for Sustainable Development (DSD). (2002). World Summit on Sustainable Development (WSSD): Johannesburg plan of implementation. Retrieved October 4, 2010, from http://www.un.org/esa/sustdev/documents/WSSD_POI_PD/English/POIToc.htm

United Nations Environment Programme (UNEP). (2008). The global atmospheric mercury assessment: Sources, emissions and transport. Retrieved October 5, 2010, from http://www.chem.unep.ch/mercury/Atmospheric_Emissions/Atmospheric_emissions_mercury.htm

Common Heritage of Mankind Principle

The "common heritage of mankind" is an ethical concept and a general concept of international law. It establishes that some localities belong to all humanity and that their resources are available for everyone's use and benefit, taking into account future generations and the needs of developing countries. It is intended to achieve aspects of the sustainable development of common spaces and their resources, but may apply beyond this traditional scope.

When first introduced in the 1960s, the "common heritage of mankind" (CHM) was a controversial concept, and it remains so to this day. This controversy includes issues of scope, content, and status, together with CHM's relationship to other legal concepts. Some commentators consider it out of fashion due to its lack of use in practice (e.g., for mining of seabed resources) and its subsequent rejection by modern environmental treaty regimes. In contrast, other commentators consider it a general principle of international law with enduring significance.

Escalating global ecological degradation, and ongoing inability to arrest the so-called tragedy of the commons (Hardin 1968), will ensure the continued relevance of the common heritage concept, despite the difficulties surrounding its acceptance by states. Evidence for this can be found in a range of efforts to apply CHM to natural and cultural heritage, marine living resources, and global ecological systems such as the atmosphere (Taylor 1998) or climate system.

Origins of the Principle

Legal discussion of CHM generally begins with the speech of the Maltese ambassador Arvid Pardo (1914–1999) to the United Nations in 1967. In this speech he proposed that the seabed and ocean floor, beyond national jurisdiction,

be considered the CHM. This was an important event that triggered the later negotiation of the 1982 Law of the Sea Convention (UNCLOS III) and other legal developments that subsequently earned Arvid Pardo the title "father of the law of the sea." But CHM has a much longer history, and Pardo drew upon this in developing CHM as a legal concept for the oceans. Other people, including the writer and environmentalist Elisabeth Mann Borgese (1918–2002), considered CHM an ethical concept central to a new world order, based on new forms of cooperation, economic theory, and philosophy.

This history is important to elucidating the ethical core of CHM: the responsibility of humans to care for and protect the environment, of which we are a part, for present and future generations. A 1948 draft World Constitution provided that the Earth and its resources were to be the common property of mankind, managed for the good of all. Concern about the use of nuclear technology and resources, for military and peaceful purposes, also led to an early proposal that nuclear resources be collectively owned and managed, and not owned by any one state. Traces of CHM are also found in the UN Outer Space Treaty (1967), which governs state exploration and use of outer space, the moon, and other celestial bodies. CHM, however, achieved prominence in the context of the evolving law of the sea. The 1967 World Peace through Law Conference referred to the high seas as "the common heritage of mankind" and stated that the seabed should be subject to UN jurisdiction and control.

Revolutionizing Law of the Sea

Concern about the impact of new technologies upon the oceans, militarization, and expanding state claims to ownership of parts of the oceans (e.g., continental shelf and exclusive economic zones), together with growing economic disparity and associated harm to long-term human security, prompted Arvid Pardo to develop the idea that all ocean space (i.e., surface of the sea, water column, seabed and its subsoil, and living resources) should be declared the CHM, irrespective of existing claims to national jurisdiction.

The intention was to replace the outdated legal concept of "freedom of the high seas" by proclaiming ocean areas an international commons. (Areas with significant natural resources that are acknowledged to be beyond the limits of exclusive territorial jurisdiction of sovereign states are known as international commons.) Freedom of the high seas, developed by the Dutch jurist Hugo Grotius (1583–1645), creates an open access regime allowing for its laissez-faire use. The few restrictions that exist serve only to protect the interests of other states and their exercise of free use.

In contrast, as the CHM, ocean space and its resources would be a commons that could not be owned by states beyond a certain limit (e.g., 200 nautical miles from the coast). As a commons it would be open to the international community of states, but its use would be subject to international administration and management for the common good of all humanity. Where areas of ocean space and resources existed within national jurisdiction, states would regulate and manage use on behalf of all mankind, not solely for the benefit of national interests.

This approach recognized the unity of the oceans' ecological systems and rejected both laissez-faire freedom and unfettered state sovereignty. It included efforts to simplify ocean jurisdiction by establishing one single line of demarcation between national and international ocean space (Draft Ocean Space Treaty of 1971) and prevent gradually expanding claims to national jurisdiction.

The CHM was originally intended as a concept that would revolutionize the law of the sea by applying to all ocean space and resources. But in 1967 Arvid Pardo recognized that this would be rejected by the powerful states who were attempting to extend their sovereign claims to more ocean space and resources. By focusing on the legal status of the much more limited entity of the "seabed" beyond national jurisdiction, it was thought that CHM could gain an important foothold within the UN system.

The 1967 Maltese proposal lead to a number of important developments, including the 1970 UN General Assembly Declaration of Principles Governing the Sea-Bed and the Ocean Floor and the Subsoil Thereof, Beyond the Limits of National Jurisdiction. This declaration set out the legal principles needed to implement the notion that the seabed and its resources are the CHM, and it helped create consensus for the negotiation of a new law of the sea convention: UNCLOS III. The ultimate outcome was a much more limited application of CHM than ever intended by its advocates. As will be explained immediately below, UNCLOS III restricted the application of CHM to a few rocks (e.g., mineral resources such as manganese nodules) sitting on the bottom of the deep seabed. For Pardo, the limited application of CHM, to "ugly little rocks" (his words), was a debasement of the phrase.

UNCLOS III

Part XI of the UN Convention on the Law of the Sea (UNCLOS III) deals with the seabed and ocean floor and subsoil thereof (the "Area") beyond the limits of national jurisdiction. Article 136 declares the Area and its resources (only) to be the "common heritage of mankind." The Area and its resources cannot be claimed, appropriated, or owned by any state or person (Article 137). All rights to resources belong to mankind as a whole, with the International Seabed Authority (ISA) acting on mankind's behalf (Article 140). The ISA must ensure the equitable sharing of financial and other benefits arising from activities in the Area, taking into particular account the needs and interests of developing states and others. Promotion of research, transfer of technology

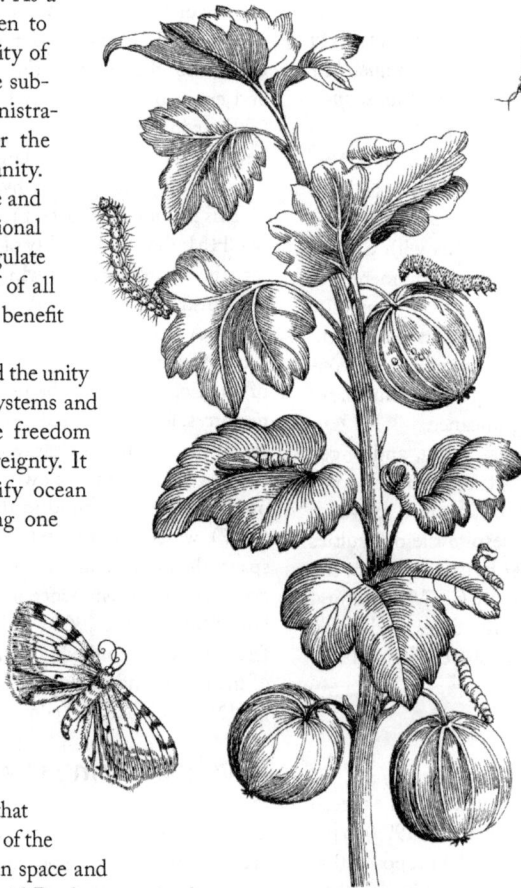

to developing states, and protection of the marine environment's ecological balance are all important functions of the ISA (Articles 143–145).

Part XI provisions create an international administration and management regime for only a small part of the international commons (the Area and its resources). It does not generally replace the freedom of the high seas (Part VII); thus the intended revolution of the law of the sea was not achieved. In the 1970s, the most commercially viable mineral resources of the Area were thought to be manganese nodules, hence Pardo's view that CHM was reduced in its application to "ugly little rocks lying in the darkest depths of all creation." Despite this serious limitation, the use of CHM was revolutionary enough to be one of the reasons why the United States of America refused to adhere to UNCLOS III.

To date, commercial use of the Area and its resources has not occurred. Further, the traditional fragmented approach to jurisdiction over separate elements of ocean space and resources endures despite the irrefutable unity of ecological systems.

1979 Moon Treaty

As noted above, aspects of CHM appeared in the 1967 Outer Space Treaty. But it was not until 1979 that a clear statement appeared in the Moon Treaty (a treaty to govern exploration and exploitation of the moon's resources). Article 11(1) declares that the moon and its natural resources are the CHM. Disputes concerning the details of an international system for resource exploitation, including provision for equitable benefit sharing, were resolved by deferring the details of a management regime for the future. The Moon Treaty has been ratified by only a few states; nevertheless it has been used to reject claims to property rights on the basis that it creates a general principle of law, applicable to the whole of the international community and not just states that ratified the treaty.

Core Elements

There is no concise, fully agreed upon definition of CHM. Its features depend upon the details of the regime applying it or the space/resource to which it is applied. There are a number of core elements, however:

• No state or person can own common heritage spaces or resources (the principle of non-appropriation). They can be used but not owned, as they are a part of the international heritage (patrimony) and therefore belong to all humankind. This protects the international commons from expanding jurisdictional claims. When CHM applies to areas and resources within national

jurisdiction, exercise of sovereignty is subject to certain responsibilities to protect for the common good.

• The use of common heritage shall be carried out in accordance with a system of cooperative management for the benefit of all humankind (i.e., for the common good). This has been interpreted as creating a type of trustee relationship for explicit protection of the interests of humanity, rather than the interests of particular states or private entities.

• There shall be active and equitable sharing of benefits (including financial, technological, and scientific) derived from the CHM. This provides a basis for limiting public or private commercial benefits and prioritizing distribution to others, including developing states (intragenerational equity between present generations of humans).

• CHM shall be reserved for peaceful purposes (preventing military uses).

• CHM shall be transmitted to future generations in substantially unimpaired condition (protection of ecological integrity and intergenerational equity between present and future generations of humans).

In recent years, these core elements have ensured that CHM remains central to the efforts of international environmental lawyers. It is recognized as articulating many key components of sustainability.

Some Controversies

Controversies surround virtually all elements of CHM. This is because, as one commentator describes, it questions the regimes that apply to resources of global significance, irrespective of where they are situated. It therefore challenges traditional international law concepts such as acquisition of territory, sovereignty, sovereign equality, and international personality, as well as the allocation of planetary resources and consent-based sources of international law (Baslar 1997). Further, it has long been recognized that the precedent established for oceans management has the potential to form the basis for the future organization of an increasingly interdependent world.

One overriding issue concerns the extent to which CHM can prevent further fragmentation and privatization of the commons (or enclosure) and replace this trend with more communitarian values and legal protection of the common good. There is a wide divergence of views on whether the core element of non-appropriation prevents CHM from applying to globally significant spaces and resources that exist within the sovereign territory of states (e.g., rainforests and their flora and fauna).

The equitable utilization element (or equitable benefit sharing), which requires the sharing of financial, technological, and scientific benefits of use of the CHM, has also proved divisive especially between developed and developing states and corporate actors. Developing states tend to view this element of CHM as pivotal to the achievement of distributive justice. Developed states and commercial interests see this element as a potential impediment to investment and the use of market incentives (e.g., property rights) to achieve economic and environmental benefits. They favor, for example, exploitation by private enterprise conducted under licensing arrangements. The 1994 Implementation Agreement (amending UNCLOS III, Part IX) was generally viewed as having eroded the distributive elements of the original regime, in favor of protection of commercial interests.

The impact of these and other issues saw CHM rejected as a concept to guide UN treaty regimes for climate change and for conservation of biological diversity. The 1992 UN Framework on Climate Change refers to the *problem of climate change* as being the "common *concern* of humankind." The original Maltese proposal was for a treaty declaring the global climate system as a part of the CHM, but this was rejected. Developing states rejected the use of CHM in the 1992 UN Convention on Biological Diversity, perceiving it as a potential threat to their sovereign rights to use and benefit from biological resources within their own territories. They were suspicious of interference under the guise of environmental protection or via the acquisition of intellectual property rights.

Extended Applications

Over the years CHM has been applied to a range of resources and spaces: fisheries, Antarctica, the Arctic landscape, geostationary orbit, genetic resources (the genetic material of plants, animals and life forms, that are of value), and basic food resources. In recent years, the United Nations Educational, Scientific and Cultural Organization (UNESCO) has robustly supported CHM through a wide range of initiatives (e.g., declarations, conventions, and protocols) that recognize natural and cultural heritage as the CHM. Although difficult to define, "natural and cultural heritage" includes tangible and intangible elements, ranging from archeological sites and historic monuments to

cultural phenomena (such as literature, language, and customary practices) and natural systems including islands, biosphere reserves, and deserts. One new area of potential application is the human genome (heritage of humanity). This may prevent the patenting of the human genome by corporate interests.

In an ecological and generational context, it is possible to argue that the Earth itself is a global commons shared by each generation and that CHM should "extend to all natural and cultural resources, wherever located, that are internationally important for the well-being of future generations" (Weiss 1989; Taylor 1998).

Future Outlook

In the short term and from the perspective of state practice and treaty negotiation, the future use of CHM is likely to be limited. International lawyers tend to treat its use—beyond the UNCLOS III and Moon Treaty—as merely political and aspirational. Issues that will shortly test the commitment of states to CHM include the status of marine living resources (of the "Area" and high seas), claims to the seabed under the melting Arctic ice, and the status of oil reserves under the deep seabed. In the context of the oceans, CHM provides the only current alternative to either freedom of use by all states or the acquisition and exercise of sovereign rights. It also recognizes the interdependence of ecosystems and acknowledges human use. It therefore has much in common with ecosystem management approaches that aim to move away from piecemeal resource-specific management regimes.

CHM is also relevant to the wider debate on transforming the role of the state from exclusive focus on protection of national interests to include responsibility to protect ecological systems, wherever they are located, for the benefit of all.

States might be reticent to embrace the possible applications of CHM, but international law is no longer the sole province of states and international lawyers. Global civil society is playing an increasing role in the development of, and advocacy for, concepts such as CHM. It is linked to renewed interest in cosmopolitanism, global ecological citizenship and justice, and the search for shared ethical principles to guide progress towards a more peaceful and sustainable future for all (Earth Charter Initiative 2000).

Prue TAYLOR

University of Auckland

See also in the *Berkshire Encyclopedia of Sustainability* Environmental Law—Antarctic; Environmental Law—Arctic; Environmental Law, Soft vs. Hard; Intergenerational Equity; International Law; Precautionary Principle; Principle-Based Regulation; Law of the Sea; Ocean Zoning; United Nations—Overview of Conventions and Agreements

FURTHER READINGS

Anand, Ram Prakash. (1997). The common heritage of mankind: Mutilation of an ideal. *The Indian Journal of International Law, 37*(1), 1–18.

Baslar, Kemal. (1997). *The concept of the common heritage of mankind in international law.* The Hague, The Netherlands: Kluwer Law International.

Bedjaoui, Mohammed. (2004). The convention for the safeguarding of intangible cultural heritage: The legal framework and universally recognized principles. *Museum International, 221/222,* 150–155.

Boda, Zsolt. (2003). Global environmental commons and the need for ethics. *Society and Economy, 25*(2), 213–224.

Borg, Simone. (Ed.). (2009). *Climate change.* Ministry of Foreign Affairs and University of Malta. [monograph]

Borgese, Elisabeth Mann. (2000). Arvid Pardo (1914–1999): In memoriam. In Elisabeth Mann Borgese et al. (Eds.), *Ocean yearbook* (14th ed., pp. xix–xxxviii). Chicago: University of Chicago Press.

Borgese, Elisabeth Mann. (2002). The common heritage of mankind: From non-living resources and beyond. In Shigeru Oda, Nisuke Andō, Edward McWhinney, & Rüdiger Wolfrum (Eds.), *Liber amicorum Judge Shigeru Oda* (Vol. 2, pp. 1313–1334). The Hague, The Netherlands: Kluwer Law International.

Borgese, Elisabeth Mann. (2004). The years of my life. In Aldo Chircop & Moira L. McConnell (Eds.), *Ocean yearbook* (18th ed., pp. 1–21). Chicago: University of Chicago Press.

Byk, Christian. (1998). A map to a new treasure island: The human genome and the concept of common heritage. *The Journal of Medicine and Philosophy, 23*(3), 234–246.

Committee to Frame a World Constitution. (1948). *Preliminary draft of a world constitution, as proposed and signed by Robert M. Hutchins [and others].* Chicago: The University of Chicago Press.

Danilenko, Gennady M. (1988). The concept of the "common heritage of mankind" in international law. *Annals of Air and Space Law, XIII,* 247–263.

Elferink, Alex G. Oude. (2007). The regime of the area: Delineating the scope of application of the common heritage principle and freedom of the high seas. *International Journal of Marine and Coastal Law, 22*(1), 143–176.

Forrest, Craig. (2009). *International law and the protection of cultural heritage.* Abingdon, UK: Routledge.

Francioni, Francesco, & Scovazzi, Tullio. (2006). *Biotechnology and international law.* Oxford, UK: Hart Publishing.

Goldwin, Robert A. (1983). Common sense vs. "the common heritage." In Bernard H. Oxman; David D. Caron; & Charles L. O. Bunderi (Eds.), *Law of the sea: US policy dilemma* (p. 59). San Francisco: ICS Press.

Gorove, Stephen. (1972). The concept of "common heritage of mankind": A political, moral or legal innovation? *San Diego Law Review, 9,* 390–403.

Hardin, Garrett. (1968). The tragedy of the commons. *Science, 162*(3859), 1243–1248.

Inglott, Peter Serracino. (2004). Elisabeth Mann Borgese: Metaphysician by birth. In Aldo Chircop & Moira L. McConnell (Eds.), *Ocean yearbook* (18th ed., pp. 22–74). Chicago: University of Chicago Press.

Joyner, Christopher. (1986). Legal implications of the concept of the common heritage of mankind. *International and Comparative Law Quarterly, 35*(1), 190–199.

Kiss, Alexandre. (1984–1985). The common heritage of mankind: Utopia or reality? *International Journal, 40,* 423–441.

Matz-Lück, Nele. (2010). The concept of the common heritage of mankind: Its viability as a management tool for deep sea genetic resources. In Erik J. Molenaar & Alex G. Oude Elferink (Eds.), *The international legal regime of areas beyond national jurisdiction: Current and future developments* (Nova et Vetera Iuris Gentium Series No. 26, pp. 61–75). The Hague, The Netherlands: Martinus Nijhoff Publishers/Brill Academic.

Nicholson, Graham. (2002). The common heritage of mankind and mining: An analysis of the law as to the high seas, outer space, the Antarctic, and world heritage. *New Zealand Journal of Environmental Law, 6,* 177–198.

Pardo, Arvid. (1967). Address to the 22nd session of the General Assembly of the United Nations, UN GAOR, 22nd sess., UN Doc. A/6695 (18 August 1967).

Pardo, Arvid. (1972). New horizons in ocean science and law. In Elisabeth Mann Borgese (Ed.), *Pacem in maribus* (pp. 249–253). New York: Dodd, Mead & Co.

Pardo, Arvid. (1975). *The common heritage: Selected papers on oceans and world order 1967–1974.* Malta: Malta University Press.

Pardo, Arvid, & Christol, Carl Q. (1983). The common interest: Tension between the whole and the parts. In Ronald St. J. MacDonald & Douglas M. Johnston (Eds.), *The structure and process of international law: Essays in legal philosophy doctrine and theory* (pp. 643–660). The Hague, The Netherlands: Martinus Nijhoff Publishers.

Payoyo, Peter B. (1997). *Cries of the sea: World inequality, sustainable development and the common heritage of humanity.* The Hague, The Netherlands: Martinus Nijhoff Publishers.

Sand, Peter H. (2004). Sovereignty bounded: Public trusteeship for common pool resources? *Global Environmental Politics, 4*(1), 47–71.

Sand, Peter H. (2006). Global environmental change and the nation state: Sovereignty bounded? In Gerd Winter (Ed.), *Multilevel governance of global environmental change: Perspectives from science, sociology and the law* (pp. 519–538). Cambridge, UK: Cambridge University Press.

Shackelford, Scott James. (2009). The tragedy of the common heritage of mankind. *Stanford Environmental Law Journal, 28*(1), 109–169.

Taylor, Prue. (1998). *An ecological approach to international law: Responding to challenges of climate change.* London: Routledge.

Tuerk, Helmut. (2010). The idea of common heritage of mankind. In Norman A. Martínez Gutiérrez (Ed.), *Serving the rule of international maritime law: Essays in honour of Professor David Joseph Attard* (pp. 157–175). Oxfordshire, U K: Routledge.

Weiss, Edith Brown. (1989). *In fairness to future generations: International law, common patrimony, and intergenerational equity.* Tokyo: United Nations University / Dobbs Ferry, NY: Transnational Publishers.

Wolfrum, Rüdiger. (2008). Common heritage of mankind. Retrieved July 2, 2010, from http://www.mpepil.com.

TREATIES AND RESOLUTIONS

Agreement Governing the Activities of States on the Moon and Other Celestial Bodies (adopted 5 December 1979, entered into force 11 July 1984) 1363 UNTS 3.

Agreement Relating to the Implementation of Part XI of the United Nations Convention on the Law of the Sea of 10 December 1982 (done 28 July 1994, entered into force 28 July 1996) 1836 UNTS 41.

Antarctic Treaty (signed 1 December 1959, entered into force 23 June 1961) 402 UNTS 71.

Convention for the Protection of Cultural Property in the Event of Armed Conflict (signed 14 May 1954, entered into force 7 August 1956) 249 UNTS 240.

Convention for the Protection of the World Cultural and Natural Heritage (adopted 16 November 1972, entered into force 17 December 1975) 1037 UNTS 151.

Convention on Biological Diversity (adopted on 22 May 1992, entered into force on 29 December 1993).

Draft Ocean Space Treaty, Working Paper, submitted by Malta, UNGA Doc. A/AC 138/53 (23 August 1971).

The Earth Charter Initiative. (2000). The Earth Charter. Retrieved August 2, 2010, from http://www.earthcharterinaction.org/content/pages/Read-the-Charter.html

First Protocol to the Convention for the Protection of Cultural Property in the Event of Armed Conflict (signed 14 May 1954, entered into force 7 August 1956) 249 UNTS 358.

Protocol on Environmental Protection to the Antarctic Treaty (done 4 October 1991, entered into force 14 January 1998) (1991) 30 ILM 1455.

Second Protocol to the Convention for the Protection of Cultural Property in the Event of Armed Conflict (signed 26 March 1999, entered into force 9 March 2004) (1999) 38 ILM 769.

Treaty on Principles Governing the Activities of States in the Exploration and Use of Outer Space, including the Moon and other Celestial Bodies (signed 27 January 1967, entered into force 10 October 1967) 610 UNTS 205.

United Nations Convention on the Law of the Sea (concluded 10 December 1982, entered into force 16 November 1994) 1833 UNTS 397.

United Nations Educational, Scientific and Cultural Organization (UNESCO). (1997, November 12). Declaration on the Responsibilities of the Present Generations Towards Future Generations. Retrieved July 2, 2010, from http://portal.unesco.org/en/ev.php-URL_ID=13178&URL_DO=DO_TOPIC&URL_SECTION=201.html

United Nations Framework Convention on Climate Change (adopted on 9 May 1992 and entered into force 21 March 1994).

United Nations General Assembly Resolution 1962 (XVIII) Declaration of Legal Principles Governing the Activities of States in the Exploration and Use of Outer Space (13 December 1963) GAOR 18th Session Supp. No.15, 15.

United Nations General Assembly Resolution 2749 (XXV) Declaration of Principles Governing the Seabed and the Ocean Floor, and the Subsoil Thereof, beyond the Limits of National Jurisdiction, UN GAOR, 25th Sess., Supp. No. 28, 24. UN Doc. A/8028 (1970).

Customary International Law

Since the mid-twentieth century, human rights and environmental issues have come to the forefront of international law. Balancing the customs and laws of many different nations to protect the good of the global population, international law must continue to harmonize the rights of sovereign states with the need to protect the environment and individual rights.

Law combines conventional processes and critical principles that institutions of governance synthesize to balance the good of the community with the rights of individuals. Most municipal or national systems of law accomplish this through a definitive constitutional governance structure with legislation, administrative rules, and judges' decisions contributing to a closed system of legal enforcement. The international legal system is different.

Specifically, the governance structure of the international legal system is not constitutional, but largely conventional, based on social practices evolved over centuries and continually tested by the standard of allowing peaceful coexistence to persist over time. All systems of social convention exist to maintain the means of cooperation, and international law is no different. State sovereignty, or the idea that states are autonomous, independent entities with a capacity, ability, and purpose all their own, is the norm that holds the conventional processes of international relations together. This concept also necessitates its own definition of justice. Although the modern international system is now recognized to include more than states, and while nongovernmental organizations (NGOs), individuals, and international organizations are gaining status in the law of transnational relations, the sovereignty of states remains the pertinent standard that maintains the cooperative core of the conventional or customary international system.

Custom as a Source of International Law

Article 38 of the Statute of the International Court of Justice (1945) provides three valid sources for international law: treaty, customary international law, and principle. The latter two sources directly affect a sustainable environment. Both custom and principle are intimately connected to one another in terms of how custom evolves and from where custom derives its core ideas for positive international rules.

Customary, or general, international law is defined principally by two characteristics, one ancient, one modern. The ancient characteristic is *practice*, and the modern is what is called *opinio juris*. Practice is simply how many and what cross section of states act in a certain way. This is the component of international law directly based on the evolution of transnational social conventions, or customs focused on the maintenance of nonviolent cooperation over time. Social conventions are usually, at first, unconscious and establish themselves over many iterations of the same set of interactions. Eventually the initial act of one state becomes the practice of "many" and when this "many" represents an adequate mix of political, economic, geographical, and interested parties, it can be recognized, usually by international courts or tribunals, or in the foreign policies of states, as a positive rule of customary international law. Practice gives international custom its universal character; once recognized as a rule of custom, the positive legal validity of a rule is considered applicable to all states, whether or not they have participated in the practice.

Opinio juris is a more modern, and less well-defined, characteristic of international customary law. It requires that any practice by a state in conformity to a rule of customary international law be acknowledged as an action *obligated* by that rule of law. On one level, *opinio juris* is a consent fail-safe so that sovereign states are not held to a rule of international customary law without accepting an obligation to that said rule. On another level, however, *opinio juris* can be assumed unless specifically disavowed by a state. This assumption connects *opinio juris* to the idea of the *persistent objector* in international law. The International Court of Justice (ICJ) has recognized that any state that publically, specifically, and consistently objects to a proposed or active rule of customary international law, may, by these persistent objections, be exempt from that rule (Fisheries Jurisdiction 1974). Therefore, two modern caveats limit the universality of customary international law. First, a rule of general international law may not apply if the state has not actively or passively acknowledged an *opinio juris* obligation to it. Second, a state, in anticipation of a rule of international customary law, may persistently object to, and remove itself from, its jurisdiction.

Detecting a breech of customary law is a matter of the reaction, or lack thereof, from the other states and agents in the international system. Many times an agent will violate a custom and then make an argument in its own defense that, in fact, reinforces that custom. But customary international law is, unlike treaty law that applies only to the signatories, normally considered to apply to everyone in the international community. In this way, although there is not an established hierarchy among the legal sources, customary international law is considered a sound basis for treaty. If a treaty codifies or becomes "declaratory" of customary international law, for example, the Vienna Convention on the Law of Treaties (VCLT) of 1969, it is considered more persuasive law.

Two important judicial cases on the modern status of customary international law, both decided by the ICJ, are the 1986 Nicaragua Case and the North Sea Continental Shelf Cases of 1969. The former established that even when a treaty is declaratory of custom, this does not make either source of law moot. Two rules exist in parallel; one is treaty based and binding only on the parties, and one is customary and binding for all. The latter case established that a rule of customary law, while not having a "mathematical formula" for its recognition, should be of a "norm-creating character" and be in "both extensive and virtually uniform" practice.

Origins of Customary Law in Principle

Principle exists as a source of international law so that a supply of fundamental legal norms are available that can be drawn on by legal institutions for the progressive codification of the law and to prevent a *non liquet*, where no law exists to settle a dispute. Principle as a source of international law under Article 38 is couched in the context of the principles of "civilized nations." While it is tempting to dismiss this definition as an anachronism of the age of colonialism (which to some extent it is), one should also try to understand the implications for this connotation in terms of the connection of "civilized" principle to custom, and the foundation of both in social convention. Through this lens, *civilized* implies principle that finds its meaning in the practices of the major players of the international system and the particular contextual definitions of such principles (e.g., self-defense of sovereignty) that act as supporting law for the coordination of the international system as it is. *Civilized* denotes that only those principles that are contextual in support of the current system of coordinating sovereign states are suitable as a basis for positive international law. In effect, contextual principle and custom become two manifestations of a single source of nontreaty international law, both based on the social conventions of the state system. Since customary international law, as it stands, is conventionally predisposed toward the sovereignty of states and their contextual obligations to control their native environment, new environmental principles seeking to become customary law (i.e., sustainability, precaution) will have to contend with this status quo.

In order to understand the relationship of custom and principle as sources of international law, it is advantageous to assume that all law follows a pattern of evolution that has three prominent stages, which are, in order: conventional justice, restorative justice, and constitutional justice. The first positive or codified law is derived from the social conventions that have established initial social order and coordination. At this stage, the process of cooperation is an end in itself, and the law draws directly from practice that supports that process.

Law, however, is not only process (i.e., convention and contextual principle) but is also critical principle. The evolution of law is a creature of the tension between the good of social order, represented in social convention/contextual principle, and the independent status of persons or of nature, with the critical principles that represent that special status in the positive law. During the first stage of legal evolution, social convention brings its own type of principle with it (e.g., self-defense and nonintervention as determined by the social convention of state sovereignty), but these are contextual to the conventions themselves rather than critical or independent of it. Critical principle that is in full tension or dialectic with conventional process has an independent justification in human reason rather than social convention, custom, or practice. For example, a concern for human rights grounded in reason has the integrity of the person, not the process equilibrium of sovereign states, as its justification.

Restoring the critical status of humanity and nature to the established legal structure of social convention and contextual principle is the task of the second stage of legal evolution: restorative justice. Unlike most national systems, international law has not yet evolved to the third stage where constitutional institutions enforce the synthesis of conventional process and critical principle. Thus the principle of sustainability remains in this second stage while becoming a legally valid rule of customary international law. Here, the effort of a restorative international legal system is to find a voluntary means to define customary law as a synthesis of contextual and critical principles that do not destabilize the conventional equilibrium of the global system.

Sustainability: Contextual or Critical Principle?

Since the end of World War II, there has been an increasingly more successful effort to integrate concepts of human and environmental rights into international law. These critical rights are not primarily concerned with the stability of the cooperative international system as it is, but with the restoration of it in terms that synthesize the integrity of humanity and nature into customary legal process. The most successful of such efforts have produced the category of *jus cogens* principles. These are noncontextual critical principles of international law that are "peremptory norms of general [or customary] international law" and, according to Articles 53 and 64 of the VCLT, cannot be violated by any treaty. These critical principles are recognized to include nonaggression and self-determination, as well as bans on slavery, the slave trade, genocide, discrimination, and torture.

While these human rights have been validated in "peremptory" law, the effort to create international customary law to support a more sustainable global environment has been less successful. Specifically, sustainability is at a crossroads where the contradictions between what can be called its inherent contextual principles justified by sovereign process (e.g., the right to resources, right to development, common but differentiated responsibilities) is in dialectic with its more critical components (e.g., the precautionary principle, prevention, the human right to a clean environment) that are critically justified independently of sovereignty and may, therefore, compromise it. These latter, critical principles are not yet considered *jus cogens*, because even their rudimentary inclusion in universal customary law would demand the amendment of current custom and contextual principle, both nationally and internationally. It is also this tension between the contextual and critical dimensions of the idea of sustainability that deprive it of the definitive "norm-creating character" required of customary international law.

Although in the contemporary era of international restorative practice, critical principles related to a *jus cogens* definition of sustainability are being considered in legal discourse, if humanity's or nature's integrity are to be judged necessary to the full integration of sustainability into international customary law, it will inevitably clash with a policy maker's predisposition toward the sovereignty of states. If sustainability is to mean more than a state's sovereign right to control and develop its resources, the current global synthesis of convention, contextual, and critical environmental principles will need to be resynthesized. This makes the future definition of sustainability within international customary law an issue of whether its contextual or critical dimension provides its "normative character" in codification. If the former is codified, then sustainability will find legal expression within the established cooperative equilibrium where sovereign process trumps ecosystem integrity. If the latter is codified, a cooperative means will have to be found for states to surrender a degree of sovereignty for the protection of the global environment, as has happened, for example, in the case of states transferring a degree of sovereignty over global trade for membership in the World Trade Organization.

John Martin GILLROY
Lehigh University

See also in the *Berkshire Encyclopedia of Sustainability* Environmental Law, Soft vs. Hard; International Law; Law of the Sea; Principle-Based Regulation; Weak vs. Strong Sustainability Debate; World Constitutionalism

FURTHER READINGS

Allott, Philip. (2002). *The health of nations: Society and law beyond the state.* Cambridge, UK: Cambridge University Press.

Brown, Chester. (2007). *A common law of international adjudication.* Oxford, UK: Oxford University Press.

Byers, Michael. (1999). *Custom, power and the power of rules.* Cambridge, UK: Cambridge University Press.

Gillroy, John Martin. (2006). Adjudication norms, dispute settlement regimes and international tribunals: The status of "environmental sustainability" in international jurisprudence. *Stanford Journal of International Law, 42*(1), 1–52.

Gillroy, John Martin. (2007). Justice-as-sovereignty: David Hume and the origins of international law. *The British Year Book of International Law, 78,* 429–479.

Gillroy, John Martin; Holland, Breena; & Campbell-Mohn, Celia. (2008). *A primer for law and policy design: Understanding the use of principle and argument in environment and natural resource law.* St. Paul, MN: West Casebook Series.

Lowe, Vaughan. (1999). Sustainable development and unsustainable arguments. In Alan Boyle and David Freestone (Eds.), *International law and sustainable development: Past achievements and future challenges* (pp. 19–38). Oxford, UK: Oxford University Press.

Sands, Philippe. (2003). *Principles of international environmental law* (2nd ed.). Cambridge, UK: Cambridge University Press.

Shaw, Malcolm. (2008). *International law* (6th ed.). Cambridge, UK: Cambridge University Press.

TREATIES / RESOLUTIONS / COURT CASES

Fisheries Jurisdiction (*United Kingdom v. Iceland*), Merits, Judgment, I.C.J. Reports 1974, p. 3.

Military and Paramilitary Activities in and against Nicaragua (*Nicaragua v. United States of America*). Merits, Judgment. I.C.J. Reports 1986, p. 14.

North Sea Continental Shelf (*Federal Republic of Germany v. Denmark; Federal Republic of Germany v. The Netherlands*), Judgment, I.C.J. Reports 1969, p. 3.

Statute of the International Court of Justice (adopted 26 June 1945, entered into force 24 October 1946) 3 Bevans 1179; 59 Stat. 1031; T.S. 993; 39 AJIL Supp. 215 (1945).

Environmental Law—Africa, Saharan

Separated from sub-Saharan Africa by the Sahara Desert, the region of Saharan Africa (also known as North Africa) is confronting a range of environmental issues stemming from a confluence of geography, climate, and economic development. Defined here to include the countries of Algeria, Egypt, Libya, Mauritania, Morocco, and Tunisia, the region presently faces water contamination and limited freshwater resources, soil erosion and desertification, overgrazing, deforestation, and oil pollution, among other problems.

The countries of Saharan Africa—Algeria, Egypt, Libya, Mauritania, Morocco, and Tunisia—have developed an array of laws and regulations to address a variety of pressing environmental issues. Environmental legislation must continue to evolve in order to balance the need for economic development with the principles of environmental protection.

Legal Systems

The legal systems of Saharan Africa are based on French civil law and Islamic law but also derive influences from treaties and conventions, customary law, principles of natural law, rules of equity, and Spanish and Italian civil law. Each country draws its legal code from a mix of sources. The Algerian, Mauritanian, and Tunisian legal systems are based largely on French civil and Islamic law. Egyptian law is a combination of Islamic and civil law, particularly Napoleonic codes. Libyan law is influenced by Italian and French civil law as well as Islamic law. Moroccan law is derived from Islamic law and French and Spanish civil law. The predominance of civil law in the region is reflected in an emphasis on legislation rather than case law, with a comparatively weaker judicial system than in common law

countries. As a result, enforcement or protection of rights by citizens, especially against government action, may be difficult to pursue.

Regional and International Agreements

The countries of Saharan Africa are party to numerous environmental agreements at the regional and international levels. These include, at the international level, the Convention on Biological Diversity (CBD), the United Nations Framework Convention on Climate Change (UNFCCC), the United Nations Convention to Combat Desertification (UNCCD), the Convention on International Trade in Endangered Species (CITES), the Basel Convention on Hazardous Wastes, the United Nations Convention on the Law of the Sea (with the exception of Libya, which signed but did not ratify the agreement), the Ramsar Convention on Wetlands, and the International Convention for the Prevention of Pollution from Ships, as modified.

Regionally, all countries except Morocco are members of the African Union, and all were signatories to the 1968 African Convention on the Conservation of Nature and Natural Resources, although only Libya has signed the Revised Convention of 2003. Algeria, Egypt, Mauritania, and Tunisia are also parties to the 1991 Bamako Convention on the Ban of the Import into Africa and the Control of Transboundary Movement and Management of Hazardous Wastes within Africa. In addition, all countries except Mauritania are party to either the Convention for the Protection of the Mediterranean Sea against Pollution (Barcelona Convention) or the Jeddah Convention (Red Sea and Gulf of Aden). Egypt is a party to both agreements. It is also the only country to have ratified the 1967 Phyto-Sanitary Convention for Africa.

Despite being signatories to so many international environmental agreements, the countries of Saharan Africa face many implementation challenges, including full incorporation of the agreements into domestic legislation. Nevertheless, the agreements attest to the involvement of the region in international environmental processes, including those focused specifically on issues in Africa.

Several bilateral agreements also exist within the region. The General Agreement Between Libya and Tunisia on Marine Fishing was executed in August 1988, and seeks to harmonize the countries' approaches to the exploitation and protection of resources in the Mediterranean Sea. The agreement addresses best practices in marine harvesting; processing, handling, and marketing of fish products; and joint technical and scientific research. Egypt has signed bilateral agreements in the areas of veterinary and animal health with Algeria (Cooperative Agreement on Animal Health between Egypt and Algeria, January 1998) and Morocco (Cooperation Agreement between Egypt and Morocco in the Field of Veterinary and Animal Health, June 1999).

The countries of Saharan Africa also participate in two continent-wide interministerial forums: the African Ministerial Conference on the Environment (AMCEN) and the African Ministers' Council on Water (AMCOW). AMCEN, established in 1985, is a permanent forum that brings together African ministers of the environment to work on environmental issues, including the development, improvement, and implementation of environmental legal frameworks. AMCOW was formed in 2002 and seeks "to provide political leadership, policy direction and advocacy in the provision, use and management of water resources for sustainable social and economic development and maintenance of African ecosystems" (AMCOW 2008). There is currently a process, supported by the United States and European nations, to build the capacity of AMCOW as part of a broader effort to ensure that newly formed laws and institutions are effective. The recognition of AMCOW as a Specialized Technical Committee of the African Union in 2009 reflects its continued institutional advancement.

Institutions

National institutions play a key role in implementing environmental laws. The surveyed countries have all designated specific environmental ministries and/or agencies. These include, in Algeria, the Ministry of Land Use Planning and Environment; in Egypt, the Egyptian Environmental Affairs Agency, located at the Ministry of State for Environmental Affairs; in Libya, the Environment General Authority; in Mauritania, the Ministry of Development and Environment; in Morocco, the Department of Environment; and in Tunisia, the Ministry of Environment and Sustainable Development and the National Environmental Protection Agency.

Several countries have established additional institutions to address specific media or environmental issues. Morocco's 1995 Water Law designated a High Council of Water and Climate (Conseil Superieur de l'Eau et du Climat) that is charged with developing a national policy on water and climate. Tunisia's Ministry of Environment and Sustainable Development oversees the National Office of Sanitation, National Environment Protection Agency, National Agency for Coastal Protection, Tunis International Center for Environment Technologies, and the National Renewable Energies Agency.

Framework Environmental Laws

Framework national environmental laws can set the foundation for environmental protection by addressing a comprehensive set of issues and threats in a manner tailored to a country's needs and capacities. Most of the countries within the region have enacted framework environmental laws. For example, Morocco's Law No. 11-03, Protection and Enhancement of the Environment (19 June 2003), requires pollution control measures for specified facilities; mandates protection of soils from desertification, floods, erosion, loss of arable land and forests, and pollution; provides for the protection of fauna and flora, including the establishment of lists of protected species; and includes other provisions regarding forests, water, air, coastal resources, and protected areas. The law also addresses hazardous substances, sets environmental standards, establishes the National Fund for the Protection and Enhancement of the Environment, and calls for the development of regulations to implement its objectives.

Egypt's Law Number 4/1994, Promulgating the Environment Law, and revised by Law Number 9/2009,

establishes an Environmental Affairs Agency and Environmental Protection Fund. The law also sets forth measures to protect land, air, and water resources from pollution, including provisions on wildlife protection, hazardous waste management, the development of a contingency plan for environmental disasters, and extensive requirements for ships and other ocean vessels. The law's implementing regulations address these legal requirements in greater detail, including the mechanics of a licensing system for various types of activities, such as development, hunting, and hazardous waste disposal.

In Libya, the 1982 Legislative Act No. 7 Concerning Protection of the Environment addresses air quality, freshwater resources, ocean and marine resources, cultivated foods, contagious diseases, soil and plant protection, and wildlife protection. The law also establishes the Technical Centre for the Protection of the Environment and authorizes the Centre to develop programs to address environmental protection. In addition, it calls for regulations to address the responsibilities of different sectors in Libya for implementing the Act.

Mauritania's Law No. 200-45 Framework Environmental Law (2000) broadly addresses conservation of biodiversity and the rational use of natural resources, desertification, pollution and nuisances, improvement and protection of the framework of life, and the harmonization of development with protection of the natural environment. The law also establishes the National Environment and Development Council and calls for a national plan of environmental action to coordinate environmental protection measures, including the fight against desertification. It further envisions the development of regulations to help enact the country's national environmental policy.

Algeria's Act No. 03-10 of 19 July 2003, concerning protection of the environment in the context of sustainable development, establishes a system to collect environmental information as well as public rights to access that information; provides for the establishment of protected areas; and establishes requirements for the protection of biodiversity, air and the atmosphere, water and aquatic environments, land and subsoil, desert environments, and all life in general. The law calls for the development of regulations to implement its provisions.

In addition to their framework environmental laws, most countries in the region have also enacted laws on water, forests, soil conservation, protected areas, wildlife protection, and many other natural resource and environmental issues. For example, Tunisia has a water pollution law, a wildlife protection law, a marine pollution law, and an air pollution and noise emissions law. Instead of a framework environmental law, the country has consolidated its environmental legislation and programs through the National Action Plan for the Environment, which delineates a strategy for natural resource conservation, pollution control, and land-use management.

Environmental Impact Assessment

Environmental Impact Assessment (EIA) is an important tool used to prevent or minimize adverse environmental effects associated with industrial and manufacturing activity, development of infrastructure, agriculture, and a wide range of other activities. Put simply, EIA requires an examination of a project's potential environmental impacts before it may proceed. In some countries, EIA is merely a procedural requirement, thus ensuring that environmental impacts are examined, while in others it is a substantive requirement that can be used to prevent environmentally harmful projects from proceeding. EIA can also provide an important opportunity for members of the public to participate in the environmental review process.

Most of the countries in Saharan Africa address EIA to some extent, either through stand-alone laws or through their framework environmental laws. Mauritania, Morocco, and Algeria have all passed separate laws that require EIAs for specific projects. For example, Mauritania's Decree No. 2004-094 (24 November 2004) establishes three categories of activities that determine the need for an EIA: (1) activities that require an environmental impact study, (2) activities that require a notice of environmental impact, and (3) activities that require neither an environmental impact study nor a notice of environmental impact. The law specifies the elements that must be included in an environmental impact study and requires public notice and comment.

In Morocco, Law 12-03, Study of Environmental Impacts (12 May 2003), includes a list of projects that require EIAs and sets forth the information that must be included in the assessment. The law also provides for public notice and comment, requires monitoring of a project's impacts, and establishes national and regional committees to examine the environmental impacts of proposed projects. Only projects that are deemed environmentally acceptable may proceed.

In Algeria, Decree 07/145 (2007) and its appendices replaced Executive Decree No. 90-78 (1990), the country's first law on EIA. The new law defines which projects are subject to an environmental impact study and sets forth additional elements that must be included in the study, such as the consideration of alternatives; an evaluation of direct, indirect, and cumulative impacts; and a plan for any mitigation measures. The law also details the procedure by which an environmental impact study must be completed and authorized. Both Algeria and Morocco require some public participation in the EIA process, including public access to information about proposed projects and an opportunity to comment on a draft EIA.

In contrast, Egypt's EIA provisions are located within its framework environmental law and implementing regulations. Together, the law and regulations require an environmental impact assessment for establishments specified in Annex 2 of the regulations. Establishments falling under one of the following four categories will be subject to the EIA requirement: (1) type of activity, such as industrial and oil facilities; (2) extent of depletion of natural resources, especially water, agricultural land, and mineral wealth; (3) location, such as on the banks of the Nile; and (4) type of energy used, such as nuclear fuel. The law also requires owners of covered facilities to keep a written record of the facility's impact on the environment and to implement any mitigation measures proposed by the Egyptian Environmental Affairs Agency.

Examining a Key Regional Issue: Water

Water availability in Saharan Africa is a central environmental and economic issue, with a disproportionate amount of water used for agriculture, despite growing desertification and scarcity. In response to the critical shortage of water, countries throughout the region have developed laws, regulations, and institutions governing water management and use. These laws address everything from water rights and permits to pollution control, wastewater reuse, and water management plans. Public participation, institutional approaches, and monitoring and enforcement are also reflected, to varying extents, in the region's water laws. Within the region, the legal frameworks of Morocco and Tunisia emerge as particularly strong examples of regulating and managing water, while the laws of Egypt and Algeria also contain some robust provisions.

A number of laws in the region address water quality through the creation of water quality standards and the use of a permitting process for polluting discharges. For example, Algeria, Egypt, and Morocco have each established drinking water quality standards based on those of the World Health Organization (WHO). These countries have also authorized the establishment of ambient water quality standards at the agency or ministry level, with Algeria's Water Law (Art. 38) requiring that three different standards be set according to the actual use of a water body. In addition, Morocco, Tunisia, and Egypt all regulate the discharge of harmful substances into public waters. Under Morocco's *Décret* No. 2-04-553, a permit is required for any discharge into surface water or groundwater that is likely to alter the chemical, biological, thermal, or physical characteristics of the water body. In Egypt, entities that discharge waste into water channels must obtain licenses from the Ministry of Irrigation and Water Resources. Egypt also has passed regulations addressing the discharge of industrial liquid waste into fresh water, including the country's sewer system and the Nile River, and has enacted legal authority requiring the Ministry of Agriculture to protect waterways from pesticides and herbicides.

Countries have also adopted institutional approaches to managing water availability and quality. Egypt, Morocco, and Tunisia have all developed plans to address water quantity and use. Egypt and Morocco's plans are aimed at redistributing water from agriculture to domestic and industrial purposes, while Tunisia's reallocation plan seeks to divert water from high- to low-availability areas and from agriculture to cities and tourism, as well as to manage water resources in individual basins (Article 20). Morocco and Yemen also require that water management authority be transferred from the central government to local agencies. Article 20 of Morocco's 1995 Water Law establishes a network of independent Basin Agencies to manage water catchments. Among other things, the Basin Agencies are responsible for developing integrated water resource development plans at both the catchment and basin level, monitoring water-use practices and plan implementation, and issuing authorizations and concessions for water use. In Tunisia, interested water users or authorities can establish water user associations to manage irrigation or drinking water systems. In Algeria, water management is established at the basin level or within each hydrological unit, with the country's water law requiring the development of a master plan for each hydrological unit. The plan should address domestic, agricultural, and industrial water use, as well as the protection of surface and subsurface water quality.

Water scarcity has also given rise to transboundary tensions in Saharan Africa, particularly around the Nile Basin. Although the Nile River originates in Ethiopia, the Nile Water Agreement of 1929 allocates most of its water to Egypt. The Nile Basin Initiative (NBI), a partnership forged by the riparian states of the Nile River, "seeks to develop the river in a cooperative manner, share substantial socioeconomic

benefits, and promote regional peace and security" (NBI 2010). Its members include Egypt, Sudan, Ethiopia, Burundi, Democratic Republic of Congo, Kenya, Rwanda, Tanzania, and Uganda. Members of the NBI upstream of the Nile have sought to revisit the issue of how the river's water is allocated. In May 2010, Rwanda, Ethiopia, Uganda, and Tanzania signed the Nile Basin Cooperative Framework Agreement, which could limit the flow of water into Egypt. Kenya has also issued a statement in support of the measure. With the two downstream countries (Egypt and Sudan) having filed objections to the agreement, the status of water governance in the Nile Basin has become tenuous.

Assessment

Confronted with pressing environmental concerns such as desertification, oil pollution, and water scarcity, the countries of Saharan Africa have assembled an impressive array of environmental laws and institutions. These laws generally adopt a comprehensive approach to protecting land, biodiversity, air, and water by establishing standards and procedures for activities that may cause environmental harm. Yet laws on the books alone are not enough; implementation and enforcement are also necessary. In addition to the executive and judicial branches, civil society and the public can play important roles in ensuring that environmental laws are carried out and upheld. In the face of growing pressures to reconcile economic development with environmental protection, the continued evolution of environmental law holds important implications for the well-being of Saharan Africa.

Lisa GOLDMAN
Environmental Law Institute

The author would like to thank Jessica Troell and Carl Bruch for their help with outlining and reviewing this article.

Editors' note: this article was written before the Arab Spring, which, starting in 2010, led to several regime changes.

See also in the *Berkshire Encyclopedia of Sustainability* Convention on Biological Diversity; Convention on International Trade in Endangered Species; Convention on Wetlands; Convention to Combat Desertification; Environmental Law—Africa, Sub-Saharan; Environmental Law—Arab Region; International Law; National Environmental Policy Act; Transboundary Water Law; Waste Shipment Law

FURTHER READINGS

Abdel Wahab, Mohamed S. E. (2008). UPDATE: An overview of the Egyptian legal system and legal research. *GlobaLex.* Retrieved November 16, 2010, from http://www.nyulawglobal.org/Globalex/Egypt1.htm

Africa Union. (2010). Homepage. Retrieved November 16, 2010, from http://www.africa-union.org/root/au/index/index.htm

African Ministers' Council on Water (AMCOW). (2008). Homepage. Retrieved November 30, 2010, from www.amcow.net

Bruch, Carl; Altman, Stephanie; Al-Moumin, Mishkat; Troell, Jessica; & Roffman, Elana. (2007). Legal frameworks governing water in the Middle East and North Africa. *International Journal of Water Resources Development, 23*(4), 595–624.

Central Intelligence Agency (CIA). (2010). The world factbook. Retrieved November 16, 2010, from https://www.cia.gov/library/publications/the-world-factbook/

ECOLEX. (2010). Homepage. Retrieved November 16, 2010, from http://www.ecolex.org/start.php

Egyptian Environmental Affairs Agency. (2010). Homepage. Retrieved November 16, 2010, from http://www.eeaa.gov.eg

FAOLEX. (2010). Homepage. Retrieved November 16, 2010, from http://faolex.fao.org/

Mauritania Ministry of Development and Environment. (2006). Homepage. Retrieved November 16, 2010, from www.minenv.gov.ma

Mechantaf, Khalil, & Touchent, Dahmène. (2010). Update: A guide to the Tunisian legal system. *GlobaLex.* Retrieved November 16, 2010, from http://www.nyulawglobal.org/globalex/Tunisia1.htm

Nile Basin Initiative. (2010). Homepage. Retrieved November 16, 2010, from http://www.nilebasin.org/

Serge, Zelezeck Nguimatsa. (2009). Researching the legal system and laws of the Islamic Republic of Mauritania. *GlobaLex.* Retrieved November 16, 2010, from http://www.nyulawglobal.org/globalex/mauritania.htm

Simpkins, John L. S. (2008). Libya's legal system and legal research. *GlobaLex.* Retrieved November 16, 2010, from http://www.nyulawglobal.org/globalex/Libya.htm

Touchent, Dahmène. (2006). Algerian law guide. *GlobaLex.* Retrieved November 16, 2010, from http://www.nyulawglobal.org/globalex/algeria.htm

Touchent, Dahmène. (2006). Introduction to the Moroccan legal system. *GlobaLex.* Retrieved November 16, 2010, from http://www.nyulawglobal.org/globalex/morocco.htm

Tunisia Online. (n.d.). Environment. Retrieved November 16, 2010, from http://www.tunisiaonline.com/environment/index.html

United Nations Environment Programme (UNEP). (n.d.). Launch of the Africa Environment Outlook (AEO) 2. Retrieved November 16, 2010, from http://www.unep.org/DEWA/Africa/AEO2_Launch/

United Nations Environment Programme (UNEP) & the Partnership for the Development of Environmental Law and Institutions in Africa (PADELIA). (n.d.). Publications: Environmental laws. Retrieved November 16, 2010, from http://www.unep.org/padelia/publications/publication.htm

The World Law Guide (Lexadin). (n.d.). Homepage. Retrieved November 16, 2010, from http://www.lexadin.nl/wlg/

Environmental Law—Africa, Sub-Saharan

Environmental degradation is just one of many issues facing the continent of Africa; it is especially critical since many Africans depend on natural resources for their livelihoods. Although a commitment to sustainable development exists on international, regional, and national levels largely because of organizations such as the African Union, the effectiveness of these treaties, protocols, and conventions is questionable since noncompliance and lack of enforcement remain overriding issues.

Africa is the world's poorest and most underdeveloped continent, and it is characterized by the occurrence of deadly diseases, governments that commit serious human rights violations, military conflict, abject poverty, illiteracy, malnutrition, inadequate water supply and sanitation, poor health, and environmental degradation. While the continent is in dire need of sustainable development, this ideal remains elusive for most African countries. Africa suffers particularly from numerous environmental challenges, including deforestation, desertification, the loss of soil fertility, the loss of biodiversity, the effects of climate change, and water pollution. It is these challenges that hinder many African countries from making progress with regard to sustainable development.

But African governments have committed themselves to international, regional, subregional, and national norms aimed at the protection and conservation of the environment. This chapter briefly examines the regional (i.e., African Union, or AU) normative environmental legal framework and relevant institutions, and a discussion of subregional law follows. Finally, this chapter briefly investigates environmental law and governance in South Africa as a member state of the AU and the Southern African Development Community (SADC).

African Union (AU)

The limited capacity of African countries, coupled with the dependence of their citizens on natural resources for their livelihoods, highlights the importance of regional cooperation to the attainment of sustainable development. Regional integration may facilitate the development of consensus around concerns such as environmental degradation and provide a framework for cooperation on shared resources and shared environmental problems.

African states previously experimented with the idea of pan-African regional cooperation in the form of the Organisation of African Unity (OAU), which was established in May 1963 in Addis Ababa, Ethiopia. The OAU, however, applied a policy of nonintervention and did not succeed in its efforts to influence the policies of its member states. The OAU Assembly Heads of State and Government convened in September 1999 in Sirte, Libya, with a view to establishing the African Union (AU) as the successor to the OAU. The Constitutive Act of the AU was subsequently signed on 11 July 2000 and entered into force on 26 May 2001; it was officially inaugurated on 9 July 2002. The AU was established primarily to confront the various challenges that the continent faces, including socioeconomic and environmental problems. One of the specific objectives of the AU is therefore to promote sustainable development (Constitutive Act of the AU, Article 3(j)). To this end, the OAU and AU have adopted various treaties, resolutions, declarations, and charters concerning environmental protection and conservation, which cumulatively constitute the regional African normative environmental law framework. The following sections briefly canvass the most important elements of this framework.

Environmental Conventions

The Phyto-Sanitary Convention for Africa of 1967 was a development of the International Plant Protection Convention of 1961. It is concerned with preventing the introduction of diseases, insects, pests, and other threats to plants into Africa, and their eradication or control. Articles II–V prescribe protective measures such as quarantining, certification, and inspection. The administration of the convention is the responsibility of the Inter-African Phytosanitary Council (IAPC) / African Plant Protection Organisation (APPO).

Article XXIV of the African Convention on Nature and Natural Resources of 1968 (Algiers Convention) makes provision for the revision of the convention five years after its entry into force. A substantially revised version was subsequently adopted on 11 July 2003. The 2003 convention is not in force yet as it awaits ratification. It is, however, important to reflect on the most important provisions of the revised convention. Article II describes the objectives of the convention, which include the enhancement of environmental protection, the fostering of the conservation and sustainable use of natural resources, and the harmonization and coordination of national environmental policies. The revised convention includes obligations pertaining to land and soil protection, water conservation, vegetation cover, species and genetic diversity, protected species, trade in specimens and the products thereof, conservation areas, processes and activities affecting the environment, sustainable development and natural resources, military and hostile activities, as well as clauses dealing with compliance and liability. Africa frequently serves as the dumping ground for the world's largest disposers of waste, and African states were of the opinion that the Basel Convention on the Transboundary Movement of Hazardous Wastes and their Disposal (signed 1989; entered into force 1992) did not adequately address their concerns. The Bamako Convention on the Ban on the Import into Africa and the Control of Transboundary Movement and Management of Hazardous Wastes within Africa (signed 1991; entered into force 1998) was therefore adopted. The Bamako Convention has three objectives: a ban on hazardous waste imports into Africa and on the export of waste from Africa, and the regulation of the transfer of hazardous waste between African states. The convention established a secretariat and Conference of the Parties (COP). The effectiveness of the convention is demonstrably questionable, as some African states continue to attract illegal dumping practices.

The African Economic Community Treaty of 1991 (Abuja Treaty / AEC) is principally aimed at promoting economic, social, and cultural development and economic integration on the African continent. It contains various references to the environment, since the coordination of environmental governance is seen as a mechanism to pursue the objectives of the AEC (Article 4(2)(h)). Article 25 establishes the Committee on Industry, Science and Technology, Energy, Natural Resources and Environment, which among other functions prepares projects and programs for the community. Article 51(1)(b) states that member states shall ensure the proper application of technology and science in respect of environmental conservation. In the context of a common energy policy, member states are to acquire a sound knowledge and assessment of their natural resources (Article 55(2)(a)). Article 58 obliges member states to adopt policies, programs, and strategies as well as establish institutions for the protection and enhancement of the environment. Article 59 also contains an undertaking concerning the control of hazardous waste.

The Convention of the African Energy Commission of 2001 establishes the African Energy Commission (AFREC) and includes as a guiding principle the "development and utilization of sustainable and environmentally friendly energy" (Article 3(c)). Article 4 stipulates that it is one of the functions of AFREC to promote the identification, adoption, and implementation of effective measures to prevent pollution in relation to African energy resources.

The African Charter on Human and People's Rights of 1981 (African Charter) includes an environmental right that provides for people's entitlement to a "general satisfactory environment favourable to their development" (Article 24). This is one of the few treaties in the world to explicitly provide for an environmental right, and it has been influential in Africa in guiding domestic formulations and the adoption of environmental rights. In the case of *Social and Economic Rights Action Center and the Center for Economic and Social Rights v. Nigeria*, ACHPR, 155/96 (2002) (SERAC case), the African Commission on Human and

Peoples Rights (a quasi-judicial body) held, for instance, that Article 24 of the African Charter imposes an obligation on the state to take reasonable measures "to prevent pollution and ecological degradation, to promote conservation, and to secure ecologically sustainable development and use of natural resources."

The Preamble and Articles 15, 16, 18, and 19 of the Protocol to the African Charter on Human and Peoples' Rights on the Rights of Women in Africa of 2003 deal with environmental issues and women's rights. In this regard, member states incur obligations to implement measures pursuant to the promotion of the "right to sustainable development" and the "right to a healthy and sustainable environment."

The African Charter on the Rights and the Welfare of the Child of 1990 provides children with a right to education that must, among other requirements, be directed in terms of Article 11 to the development of respect for the environment and natural resources.

The above exposition demonstrates that the AU and its predecessor have developed an impressive array of international agreements pursuant to the goal of sustainable development. But national implementation of these instruments in general is a problem, since effective compliance and enforcement mechanisms are often lacking or are ignored completely. This might lead one rightly to question the effectiveness of these agreements.

Soft Law and AU organs

Certain organs of the AU generate resolutions, decisions, declarations, principles, and guidelines that constitute environmental "soft law." These instruments are nonbinding but may form the basis for subsequent binding treaties or influence state practice pursuant to the forming of binding customary international law. While these instruments are too many to canvass here, a brief summary of the most important "authors" or institutions of soft law follows below.

The Assembly is the supreme organ of the AU and consists of heads of state and government or their duly accredited representatives. The Assembly determines the common policies of the AU and monitors the implementation of policies and decisions of the Union. At each ordinary session the Assembly adopts decisions, declarations, and resolutions on issues of common concern. It has already adopted a vast array of instruments relating to environmental matters. For example, it made important decisions during the eighth (January 2007), twelfth (February 2009), and thirteenth (July 2009) sessions, which sparked the development of a common position on climate change.

The Assembly's Executive Council consists of the ministers of foreign affairs or such other ministers or authorities as are designated by the governments of the member states. The Executive Council coordinates and adopts policy decisions on areas of common interest, which includes environmental protection, and has to date adopted a vast range of resolutions concerning the environment. This includes, for example, the Nairobi Declaration on the African Process for Combating Climate Change, which was adopted during the Executive Council's fifteenth ordinary session (June 2009).

Various institutions were established with the formal adoption of the New Partnership for Africa's Development (NEPAD) Strategic Framework in July 2001. NEPAD is a development program, and its primary objective includes sustainable growth and development for African countries. Environment and Climate Change is one of the priority areas of NEPAD, which is significant because NEPAD hereby acknowledges the importance of environmental protection in future developmental strategies. The secretariat is responsible for coordinating and facilitating the preparation and implementation of the NEPAD Environment Action Plan (EAP) and the Sub-Regional Environmental Action Plans (SREAPs). The EAP was prepared under the auspices of the African Ministerial Conference on the Environment (AMCEN), which was established in December 1985 by the United Nations Environment Programme (UNEP). Its mandate includes advocating environmental protection in Africa. Since its creation it has fulfilled several roles, such as the development of common positions pursuant to negotiations of international environmental treaties, and capacity building in the field of environmental governance. AMCEN has notably played an important role concerning the African response to climate change. The role of AMCEN in relation to regional environmental initiatives on the African continent is also noteworthy, since it is expected that AMCEN would ultimately become a Specialised Technical Committee (STC) of the AU Commission

Southern African Development Community (SADC)

Regional Economic Communities (RECs) such as the Southern African Development Community (SADC) constitute the instruments for the achievement of the objectives of the AU, and it is envisaged that SADC will play a key role in the implementation of environmental measures under the leadership of the AU. SADC was established by means of the Windhoek Treaty (Declaration and Treaty Establishing the Southern African Development Community, 1992, as amended in 2001). Its member states include Angola, Botswana, the Democratic Republic of Congo, Lesotho, Madagascar, Malawi, Mauritius, Mozambique, Namibia, South Africa, Swaziland, United Republic of

Tanzania, Zambia, and Zimbabwe. While SADC's main objective was to establish a free trade area by 2008, the ultimate goal of member states remains the creation by 2034 of a complete economic union with integrated monetary and fiscal systems and a regional parliament. Member states realize that deeper economic integration requires coordination in other spheres, such as the environment, and several SADC instruments, institutions, and protocols are relevant to environmental governance. This is evident from Article 5(1)(g) of the SADC Treaty, which affirms that one of its objectives is to promote the sustainable use of natural resources and the effective protection of the environment.

The SADC Treaty

The Summit is the supreme policy-making institution of SADC. It consists of the heads of state or government of all member states. It is responsible for the overall policy direction and control of the functions of SADC and adopts legal instruments, some of which take the form of environmental protocols pursuant to the protection of the environment.

Article 21(2) of the Windhoek Treaty provides that all member states must, through appropriate institutions of SADC, coordinate, rationalize, and harmonize their overall macroeconomic policies and strategies. One of the agreed areas of cooperation is "natural resources and environment." The secretariat is responsible for the harmonization of the policies of member states and the submission of coordinated policies and programs to the council for consideration and approval. The secretariat is therefore the principal executive institution of SADC. It consists of one minister from each member state. It is one of the responsibilities of this organ to oversee the implementation of the policies of SADC, including environmental policies.

Institutional and governance difficulties experienced in SADC recently led to the adoption of a "Report on the Restructuring of SADC Institutions." A Regional Indicative Strategic Development Plan (RISDP) has been developed in accordance with the report in order to provide strategic direction to SADC. The process has restructured the previous coordinating units into four directorates: (1) Trade, Industry, Finance and Investment (TIFI); (2) Infrastructure and Services; (3) Food, Agriculture and Natural Resources (FANR); and (4) Social and Human Development and Special Programmes (SHDSP). The plan also includes a selection of so-called intervention areas, and environment and sustainable development has been designated as one of these priority areas. The overall goal of the environment intervention effort is to ensure that natural resources and the environment are preserved for future generations.

Environmental Protocols

The main instruments by means of which cooperation in the environmental field is to be achieved by SADC member states, at least at a normative level, are protocols, which must "spell out the objectives and scope of, and institutional mechanisms for, co-operation and integration" (Article 22 of the SADC Treaty). The state of implementation, compliance with, and enforcement of these protocols, however, remains a challenge in the region. While an assessment of the effectiveness of the protocols falls outside the scope of this enquiry, the following paragraphs briefly outline in chronological order those protocols and their provisions directly relevant to natural resources and environmental protection.

Southern Africa is one of the world's regions with the most shared watercourses. It is therefore not surprising that the Protocol on Shared Watercourses (1995, revised in 2000) is the oldest and arguably most comprehensive environment-related normative instrument in SADC. The protocol is crucial in an extremely water-scarce region of the world. (This discussion focuses on the 2000 revision, since it is expected that it will soon come into force.) The general objective of the protocol is to promote cooperation for the judicious, sustainable, and coordinated management, protection, and utilization of shared watercourses in the SADC Region (Article 2). It makes provision for a broad range of instruments and institutions to realize this objective. These include planned measures; environmental protection and preservation; the management of shared watercourses; and the prevention and mitigation of harmful conditions and emergency incidents (Article 4). The institutional framework for its implementation consists of SADC water sector organs; shared watercourse institutions; the Committee of Water Ministers; the Committee of Water Senior Officials; and the Water Sector Co-ordinating Unit (Article 5). Article 6 allows member states to conclude shared watercourse agreements to realize the co-management of shared watercourses.

The Protocol on Energy (1996) sets out provisions for the optimal use of energy in the southern African region. Its purposes are to support economic growth and development, to alleviate poverty, and to improve the standard and quality of life, while promoting the self-reliance of member states in terms of energy needs (Articles 2(1) and 2(2)). While the protocol encourages scientific and technological developments with regard to energy, Article 2(8) specifically provides that the development and use of energy must be environmentally sound. Its main objectives include cooperation in the development and utilization of energy with respect to wood fuel, petroleum and natural gas, electricity, coal, new and renewable energy sources, energy efficiency, and energy conservation (Article 3(3) and items 1–6 of Annex I). The protocol arguably makes it incumbent on SADC member states to devise and implement cooperative strategies with respect to the provision, environmentally sound management, and further development of the forgoing energy sectors, which will be important considerations in SADC's response to climate change governance and the international drive toward "greener" forms of energy and energy conservation. A commission and various substructures are responsible for implementing the protocol (Article 4). While containing no specific provisions on how its objectives are to be achieved, it provides in broad terms for the reporting of data and information exchange between member states (Article 6), cooperation with non-SADC states and organizations (Articles 7 and 8), and research development and training (Article 9).

Most southern African countries are rich in mineral resources, and mining forms the backbone of various economies in the region. While mining has the potential to create enormous wealth, the effect of mining on the environment is often devastating. It is with this in mind that the Protocol on Mining (1997) aims to maximize the socioeconomic benefits resulting from mining while aiming to protect the environment against its harmful effects (Article 2). The effectiveness of the environmental protection component is questionable, however, as economic and political motives arguably often prevail against environmental considerations in decisions related to mining in the region. In Article 2(10), member states undertake to observe internationally accepted standards of health, mining safety, and environmental protection. Article 8 specifically provides for environmental protection, in that member states must promote sustainable development by ensuring that a balance between mineral development and environmental protection is attained; encourage a regional approach in conducting environmental impact assessments, especially in relation to shared systems and cross-border environmental effects; collaborate in the development of programs to train environmental scientists in fields related to the mining sector; and share information on environmental protection and environmental rehabilitation.

Human health is an important component of the broader environmental governance effort, and the Protocol on Health (1999) recognizes this fact. While not concerned primarily with environmental health, the protocol provides in Article 23 for member states to collaborate, cooperate, and assist one another in a cross-sectoral approach in addressing regional environmental health issues and other concerns, including those of toxic waste; waste management; port health services; the pollution of air, land, and water; and the degradation of natural resources. Other provisions of this protocol that relate directly to environmental health include provisions on malaria control (Article 11) and emergency health services during natural disasters (Article 25).

The Protocol on Wildlife Conservation and Enforcement (1999) recognizes in its preamble that the viability of wildlife resources (excluding forests and fisheries resources, which are regulated by other protocols) in southern Africa requires collective action by all SADC member states. To this end, each member state must ensure the conservation and sustainable use of wildlife resources under its jurisdiction (Article 3). Specific objectives of the protocol include promoting the sustainable use of wildlife; harmonizing legal instruments governing wildlife use and conservation; enforcing wildlife laws within, between, and among member states; facilitating the exchange of information; assisting in the building of capacity for wildlife management, conservation, and the enforcement of wildlife laws; promoting the conservation of shared wildlife resources through the establishment of transfrontier conservation areas; and facilitating community-based natural resources management practices (Article 4). While Article 5 establishes the institutional structure for the implementation of the Protocol, Article 6 obliges member states to create legal instruments to ensure conservation and the sustainable use of wildlife. Wildlife management and conservation programs must also be established, and these and the other relevant measures (Articles 7–9), cumulatively, must ensure optimal cooperation for the sustainable regional management of wildlife resources.

The Protocol on Fisheries (2001) recognizes the need for the sustainable use and protection of fisheries (Preamble) with a view to eradicating poverty, sustaining livelihoods, and ensuring the availability of aquatic resources for future generations (Article 3). Its provisions apply to living aquatic resources, aquatic ecosystems, and fishing

activities (Article 2). While the implementation obligation of the protocol is primarily at national level, regional cooperation is especially required with respect to shared resources (Articles 4 and 5). Article 6 highlights the need for common positions and both coordinated and complementary actions at the regional level with respect to international and other instruments related to the protocol—for example, the 1982 United Nations Convention on the Law of the Sea (UNCLOS). To realize the effective management of shared resources, Article 7 provides for dispute resolution between member states, information sharing, the establishment of institutions and instruments for co-management, the establishment of co-management plans, and measures to prevent and eliminate overfishing. It places significant emphasis on the creation and harmonization of national laws to regulate aquatic resources (Article 8) and law enforcement in this respect (Article 9). Article 12 provides for artisanal, subsistence, and small-scale commercial fishing, and emphasizes the need to promote the socioeconomic uses of aquatic resources while at the same time protecting these resources. Further provisions of the protocol relate to the promotion of aquaculture and the protection of aquatic resources, trade and investment activities related to aquatic resources, science and technology, and information exchange between member states (Articles 13–18).

There are many forest areas in southern Africa, and apart from providing people with fuel and general sustenance, they also constitute an important part of the entire regional ecosystem. It is not surprising therefore that SADC places a high premium on the sustainable management of forests. This is to be achieved by means of the Protocol on Forestry (2002), which is applicable to all activities relating to the development, conservation, sustainable management, and utilization of all types of forests and trees, and trade in forest products in the region (Articles 2 and 3). Member states must assist and support one another in addressing common issues related to deforestation, genetic erosion, climate change, forest fires, pests, diseases, alien invasive species, and law enforcement (Article 3). The protocol explicitly provides for security of land tenure; the establishment of a subcommittee to oversee the implementation of the protocol; the development of national forest policies, programs, and plans; measures to undertake national forest assessments; and the development and enforcement of national legal and administrative measures (Articles 5–11). The specific roles of local communities, traditional knowledge, and women are also recognized in Articles 12, 13, and 16. Because some forests in the region traverse borders, Article 14 makes explicit provision for the transboundary management of forests. The remainder of the protocol makes provision for the regulation of sylvan genetic resources; industry, trade, and investment activities related to forests; capacity building and public awareness raising;

research and development; and reporting and information exchange obligations (Articles 17–21).

South African Environmental Law and Governance

The Republic of South Africa is considered one of the leading countries on the African continent. As a regional powerhouse it plays a vital role in the AU and SADC in terms of setting norms, leadership, and institution building. While it very actively influences the development of regional and subregional environmental law, its domestic environmental law regime is itself continuously being influenced by regional and subregional environmental law in accordance with domestic constitutional imperatives for domestic law to incorporate and heed international law (Constitution of the Republic of South Africa 1996, sections 39, 231–233). Since its reintegration into the international arena following decades of isolation during apartheid, South Africa has developed a comprehensive environmental law and governance regime that provides for the establishment of a host of institutions responsible for environmental governance. Despite these positive developments, challenges in upholding the rule of environmental law remain plainly evident in South Africa's daily struggle with the realities of sustainability. The country's socioeconomic and environmental welfare is balanced in a delicate yet complex equilibrium and is under significant strain as a result of a number of pressures, including the unsustainable exploitation of marine resources, increased threats to fauna and flora, soil erosion, uncontrolled and ever-expanding mining and agricultural activities, rapid urbanization and population growth, the proliferation of waste disposal sites, and the impacts of climate change. The prevalence of HIV/AIDS, insufficient access to environmental resources such as water and sanitation, a lack of adequate housing, and pervasive poverty are only some of the socioeconomic challenges plaguing the majority of the population while simultaneously compounding many of the forgoing ecological challenges. Environmental law plays an indispensable role in addressing these challenges and redirecting South Africa onto a sustainable path.

Historical Developments

Environmental concerns were raised in South Africa as early as the seventeenth century, albeit to further the well-being of a struggling European community. The twentieth century saw few initiatives to enhance environmental protection. Legislation focused primarily on preventing illegal hunting. In the period between 1800 and the establishment of the Union of South Africa in 1910, legislative measures emerged to regulate fishing, noxious weeds, and the demarcation of forests as the first formally protected areas in South Africa. The first environmental control at the national level came into being with the enactment of the Irrigation and Conservation of Waters Act 8 of 1912, and some other statutes followed. In alignment with growing global environmental awareness, it was between 1940 and 1969 that further legislation was promulgated to address environmental challenges more comprehensively. The period since 1970 has seen the most significant development of environmental law, and a host of regulatory institutions has been created.

The Legal Framework

Section 24 of the Constitution of the Republic of South Africa (1996) provides for environmental responsibility and states that everyone has the right to an environment that is not harmful to their health or well-being; and to have the environment protected, for the benefit of present and future generations, through reasonable legislative and other measures that (1) prevent pollution and ecological degradation; (2) promote conservation; and (3) secure ecologically sustainable development and use of natural resources while promoting justifiable economic and social development.

This is a basic fundamental right, and while it elevates environmental protection to the constitutional level, it also provides the foundation for the entire South African environmental law and governance effort. It is frequently invoked in domestic courts by proponents of environmental protection and contributes significantly to the development of sustainability jurisprudence in the country.

The National Environmental Management Act 107 of 1998 (NEMA) is South Africa's primary environmental framework law. It contains generic provisions applicable to all actions that may affect the environment, including provisions related to environmental impact assessment (EIA); South Africa's international environmental obligations, including the ratification of environmental treaties; compliance, enforcement, pollution prevention, and remediation; and South Africa's primary environmental enforcement agency, the Environmental Management Inspectorate (EMI). It also specifically provides for a "duty of care" and obligations to avoid, minimize, and remediate pollution; the protection of workers refusing to do environmentally hazardous work; the control of emergency incidents; access to environmental information and the protection of whistle-blowers; the legal standing to enforce environmental laws; and private prosecution and criminal proceedings. Duty of care entails that people should apply proper (environmental) care in all their activities, products, and services that may have the potential to negatively affect the environment (including people living in the environment). Complying with environmental law provisions is a prerequisite for adhering to the duty of environmental care and where there is non-compliance, certain sanctions and liability will follow.

Besides the generic regulation represented by NEMA, South Africa has various sectoral environmental laws that aim to regulate subject-specific issues. Mining is regulated by the Mineral and Petroleum Resources Development Act 28 of 2002; water resources by the National Water Act 36 of 1998 and the Water Services Act 108 of 1997; air quality by the National Environmental Management: Air Quality Act 39 of 2004; protected areas by the National Environmental Management: Protected Areas Act 57 of 2003; biodiversity by the National Environmental Management: Biodiversity Act 10 of 2004; waste by the National Environmental Management: Waste Act 59 of 2008; the coastal zone and resources by the National Environmental Management: Integrated Coastal Management Act 24 of 2008; marine resources by the Marine Living Resources Act 18 of 1998; nuclear energy by the National Nuclear Regulator Act 47 of 1999 and the Nuclear

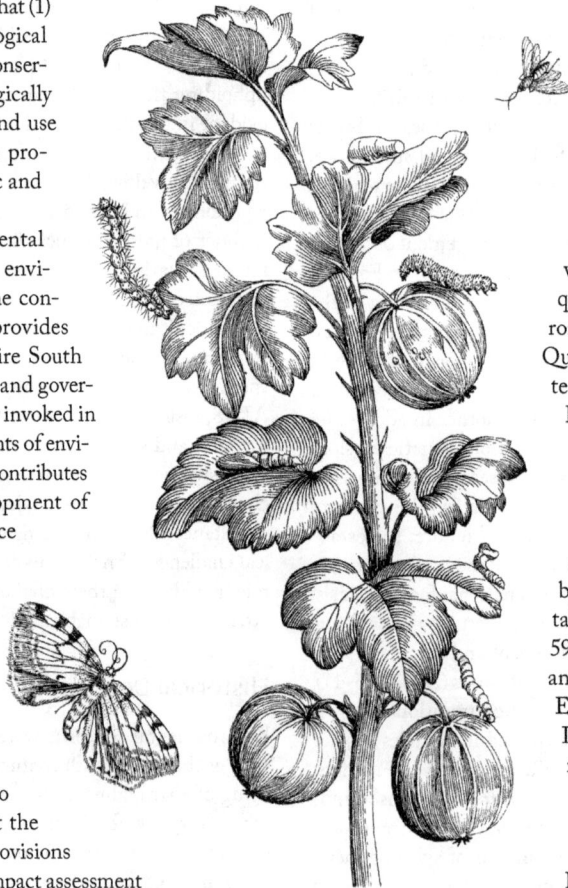

Energy Act 46 of 1999; land use and planning mainly by the Development Facilitation Act 67 of 1995 and Chapter 5 of NEMA dealing with EIAs; and cultural heritage resources by the National Heritage Resources Act 25 of 1999. Apart from these national laws, some other incidental national laws and many provincial and local environmental bylaws exist, regulating a diverse range of environmental issues. These laws comprehensively cover a wide range of environmental issues, and while they are not unique compared to environmental statutes in other jurisdictions, they are fairly recent, up-to-date, and modern in the sense that they compare with the best in the world. Unfortunately, in many instances, these statutory provisions remain paper tigers since their effective enforcement is compromised by lack of environmental awareness and insufficient or lack of public-sector enforcement resources, among others.

In addition to statute law, common law is also a source of South African environmental law, albeit to a limited extent. The common law rules regulation issues of nuisance and neighbor law apply and include, for example, the *sic utere tuo ut alienum non laedas* rule, which requires a person to use his or her property in such a manner that another person's enjoyment and use of his or her own property is not hindered. It effectively disallows unbridled use of property (including environmental resources) to the detriment of others.

Institutions

A multitude of environmental authorities exists in South Africa, and cumulatively they are responsible for environmental governance there. The Department of Environment and Water Affairs is the principal institution in this respect, and the Department of Minerals and Energy also significantly influences environmental governance matters in the country. Some argue that the plethora of institutions creates a fragmented approach to environmental governance with the overlap in their functions giving rise to turf wars that consume time and costly effort in both the private and the public sectors.

The judiciary plays an important part in environmental governance. South Africa's hierarchy of courts includes one Constitutional Court, one Supreme Court of Appeal, 13 High Courts, 250 Magistrates' Courts, and other courts established or recognized in terms of an act of Parliament. South Africa does not have a specialized environmental court, a trend that is not uncommon on the African continent. Judging from the environmental jurisprudence that has emerged during the course of the past fifteen years, one can conclude that the judiciary is increasingly asserting itself in the realm of environmental governance by interpreting environmental legislation, pronouncing on the validity of executive and legislative action, resolving civil environmental disputes and disputes between the public and private sector, and sanctioning noncompliance with environmental laws.

Future Challenges

It is evident that environmental law is steadily developing in Africa at both regional and subregional levels. While the African continent and its many countries face numerous challenges, it is encouraging to observe that there are some very conscious legal efforts underway to achieve the ideal of sustainability. But compared with other regional and subregional structures, such as the European Union (EU), the AU and SADC are lagging behind, and much more is required of them in terms of capacity building, fostering good governance practices, and designing and implementing environmental laws that effectively address ecological and socioeconomic concerns in a balanced manner.

South Africa functions as part of a regional and subregional framework, and performs fairly well in terms of the rule of environmental law. But like most of its African counterparts, many legal, political, and governance challenges remain. These require careful, continuous attention, especially in the wake of unpredictable environmental impacts such as climate change, and the myriad socioeconomic challenges facing the country.

Louis J. KOTZÉ and Werner SCHOLTZ
North West University

See also in the *Berkshire Encyclopedia of Sustainability* Armed Conflict and the Environment; Convention on Biological Diversity; Convention to Combat Desertification; Environmental Law—Africa, Saharan; Development, Sustainable—Overview of Laws and Commissions; International Law; Justice, Environmental; Soil Conservation Legislation; Transboundary Water Law; Waste Shipment Law; Water Security

FURTHER READINGS

African Union. (2010). Homepage. Retrieved June 16, 2010, from http://www.africa-union.org/
Biegon, Japhet, & Killander, Magnus. (2009). Human rights developments in the African Union in 2008. *African Human Rights Law Journal, 9*(1), 295–311.
Chaytor, Beatrice, & Gray, Kevin R. (Eds.). (2003). *International environmental law and policy in Africa*. Dordrecht, The Netherlands: Kluwer Publishing.
Chigara, Ben. (2003). The contest for labels in the Southern African development community (SADC) land issue. *Nordic Journal of International Law, 72*(1), 369–397.
Department of Environmental Affairs, Republic of South Africa. (2010a). Homepage. Retrieved June 18, 2010, from http://www.environment.gov.za/
Department of Environmental Affairs, Republic of South Africa. (2010b). State of the environment. Retrieved June 18, 2010, from http://soer.deat.gov.za/widepage.aspx?m=16

Evans, David; Holmes, Peter; & Mandaza, Ibbo. (1999). SADC: The cost of non-integration. Harare, Zimbabwe: Sapes Books.

Kidd, Michael. (2008). *Environmental law*. Cape Town, South Africa: Juta.

Kotzé, Louis J. (2007). The judiciary, the environmental right and the quest for sustainability in South Africa: A critical reflection. *Review of European Community and International Environmental Law, 16*(3), 298–311.

Kotzé, Louis J., et al. (2008). *South African environmental law through the cases*. Durban, South Africa: LexisNexis Butterworths.

Kotzé, Louis J. (2008). The Southern African Development Community (SADC) experience in shared watercourse governance. In Sharelle Hart (Ed.), *Shared resources: Issues of governance* (pp. 57–76). Gland, Switzerland: International Union for Conservation of Nature.

Kotzé, Louis J., & Paterson, Alexander R. (2009). South Africa. In Louis J. Kotzé & Alexander R. Paterson (Eds.), *The role of the judiciary in environmental governance: Comparative perspectives* (pp. 557–601). Alphen aan den Rijn, The Netherlands: Kluwer Law International.

Lebotse, Kabelo Kenneth. (1999). Southern African development community protocol on shared watercourses: Challenges of implementation. *Leiden Journal of International Law, 12*(1), 173–181.

Lubbe, Willem D. (2007). Straddling borders and legal regimes: The case for co-operative trans-frontier biodiversity conservation in SADC. *Oxford Yearbook of International Environmental Law, 18*, 126–152.

Maluwa, Tiyanjana. (2004). The African Union, the Southern African development community, and the new partnership for Africa's development: Some observations on South Africa's contribution to international law-making and institution building in Africa, 1994–2004. *South African Yearbook of International Law, 29*, 5–23.

Mboya, Tom. (2009). Conflict between state sovereignty and the right of intervention under the constitutive act of the African Union. *Africa Insight, 39*(2), 77–89.

Murithi, Timothy. (2007). Institutionalising Pan-Africanism: Transforming African Union values and principles into policy and practice. *Institute for Security Studies, 143*, 1–16.

Murithi, Timothy. (2005). *The African Union Pan Africanism peace-building and development*. Aldershot, UK: Ashgate.

Ndulo, Muna. (1999). African integration schemes: A case study of the Southern African development community (SADC). *African Yearbook of International Law, 7*, 3–30.

Olivier, Gerrit, & Olivier, Michele. (2004). Models of regional integration: The European Union and the African Union. *South African Public Law, 19*(2), 351–364.

Oosthuizen, Gabriel H. (2006). *The Southern African development community: The organisation, its policies and prospects*. Midrand, South Africa: Institute for Global Dialogue.

Packer, Corinne A. A., & Rukare, Donald. (2002). The new African Union and its constitutive act. *American Journal of International Law, 96*(2), 365–379.

Paterson, Alexander R., & Kotzé, Louis J. (Eds.). (2009). *Environmental compliance and enforcement in South Africa: Legal perspectives*. Cape Town, South Africa: Juta.

Scholtz, Werner. (2010). The promotion of regional environmental security and Africa's common position on climate change. *African Human Rights Law Journal, 1*(10), 1–25.

Scholtz, Werner. (2009). Economic law as an economic good: Its rule function and its tool function in the competition of systems. In Karel Meesen et al. (Eds.), *Environmental harmonisation in the SADC region: An acute case of asymmetry* (pp. 385–397). Munich, Germany: Sellier European Law Publisher.

Shelton, Dinah. (2003). Decision regarding communication 155/96. *American Journal of International Law, 4*(96), 937–942.

Sirota, Benjamin. (2004). Sovereignty and the Southern African development community. *Chicago Journal of International Law, 5*(1), 343–353.

Situma, Francis D. P. (2000). Africa's potential contribution to the implementation of international environmental law. *Transnational Law and Contemporary Problems, 10*(2), 385-421.

South African Government. (2010). National departments. Retrieved June 18, 2010, from http://www.info.gov.za/aboutgovt/dept.htm

Southern African Development Community. (2010). Homepage. Retrieved June 16, 2010, from http://www.sadc.int/

Strydom, Hennie, & King, Nick. (Eds.). (2009). *Fuggle and Rabie's environmental management in South Africa* (2nd ed). Cape Town, South Africa: Juta.

Sturman, Kathryn. (2007). New growth on deep roots: Prospects for an African Union government. *Institute for Security Studies Papers Issue, 146*, 1–12.

Tieku, Thomas Kwasi. (2007). African Union promotion of human security in Africa. *African Security Review, 16*(2), 26–37.

Tladi, Dire. (2000). The quest to ban hazardous waste import into Africa: First Bamako and now Basel. *The Comparative and International Law Journal of Southern Africa, 33*(2), 210–226.

United Nations Environment Programme (UNEP). (2006). *Africa environment outlook 2: Our environment, our wealth*. Nairobi, Kenya: UNEP.

Van der Linde, Morne. (2002). Review of the African Convention on Nature and Natural Resources (1969–2001). *African Human Rights Law Journal, 2*(1) 33–59.

Van der Linde, Morne, & Louw, Lirette. (2003). Considering the interpretation and implementation of the African Charter in light of the SERAC/CESR communication. *African Human Rights Law Journal, 3*(1), 167–187.

Zondi, Siphamandla, & Mulaudzi, Christopher. (2010). SADC integration and poverty eradication in Southern Africa: An appraisal. *Africa Insight, 39*(4), 35–52.

Environmental Law—Antarctica

Because of unresolved territorial sovereignty south of 60° south, a large part of Antarctica has no generally recognized laws of its own; it is regulated through a combination of individual state laws, international treaty law, soft law, and political norms around the Antarctic Treaty System (ATS). Antarctica has great environmental value and natural resources, and provides globally significant research opportunities. Balancing resource interests with environmental protection remains the central challenge.

Antarctica is often thought of as a continent and its immediately surrounding islands, but biophysically, geopolitically, and legally it is something more. In our context, Antarctica includes (1) the continent, surrounding islands, and oceanic area south of latitude 60° south and (2) the sub-Antarctic islands and ocean south of the Antarctic Convergence or Polar Front (ACPF), which variably bounds Antarctica at 45° to 60° south. The area south of 60° is the area of application of the Antarctic Treaty and all but one of the subsequent legal instruments that form the Antarctic Treaty System (ATS), which is the core of the present Antarctic environmental law arrangements. The ocean south of the ACPF, historically referred to as the Southern Ocean, is the area of application of the Convention for the Conservation of Antarctic Marine Living Resources (CCAMLR). Accordingly, the CCAMLR boundary provides a useful working border for our consideration of Antarctica. (See figure 1 on the following page.)

Three clusters of law apply interactively in the area: metropolitan law of individual states; globally applicable international law, such as the UN Convention on the Law of the Sea (UNCLOS); and international law adopted under the regionally focused ATS. All states can apply their metropolitan law to their nationals. States that assert sovereignty over territory also seek to apply their metropolitan law to all other nationals in these areas.

Territorial Claims and Coastal States

Discovery and exploration of Antarctica extended from the late eighteenth century into the immediate post–World War II period, but most of the continent and all of its surrounding islands were claimed by different states before 1950. (See figure 2 on page 47.) The sub-Antarctic islands, all lying north of the Antarctic Treaty Area, are subject to national jurisdiction, although Argentina disputes two groups—South Georgia and the South Sandwich Islands, which are claimed by the United Kingdom—as part of the wider Falklands/Malvinas imbroglio. For sub-Antarctic islands, environmental law obligations are provided under metropolitan and/or territorial legislation. Most have some protected-area status under such law—for example, Australia's Heard and McDonald islands are managed as an International Union for Conservation of Nature (IUCN) category 1a nature reserve under the 1987 Heard Island and McDonald Islands Environment Protection and Management Ordinance, with a marine reserve for the surrounding marine environment enabled under the 1999 Environment Protection and Biodiversity Conservation Act.

Sub-Antarctic island groups have also been considered as natural properties under the 1972 World Heritage Convention, which is concerned with the protection of the world's cultural and natural heritage; a list of significant sites is maintained by the World Heritage Committee, with new nominations accepted annually. Heard and McDonald Islands were added to the World Heritage list in 1997, and South Africa's King Edward Islands was

Figure 1. Antarctica

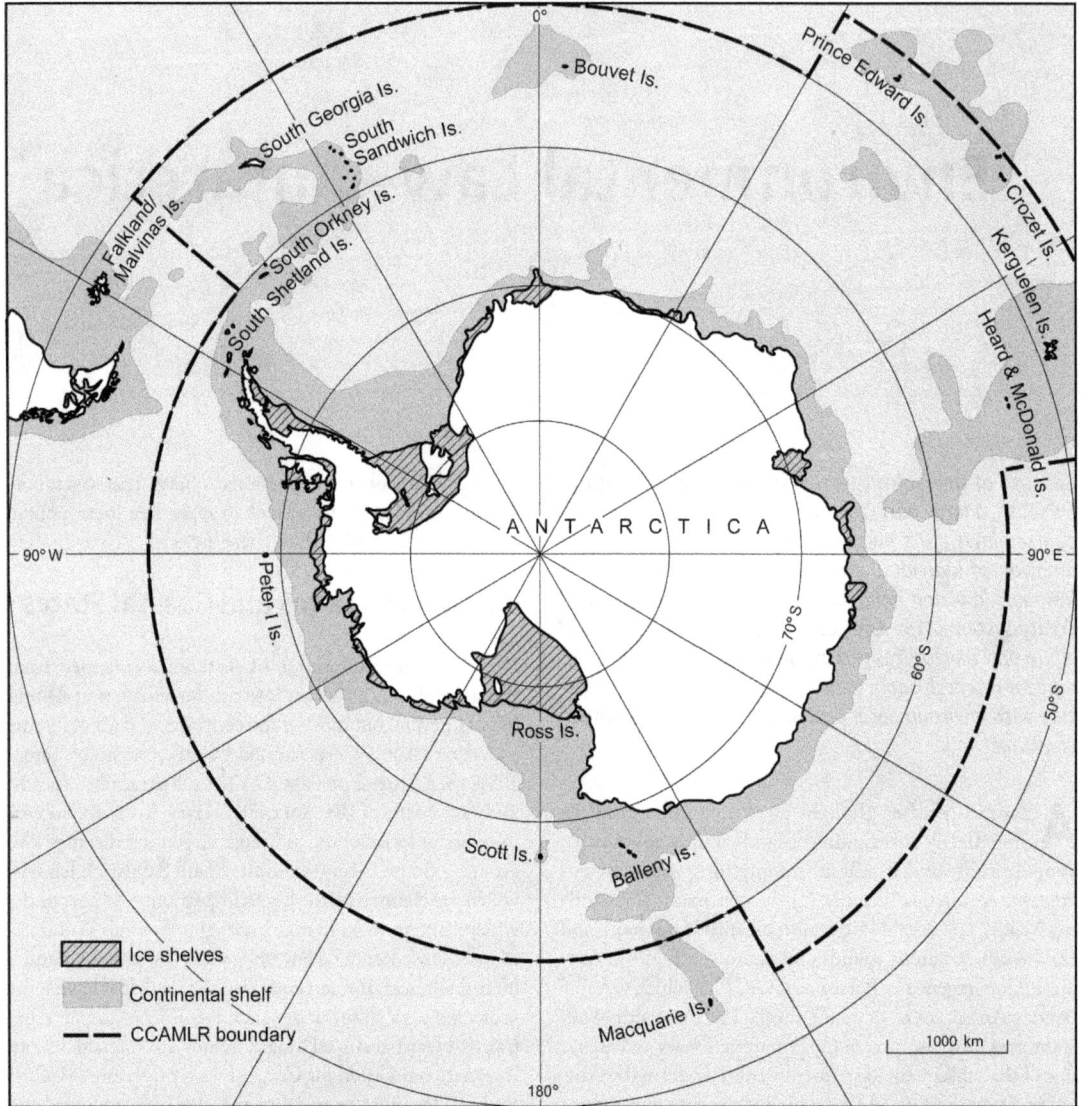

Source: Figure prepared by Philip Stickler for Alan D. Hemmings and Tim Stephens in the Antarctic Continental Shelf project

Note: The northern boundary of the Convention for the Conservation of Antarctic Marine Living Resources (CCAMLR) approximates the position of the Antarctic Convergence or Polar Front (ACPF), which in turn is often taken as an appropriate biophysical boundary for "Antarctica."

nominated in 2009. But given the unresolved territorial sovereignty issues within the Antarctic Treaty area, periodic generic advocacy for World Heritage listing of sites within the region has foundered on the requirement that properties are in the territory of states parties.

The seven claimant states (Argentina, Australia, Chile, France, New Zealand, Norway, and the United Kingdom)

apply at least some of their metropolitan environmental law to their asserted Antarctic territories, although sometimes with discretionary clauses in relation to non-nationals; this avoids difficulties with states that do not recognize their jurisdiction or disagreements with obligations under the Antarctic Treaty. Nonclaimant states variably apply their metropolitan environmental law in Antarctica, consistent

Figure 2. Antarctic Territorial Claims. Seven states assert sectoral territorial claims to the Antarctic continent, three of which substantially overlap in the Antarctic Peninsula. One "sector" between 90° and 150° west longitude remains unclaimed.

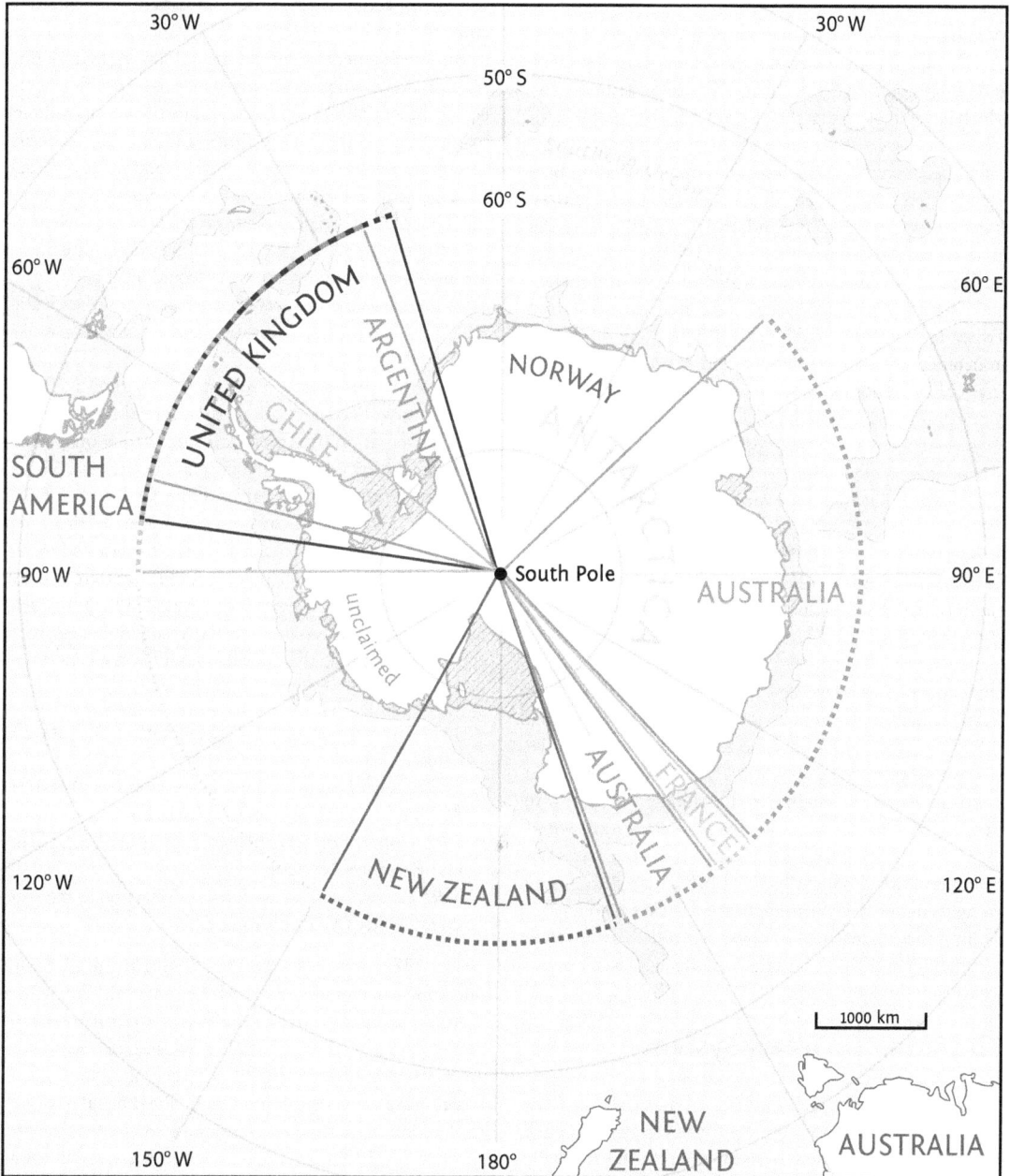

Source: author.

with their extraterritorial jurisdiction capacities, but usually not to the extent of claimants. But some issues, such as marine mammal protection, particularly regarding cetaceans (whales, dolphins, porpoises, etc.), evoke common responses from both claimants and nonclaimants (e.g., New Zealand's Marine Mammals Protection Act 1978 and the US Marine Mammal Protection Act 1972 both apply in Antarctica).

Whaling Regulations

The 1946 International Convention for the Regulation of Whaling (ICRW) and its International Whaling Commission (IWC) predate the Antarctic Treaty (signed in 1959) and remain outside the Antarctic Treaty Systems (ATS), which has sought to quarantine itself from the problematical whaling issue. Arguments about jurisdictional demarcation between the IWC and ATS around whaling have been bolstered by state practice, which has seen Antarctic states not applying ATS standards to whaling activities or reviewing those activities in ATS forums. Antarctic Treaty Consultative Parties, the category of decision-making states (currently twenty-eight) under the Antarctic Treaty, have viewed whaling expeditions quite differently from other Antarctic expeditions, and accordingly standard environmental norms—such as advance notification, environmental impact assessment (EIA), or other developing environmental management tools—have not been applied for any aspects of whaling.

Environmental nongovernmental organizations (NGOs) have tried to raise aspects of Japan's "scientific" or Special Permit (JARPA II) whaling in the Antarctic in the context of the ATS's particular duties relating to environmental protection there; New Zealand also has attempted to initiate a discussion at the Antarctic Treaty Consultative Meeting regarding an accident in Antarctica involving a Japanese whale support vessel. Both were blocked by Japan and others on the grounds that the forum was not an appropriate one in which to discuss whaling-related issues. Finally, it may be noted that although Australia has initiated action against Japan in the International Court of Justice in relation to its whaling in Antarctica, arguing that Japan is in breach of various international obligations and particularly is abusing its rights under ICRW, its application makes no reference to any duties under the ATS, or to Australia's assertion of jurisdiction over the Antarctic waters in which this activity frequently takes place.

The Antarctic Treaty System

The 1959 Antarctic Treaty addressed and stabilized the key problem of territorial sovereignty. Seven states claimed territories, three of these overlapped and were mutually contested, two other states (the United States and the USSR) rejected these claims but asserted their own basis to claims, and the few other active Antarctic states did not recognize any claims. Building on the scientific cooperation in Antarctica during the 1957–1958 International Geophysical Year, the Antarctic Treaty "froze" positions on territorial sovereignty through its Article IV, established science as the basis for Antarctic presence and cooperation with free access to terrain and scientific data, and essentially demilitarized the continent and established a reassuring inspection regime. While focused on geopolitical ends, the Antarctic Treaty made significant contributions to the development of environmental law. Article I's prohibition of measures of a military nature—specifically, the establishment of military bases and fortifications, military maneuvers, and weapons testing—and Article V's contingent prohibitions of nuclear explosions and waste disposal, were not only directly important for the Antarctic environment but established precedents for restraining problematical activities there. Article IX established administrative arrangements whereby the parties would meet periodically after the treaty's entry into force, concerning, inter alia, measures regarding "preservation and conservation of living resources in Antarctica."

By 1964 this treaty allowed the Antarctic Treaty Consultative Parties to adopt the Agreed Measures for the Conservation of Antarctic Fauna and Flora, which declared the area a special conservation area, established the general duty to avoid harmful interference with fauna and flora, and created categories of Specially Protected Species and Specially Protected Areas (the last designated solely on the basis of "outstanding scientific interest"). The principles established here were developed in subsequent instruments adopted as particular resource issues arose, collectively forming the basis for the ATS, the consensus-based core of Antarctic governance today:

- 1972 Convention for the Conservation of Antarctic Seals
- 1980 Convention for the Conservation of Antarctic Marine Living Resources (CCAMLR)
- 1988 Convention on the Regulation of Antarctic Mineral Resource Activities
- 1991 Protocol on Environmental Protection to the Antarctic Treaty (Madrid Protocol)

The 1972 seals convention was negotiated to deal with uncertainties about the reach of the Antarctic Treaty into the marine environment in the face of a possible renewal of commercial sealing, which has not, in fact, eventuated. Aside from reporting obligations in relation to some scientific research on seals, it is moribund. The mineral resources convention, which was an environmental cause célèbre through the 1980s, was abandoned in the early 1990s as environmentally and economically unacceptable to parties, with the perceived risks of mineral extraction, particularly oil, being seen to pose severe risks of environmental damage through both chronic and catastrophic misadventure that could not easily be responded to or remediated in this severe and remote location. Further, some Antarctic states were concerned that the availability of resources from Antarctica might make it a competitor with their own domestic minerals production. The Madrid Protocol, which replaced it, specifically prohibits mineral-resource activities apart from research, and updates and expands earlier standards in relation to environmental protection. Generic obligations toward the environment are established in the main body, in particular in the principles of Article III. The technical standards are provided in updatable annexes. Five annexes that address different topics are currently in force: I Environmental Impact Assessment, II Conservation of Antarctic Fauna and Flora (amended in 2009), III Waste Disposal and Waste Management, IV Prevention of Marine Pollution, and V Area Protection and Management. Annex VI—Liability Arising from Environmental Emergencies, adopted in 2005—is not yet in force.

The protocol's objective is the "comprehensive protection of the Antarctic environment and dependent and associated ecosystems," although these terms remain undefined. The area is designated "a natural reserve, devoted to peace and science." Values to be protected extend across the range of intrinsic, wilderness, aesthetic, and scientific (in particular, research essential to understanding the global environment). Some precautionary focus is evident in the environmental principles, which include injunctions to avoid significant adverse environmental effects and guidelines to plan and conduct activities "on the basis of information sufficient to allow prior assessments of, and informed judgements about, their possible impacts on [the environment]." The primary active mechanism for doing so is the EIA, using a three-tiered system predicated on whether the likely impacts will have less than, no more than, or more than "a minor or transitory impact" (with subsequent work on how to define these parameters by the advisory Committee for Environmental Protection established under the protocol).

The protocol saw a broadening of the criteria on which protected areas might be based as well as requirements for legally binding management plans. It also saw an expansion of scope beyond the historically terrestrial focus to allow marine protected areas—although this in fact proved problematical because of its perceived intrusion on CCAMLR prerogatives (and more substantively the resistance of fishing states therein

to area closures); it now requires a joint sign-off by both CCAMLR and the Antarctic Treaty Consultative Meeting. CCAMLR itself has been slow to designate marine protected areas in its own right, despite having this capacity through its conservation measures.

While the three conventions considered above all have the same area of application as the Antarctic Treaty, the marine living resources convention applies to a much larger ecosystem—the entire marine area south of the ACPF. CCAMLR was negotiated to create a mechanism for the regulation of then-emerging krill and finfish fisheries in Antarctica, and so in a sense it was an early Regional Fisheries Management Organisation (RFMO). But its ecosystem focus, objective of conserving Antarctic marine living resources (even with its definition of conservation including "rational use"), and coupling with the wider ATS makes it more than an RFMO.

Global Environmental Instruments

Notwithstanding the existence of a specific regional body of international environmental law, the Antarctic is part of the wider world to which environmental agreements apply.

Whereas CCAMLR is responsible for, inter alia, all marine harvesting within a defined area, the Convention for the Conservation of Southern Bluefin Tuna (CCSBT) is responsible for management of a single species, *Thunnus maccoyii*, wherever that occurs. Bluefin tuna generally inhabit a belt across the South Pacific and South Indian oceans immediately north of the CCAMLR area. In 2005 Japan (party to both conventions) was discovered harvesting tuna within the CCAMLR area, nominally under cover of CCSBT but without explicit consideration under either, let alone coordination between them over respective management roles, despite this scenario being anticipated. Exchanges between secretariats that began in 2005 had not led to any resolution five years on, which suggests the administrative complexity actually entailed in ensuring consistency between international instruments in areas of common interest.

The Agreement on the Conservation of Albatrosses and Petrels (ACAP), negotiated between range states (the

countries in which a particular species is usually found) of the Southern Hemisphere species, had roots in both the Convention on the Conservation of Migratory Species of Wild Animals, and the ATS. One species presently listed by ACAP breeds within the Antarctic Treaty Area, several others breed on sub-Antarctic islands, and more forage within our defined area of Antarctica. This convention, explicitly applying the precautionary approach in its project of preserving a "favourable conservation status" for albatrosses and petrels has, in contrast to CCSBT, rapidly developed a close working relationship with the ATS, and particularly with CCAMLR, consistent with the latter's ecosystem focus.

Two global agreements, the Convention on Biological Diversity (CBD) and the United Nations Convention on the Law of the Sea (UNCLOS) present particular challenges for the Antarctic regional dispensation. The CBD rubs against the ATS in the commercial realization of biodiversity through bioprospecting (where the Polar Regions are of particular interest). The ATS has not yet reached consensus on any particular regulatory approach to bioprospecting and has left it subject only to Antarctic Treaty rules pertaining to the management of science, and to environmental obligations under the Madrid Protocol and CCAMLR. In its wider discussion of global biodiversity, the CBD has periodically touched on the emerging interest in bioprospecting in the Antarctic, raising the specter of turf wars over jurisdiction.

The most obvious contact between the ATS (and member states) and global instruments has occurred in relation to extended continental shelf (ECS) issues. Under Article 76 of UNCLOS, a coastal state may submit data concerning any extension beyond 200 nautical miles for consideration by a Commission on the Limits of the Continental Shelf (CLCS). If successful, the coastal state acquires preclusive rights to that further shelf area. States exercising sovereignty over sub-Antarctic islands, and/or asserting sovereignty over continental claims, identify themselves as coastal states in Antarctica. The difficulty arises through nonrecognition of continental claims by most other states and interpretations of Article IV of the Antarctic Treaty. With the exception of Argentina, claimants have flagged their ECS interests while avoiding actual consideration of these areas by the CLCS (Argentina's unqualified data submission will be placed in limbo through the CLCS rules of procedure as relating to a disputed area). Where an ECS attaches to sub-Antarctic islands, positive recommendations from the CLCS may still effectively remove shelf areas from collective governance within the CCAMLR area, and (in two cases where sub-Antarctic ECS extends into the Antarctic Treaty Area) for the first time the CLCS provides international sanction for the assignation of areas to particular states south of 60°.

An Assessment

In 1959 only twelve states were active in Antarctica; today more than fifty are. Although this is still a minority of the 192 UN states, a far larger number of actors and activities are underway in Antarctica than ever before. In-area activities and the externally generated pressures of climate change, ozone depletion, and pollution mean that Antarctica is under increasing environmental challenge from human agency, notwithstanding the ending of sealing, unrestricted whaling, and manifestly more-sensitive individual human behavior there. Levels of compliance with environmental law are variable but vastly better than even a decade ago, and grounded in standards, operational practice, and administrative capacities unthinkable twenty years earlier. As is true everywhere around the world, environmental standards are both higher and more consistently complied with ashore than in the marine environment.

Sustainability is nowhere mentioned in the ATS, although increasingly it is evident in national and global environmental laws that also apply in Antarctica. But sustainability is the subtext to contemporary environmental management in Antarctica, even when not explicit. How to balance environmental protection with resource interests remains the central challenge in the region. The abandonment of a minerals convention in the early 1990s does not mean that mining interests are abandoned for all time (the interest in Antarctic ECS suggests as much), and it has not prevented other resource issues from subsequently emerging. The past twenty years have seen a massive expansion in marine harvesting and tourism in Antarctica, along with the emergence of bioprospecting. Reserving ECS rights under UNCLOS, and even some lines of attack in the anti-whaling campaign, suggest the mobilization of nationalism is still possible in Antarctica around territorial claims and resources, fifty years after the adoption of the Antarctic Treaty.

Viewed overall, environmental law in Antarctica reveals certain characteristics that are perhaps peculiar to this region. This has been predicated on a view of Antarctica as a special environment, meaningfully distinct from other places. A wider Antarctic exceptionalism has been evident, with high profile resource or environmental issues (successively: sealing, fishing, mining, and generic environmental standards) addressed in stand-alone and regionally focused instruments. It also has been characterized to a degree by a sort of minimalism, with only those issues seen (across an ATS where decision making is by consensus) as presenting a clear and present danger justifying new legal infrastructure, and with each new instrument being without prejudice to preceding instruments. Revision of instruments once adopted has not been attempted, and thus the emerging edifice of the ATS is sometimes internally inconsistent. Critically, each new environmental instrument (and many of the second-level agreements reached under these) has been tied to the 1959 Antarctic Treaty and its core concerns. The development of the ATS has created some difficulties in relation to the use of global environmental instruments in Antarctica since, whilst formally conceding their legitimate application to Antarctica, Antarctic states have in practice sought to limit their application there.

Environmental law in Antarctica has plenty of issues still to address. The question for the next decade is whether advances in Antarctic environmental law will be achieved through the regional ATS or through further development of global environmental instruments and practice.

Given the globally significant achievements of international peace, security, and, more recently, relative environmental sensitivity that have evolved over the past fifty years through the ATS, as well as the continuing intractability of the territorial issue in Antarctica, the case for continuing to view Antarctica as a place apart from our increasingly globalized world appears compelling. Applying general global rules to Antarctica looks a risky proposition, given its physical and geopolitical peculiarities. Without resident populations or recognized government standing in relation to Antarctica, shorn of its collective governance system—the ATS—Antarctica would, for all its size and severity, be adrift in an international context where, inevitably, its interests would not be the prime determinant of global rules or norms.

Alan D. HEMMINGS
University of Canterbury

See also in the *Berkshire Encyclopedia of Sustainability* Convention on Biological Diversity; Environmental Law (several articles: Arctic; Australia and New Zealand; East Asia; South America); Fishing and Whaling Legislation; International Court of Justice; Law of the Sea; Montreal Protocol on Substances That Deplete the Ozone Layer; Natural Resources Law; United Nations—Overview of Conventions and Agreements.

FURTHER READINGS

Agreement on the Conservation of Albatrosses and Petrels (ACAP). (2010). Homepage. Retrieved September 13, 2010, from http://www.acap.aq/

Bastmeijer, Kees. (2003). *The Antarctic environmental protocol and its domestic legal implementation*. The Hague, The Netherlands: Kluwer Law International.

Bastmeijer, Kees, & Roura, Ricardo. (2004). Regulating Antarctic tourism and the precautionary principle. *The American Journal of International Law, 98*(4), 763–781.

Convention on the Conservation of Antarctic Marine Living Resources (CCAMLR). (n.d.). Homepage. Retrieved from http://www.ccamlr.org/default.htm

Francioni, Francesco, & Scovazi, Tullio. (Eds.). (1996). *International law for Antarctica*. The Hague, The Netherlands: Kluwer Law International.

Goldsworthy, Lyn, & Hemmings, Alan D. (2008). The Antarctic Protected Area approach. In Sharelle Hart (Ed.), *Shared resources: Issues of governance* (Environmental Policy and Law Paper No. 72, pp. 105–128). Gland, Switzerland: International Union for Conservation of Nature and Natural Resources.

International Court of Justice (ICJ). (2010). Application instituting proceedings against the government of Japan. Retrieved May 31, 2010, from http://www.icj-cij.org/docket/files/148/15951.pdf

Hemmings, Alan D. (2009). From the new geopolitics of resources to nanotechnology: Emerging challenges of globalism in Antarctica. *The Yearbook of Polar Law, 1*, 53–72.

Hemmings, Alan D., & Kriwoken, Lorne K. (2010). High-level Antarctic EIA under the Madrid Protocol: State practice and the effectiveness of the comprehensive environmental evaluation process. *International Environmental Agreements, 10*(3), 187–208.

Hemmings, Alan D., & Stephens, Tim. (2010). The extended continental shelves of sub-Antarctic islands: Implications for Antarctic governance. *Polar Record, 46*(4), 312–327.

International Whaling Commission (IWC). (2010). Homepage. Retrieved September 13, 2010, from http://iwcoffice.org/index.htm

Leary, David. (2009). Bioprospecting in Antarctica and the Arctic. Common challenges? *The Yearbook of Polar Law, 1*, 145–174.

Prescott, Victor, & Triggs, Gillian D. (2008). *International frontiers and boundaries: Law, politics and geography*. Leiden, The Netherlands: Martinus Nijhoff.

Rothwell, Donald R. (1996). *The polar regions and the development of international law*. Cambridge, UK: Cambridge University Press.

Secretariat of the Antarctic Treaty. (2010). Homepage. Retrieved September 13, 2010, from http://www.ats.aq/index_e.htm

Triggs, Gillian, & Riddell, Anna. (Eds.). (2007). *Antarctica: Legal and environmental challenges for the future*. London: British Institute of International and Comparative Law.

Environmental Law—Arab Region

In most modern Arab states, ecosystem management has been left in the hands of institutions and public sector officials unwilling to enforce compliance to unfocused legislation. But the Arab region, straddling both Africa and Asia, is in a position to inspire millions of people toward more environmentally sustainable behavior as it examines lessons learned in recent years about formulating effective environmental laws.

The Arab region (AR), which stretches from Morocco and Mauritania in the west, through northern Africa and the islands of Comoros, to the Levant and the Arabian/Persian Gulf in the east, is a region facing daunting environmental challenges. (See map on the following page.) This area, where civilizations originated and first began to make use of the natural world, faces growing resources demands. The AR is one of the driest part of the world, and environmental challenges include soil degradation and desertification, deforestation, marine and coastal degradation, species loss, water scarcity, air pollution, and solid waste management.

Domestic Environmental Laws

The environmental laws in the AR are often set in conformity with those applied in developed countries, and are in many cases rigid and uniform, unreflective of the environmental conditions and economic/technical situations in most Arab states. This issue makes it difficult, from an economic perspective, to abide by these regulations or make them functional.

Problems also exist in institutions that enforce environmental legislation, either because of limited expertise or a lack of awareness and training for public sector personnel. In addition, the efforts of public authorities or institutions in charge of enforcing environmental laws often lack coordination and thus foster noncompliance. Some Arab states have environment ministries, others have general directorates and/or councils or agencies for environment, but only a few have both (e.g., Egypt, United Arab Emirates, and Yemen).

The legislation itself often lacks provisions for effective punishment, since apprehension exists regarding the social and economic pressures of implementing penalties and fines. Furthermore, most legislation tends to disregard the use of economic incentives to ensure environmental compliance, and rarely do Arab states entrust specialized police to protect and monitor environmental standards.

Multilateral Environmental Agreements

Against the backdrop of the Arab states' heightened interest in the environment, Multilateral Environmental Agreements (MEAs) have provided the political motivation to address domestic environmental concerns. For instance, ratification of the Basel Convention on the Control of Transboundary Movements of Hazardous Wastes and Their Disposal (Basel Convention) has driven the process resulting in the legal banning of trade in hazardous wastes in Arab states. Some MEAs set up standing committee/technical and scientific bodies to facilitate and monitor the implementation of the agreement.

The degree of importance attributed to MEAs by Arab states varies both among states and between the MEA in question. Among the MEAs most important to the Arab states are the UN Convention to Combat Desertification (UNCCD), the United Nations Convention on Biological Diversity (UNCDB), the United Nations Framework Convention on Climate Change (UNFCCC), and the Kyoto Protocol. Other global conventions of significant

The Arab Region.

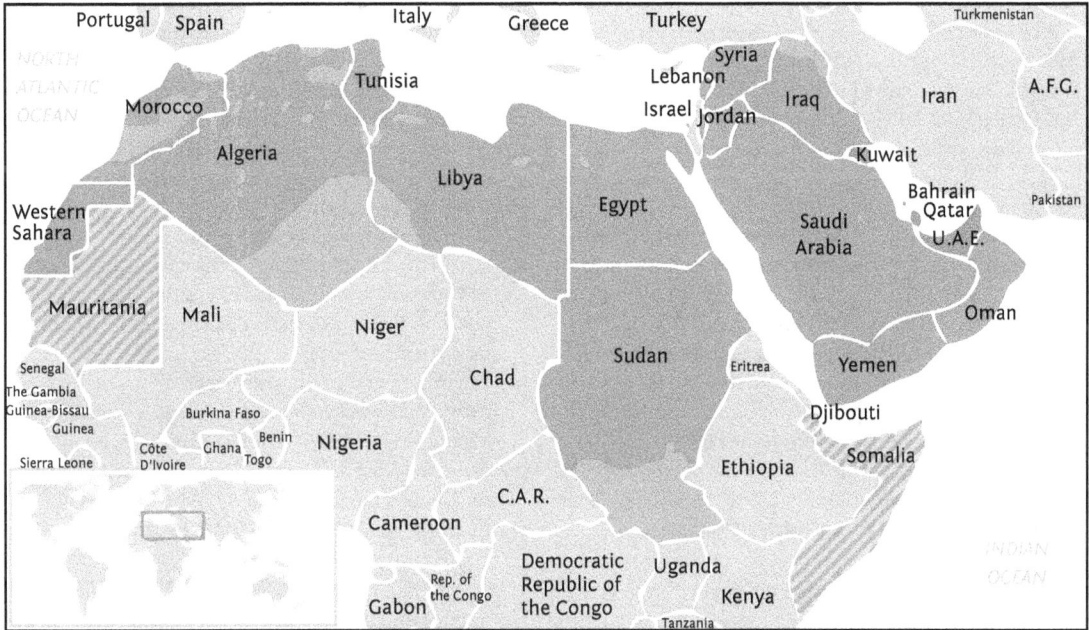

- Arab League States members
- Non-Arabic speaking areas of Arab League States members
- Arab League States with low Arabic Speaking population

Source: Berkshire Publishing. Note: this map predates the existence of South Sudan, which separated from Sudan in 2011.

importance to the region are the Vienna Convention on the Protection of the Ozone Layer (Vienna Convention), the Montreal Protocol on the Substances that Deplete the Ozone Layer (Montreal Protocol), and the Basel Convention. Apart from Arab states that experience political turmoil—such as Iraq, Palestine, Somalia, and (in some cases) Lebanon—most others have already ratified these conventions. Saudi Arabia, however, has not yet ratified the Stockholm Convention on Persistent Organic Pollutants (POPs).

The ratification and implementation of MEAs in the AR has not been ideal. In most cases, Arab states have joined international treaties only after their entry into force; this can be attributed both to the lack of involvement of Arab states in the drafting of such treaties, and to the slow ratification process in the respective states. Among the various MEAs, the Montreal Protocol has been most successfully implemented in the region, and this can be directly attributed to the availability of financial and technical resources allocated for this purpose and made available to Arab states. The main hindrances to the satisfactory implementation of MEAs in the region are inadequate national resources, infrastructure, and expertise.

In general, MEAs have spurred Arab states into promulgating more environmental legislation and creating new environmental institutions. Arab involvement in MEAs has been most strong with the UNFCCC and the Kyoto Protocol, both during the negotiation and implementation stages, as the region is highly vulnerable to the potential impacts of climate change. But some other MEAs, such as the UNCDB and the UNCCD, which also deserve strong Arab involvement and interest, have achieved limited success in the region because of lack of resources.

Regional and Subregional Environmental Agreements

Regional and Subregional Environmental Agreements (RSEAs) have generally achieved a greater level of ratification and compliance in the AR since they deal with issues that directly interest certain Arab states. As such, it is easier to secure national political support. Key agreements include the regional seas conventions, namely the Mediterranean Action Plan (MAP; Barcelona, 1976)—the first-ever Regional Seas Program under the auspices of the United Nations Environment Programme (UNEP)—the

Regional Organization for the Protection of the Marine Environment (ROPME; Kuwait, 1978) in the Arabian Gulf, and the Protection of the Environment in the Red Sea and Gulf of Aden (PERSGA; Jeddah, 1982). These conventions have proven to be useful instruments for the protection and sustainable use of regional marine and coastal resources.

For the last two decades, RSEAs and MEAs have catalyzed regional coordination on common environmental concerns through several Arab ministerial forums, such as the Council of Arab Ministries Responsible for the Environment (CAMRE). CAMRE, in collaboration with the UNEP-Regional Office for West Asia and the UN-ES-CWA, has been trying to coordinate activities in the AR related to some of the MEAs. Three standing committees were established, one for the UNFCCC and the Kyoto Protocol, the second for chemical management, and the third for the ozone layer. Although these committees discuss provisions at stake, exchange expertise, and coordinate positions, they do not always reach consensus.

Environmental Legislation: Development and Application

A study conducted by CAMRE in 2007 indicated that the policy of environmental law in the AR has emerged in a piecemeal fashion, based on selective laws and regulations issued to cope with particular situations. Until recently, no law-making body in any Arab state passed well-defined legislation designated as environmental legislation per se. General legislation over time has instead subsumed environment-related issues tangential to the primary reason for its enactment.

Arab-region policy makers face a challenge: finding a way to integrate and develop a coherent domestic environmental policy conducive to holistic environmental legislation (i.e., all-embracing legislation aimed at protecting the environment). Experience gathered thus far can teach the following lessons.

- A comparison of national-level environmental legislation (and its ramifications) in select Arab and non-Arab states should be conducted before and during the drafting process.

- Adopting terminology that has been tested in previous controversies is often beneficial, as is avoiding ambiguity and uncertainty among more than one environment-related law.
- Environmental legislation should be socially acceptable (as, for example, with Egyptian Law n° 4/1994); administratively feasible (meaning that institutions don't overlap responsibilities or functions regarding enforcement); and economically viable (by viewing compliance as opportunity, by developing and applying technologies that are environmentally sustainable for both poor and affluent consumers, and by creating next-generation practices that enable individuals and businesses to aim for eco-efficiency).
- Environmental legislation needs to strike a balance between completeness and flexibility; it should provide a framework to be subsequently developed by means of by-laws/decrees/administrative acts that can be adapted to changing circumstances.
- Existing indigenous rights ought to be smoothly revisited and options for transitional provisions made.
  - Domestic environmental legislation must be compatible with the more than 150 environmental international conventions (existing as of 2010).

Despite some progress, no major advance in developing these legal frameworks has been made. Environment enforcement officials have been reluctant to be tough on issues of compliance. Judges and prosecutors often possess little knowledge of the complex and abundant technical information involved in non-compliance cases. The execution of court decisions within a reasonable period of time, however, adds to the effectiveness of relevant environmental law and can be utilized to increase public awareness. Moreover, execution can be facilitated through the merger of both statutory provisions and customary arrangements.

Outlook in the Twenty-First Century

Despite huge investments made in some Arab states toward preserving the environment, overall immediate results have been unsatisfactory and unsustainable

because the underlying institutional and legislative foundations have been lacking or ineffective. In most Arab states, legislation is often unresponsive to the demands of stakeholders and civil society. Moreover, ecosystem management has usually been left in the hands of institutions implementing a top-down approach, which has increasingly been questioned for its lack of legitimacy and effectiveness.

This article has suggested that some Arab states are updating existing environmental laws or formulating new legislation in order to sustain ecosystem management. But some believe the substance and scope of these environmental laws/legislation may fall short of expectations. Environment legislation is multilayered, reflecting different national dynamics and priorities as well as customary arrangements and statutory provisions. Several Arab states have focused on the use of statutory provisions, although some of them have relied upon diverse arrangements based on culture and tradition.

Yet can ancient ideas help secure environmental future? The old adage, "There can be no destiny without a sense of History," addresses that question. To the degree that the AR's destiny is inextricably tied to the state of its environment, Arab states should be looking to their celebrated pasts (as, for example, the ancient Aflaj irrigation systems still preserved in Oman, and Himā (literally, "protected/forbidden place" in Islamic tradition), the approach to conservation dating back some 1,500 years in present-day Saudi Arabia). To an alarming degree, most states have not called on one of their great resources, their rich environmental history, to help them build this new sense of destiny. Looking at the past is essential if Arab states are to actively build a sustainable development, fusing a cultural identity with recent developments in environmental science as a way to achieve a sustainable environmental future.

Arab states can be reactive or choose to be proactive. To do nothing is likely to invite dysfunctional management. To be proactive carries tremendous responsibility and can be daunting, but Arab states must address the greatest sustainability challenges that governments and individuals around the globe continue to face.

The situation is not entirely bleak. In celebration of Earth Day's fortieth anniversary, Morocco announced an unprecedented National Charter for Environment and Sustainable Development, the first commitment of its kind in Africa and the AR. This charter, which has undergone a nationwide public consultative process, will form the framework for domestic environmental laws.

Mapping the road ahead will save Arab states time—and could be critical, because the clock is ticking. The AR, which straddles Africa and Asia, could lead both continents in groundbreaking environmental practices, inspiring millions of people toward more environmentally sustainable behavior.

Tarek MAJZOUB
Beirut Arab University

Fabienne Quilleré-MAJZOUB
University of Rennes 1

Editors' note: this article was written before the Arab Spring, which, starting in 2010, led to several regime changes.

See also in the *Berkshire Encyclopedia of Sustainability* Convention on Biological Diversity; Convention to Combat Desertification; Environmental Law—Africa, Saharan; Environmental Law—Israel; International Law; Kyoto Protocol; Transboundary Water Law

FURTHER READINGS

Al-Hassani, Salim T. S. (2009). 1000 years amnesia: Environment tradition in Muslim heritage. Retrieved August 20, 2010, from http://muslimheritage.com/topics/default.cfm?ArticleID=1167

Al Shaqsi, Saif Bin Rashid. (1996). *Aflaj management in the Sultanate of Oman: Case study of Falaj Al-Hamra (Dawoodi) and Falaj Al-Kasfah (Aini).* Bangor, UK: University of Wales, Centre for Arid Zone Studies.

Arab Forum for Environment and Development (AFED). (2008). Arab environment: Future challenges. Beirut, Lebanon: AFED.

Arab Forum for Environment and Development (AFED). (2010). Arab environment: Water. Beirut, Lebanon: AFED. Retrieved November 30, 2010, from http://www.afedonline.org/

Basel Convention Regional Centre for Training and Technology Transfer for Arab States in Egypt. (2010). Project progress 01/07–31/12/2009.

Convention on Biological Diversity (CBD). (2009). Sustaining life on Earth. Retrieved September 30, 2010, from http://www.cbd.int/convention/guide.shtml

Foltz, Richard C.; Denny, Frederick M.; & Baharuddin, Azizian. (Eds.). (2003). *Islam and ecology: A bestowed trust.* Cambridge, MA: Harvard University Press.

The Forum on Religion and Ecology. (2004). Islam and ecology bibliography. Retrieved August 20, 2010, from http://fore.research.yale.edu/religion/islam/islam.pdf

Majzoub, Tarek. (2005). Potential 'legislative water governance' in the ESCWA region. Seminar on water governance: The role of stakeholders and civil society institutions, November 14–18, Beirut, Lebanon.

Majzoub, Tarek; Mokorosi, Palesa Selloane; García-Pachón, Maria del Pilar; Leendertse, Kees; & Indij, Damian. (2010). *Streams of law—A training manual and facilitators' guide on water legislation and legal reform for integrated water resources management.* Pretoria, South Africa: Cap-Net.

Majzoub, Tarek, & Quilleré-Majzoub, Fabienne. (2009, Summer). "Cloud Busters": Reflections on the Right to Water in Clouds and A Search for International Law Rules. *Colorado Journal of International and Environmental Law Policies (CJIELP), 20*(3), 321-365.

Ministry of Regional Municipalities & Water Resources. (2008). Aflaj Oman in the world heritage list. Muscat, Sultanate of Oman.

The Multilateral Fund Secretariat. (2007). Multilateral Fund for the Implementation of the Montreal Protocol. Country programme and compliance summary sheets. Retrieved December 6, 2010, from http://ozone.unep.org/Publications/country-programme-and-compliance-sheets-july07.pdf

Regional Office for Science and Technology for the Arab States (ROSTAS). (1986). *The major regional project on rational utilization and conservation of water resources in the rural areas of Arab states with emphasis on traditional water systems.* (UNESCO-ROSTAS & the Arab Center for Studies of Arid Zones and Drylands (ACSAD), Trans.). Paris: ROSTAS/HYD/1/86.

The Regional Organization for the Conservation of the Environment of the Red Sea and Gulf of Aden (PERSGA). (n.d.). Consolidated Jeddah Convention 1982–2006. Retrieved August 20, 2010, from http://www.persga.org/inner.php?id=62

United Nations Economic and Social Council (ECOSOC). (2001). Arab Declaration to the World Summit on Sustainable Development. E/CN.17/2002/PC.2/5/Add.3.

United Nations Environment Programme (UNEP). (2006). Manual on compliance with and enforcement of multilateral environmental agreements. Retrieved August 20, 2010, from http://www.unep.org/dec/docs/unep_manual.pdf

United Nations Environment Programme (UNEP). (2010). Report of the Implementation Committee under the Non-Compliance Procedure for the Montreal Protocol (Forty-fourth meeting). UNEP/OzL.Pro/ImpCom/44/5.

United Nations Environment Programme Mediterranean Action Plan (UNEP/MAP). (n.d.). Barcelona Convention. Retrieved September 30, 2010, from http://www.unepmap.org/index.php?module=content2&catid=001001004

United Nations Environment Programme (UNEP) Ozone Secretariat. (2010). Reports of the Implementation Committee under the Non-Compliance Procedure for the Montreal Protocol. Retrieved September 30, 2010, from http://ozone.unep.org/Meeting_Documents/impcom/impcom_reports_index.shtml

United Nations Framework Convention on Climate Change (UNFCCC). (n.d.). Kyoto Protocol. Retrieved September 30, 2010, from http://unfccc.int/kyoto_protocol/items/2830.php

United Nations Framework Convention on Climate Change (UNFCCC). (n.d.). National Adaptation Programmes of Action (NAPAs). Retrieved August 20, 2010, from http://unfccc.int/national_reports/napa/items/2719.php

Environmental Law—Arctic

The effects of climate change are more obvious in the Arctic than anywhere else on Earth. Protecting its fragile ecosystems through laws is complicated by the fact that multilevel (and multinational) governance is a reality in the Arctic; in addition to international conventions, treaties, and agreements, there is land belonging to eight separate nations within the Arctic Circle. Global awareness of the need for Arctic-specific legislation is increasing however.

For a long time, people thought the Arctic was protected from human-induced pollution due to its general inaccessibility. This concept started to change with the increasing scientific knowledge that the Arctic ecosystems are being contaminated via air and ocean currents that transport pollutants from industrialized areas. Since the Arctic ecosystems in general are more vulnerable to human-induced pollution than more temperate areas, it is necessary to take extra protective measures regarding the Arctic environment. This vulnerability is caused by several factors, such as the general low biodiversity of Arctic ecosystems. Increasingly, the challenge is to counter the dramatic changes caused by climate change in the region. According to scientific assessments, these changes are, and have been, twice as intense in the Arctic as rest of the world (ACIA 2004).

But what is the Arctic, and in particular, where is its southernmost boundary? Several different criteria can be presented for drawing this boundary. Possible natural boundaries are, for instance, the tree line (the northernmost boundary where trees grow) or the 10°C isotherm, that is, the southernmost location where the mean temperature of the warmest month of the year is below 10°C. The Arctic Circle has been used as a criterion for full membership to the Arctic Council, an intergovernmental forum providing a means for promoting cooperation, coordination, and interaction among the Arctic nations, with only those states invited to participate that possess areas of territorial sovereignty above the Arctic Circle; the eight members include Canada, Denmark (with its Arctic constituent countries Greenland and the Faroe Islands), Finland, Iceland, Norway, Russia, Sweden, and the United States. It is therefore most convenient to use the Arctic Circle as the point of reference when defining the Arctic's southernmost border.

The Arctic and the Antarctic

Since the Polar Regions share many similarities in terms of climate, it is debatable whether similar environmental rules apply, or should apply, in both Polar Regions. If one compares the two poles, there seem to be many differences: the Arctic consists of ocean surrounded by continents, whereas the Antarctic is a continent surrounded by ocean; the Antarctic has no permanent human habitation, while the Arctic is inhabited by indigenous peoples and other local communities. Yet the two polar areas resemble each other in many respects. Both have extreme climatic conditions, receiving less radiation from the sun than other parts of the globe, and their ecosystems have adapted to very cold and dark environments with short and light growing seasons. In such conditions, the ecosystems are simple and contain only a few key species. Both regions are also relatively inaccessible, given the extreme conditions, although this is rapidly changing due to climate change. This inaccessibility functions also as a natural protection from some human-induced pollution, given that it is difficult to establish most economic activities there.

From the viewpoint of environmental protection, it is significant that the Polar Regions are indeed very similar. Their ecosystems and environments share important characteristics, suggesting that similar types of environmental protection measures might be called for. Yet, this is more easily said than done.

The Polar Regions are, in effect, opposites when it comes to enacting, implementing, and applying environmental protection rules. Of vast importance is whether the regions are under the sovereignty of nation-states or not. If a certain territory is under the sovereignty of a state, it is this state that has competence in enacting, implementing, and applying rules of environmental protection, even if it has to observe all of the international environmental law (IEL) rules, in particular multilateral environmental agreements (MEA), when doing that.

Here the Arctic and the Antarctic differ greatly. With sovereignty claims "frozen" by the 1959 Antarctic Treaty, there are no coastal states in the Antarctic that could establish maritime sovereignty and jurisdiction over the so-called Southern Ocean. (The Antarctic Treaty regulates international relations on Antarctica, establishes the continent as a scientific preserve, and bans military activity there.) Seven states had claimed parts of the Antarctic as sovereign area before the conclusion of the treaty. Yet, with this legally binding convention, these "claimant States" agreed not to consolidate these claims into full sovereignty for the duration of the treaty, which is likely to continue far into the future. The situation in the Arctic contrasts sharply with this. All of the land area—continents as well as islands—is firmly under the sovereignty of the Arctic states, and much of the Arctic waters now fall under their maritime jurisdiction. The core of the Arctic Ocean, however, remains part of the high seas and thus beyond national jurisdiction. Three high-seas areas exist in the Barents Sea, the North Atlantic, and the Bering Sea.

These great differences make it clear that the Arctic environment needs to be protected in a different manner than the Antarctic. Yet since there are similarities in their climate, it is also clear that environmental law is confronted with similar types of challenges and it is useful to look to the Antarctic for inspiration when devising environmental protection and law in the Arctic.

Legal Structure in the Arctic

Environmental protection is a complex issue in the Arctic because the competence is divided between various levels of governance, and these governance structures need to take into account international environmental law requirements. The three federal states—the Russian Federation, the United States, and Canada—each have some powers of environmental protection in their federal level and some in a subunit level (e.g., the state of Alaska in the United States or the Canadian territory of Nunavut). Even though the European Union (EU) is not a state in the eyes of international law, it is functionally very close to being one; hence it is called a *supranational organization*. Especially in environmental protection, the "federal level" of the EU has enacted a vast number of directives and regulations relevant to environmental protection in the EU's Arctic Council member states, which in the arctic region includes the northernmost parts of Finland and Sweden. (The Faroe Islands and Greenland, both self-governing overseas administrative territories of Denmark, are not part of the EU, but have strong partnership relations with it.)

There are many multilateral environmental agreements that are applicable in the Arctic simply because one or more of the Arctic nations is a party:

- The United Nations Convention on the Law of the Sea (UNCLOS) is the overarching treaty governing the Arctic marine area. All Arctic states are party to the convention, except the United States (as of 2010). UNCLOS provides basic jurisdictional rules for coastal, flag, and port states, and prescribes principles for major ocean uses and marine environmental protection.
- The 1995 Fish Stocks Agreement—one of two UNCLOS implementing agreements—has all eight Arctic states as its parties and provides rules governing straddling and highly migratory fish stocks, obligating them to establish regional fisheries management organizations.
- The Convention on Biological Diversity (entered into force 29 December 1993) is applicable to the components of biological diversity in marine areas under the national jurisdiction of the seven Arctic states that are

parties to it (which excludes the United States). The International Convention for the Prevention of Pollution from Ships, 1973, as modified by the Protocol of 1978 relating thereto (MARPOL 73/78, together with its annexes) is the main treaty governing ship-based pollution, and all the eight Arctic states are party to it and many of its annexes.

- The International Convention on Oil Pollution Preparedness, Response and Cooperation (1990) prescribes principles for responding to oil pollution accidents, according the International Maritime Organization (IMO) the governing role of the convention, and includes all of the Arctic states except Russia.

- The Espoo Convention requires parties to integrate potential transboundary pollution from proposed activities into the environmental impact assessment (EIA) procedure of the origin state. This convention currently applies to only five Arctic states, although Iceland, the Russian Federation, and the United States are still signatories.

- The Stockholm Convention on Persistent Organic Pollutants (POP) aims to protect human health and the environment from POPs and specifically acknowledges that Arctic ecosystems and indigenous peoples are particularly threatened by these substances.

Special Arctic Environmental Law

The Arctic is a prime example of a region where multilevel governance is a reality in terms of environmental policy and law. Given that most environmental law is enacted at a nation-state level, especially because MEAs are implemented through nation-state legislation, it is important to ask whether there is any Arctic environmental law tailored to unique Arctic conditions. Of the eight member states of the Arctic Council, most have their capitals far removed from their northern regions, with the notable exceptions of Iceland, Greenland with its self-governance (and possible independence in the future), and the Svalbard Islands with its special international status and strict environmental protection regime.

In fact, as the Arctic Council–sponsored study the *Arctic Human Development Report* (*AHDR*) concluded, the general trend in the area is devolving authority back to the northern and Arctic regions, thus increasing these powers in environmental policy and law, which specifically has been the case with respect to indigenous peoples residing in Alaska; the Yukon, Northwest Territories, and Inuit-dominated agreement areas in Canada; and Greenland's Inuit in Denmark. Most of the indigenous arrangements have either exclusive or mutual decision-making power (with the federal government or its subunit) in many areas of environmental protection. And some of the subunits of federal states (such as Alaska or the Yukon and Nunavut territories) also have some environmental policies and laws

It has primarily been the Arctic Council and its predecessor, the Arctic Environmental Protection Strategy (AEPS), that have injected Arctic perspective into environmental law and policy. The focus of this Arctic cooperation has been protecting the fragile environment of the Arctic. Four environmental-protection working groups were established to implement action regarding different issues. The 1996 creation of the Arctic Council broadened the mandate of cooperation to all common issues facing the region, especially those relating to sustainable development. Arctic indigenous peoples' international organizations have a unique status in the Arctic Council as its permanent participants, who need to be consulted by the member states before any decisions are made. Their status is higher in the council than the status given to major nation-states (e.g., China, Japan, and South Korea) and the EU, who are either permanent or ad hoc observers. And because the indigenous peoples' organizations have such high status in the Arctic Council, they have been able to include their views and traditional knowledge in policy and science documents produced under the auspices of the Arctic Council. The Arctic indigenous peoples traditional observations were taken into account in the *Arctic Climate Impact Assessment*, and their influence was clear when the Arctic Council's *Arctic Offshore Oil and Gas Guidelines* were revised a third time in 2009.

The main achievements of the Arctic Council in the field of Arctic law and policy have been threefold. The first is identifying via scientific assessments the main threats to the Arctic environment; this has been the task of the

Arctic Monitoring and Assessment Programme Working Group (AMAP). The actors working under the auspices of the Arctic Council made a concerted effort to influence the negotiations over the 2001 Stockholm Persistent Organic Pollutants (POPs) Convention. It was, in fact, the information that POPs end up in the Arctic, compiled by AMAP, combined with the human face put to the problem by the region's indigenous peoples that made a difference in the negotiations. The Arctic Council has been able to address only indirectly the problems of ozone depletion and climate change caused by chlorofluorocarbons and greenhouse gases respectively. But by sponsoring the *Arctic Climate Impact Assessment* (with the International Arctic Science Committee), the Arctic Council was able to feed regional scientific information to the respective global regimes tackling these problems.

Current Challenges

Whaling is regulated worldwide by the 1946 International Convention for the Regulation of Whaling. As is well-known, the resultant International Whaling Commission set up a moratorium against all whaling in 1982, which entered into force in 1986. This controversial decision is still in force, even though the scientific committee of the International Whaling Commission has studied its partial revision. Yet, since the Arctic waters host many whale species, the Arctic countries have developed special policies and laws with respect to whaling. First of all, two of the Arctic states—Canada and Iceland—withdrew from the Whaling Convention and its commission because of the moratorium on all whaling. Even though Iceland returned as a member in 2002, it made a reservation to the effect that it could commence—on the basis of sound science—commercial whaling after 2006. Norway objected to the moratorium, and is thus not legally bound by it, and has continued whaling; it has set national catch limits over minke whales for its coastal whaling operations, for instance. Aboriginal subsistence hunting is allowed in by Whaling Convention, and thus indigenous peoples of Alaska, Greenland, and Russia continue hunting on that basis.

There is even a special cooperative body established to conserve and manage cetaceans (whales and dolphins) and pinnipeds (seals and walruses) in the Arctic, established via the Agreement on Cooperation in Research, Conservation and Management of Marine Mammals in the North Atlantic (NAMMCO Agreement). The NAMMCO Commission is an international body for cooperation on the conservation, management, and study of marine mammals in the North Atlantic. The agreement was signed in Nuuk, Greenland, on 9 April 1992 by Norway, Iceland, Greenland, and the Faroe Islands.

Biodiversity protection is done in manifold manners in the Arctic. Seven of the eight Arctic states are parties to 1993's Convention on Biological Diversity (CBD), an international treaty to sustain the diversity of life on the planet. The 1973 Agreement on Conservation of Polar Bears has been working to protect this Arctic-specific species. Even if traditional protective measures have been somewhat functional, climate change may destroy the habitat of the polar bear: the sea ice.

The Arctic Council's Conservation of Arctic Flora and Fauna (CAFF) working group has advanced biodiversity in programmatic manner, mobilizing already existing resources from the member states to do this work.

As part of the final ministerial meeting of the Arctic Environmental Protection Strategy (AEPS) in 1997 in Alta, Norway, *Guidelines for Environmental Impact Assessment (EIA) in the Arctic* were adopted together with another document—*Arctic Offshore Oil and Gas Guidelines*. The EIA guidelines provide important guidance for Arctic EIAs, but as independent research has shown, the instrument has not been used, and very few nations are even aware that it exists. If revised and used by the Arctic Council and its member states, however, these could promote sustainable development in the region. The *Arctic Offshore Oil and Gas Guidelines*, which also contains strict EIA procedures for these particular types of activities, was revised a third time in the last ministerial meeting of the Arctic Council in April 2009, but it is difficult to say whether it has been made use of since the Arctic Council does not evaluate the effectiveness of the instruments that it produces.

The only legally binding article that recognizes the special vulnerability of the Arctic environment is Article 234 of UNCLOS (1982):

> Coastal States have the right to adopt and enforce non-discriminatory laws and regulations for the prevention, reduction and control of marine pollution from vessels in ice-covered areas within the limits of the exclusive economic zone, where particularly severe climatic conditions and the presence of ice covering such areas for most of the year create obstructions or exceptional hazards to navigation, and pollution of the marine environment could cause major harm to or irreversible disturbance of the ecological balance. Such laws and regulations shall have due regard to navigation and the protection and preservation of the marine environment based on the best available scientific evidence.

This provision mandates those Arctic coastal countries that control sea areas under ice coverage for most part of the year to adopt and enforce nondiscriminatory "regulations for the prevention, reduction and control of marine pollution from vessels" within the limits of their exclusive economic zones. Two Arctic states—Canada and Russia—have made use of this provision and availed themselves of stronger powers to control ship traffic to protect the marine environment. The International Maritime Organization (IMO) adopted the nonbinding Guidelines for Ships Operating in Arctic Ice-Covered Waters in 2002 for shipping that applied only in the Arctic (as had been the case for UNCLOS Article 234). These provide important guidance on construction requirements for ships entering the Arctic waters, similar to those adopted by International Association of Classification Societies (IACS). They also recommend equipment standards, various types of operational measures, and environmental protection and damage control. Recently, the IMO Assembly has adopted such guidelines to apply in both Polar Regions, and the IMO has a process in motion to consider making these legally binding by 2012.

Even if it was the Antarctic Treaty Consultative Meeting (ATCM) that adopted the Practical Guidelines for Ballast Water Exchange in Antarctic waters—which was then later adopted by IMO—these guidelines aim to make sure that vessels operating in both Polar Regions handle ballast water responsibly so that invasive marine organisms are not transported between the regions.

Future Challenges

The growing challenge for Arctic environmental policy and law is pressure from global climate change and economic globalization. With the rapid, escalating changes in the Arctic, various kinds of economic activities are entering the region; onshore mining, hydrocarbon exploitation, and other industrial activities are increasing there.

In the mid- and long-term, the consequences of climate change in the region will be dramatic: changes in the region's ecosystems; shrinking sea ice cover and a concomitant possibility of increasing economic activities in the marine areas (shipping, offshore oil and gas exploitation, and offshore tourism); and the melting of permafrost, which destabilizes building foundations and further accelerates climate change by the release of methane.

The projected consequences of climate change, especially the quickly receding and thinning sea ice, have provoked discussions on future Arctic governance. As it presently stands, the Arctic Council does not seem to be able to counter the challenges posed by a transformed Arctic with many economic activities in operation. For this reason, there are many scholarly proposals on improving the governance system, such as moving from the current soft law approach to a binding and enforceable treaty of some sort. Even the EU's European Parliament has advocated such an approach in its resolution of 9 October 2008 on Arctic governance:

The Commission should be prepared to pursue the opening of international negotiations designed to lead to the adoption of an international treaty for the protection of the Arctic, having as its inspiration the Antarctic Treaty, as supplemented by the Madrid Protocol signed in 1991, but respecting the fundamental difference represented by the populated nature of the Arctic and the consequent rights and needs of the peoples and nations of the Arctic region; believes, however, that as a minimum starting-point such a treaty could at least cover the unpopulated and unclaimed area at the centre of the Arctic Ocean;

Yet until now, the Arctic Council member states have been satisfied with the Arctic Council, which has become stronger. The strengthening of the Arctic Council is partly due to the fact that the Arctic Ocean coastal states (Canada, Denmark, Norway, Russia, and the United States) have started to organize their own informal meetings and even issued an Ilulissat Declaration in 2008, which affirmed that they were fully aware of the risks posed by climate change in the region and that they are preparing to meet the challenges by precautionary regulation in various policy areas. The coastal states also stated that the solution is not a comprehensive Arctic legal regime but a strengthening of the existing regulatory frameworks.

It is encouraging that the Arctic states have expressed willingness for precautionary regulation, that is, halting or closing certain commercial activity before further scientific studies prove that these can be done sustainably. This type of precautionary approach is exemplified by the 2009 US action—under the recommendation from its North Pacific Fishery Management Council—to close 200,000 square miles of water off the north coast of Alaska to commercial fishing until further scientific studies are done to assess the region's vulnerability.

Timo KOIVUROVA
University of Lapland

See also in the *Berkshire Encyclopedia of Sustainability* Cod Wars (*United Kingdom v. Iceland*); Convention for the Prevention of Pollution from Ships; Customary International Law; Environmental Law (several articles: Antarctica; Europe; Russia and Central Asia; United States and Canada); Fishing and Whaling Legislation; International Law; Law of the Sea; Ocean Zoning; Precautionary Principle

FURTHER READINGS

Alfredsson, Gudmundur, & Koivurova, Timo (Eds.). (2009). *The 1st and 2nd yearbook of polar law*. Leiden, The Netherlands: Martinus Nijhoff.
Arctic Climate Impact Assessment (ACIA). (2004). ACIA reports. Retrieved November 12, 2010, from http://www.acia.uaf.edu

Arctic Council. (2010). Homepage. Retrieved August 19, 2010, from http://www.arctic-council.org

Arctic Council. (2009). *Arctic offshore oil and gas guidelines 2009.* Retrieved November 10, 2010, from http://arctic-council.org/filearchive/Arctic%20Offshore%20Oil%20and%20Gas%20Guidelines%202009.pdf

Arctic Environment Protection Strategy. (1997). *Guidelines for environmental impact assessment (EIA) in the Arctic.* Helsinki, Finland: Finnish Ministry of the Environment. Retrieved September 19, 2010, from http://ceq.hss.doe.gov/nepa/eiaguide.pdf

Arctic Governance. (2010). The Arctic Governance Project: A sustainable future for the north. Retrieved August 19, 2010, from http://www.arcticgovernance.org/compendium.137742.en.html

Arctic Transform. (2008–2009). Documents. Retrieved August 19, 2010, from http://arctic-transform.org/docs.html

Baker, Betsy. (2009). Filling an Arctic gap: Legal and regulatory possibilities for Canadian-US cooperation in the Beaufort Sea. *Vermont Law Review, 34*(1), 5. Retrieved August 19, 2010 from http://lawreview.vermontlaw.edu/articles/v34/1/baker.pdf

Doelle, Meinhard. (2008). The climate change regime and the Arctic region. In Timo Koivurova, et al. (Eds.), *The capability of international governances systems in the arctic to contribute to the mitigation of climate change and adjust to its consequences.* Berlin: Springer Verlag.

Einarsson, Níels; Larsen, Joan Nymand; Nilsson, Annika; & Young, Oran R. (Eds.) (2004). *Arctic human development report (AHDR).* Retrieved September 19, 2010, from http://www.svs.is/AHDR

European Parliament Resolution of 9 October 2008 on Arctic governance. (2008). Retrieved November 10, 2010, from http://www.europarl.europa.eu/sides/getDoc.do?type=TA&reference=P6-TA-2008-0474&language=EN

Heinämäki, Leena. (2004). Environmental rights protecting the way of life of arctic indigenous peoples: ILO Convention No. 169 and UN draft declaration on indigenous peoples. *Arctic Governance,* 231–259.

Heinämäki, Leena. (2006). The protection of the environmental integrity of indigenous peoples in human rights law. *Finnish Yearbook of International Law, 17,* 187–232.

Heinämäki, Leena. (2010). *The right to be a part of nature: Indigenous peoples and the environment.* Rovaniemi, Finland: Lapland University Press.

International Maritime Organization (IMO). (2002). Guidelines for ships operating in Arctic ice-covered waters. Retrieved November 10, 2010, from http://www.imo.org/includes/blastDataOnly.asp/data_id%3D6629/1056-MEPC-Circ399.pdf

Koivurova, Timo. (2002). *Environmental impact assessment in the arctic: A study of international legal norms.* London: Ashgate Publishing.

Koivurova,Timo. (2003). The importance of international environmental law in the arctic. *Finnish Yearbook of International Law, 14,* 341–351.

Koivurova, Timo. (2008). Transboundary environmental assessment in the arctic. *Impact Assessment and Project Appraisal, 26*(4), 265–275.

Koivurova, Timo. (2005). Environmental protection in the Arctic and the Antarctic: Can the polar regimes learn from each other? *International Journal of Legal Information, 33*(2), 204–218.

Koivurova, Timo. (2010). Environmental protection in the Arctic and Antarctica. In Natalia Loukacheva (Ed.), *Polar law textbook* (pp. 23–44). Kaliningrad, Russia: Nordic Council of Ministers.

Koivurova, Timo. (2008). Implementing guidelines for environmental impact assessment in the arctic. In Kees Bastmeijer & Timo Koivurova (Eds.), *Theory and practice of transboundary environmental impact assessment* (pp. 151–173). Leiden, The Netherlands: Martinus Nijhoff.

Koivurova, Timo. (2009). Governance of protected areas in the arctic. *Utrecht Law Review, 5*(1), 44–60.

Koivurova, Timo; Keskitalo, Carina; & Bankes, Nigel. (Eds.). (2009). *Climate governance in the Arctic.* New York: Springer.

Koivurova, Timo, & Molenaar, Erik. (2009). *International governance and regulation of the marine Arctic.* Oslo, Norway: WWF International Arctic Program.

Koivurova, Timo, & VanderZwaag, David. (2007). The Arctic Council at 10 years: Retrospect and prospects. *University of British Columbia Law Review, 40*(1), 121–194.

Leary, David. (2009). Bioprospecting in the Antarctic and the Arctic: Common challenges? *Yearbook of Polar Law, 1,* 145–174.

Nowlan, Linda. (2001). *Arctic legal regime for environmental protection* (IUCN environmental policy and law paper No. 44). Retrieved August 20, 2010, from http://data.iucn.org/dbtw-wpd/edocs/EPLP-044.pdf

Rothwell, Donald. (1996). *Polar Regions and the development of international law.* Cambridge, MA: Cambridge University Press.

United Nations Convention on the Law of the Sea (UNCLOS) (concluded 10 December 1982, entered into force 16 November 1994) 1833 UNTS 397.

VanderZwaag, David; Huebert, Rob; & Ferrara, Stacey. (2002). The Arctic environmental protection strategy, Arctic Council and multilateral environmental initiatives: Tinkering while the Arctic marine environment totters. *Denver Journal of International Law and Policy, 30*(2), 166–171.

VanderZwaag, David. (2006). The Arctic. *Yearbook of International Environmental Law, 17,* 386–391.

Environmental Law—Australia and New Zealand

Environmental law in Australia and New Zealand is based upon the principle of common law, built on judicial precedent. The extreme eco-diversity of these nations has prompted far-reaching legislation—in Australia with the Environment Protection and Biodiversity Conservation Act 1999 and in New Zealand with the Resource Management Act 1991, which places sustainable management at its core. The two national governments cooperate extensively on environmental matters.

Australia and New Zealand were both settled by the British, and both have inherited the British common law system whereby laws are built on judicial precedent. Both nations have developed varying strategies for legal protection of their respective environments, which span several climate zones. New Zealand is characterized by dramatically differing microclimates encompassing climatic zones ranging from the subtropical north through temperate, desert, fjord, and high alpine in the southern longitudes. Australia's climate spans equatorial and tropical zones in the north of the continent through subtropical, desert, grasslands, and temperate in the south. Australia has a highly variable climate with regional variations in rainfall and extensive periods of drought. It is considered "mega-diverse" in respect to its biodiversity. (The United Nations Environment Programme's World Conservation Monitoring Centre defines "mega-diverse countries" as those nations, mainly in the tropics, which account for a high percentage of the world's biodiversity because of their very large numbers of species.)

Australia

Australia's exports contribute approximately 20 percent of gross domestic product, over half of which comprises natural resource–based exports, principally from mining and agriculture. It also is the driest continent on Earth (after Antarctica), with water scarcity, dry land salinity, and land degradation creating the key issues for environmental management. The major sources of pressure on the Australian environment and its natural resources include land clearing, invasive species, increasing population density in coastal areas, climatic variability (particularly drought), extractive industries (mining, agriculture, transport, manufacturing and energy production and consumption), and climate change.

Legal System and History

Australia is a constitutional monarchy and parliamentary democracy. The Australian Constitution 1901 established a federal system of government that comprises a national government (the Commonwealth), six states, and three self-governing territories. Each of these governments has lawmaking powers determined by the division of powers under the Australian Constitution. The Commonwealth Government has jurisdiction to enact legislation in relation to areas specified in the Constitution with the residue of powers resting with state parliaments.

Australia inherited the common law and legislation of Britain following settlement. Under the common law system, the Crown enjoyed absolute ownership of all land in the colony and all rights to land were derived from the Crown. This position is based on the assumption that when settled, Australia was *terra nullius*, that is, the land belonged to no one. In the landmark case of *Mabo v. Queensland* (1992), however, the High Court rejected *terra nullius* as a basis for denying aboriginal entitlement to land at common law. The finding specified that a form of native title could survive colonization until that title is extinguished by an inconsistent exercise of sovereign power (for example, through the grant of freehold title to others or by specific legislation that shows clear intention to affect native title rights and interests). In response to the *Mabo* decision and to provide certainty to the holders of past Crown grants of title and permits to access land and natural resources, the Commonwealth enacted the Native Title Act 1993. This legislation provides a framework for recognizing and protecting native title and determining claims for native title.

Constitutional Power and Environmental Legislation

State governments have traditionally held legal responsibility for natural resource management and land use determinations within their jurisdictions. Accordingly, most environmental legislation in Australia has been enacted at the state level, covering areas including biodiversity, native vegetation, environmental planning and assessment, pollution and waste, water, natural and cultural heritage, energy, biotechnology, and natural resources management.

The Commonwealth Government has no direct constitutional power with respect to the environment, but legislation to achieve environmental objectives may be enacted by the Commonwealth in a number of ways. For example, the Constitution provides for the states to refer their powers to enact legislation to the Commonwealth Government. Such a referral of powers enabled the Commonwealth to enact the Water Act 2007 to implement water resource management in the Murray-Darling Basin, the largest river system in Australia, extending over four states and one territory.

The Commonwealth has also enacted legislation to achieve environmental objectives through reliance on its powers under the Constitution relating to external affairs, trade and commerce, corporations, finance and taxation, and "people of any race." In the key case of *Commonwealth v. Tasmania* (1983), the High Court of Australia upheld the validity of Commonwealth legislation enacted to implement Australia's obligations under the World Heritage Convention, which had the effect of preventing a proposed hydroelectric power development authorized by the Tasmanian state government. The validity of Commonwealth power

with respect to environmental matters was confirmed in a number of further decisions of the High Court of Australia during the 1980s.

A framework for a cooperative approach to federalism in environmental conservation and management was agreed between the Commonwealth and state/territory governments in the 1990s under which the respective spheres of Commonwealth and state environmental responsibility were determined. The Intergovernmental Agreement on the Environment 1992 recognized that the states have primary responsibility for environmental management within their jurisdictions while the Commonwealth has a legitimate role with respect to national environmental issues, such as those relating to international obligations, environmental effects that reach beyond one state or into the marine environment, and those enabling the development of national environmental standards and guidelines.

The respective governments also agreed that the development and implementation of environmental policy and programs by all levels of government should be guided by the principles of ecologically sustainable development. These principles—the precautionary principle, intergenerational equity, conservation of biological diversity and ecological integrity, and improved valuation, pricing, and incentive mechanisms—are included in the majority of environmental legislation at both national and state/territory levels (usually in clauses outlining the objectives of the statute).

Environmental Legislation

The key national environmental legislation is the Environment Protection and Biodiversity Conservation Act (EPBC) 1999. This Act codifies the Commonwealth's powers with respect to matters of national environmental significance, namely World Heritage properties, Ramsar wetlands of international importance (those protected by the Convention on Wetlands, signed in Iran in 1971), listed nationally threatened species and communities, listed migratory species protected under international agreements, nuclear actions, commonwealth marine environment, and national heritage. The Commonwealth Government has to date resisted calls to incorporate greenhouse gas emissions or land clearance as matters of national environmental significance, which has triggered environmental impact assessment and approval processes under the EPBC Act.

The objects of this "one-stop-shop" legislation include promoting ecologically sustainable development through the conservation and ecologically sustainable use of natural resources. Where an action would be likely to have a significant impact on a matter of national environmental significance, it will be prohibited unless approved by the Commonwealth Minister for the Environment or otherwise exempted from needing approval. The minister must take a range of matters into account in determining significance, and the EPBC Act provides for environmental referral, assessment, and approval processes. The minister is required to take into account the precautionary principle in relation to a wide range of decisions that may be made under the auspices of the EPBC Act. The Act also provides frameworks for the conservation of biodiversity, heritage, and protected areas that fall within the scope of Commonwealth responsibility.

The EPBC Act is administered by the Commonwealth Department of Environment, Water, Heritage and the Arts. While it provides for a range of criminal and civil penalties and other administrative remedies, enforcement has been weak, particularly in the early years of operation. Following the allocation of substantial resources by the Commonwealth Government, there has been modest improvement in enforcement of the Act.

The Commonwealth has also enacted legislation across a range of other environmental areas, including the Water Act 2007, National Greenhouse and Energy Reporting Act 2007, Gene Technology Act 2000, and the Hazardous Waste (Regulation of Exports and Imports) Act 1989. The existence of different sets of environmental legislation at the Commonwealth and state/territory levels requires extensive coordination and cooperation between governments in order to avoid duplicated efforts and wasted resources.

It should be noted that local governments play an important role in environmental management in Australia. There are 560 local government bodies that are created under state and territory legislation. Local governments are responsible for key environmental matters including the approval of applications for development, sewage and storm water management, waste disposal, pollution, and contaminated sites.

Courts and Environmental Litigation

A unique development in Australian environmental law at the state level is the creation of specialist environmental courts and tribunals to determine environmental matters. Specialist environmental courts such as the Land and Environment Court of New South Wales have been fundamental in developing environmental law jurisprudence dealing with the interpretation and application of legal principles applicable to environmental decision-making. A key example is the judgment of Justice Stein in *Leatch v. National Parks and Wildlife Service and Shoalhaven City Council* (1993), the first case to deal with the precautionary principle. Subsequent cases have found that the principles of ecologically sustainable development are relevant matters to be considered in determining application for approvals to undertake activities under other statutes. At the Commonwealth level, there are no specialist environmental courts or tribunals, and challenges to decisions are made in the Federal Court of Australia and, in relation to certain decisions, the Administrative Appeals Tribunal.

Public-interest advocacy cases in Australia play an important role in enabling public scrutiny of environmental decision making and in the development of jurisprudence dealing with the legality or merits of environmental decision making. At the Commonwealth level, the EPBC Act contains expanded legal standing for third-party applications that allows individuals and organizations engaging in environmental protection and/or conservation activities to commence judicial review applications. In some state and territory environmental legislation, open standing provisions confer standing on all members of the public. Substantive access to justice has also been addressed through the development of jurisprudence around costs, security for costs, and undertakings for damages. For example, in the case of *Oshlack v. Richmond River Council* (1998), the High Court confirmed that a court may depart from the general principle in judicial proceedings so that the successful party is entitled to its costs where the proceedings are brought in the public interest.

New Zealand / Aotearoa

New Zealand, also known by the Māori word "Aotearoa," which is generally accepted to mean "long white cloud," comprises three main islands: the North Island

(Te Ika-a-Māui), the South Island (Te Wai Pounamu), and Stewart Island (Rakiura). Aotearoa is thought to have originally specified the North Island. It has a very lengthy coastline, estimated at between 15,000 and 18,000 kilometers in length (compared to around 25,000 kilometers for Australia, which has nearly twenty-nine times the land area of New Zealand) and possesses a correspondingly vast exclusive economic zone (EEZ), the fourth largest in the world. Given these conditions, protection and management of New Zealand's marine resources are a high priority.

Agriculture is the largest export sector in New Zealand, accounting for over two-thirds of exported goods. Forestry and fisheries are also major industries. As a result, many of the country's most pressing environmental issues center around land use, clearing of native forests for farmland, loss of biodiversity, invasive weed species, and the deleterious effects of livestock effluent and fertilizer runoff on waterways. These problems have been exacerbated by a shift in recent years from traditional wool production to more intensive dairy farming.

Legal System and History

Aotearoa / New Zealand is a constitutional monarchy and a parliamentary democracy. It is a unicameral system with Parliament as the sole law-giving body, the upper house having been abolished in 1951. The legal system of New Zealand, like Australia, is based on that of the United Kingdom. New Zealand is one of only three countries in the world (along with the United Kingdom and Israel) without a constitution written as a single document. New Zealand's constitution is recognized as being contained in several pieces of legislation, conventions, letters patent of the Governor-General, the Treaty of Waitangi, some imperial enactments from England, and principles of rule of law as developed in the common law courts. It is also unique in having sovereignty "shared" between the indigenous Māori people and Pākehā (non-Māori), as specified by the founding constitutional document, the Treaty of Waitangi / Te Tiriti o Waitangi (the Treaty), signed in 1840 between the representatives of the British Crown and Māori chiefs. Prior to the signing of the treaty, there was no legal system in place. The Māori governed themselves according to *tikanga* (customary law) and settlers were treated as subjects of the Australian state of New South Wales. Despite its fundamental constitutional status, the treaty was long considered to be a "simple nullity" (per Chief Justice Prendergast in *Wi Parata v. The Bishop of Wellington* (1877)) and was only reincorporated into the law of New Zealand by inclusion in the State Owned Enterprises Act 1986, which required that effect be given to "the principles of the Treaty of Waitangi." These principles were defined by the Court of Appeals in the 1987 case, *New*

Zealand Māori Council v. Attorney-General. References to the principles of the treaty are now included in numerous other acts. The recognition of "*tikanga* Māori" (Māori customs) and indigenous approaches to environmental governance have become well established in New Zealand environmental law.

Environmental Legislation

The core piece of environmental legislation, the Resource Management Act 1991 (RMA), places "sustainable management" at the center of New Zealand's environmental law. Specifically, this incorporates the two goals of integrated resource management and sustainable development. In 1993 the Ministry for the Environment defined the term "integrated resource management" as integration across media (water, air, land); integration across agencies (local, regional, and territorial authorities); and integration across time (accumulation of activities and effects over time). The RMA acts as a framework law, providing few rules regarding the management of natural resources, and leaving specific provisions to subordinate legislation, adjudication, and review in the courts.

The New Zealand approach to sustainable management is codified in section 5 of the RMA with the following provisions.

1. The purpose of this Act is to promote the sustainable management of natural and physical resources.
2. In this Act, "sustainable management" means managing the use, development and protection of natural and physical resources in a way, or at a rate, that enables people and communities to provide for their social, economic and cultural well-being and for their health and safety while: (a) sustaining the potential of natural and physical resources (excluding minerals) to meet the reasonably foreseeable needs of future generations; (b) safeguarding the life-supporting capacity of air, water, soil and ecosystems; and (c) avoiding, remedying, or mitigating any adverse effects of activities on the environment.

Sections 6, 7, and 8 provide guiding principles to be considered by decision makers in their application of section 5. Section 6 outlines matters of national importance such as the protection of coastal environments, indigenous flora and fauna, and special recognition of the relationship between Māori and the land. Section 7 includes other matters; these include *kaitiakitanga* (roughly "guardianship" or "collective custodianship"), recognition of the intrinsic worth of ecosystems, and the efficient use and development of physical resources. Section 8 affirms the importance of adhering to the principles of the Treaty of Waitangi when making decisions on behalf of the act.

Remarkably, the RMA cannot be used to consider the effects of greenhouse gas emissions. A proposed 2006 amendment bill would have brought greenhouse gases within the ambit of the RMA, but it was set aside to allow for the imposition of a carbon tax. The government then changed its position on carbon tax and is now committed solely to an emissions trading scheme as a way to mitigate climate change.

The Local Government Act 2002 (LGA) takes a stronger ecological approach to local authority decisions by incorporating a definition of "sustainable development" as opposed to the milder environmental approach of "sustainable management" promulgated in the RMA. For example section 14(1)(h) of the LGA provides that when framing a regional plan for sustainable development, a local authority should take into account:

- the social, economic and cultural well-being of people and communities;
- the need to maintain and enhance the quality of the environment; and
- the reasonably foreseeable needs of future generations.

Substantial changes have been made to the RMA with the Resource Management (Simplifying and Streamlining) Amendment Act 2009. These amendments are intended to:

- improve mechanisms for the management of frivolous or vexatious objections and appeals;
- improve trade competition;
- improve the processing of applications for proposals of national significance;
- establish an Environmental Protection Authority (EPA) to act as a central authority for consents best handled on a national basis; and
- improve plan development and change processes which many have argued have become unwieldy and expensive.

There is concern, however, that public participation and consultation will be diminished by these reforms.

Courts and Environmental Litigation

Constituted under the Resource Management Amendment Act 1996, the Environment Court is New Zealand's primary institution for the adjudication and review of resource management decisions. Its jurisdiction includes the operation of multiple statutes including the RMA; Historic Places Act 1993; Forests Act 1949; Local Government Act 1974; Transit New Zealand Act 1989; Crown Minerals Act 1991; and Public Works Act 1981. The court has jurisdiction under the RMA to hear appeals of relevant decisions of lower courts and to review the content of regional and district statements and plans, resource consents, subdivisions, environmental effects of mining, and non-notification of resource consents. The court lacks the power, however, to initiate an inquiry or investigation and is thus limited to a purely reactive role, responding only to previous decisions. Nonetheless, the jurisprudence of the Environment Court has contributed significantly to the definition and refinement of sustainable management as the key concept of New Zealand environmental law.

There has been a substantial amount of jurisprudence around the meaning of "sustainable management" in section 5 of the RMA. The Environment Court has developed two approaches to interpretation of section 5: the "environmental bottom line" approach and the "overall judgment approach." The distinction between these two approaches turns on the interpretation of the word "while" in section 5(2).

The bottom line approach, as exemplified in the High Court decision of *New Zealand Rail Ltd v. Marlborough District Council* (1994), initially favored and construed "while" to mean that all the safeguards—(a), (b) and (c), as listed under number 2 above—are not competing priorities to be balanced against each other but that they must all be satisfied for the object of the section to be considered fulfilled. A weaker approach to sustainability, the "overall broad judgment" approach has also developed in a line of cases beginning with *North Shore City Council v. Auckland Regional City* (1997). In this case the court reasoned that "[s]uch judgment allows for comparison of conflicting considerations and the scale and degree of them, and their relative significance or proportion in the final outcome."

Cooperation

There has been extensive cooperation with respect to policy development on environmental matters between the Australian and New Zealand governments. For example, the Natural Resources Ministerial Council comprises the Australian, state, territory, and New Zealand ministers responsible for primary industries, natural resources, environment, and water policy. It is the key government body in relation to consultation and coordination of responses to natural resource issues in Australia and New Zealand.

Susan SHEARING
University of Sydney

Vernon TAVA
University of Auckland

See also in the *Berkshire Encyclopedia of Sustainability* Convention for the Prohibition of Fishing with Long Drift Nets in the South Pacific; Development, Sustainable—Overview of Laws and Commissions; Environmental

Law—Pacific Island Region; Intergenerational Equity; International Law; Natural Resources Law; New Zealand Nuclear Free Zone, Disarmament, and Arms Control Act; Precautionary Principle

FURTHER READINGS

Bates, Gerry M. (2010). *Environmental law in Australia* (7th ed.). Sydney: LexisNexis Butterworths.

Godden, Lee, & Peel, Jacqueline. (2010). *Environmental law: Scientific, policy and regulatory dimensions*. South Melbourne, Australia: Oxford University Press.

Bonyhady, Tim. (Ed.). (1992). *Environmental protection and legal change*. Sydney: Federation Press.

Department of Infrastructure and Planning. (2010). *A guide to the Local Government Act 2009 for mayors and councillors*. Retrieved December 4, 2010, from http://www.dip.qld.gov.au/resources/guideline/local-government/guide-to-act-for-mayors-and-councillors.pdf

Dovers, Stephen, & Wild River, Su. (Eds.). (2003). *Managing Australia's environment*. Sydney: Federation Press.

Dovers, Stephen. (Ed.). (2000). *Environmental history and policy: Still settling Australia*. Melbourne, Australia: Oxford University Press.

Fisher, Douglas E. (2010). *Australian environmental law: Norms, principles and rules* (2nd ed.). Sydney: Thompson Reuters.

Harding, Ronnie; Hendriks, Carolyn M.; & Faruqi, Mehreen. (2009). *Environmental decision-making: Exploring complexity and context*. Sydney: Federation Press.

Harris, Rob. (Ed.) (2004). *Handbook of environmental law* (1st ed.). Wellington, N.Z.: Royal Forest and Bird Protection Society of New Zealand, Inc.

Nolan, Derek. (Ed.) (2005). *Environmental and resource management law*. Wellington, N.Z.: LexisNexis.

Peel, Jacqueline. (2005). *The precautionary principle in practice: Environmental decision-making and scientific uncertainty*. Sydney: Federation Press.

Salmon, Peter. (Ed.). (2005). *Salmon Resource Management Act 1991*. (Brookers). Retrieved November 29, 2010, from https://www.thomsonreuters.co.nz/media/pdfs/Salmon%20Resource%20Management%20Act%20Lslf%20Feb%202009.pdf

Thomas, Ian. (2005). *Environmental management: Processes and practices for Australia*. Sydney: Federation Press.

Tunks, Andrea. (1997). Tangata Whenua ethics and climate change. *New Zealand Journal of Environmental Law 1*(1), 67-124.

Williams, David A. R. (Ed.). (1997). *Environmental and resource management law in New Zealand*. (2nd ed.) Wellington, N.Z.: Butterworths.

Wilson, Vivienne, & Salter, Jonathan. (2003). *A guide to the Local Government Act 2002*. Wellington N.Z.: Brookers.

COURT CASES

Commonwealth v. Tasmania (1983) 46 ALR 625

Leatch v. National Parks and Wildlife Service and Shoalhaven City Council (1993) 81 LGERA 270

Mabo v. Queensland (1992) 175 CLR 1

Oshlack v. Richmond River Council (1998) 193 CLR 72

New Zealand Māori Council v. Attorney-General [1987] 1 NZLR 687

New Zealand Rail Ltd v. Marlborough District Council [1994] NZRMA 70

North Shore City Council v. Auckland Regional City [1997] NZRMA 59

Wi Parata v. The Bishop of Wellington (1877) 3 NZ Jur (NS) SC 72)

Environmental Law—Central America and the Caribbean

Scattered attempts at protecting specific natural resources in Central America and the Caribbean countries began to cohere into broader, national environmental laws in 1972, after the First United Nations Conference on Environment and Development. A second conference in 1992 reinforced the trend, but environmental law remains incomplete and irregular across the region owing to disparities in legal structure between countries.

Environmental law is far from homogeneous in the Central American and Caribbean countries, despite their proximity. The majority of Central American countries belong to the civil law tradition of most of Europe, whereas in Belize and in many Caribbean countries, the common law tradition (the system of law in the United Kingdom and its former colonies) rules the legal system. Environmental law is more developed in countries such as Mexico or Costa Rica; in others, such as Saint Kitts and Nevis or Nicaragua, initial environmental laws have only recently been implemented. In underdeveloped countries, such as Haiti, no specific environmental law has yet been passed.

In fact, in many of the countries analyzed in this article, environmental law was practically nonexistent before 1972. In that year, the United Nations Conference on Human Environment and Development, as well as the Stockholm Declaration that was signed by participating national states, encouraged governments to legislate in environmental matters and include environmental provisions in their national constitutions. (See table 1 on the following page.)

After 1972, a number of Central American and Caribbean countries started passing pieces of legislation to specifically address environmental issues. Some scholars identify this process as the first generation of environmental law (see Robinson 2003). In the same vein, environmental legislation

was accompanied by the creation of administrative agencies in charge of enforcing such laws.

A second stage in the evolution of environmental law took place after the Rio Conference in 1992. At the conference, 179 heads of state met in Rio de Janeiro, Brazil, for the second International Earth Summit, which was convened to address urgent problems on environmental protection and socioeconomic development. The assembled leaders signed the 1992 United Nations Framework Convention on Climate Change and the Convention on Biological Diversity; endorsed the Rio Declaration and the Forest Principles; and adopted Agenda 21, a three-hundred-page plan for achieving sustainable development in the twenty-first century.

The Rio Declaration contains twenty-seven principles that commit signatory parties to introducing certain tools of environmental policy into their national laws. The Framework Convention on Climate Change set the goal, spelled out in Article 2, of "stabilization of greenhouse gas concentrations in the atmosphere at a level that would prevent dangerous anthropogenic interference with climate system," and consequently encourages states to establish new legal instruments aimed at achieving that goal. The United Nations Convention on Biological Diversity has three basic goals, as put forth in Article 1: "the conservation of biological diversity, the sustainable use of its components and the fair and equitable sharing of benefits arising out of the utilization of genetic resources." It implies that signatory parties should update their legislation to fulfill these objectives as well.

The commitment to updating legislation is expressly established by principle 11 of the Rio Declaration. According to this principle, signatory parties "shall enact efficient laws on environment. Environmental standards, management objectives, and priorities should reflect environmental and

Table i. Environmental Agencies in Central American and Caribbean Countries

Country	Agency	Year of Creation
Belize	Department of the Environment	1992
Costa Rica	Ministry of Energy and Environment	1990
	Environmental Comptroller Administrative	1995
	Environmental Court	1995
Dominican Republic	Ministry of Environment and Natural Resources	2000
El Salvador	Ministry of the Environment and Natural Resources	1998
Guatemala	National Commission of the Environment	1980
	Ministry of the Environment and Natural Resources	2000
Honduras	Secretary of the Environment and Natural Resources	1996
Jamaica	Natural Resources Conservation Authority	1975
	Natural Resources Conservation Department	1975
	National Resources Conservation Authority	1992
Mexico	Under Ministry of Environment Improvement	1971
	Ministry of Urban Development and Environment	1982
	Ministry of Social Affairs	1992
	Ministry of the Environment, Natural Resources and Fishing	1996
	Ministry of Environment and Natural Resources	2000
Nicaragua	Ministry of the Environment and Natural Resources	1994
	National Resources Conservation Authority	1996
Panama	National Institute of Renewal Natural Resources	1986
	National Authority of the Environment	1998
Saint Kitts and Nevis	Department of the Environment	1996
Saint Lucia	National Conservation Authority	1999
Trinidad and Tobago	Environmental Management Agency	2000

Source: Author

development context to which they apply. Standards applied by some countries may be inappropriate and of unwarranted economic and social cost to other countries, in particular developing countries." By 1996, the United Nations Program for Environmental Protection, Regional Office for Latin American and Caribbean, had conducted a study indicating that most of the Latin American countries, including those in Central America, had enacted new environmental laws aimed at fulfilling such commitment (see González 2006). Data regarding Caribbean countries, however, showed that the legislative process was slower in this area.

Partly in response to the study, Central American and Caribbean countries enacted new environmental legislations or amended those previously passed after the Rio Earth Summit. Table 2 (on the following pages) shows the countries that passed new environmental laws after 1992 or modified their antique environmental laws.

Despite these improvements, environmental law in the region has not yet achieved homogeneity. First, in many countries environmental legislation is still focused on specific environmental problems, as is the case in Antigua and Barbuda, Bahamas, Dominica, Jamaica, Saint Lucia, and

TABLE 2. New Environmental Laws Enacted by Countries after the Rio Earth Summit of 1992

Country	Law	Year
Antigua and Barbuda	Oil Pollution of Maritime Areas Act	1995
Bahamas	Conservation and Protection of the Physical Landscape of Bahamas Act	1997
	Archipelagic Waters and Maritime Jurisdiction Act	1993
	Antiquities, Monuments and Museum Act	1998
Barbados	Environmental Levy Act	1996
	Shipping (Oil Pollution) Act	1994
	Coastal Management Act	1998
	Marine Pollution Act	1988
	The National Conservation Commission Act	1985
Belize	Environmental Protection Act	1992
	The Maritime Areas Act	1992
	Coastal Zone Management Act	1998
Costa Rica	Act Number 317 of Wildlife Conservation	1992
	Organic Act of the Environment	1995
Dominica	Water Catchment Rules	1995
	Physical Planning Act	2002
Dominican Republic	General Act on the Environment and Natural Resources	2000
El Salvador	Environmental Act	1997
Guyana	Environmental Protection Act	1996
Guatemala	Act for Protection and Improvement of the Environment	1980
Honduras	General Act of the Environment	1993
Jamaica	The Maritime Areas Act	1996
	Natural Resources Conservation Authority Act	1991
Panama	Act Number 24 Wildlife	1995
	General Act of Environment	1998
Nicaragua	General Act of the Environmental and Natural Resources	1996
Mexico	General Act of Wildlife	2000
	General of Sustainable Use of Forest	2003
	General Act for Prevention and Integral Management of Waste	2003
Saint Kitts and Nevis	National Conservation and Environmental Protection Act	1987 (as amended in 1996)
Saint Lucia	Merchant Shipping (Oil Pollution) Act	1996
	National Conservation Authority Act	1999
	St. Lucia Solid Waste Management Authority Act	1996

(Continued)

TABLE 2. **Continued**

Country	Law	Year
Saint Vincent and the Grenadines	Town and Country Planning Act	1992
	Forest Resource Conservation Act	1992
Trinidad and Tobago	Environmental Management Act	1995
	Conservation Wildlife Act	1996
	Maritime Areas Act	1996

Source: Author

Saint Vincent and the Grenadines. Second, general environmental acts passed in many countries result in different levels of development. The following section describes national legislation in those countries where laws focused on the environment as a whole have been enacted.

Central America

The legal system in Central American countries is governed by the principles of the civil law tradition. Civil law is written and codified, unlike common law, which is often formed by the opinions of judges based on historic custom. In consequence, Central American countries built their environmental laws by passing codes that initially attempted to protect the environment through the exercise of powers granted by such laws to administrative agencies. In later years, because of the international commitments adopted by these countries, environmental laws started incorporating new market-based environmental policy instruments.

Belize

Belize passed its ten-part Environmental Protection Act in 1992. This law creates the Department of the Environment and regulates its operation. The law also introduces environmental impact assessment as the main tool for environmental management and includes a system of penalties for cases of noncompliance. Additionally, it dedicates a full section to regulating dumps.

Natural resource protection in Belize continues to be regulated by different laws, such as the Wildlife Protection Act, Forest Act, Fisheries Act, Coastal Zone Management Act, and National Park System Act, all enacted since the 1920s. The effectiveness of such legal bodies has made it possible to increase the number of protected natural areas and protect the biodiversity within them. In the opinion of Winston Andersen (2002b), Belize's Environmental Protection Act has the essential purpose of overcoming the traditional fragmentation in environmental

regulation by institutionalizing broad-based environmental management.

Costa Rica

Costa Rica was one of the first Central American countries to include in its constitution the right to a healthy environment. Article 50 of the Constitution of 1949 as amended in 1994 recognizes the right of all citizens to live in a healthy and ecologically balanced environment and has standing to file an action aimed at obtaining the restoration of damaged environment. In 1995, Costa Rica approved the Organic Act of the Environment, with the objective of providing people and government with the necessary instruments to obtain a healthy and ecologically balanced environment. This act also declares that the environment is a common heritage of all the citizens of Costa Rica.

The Organic Act of the Environment regulates environmental impact assessments; protection and improvement of human settlements; land ordinances; protected natural areas; coastal maritime and wetland resources; biological diversity; and protection of forests, air, water, soil, and energy resources. It includes a section on enforcement and compliance. In the same direction, the Environmental Comptroller was created to supervise compliance with environmental law, and an Administrative Environmental Court was given jurisdiction to decide on environmental issues. In 1990, the Ministry of Energy and Environment was established in this country.

El Salvador

The Environmental Act of El Salvador was passed in 1997, and within a year El Salvador had created the Ministry of the Environment and Natural Resources. The objective of the Environmental Act is to develop constitutional provisions regarding protection, conservation, and restoration of the environment; ensure sustainable use of natural resources, making possible a better quality of life for present and future generations; rule public and private environmental management and environmental protection; and assure the application of international treaties and agreements relevant to El Salvador.

Among the main tools for environmental protection provided by the act are environmental ordinance of the territory, environmental impact assessment, access to information, public participation, environmental education, incentives and disincentives, and the Environmental Fund.

Guatemala

In Guatemala, the Act for Protection and Improvement of the Environment was passed in 1980. The act's objective is to improve the quality of life for the inhabitants of Guatemala by guaranteeing the country's ecological balance and protecting its environment. The act regulates air pollution, air quality, hydrological system protection, appropriate use of mineral resources, noise pollution, visual pollution and protection, and conservation of biotic systems. It includes a chapter regarding infractions, sanctions, and resources as well. This chapter also grants "popular action" to make a complaint before the authorities against loopholes in any action that could result in pollution, detriment, or loss of natural resources or that could affect the quality of life.

The 1980 act created the National Commission of the Environment, which reports to the President of the Republic. Guatemala also created a Ministry of the Environment and Natural Resources in 2000.

Honduras

In Honduras, a General Act of the Environment was passed in 1993. This law establishes an appropriate legal framework for orienting farming, forest, and industrial activities toward more rational and sustainable use of natural resources and environmental protection. The act also establishes instruments of environmental policy, including environmental impact assessment, public participation, and environmental education and research. In addition, this act created the Environmental Attorney General, who represents the public trust in environmental protection, whereas the Ministry of Environment formulates environmental policies.

Mexico

Mexico was one of the first countries in the region to legislate on environmental matters. The Federal Act to Prevent and Combat Pollution was passed in 1971 by the federal congress, and the first Under Ministry of Environmental Improvement was established to apply this act. The act focused on dealing with air pollution problems, but it was not effectively enforced because of multiple mistakes contained in its regulatory structure. As a consequence, it was repealed by the Federal Act for Environmental Protection in 1981. By 1982, the Ministry of Urban Development and Environment had succeeded the Under Ministry of Environmental Improvement as the federal environmental authority.

Later, the addition of Section XXIX-G to Article 73 of the Mexican Constitution gave foundation to the promulgation of the Ecological Equilibrium and Environmental Protection General Act of 1988, which for the first time allowed local governments to enact their own environmental laws.

While the laws of 1971 and 1981 concentrated on the problems associated with environmental pollution, the Ecological Equilibrium and Environmental Protection General Act focused on preserving the environment as a whole. This law defined the principles that have since ruled the environmental policy of the Mexican government, and established the instruments needed to achieve the law's objectives (including environmental impact assessment, environmental planning, and ecological standards). The act specified the powers of the various environmental authorities and established administrative and criminal sanctions for cases of noncompliance with its provisions. It also defined a system of power distribution among federal, local, and municipal governments.

The Act of 1988 has been reformed several times, but the most important modification occurred in 1996 when the law was changed to include economic instruments of environmental policy as well as the public's right to access information and participate in making policy. A key factor influencing this reform was Mexico's incorporation into the North American economy by signing the North American Free Trade Agreement. Environmental nongovernmental organizations had accused Mexico of not having effective environmental laws. This obliged the Mexican government to strengthen its environmental programs in order to demonstrate its commitment to environmental protection. The change coincided with an increase in public and private enforcement and compliance programs. By 1992, the Ministry of Urban Development and Environment was replaced by the Ministry of Social Development, which was charged with environmental protection. The Attorney General for Environmental Protection and a regulatory agency, the National Institute of Ecology, were created as specialized branches of this Ministry.

In 1996, the Ministry of Social Development was replaced by the Ministry of the Environment, Natural Resources and Fishing for the task of protecting the environment, and in 2000 it changed its name to the Ministry of Environment and Natural Resources.

In 1999, Mexico amended its federal constitution to incorporate the people's right to a healthy environment and the principle of sustainable development. Since then, the federal congress has enacted the General Act of Wildlife of 2000, the General Act for Sustainable Use of Forest of 2003, and the General Act for Prevention and Integral Management of Waste of 2003. Finally, the National Water Act was substantially modified in 2004.

Nicaragua

In 1990, the Nicaragua National Commission of Environment and Territory Ordinance was established as an Executive Advisory Office. Then in 1994, the Ministry of the Environment and Natural Resources was created. The General Act of the Environment was not passed until 1996. Political, social, and economic factors explain why this country was one of the last Central American countries to pass an environmental law. Until 1979, Nicaragua was under the domination of the Anastasio Somoza dictatorship, and during the 1980s the country was governed by the socialism doctrine.

The 1996 law sets up the rules for environmental conservation, protection, and restoration. It also created the National Commission of the Environment to coordinate the state and public in defining environmental policies. In addition, it established an Attorney General's Office in charge of enforcing the law and to represent the public interest in protecting the environment. This legal body also defined the environmental policy tools, such as environmental planning, environmental ordinance of the territory, protection of natural areas, the licensing system, environmental impact assessments, the National System of Environmental Information, environmental education and research, incentives, public investments, and the National Environmental Fund.

Panama

In Panama, the General Act of Environment was passed in 1998. This act established the National Authority of the Environment as an autonomous office in charge of enforcing laws and regulations regarding the environment and natural resources. The National Council of the Environment was also established with this act and is composed of three state ministries designated as advisory entities to the Cabinet of Ministries on environmental matters. The act also created the National Advisory Commission as an advisory entity for the National Authority of the Environment.

The General Act of Environment defined the tools for environmental policy, such as environmental ordinance, environmental impact assessment, environmental quality standards, access to information, environmental education, and research and monitoring systems.

The Caribbean

The Caribbean region comprises Caribbean sea islands, including Antigua and Barbuda, Aruba, the Cayman Islands, Cuba, Dominica, the Dominican Republic, Grenada, Guadeloupe, Haiti, Jamaica, Martinique, Puerto Rico (not included in this article, as it is a territory of the United States), Saint Kitts and Nevis, Saint Lucia, Saint Vincent and the Grenadines, Trinidad and Tobago, Turks and Caicos Islands, and the Virgin Islands. Unlike the Central American countries, the Caribbean countries (excepting Guyana, Haiti, the Dominican Republic, and Saint Lucia) are ruled by the common law system, in which the law is developed by judges through decisions of courts and similar tribunals rather than through legislative statutes or executive branch action. Nevertheless, common law countries have been developing and codifying environmental laws.

Barbados

In Barbados, an Environmental Management Act is under discussion. The bill is aimed at improving areas of environmental protection such as environmental noise, ambient air quality, and water quality control. It would also create a Ministry of Environment, Water Resources and Drainage. Previously, the Environmental Levy Act of 1996 was passed to promote efficient solid waste management and implement the "polluter pays" principle by defraying the costs of waste collection and disposal of imported goods.

Dominican Republic

In the Dominican Republic prior to 2000, the legal framework providing environmental protection comprised a hodgepodge of special laws, presidential decrees, resolutions, and administrative measures. These often contradicted each other and lacked adequate scientific character, resulting in ineffective protection of the country's natural resources.

In October 1999, the congress approved a bill for a General Act on the Environment and Natural Resources, which was passed as Law 64–00 on 18 August 2000. Law 64-00 recognizes the importance of the protection, preservation, and sustained use of natural resources for the well-being of humanity, and highlights the need for special protection of the country's rare and endangered natural resources by correcting the deforestation, dry conditions, and general degradation of the environment. It includes special laws directing areas such as tourism, electricity, and telecommunications to address environmental concerns as part of doing business.

Under Law 64–00, the state is obliged to protect the environment and must adopt integrated policies to which all institutions related to natural resources must adhere in order to ensure their effectiveness. The state's responsibility of protecting and restoring the environment is shared with society down to the individual level. In this manner, the law provides for mandatory inclusion of environmental programs in all social and economic development programs.

Furthermore, the law provides that "lack of scientific absolute certainty shall not be called as a reason not to adopt preventive effective measures in any activities having a negative influence on the environment." Law 64–00 was designed "to provide rules for the protection, improvement and restoration of the environment and natural resources, by ensuring the sustained development thereof." The law regulates across a broad spectrum, including "soil; water and air contamination; dangerous products, elements, and substances; domestic and municipal waste; human settlements; and sonic contamination." It also regulates the Secretary of State for the Environment and Natural Resources as well as municipal authorities who grant rights for the use soil and water, coast and sea, forest and cave, and minerals.

The Ministry of Environment and Natural Resources, created by Law 64–00, is responsible for drafting, executing, and supervising the implementation of national policies on the environment and natural resources; ensuring the preservation, protection, and sustained use of natural resources; improving soil, air, and water contamination rules; ensuring the proper exploration and use of mineral resources; preserving coastal and sea resources; and establishing general environmental rules for residential and industrial settings.

Haiti

Haiti has not yet passed any comprehensive laws to protect the environment (see Victor 1995). A number of legal instruments have been enacted to protect specific natural resources, such as the act organizing the Drinking Water Sector in 2008; a decree on management of the environment and on the regulation of citizens' behavior for

sustainable development; the Act of April 23 on historic, artistic, and natural and archeological heritage; an act that established measures to combat deforestation in 1936; and an act to establish national forest reserves in 1926.

Jamaica

By 1975, the Jamaican parliament had established the Natural Resources Conservation Authority and the Natural Resources Conservation Department, but it was not until 1992 that the National Resources Conservation Authority was legally constituted under the National Resources Conservation Authority Act. This agency has wide environmental functions including: holding property; regulating the conduct of environmental impact assessments; promoting public awareness; managing certain national parks, marine parks, protected areas, and public recreation facilities; taking administrative and judicial proceedings against environmental infractions; and advising the minister on general environmental policy.

Saint Kitts and Nevis

In Saint Kitts and Nevis, the National Conservation and Environmental Protection Act was passed in 1987. This act was augmented by the National Conservation and Environment Protection (amendment) Act of 1996. The Amendment of 1996 established the Department of the Environment as the leading environmental agency in the country. The Department of the Environment coordinates conservation efforts and the National Conservation Commission (an advisory and consultative body to the minister). The commission makes recommendations regarding a list of special buildings to be preserved for historic and cultural values and promotes conservation as part of long-term national economic development.

The Environmental Protection Act supports the establishment and administration of protected natural areas; establishment of national parks and historic sites; protection of coasts beaches; conservation of forestry, soil, and water; protection of wild animals and birds; and protection of antiquities and historic buildings.

Saint Lucia

In Saint Lucia, the National Conservation Authority Act was passed in 1999. It provided for the establishment of a National Conservation Authority, whose responsibilities are largely restricted to the conservation of natural beauty and topographic features, particularly in relation to beaches. The minster has powers to declare any land or water to be a protected area for the purpose of preserving or enhancing its natural beauty, fauna, or flora; or the creation of a recreational area or national park.

Trinidad and Tobago

The Environmental Management Act of Trinidad and Tobago was passed in 1995. This was later repealed by the Environmental Management Act of 2000, which is identical in most respects except for a provision on the constitutionally of the Environmental Commission. The act created an unprecedented array of institutions with varying responsibilities. The leader is the Environmental Management Agency, but there are also an Environmental Trust Fund and an Environmental Commission. The Environmental Management Agency makes recommendations for national environmental policy, develops programs and effective management strategies, coordinates environmental management functions, and improves public awareness and education.

Evaluating Environmental Law

As described, the evolution of environmental law in Central American and Caribbean countries is not homogeneous, although it is possible to identify three common characteristics in the more recent national environmental laws:

- There is a trend toward passing or framing general environmental laws with a more comprehensive perspective.
- All new legislation incorporates an environmental impact assessment process in addition to other environmental tools proposed by the Rio Declaration.
- Environmental laws include the establishment of environmental agencies in charge of the enforcement and compliance of such legal bodies.

Nevertheless, the use of market-based instruments of environmental policy are still missing in most of the Central American and Caribbean countries. These will surely arise as regional and global pressures increase on every country's environment.

José Juan GONZÁLEZ MÁRQUEZ
Metropolitan Autonomous University

See also in the *Berkshire Encyclopedia of Sustainability* Convention on Biological Diversity; Development, Sustainable—Overview of Laws and Commissions; Environmental Law—South America; Environmental Law—United States and Canada; International Law

FURTHER READINGS

Aguilar Rojas, Grethel, & Iza, Alejandro. (Eds.). (2009). *Derecho ambiental en Centro América* [Central American Environmental Law] (2 vols.). Gland, Switzerland: *Union Internationale pour la Conservation de la Nature* (UICN) [International Union for Conservation of Nature (IUCN)].

Anderson, Winston. (2002a). *Caribbean environmental law: Development and application*. Mexico City: United Nations Environment Programme, Regional Office for Latin America and the Caribbean (UNEP-ROLAC).

Anderson, Winston. (2002b, April). *The evolving role of the judiciary in environmental compliance and enforcement*. Presented at the 6th International Conference on Environmental Compliance and Enforcement, San José, Costa Rica.

Brañes Ballesteros, Raúl. (1996). *Manual de derecho ambiental mexicano* [Handbook of Mexican Environmental Law]. Mexico City: Fondo de Cultura Economica. Fundación Universo XXI.

Brañes Ballesteros, Raúl. (2001). *Informe sobre el desarrollo del derecho ambiental latinoamericano. Su aplicación después de 10 años de la Conferencia sobre Medio Ambiente y Desarrollo* [Report on the development of Latin American environmental law. Its enforcement and compliance 10 years after the Conference on Environment and Development]. México City: United Nations Environment Programme, Regional Office for Latin America and the Caribbean (UNEP-ROLAC).

Cambronero, Roxana Salazar. (1993). *El derecho a un ambiente sano: Ecología y desarrollo sostenible* [The right to a healthy environment: Ecology and sustainable development]. San Jose, Costa Rica: Libre.

González Márquez, José Juan. (1996). *La recepción en los sistemas jurídicos de los países de Américana Latina y el Caribe de los compromisos asumidos en la Conferencia de las Naciones Unidas sobre Medio Ambiente y Desarrollo (1992). Propuestas para la cooperación hemisférica* [The implementation of commitments adopted at the United Nations Conference on Environment and Development (1992) by the Latin American and Caribbean legal systems: Proposals for hemispheric cooperation]. México City: United Nations Environment Programme, Regional Office for Latin America and the Caribbean (UNEP-ROLAC).

Legal framework for business activities. (2005, August 6). Environmental protection: Law 64-00. *DominicanToday.com*. Retrieved December 3, 2010, from http://www.dominicantoday.com/dr/business-guide/2005/8/6/3438/ENVIRONMENTAL-PROTECTION-LAW-64-00

McCalla, Winston. (1995). *Compendium on environmental protection and natural resources management legislation in Belize*. Natural Resource Management and Protection Project, Final Report. United States Agency for International Development (USAID) Project No. 505–0043.

Pollard, Duke E. E. (Ed.). (1991). *Environmental laws of the Commonwealth Caribbean*. Cave Hill, Barbados: Caribbean Law Institute.

Rey Santos, Orlando. (1998). *Derecho ambiental: Principios y conceptos básicos. Tratamiento del concepto de desarrollo sostenible, como piedra angular y meta del derecho ambiental* [Environmental law: Basic principles and concepts. Analysis of the concept of sustainable development as the cornerstone and goal of environmental law]. La Habana, Cuba: Dirección de Política Ambiental. Ministerio de Ciencia, Tecnología y Medio Ambiente [Environmental Policy Office. Ministry of Science, Technology and Environment].

Robinson, Nicholas. (2003.) Challenges confronting the progressive development of a second generation of environmental laws. In Lye Lin-Heng & María del Socorro Z. Manguiat (Eds.), *Towards a "second generation" in environmental laws in the Asian and Pacific Region: Select trends* (pp. 27–32). Gland, Switzerland and Cambridge, UK: IUCN.

United Nations Convention on Biological Diversity (CBD). (1992). Full text of the convention. Retrieved November 8, 2010, from http://www.cbd.int/convention/convention.shtml

United Nations Environment Programme, Regional Office for Latin America and the Caribbean (UNEP-ROLAC). (1999). *Manual de Legislación Ambiental de Guatemala* [Handbook Environmental Law of Guatemala]. Mexico City: UNEP-ROLAC.

United Nations Environment Programme, Regional Office for Latin America and the Caribbean (UNEP-ROLAC). (2003). Global Environment Outlook (GEO) report for Latin America and the Caribbean: Environment outlook 2003. Mexico City: UNEP-ROLAC.

United Nations Framework Convention on Climate Change (UNFCCC). (1992). Full text of the convention. Retrieved November 8, 2010, from http://unfccc.int/essential_background/convention/background/items/1349.php

Victor, Jean Abdré. (1995.) Code des Lois haitiennes de L'Environnement. Port-au-Prince, Haiti: UNDP.

Environmental Law—China

Environmental legislation in China did not exist before 1979, but China's rapid development and economic growth in the latter twentieth century and large population have created significant constraints on the land and natural resources. Although many laws have been written since then, they are implemented primarily by the local governments and courts, which tend to favor local businesses (for short-term economic reasons) over enforcement of national environmental law.

Historically China has faced many human-induced environmental disasters related to water diversion projects, deforestation, and flawed agricultural policies since its prehistoric agrarian communities in the Huang (Yellow) River basin. Today, China's status as the world's most populous country and its rapid urbanization and economic growth combine to create daunting environmental challenges that impose significant constraints on the country's land and natural resources, including severe water and air pollution, soil contamination and desertification, and mounting solid waste as well as climate change.

Water pollution is an example: according to the 2008 official report on China's environment, the seven major rivers in China suffer from medium pollution (Ministry of Environmental Protection 2009, 3), and eleven out of the twenty-eight lakes and reservoirs under the central government's strict supervision have a water quality graded less than five, the lowest national standard for water quality (p. 9). This means the water is essentially unusable for any purpose. A 2009 pollution source census found that chemical oxygen demand in China's water was 30 percent higher than previously recognized (Oster 2010). (Chemical oxygen demand is a measure of organic pollutants; a higher number indicates poorer water quality.) One reason for the increase was that the survey included nonpoint source pollution (from diverse sources) from agriculture for the first time.

Environmental Administrative and Government Framework

Modern China is a unitary state, and technically all power comes from the central government in Beijing. But economic reforms over the last three decades have brought significant decentralization to the country, and in many cases the central government has been unable to rein in local government power, leading to substantial de facto autonomy for local governments.

According to the constitution, all power in the People's Republic of China (PRC) belongs to the people and is exercised through the National People's Congress (NPC) and through local people's congresses at lower levels of government. Most governmental power, however, is implemented by the Standing Committee of the Politburo of the Chinese Communist Party (CCP), and the CCP plays an important but nontransparent role in shaping China's national policy, including major decisions related to the environment, and the operation of government at all levels.

The NPC, as the supreme organ of state power, has the authority to issue laws binding across China and appoints the president of the nation, the premier, and the president of the Supreme People's Court. Within the environmental arena, NPC and its Environment and Natural Resources Protection Committee play an important role in making, revising, and interpreting environmental statutes, inspecting the implementation of environmental laws as well as supervising the work of environmental agencies and courts. The day-to-day work of operating the government is carried out by the State Council in the central government, headed by the premier. The State Council is divided into various ministries and commissions. This structure of a people's congress on one hand and a day-to-day government on the other hand is also replicated at the local government level.

At the center of China's environmental regulatory system is the Ministry of Environmental Protection (MEP) under the State Council. Prior to obtaining cabinet level ministry status in March 2008, MEP was known as the State Environmental Protection Agency. The elevation of MEP to full ministry level was intended to enhance the ability of MEP to protect China's environment and evince the Chinese government's determination to improve environmental governance. MEP's primary duties include formulating and implementing national environmental policies, drafting laws and regulations, setting national environmental quality standards, establishing pollution discharge limits, and overseeing nearly three thousand subnational environmental protection bureaus (EPBs).

MEP has a relatively small staff of less than one thousand employees; therefore the bulk of environmental monitoring and enforcement is delegated to subnational EPBs and their roughly 180,000 employees nationwide. Subnational EPBs exist at the provincial, city, county, and district levels. EPBs issue pollution permits, keep records, collect fines, conduct accident and violation investigations, and help draft local laws, regulations, and rules. While technically subordinate to MEP, EPBs actually have a substantial amount of autonomy. This autonomy is derived from the fact that local governments control the bulk of funding for EPBs as well as the promotion process and other personnel decisions, and such arrangements make EPBs more susceptible to the concerns of local governments than to those of MEP when issuing permits or taking enforcement actions. It is generally believed that local governments are more likely to favor local industry over strict enforcement of environmental law for short-term economic and tax reasons.

When a violation comes to the attention of an EPB, the law provides for numerous penalties, including revocation of discharge permits, an injunction on certain activities, facility closure, or relocation. By far the most common penalty is a fine. Because of pressure from local government or business interests, it is common for EPBs to negotiate fines with violators, even when violations are repetitive or intentional. To enhance its role in supervising local EPBs and to improve the handling of enforcement issues involving major or interjurisdictional incidents, MEP has established six regional offices across the country since 2002. These regional offices have so far played a very limited role, however, and are not permitted to conduct monitoring or direct enforcement actions within the sole jurisdiction of an EPB.

Concerned citizens and pollution victims can report polluters and persuade the local EPBs to investigate. If the EPB finds the source and determines that the pollution was harmful, the EPB may suggest that the parties engage in mediation under its guidance. If at the end of the EPB's mediation the victim is not satisfied with the outcome, or the polluter fails to perform under the agreement, the victim can file a civil action with the local court.

Environmental Legislative and Judicial Framework

China's current legal system combines a number of legal traditions, including elements from the continental European civil law tradition, substantial elements borrowed from the socialist law system of the former Soviet Union, and principles inherited from imperial Chinese law. In recent years, especially in the environmental area, American legal principles increasingly are reflected in China's legal system. The Open Door policy and reform in the late 1970s led to China's rapid economic development and ongoing transition to a market economy, which has had enormous implications for the country's legal development. The 1980s and 1990s saw a massive and rapid enactment of laws, regulations, and rules, particularly those regulating economic and commercial relations, as a tool for attracting foreign investment. Statutory laws are of key importance, and court judgments have formally no precedential effect, though they may serve as guidance.

In 1979, the Standing Committee of NPC adopted the Environmental Protection Law (for trial implementation), a basic framework law that signifies the beginning of environmental legislation in modern China. The mid-1980s witnessed the early stage of China's environmental protection legislation, but starting in the early 1990s, China's environmental regulatory framework expanded at an unprecedented pace. Numerous environmental laws, regulations, rules, and standards have been enacted or amended every year since then. So far China has adopted over two dozen environmental statutes that address pollution prevention and control, natural resources protection and conservation, and environmental impact assessment. The Chinese environmental law system also includes environmental protection provisions in other areas of legislation, as well as those international conventions and treaties focusing on environmental protection that have been ratified by the Chinese government. The addition of new laws has done little to improve overall enforcement. New and revised laws tend to be more detailed, however, and incorporate best practices from around the globe, which hold the potential for enhancing enforcement.

While the vast majority of environmental enforcement uses administrative procedures, China's court system is often relied upon as well. There are four levels of general courts in China to enforce environmental laws: the Supreme People's Court (SPC) at the central government level, the High People's Courts at the provincial levels, and the Intermediate and Basic People's Courts further down at the local level. There are also several types of specialized courts that include military courts, maritime courts (e.g., for water pollution), courts of forestry affairs (e.g., for damage to forest resources), courts of railway transportation, courts of agriculture cultivation, and most recently, environmental courts. The SPC issues judicial interpretations, essentially interpretive regulations, to clarify important environmental legal concepts and principles as well as guiding lower-level courts in the application of environmental law by retrial of important and complicated cases. For all other courts, their role in environmental governance includes hearing environmental tort litigation, conducting judicial review of decisions by environmental protection agencies, and mediating environmental disputes. Among different levels of courts, the Basic People's Courts serve as the first-instance trial court, and the Intermediate People's Courts serve as the major appellate review court for most environmental criminal, civil, and administrative cases. Basic level courts also tend to be the most susceptible to local protectionism.

Because administrative enforcement in China is lacking, many pollution casualties and public interest advocates rely on China's tort law to sue polluters for damages. Over the past decade several important environmental tort law principles have been established to help protect pollution victims. Firstly, the law imposes no-fault liability on polluters. This means that the defendant need not have been negligent or even caused the pollution discharge; if the defendant's pollution caused the harm, the defendant can be liable. Secondly, the burden of proof is reversed. The plaintiff only needs to make a prima facie case that the defendant's pollution caused the harm, and the burden then shifts to the defendant to disprove the plaintiff's allegation. Thirdly, a three-year statute of limitations for claiming compensation, starting at such time when the party becomes aware of or should become aware of losses due to pollution, applies to environmental tort cases. This is one year longer than the standard statute of limitations for tort cases in China. Unfortunately, for many pollution victims, China's courts do not always apply these favorable provisions as the law dictates. The same local protectionism that influences lax administrative enforcement can also influence judicial decisions within local courts.

Enforcement Challenges and New Initiatives

In spite of China's admirable efforts to legislate environmental law, huge gaps exist between law on the books and enforcement on the ground. Pursuit of economic development, lack of financial and human resources, local protectionism, a weak and nonindependent judiciary, weak regulatory infrastructure, and limited civil society engagement are all major barriers to enforcing China's environmental law.

In recent years, measures have been taken to promote efficient and effective environmental enforcement. This includes strengthening the local governments' responsibility for environmental protection by taking into consideration the environmental quality in their respective administrative regions to evaluate and assess the performance of local governments and officials in charge, giving environmental protection agencies broader and more effective enforcement tools, imposing tougher penalties for violation, and encouraging public participation and judicial activism in protecting the environment.

A promising new initiative is the establishment of specialized environmental courts in several cities and counties across China since 2004. The establishment of these courts helps streamline the process of hearing environmental cases, allows the cases to be heard by judges with enhanced technical expertise, and expands the standing for plaintiffs to encourage environmental public interest litigation that regular courts will not accept under current Chinese law. China's environmental situation is a global issue, and many international NGOs, foundations, and research institutions work in China on improving its environmental governance. The specialized environmental courts initiative is a good example of this kind of international effort.

Implications

China has achieved rapid economic development, but reforms in the political system and development of rule

of law lag behind. (Rule of law is a system that attempts to protect the rights of citizens from arbitrary and abusive use of government power.) But recent developments within the environmental governance arena, such as environmental courts and freedom of information laws, promote a more open and transparent government with enhanced civil society engagement. Improved activism and increased independence for the judiciary will ultimately push China a step further toward sustainable environmental governance with democratic and rule of law characteristics.

Jingjing LIU and Adam MOSER
Vermont Law School

See also in the *Berkshire Encyclopedia of Sustainability* Development, Sustainable—Overview of Laws and Commissions; Enforcement; Environmental Law (several articles: East Asia; India and Pakistan; Southeast Asia); International Law; Polluter Pays Principle; Tort Law

FURTHER READINGS

Behr, Volker. (2007). Development of a new legal system in the PRC. *Louisiana Law Review, 67*, 1161.

Chen, Jianfu. (2008). *Chinese law: Context and transformation.* Leiden, The Netherlands: Martinus Nijhoff Publishers.

Clarke, Donald. (2005). *The Chinese legal system.* Retrieved September 1, 2010, from http://docs.law.gwu.edu/facweb/dclarke/public/ChineseLegalSystem.html

Economy, Elizabeth. (2004). *The river runs black: The environmental challenge to China's future.* Ithaca, NY: Cornell University Press.

Finder, Susan. (1993). The Supreme People's Court of the PRC. *Journal of Chinese Law, 7*, 145.

Lieberthal, Kenneth, & Oksenberg, Michel. (1998). *Policy making in China: Leaders, structures, and processes.* Princeton, NJ: Princeton University Press.

Lubman, Stanley. (2000). *Bird in a cage: Legal reform in China after Mao.* Stanford, CA: Stanford University Press.

Ma, Xiaoying, & Ortolano, Leonard. (2000). *Environmental regulation in China: Institutions, enforcement, and compliance.* Lanham, MD: Rowman & Littlefield.

Ministry of Environmental Protection of the People's Republic of China. (2009). *2008: Report on the state of the environment in China.* Retrieved November 19, 2010, from http://english.mep.gov.cn/down_load/Documents/201002/P020100225377359212834.pdf

Oster, Shai. (2010, February 10). China report finds extensive pollution. *Wall Street Journal.* Retrieved November 18, 2010, from http://online.wsj.com/article/SB10001424052748704182004575054811793594150.html

Peerenboom, Randall. (2002). *China's Long March to the rule of law.* Cambridge, UK: Cambridge University Press.

Van Rooij, Benjamin. (2006). *Regulating land and pollution in China: Lawmaking, compliance, and enforcement; Theory and cases.* Leiden, The Netherlands: Leiden University Press.

Van Rooij, Benjamin. (January 2010). The people vs. pollution: Understanding citizen action against pollution in China. *Journal of Contemporary China, 19*(63), 55–77.

Wang, Alex. (2007). The role of law in environmental protection in China: Recent developments. *Vermont Journal of Environmental Law, 8*, 195.

Wang, Canfa. (2007). Chinese environmental law enforcement: Current deficiencies and suggested reforms. *Vermont Journal of Environmental Law, 8*, 159.

Environmental Law—East Asia

Following their successive, rapid economic booms, Japan, Taiwan, South Korea, and China experienced one downside of industrialization: severe pollution and its harmful health effects. Growing public demand and international pressure brought about remedial policy and considerable improvements in Japan, Taiwan, and South Korea. China, however, still struggles with environmental pollution, having many laws on the books but ineffective enforcement.

Environmental law responds to environmental destruction, which is intensified by industrial growth. Since the end of World War II, countries in the East Asian region experienced astoundingly rapid economic growth. First Japan, then South Korea and Taiwan, and now China—with GDP growth rates sometimes exceeding 10 percent a year—all earned the label "economic miracle." This rapid growth brought them unprecedented prosperity, but also cast a shadow of industrial pollution over their lands and people. The sprouting factories carelessly dumped their toxic waste into the surrounding water, air, and land. Individuals and communities suffered from pollution-induced asthma, cancer, fetal deformity, and other diseases. These horrors created social tensions, spurred protest movements, and spread doubts about the benefits of headlong growth. It cast these societies successively into a common social syndrome: the growth/environment dilemma. Tensions between groups for and against more industrial growth threatened to stalemate the growth process (Broadbent 1998). Businesses and ministries for economic development often prefer voluntary measures and weaker standards. Environmental agencies tend to support stronger standards, but often lack political clout. When available, citizens have used courts, competitive elections, and public protest to successfully press for more effective legal and regulatory controls.

In Japan, the growth/environment dilemma reached its peak and transformation point around 1970. In South Korea and Taiwan, this peak occurred around 1990 and coincided with the fall of authoritarian governments in both societies. In China, the problem is ongoing. Due to China's system of centralized authority, the victims of industrial pollution have not been able to exert public pressure on the government. The central government, however, has recognized industrial pollution as a serious problem and produced many formal laws to address it.

Environmental Law in Japan

Japan experienced very rapid economic growth after World War II, especially from the mid-1950s. This economic growth lacked effective environmental regulations and laws, bringing about serious environmental problems such as air and water pollution. Pollution-related disease events included four major incidents, including the Minamata and Niigata mercury poisonings, Itai-Itai cadmium disease, and the Yokkaichi asthma case (Ui 1992). These four major pollution problems aroused public concern and raised questions about the government's economic growth priorities. In each case, the victims sued in court for redress. Their success opened a path to judicially awarded fiscal compensation for the victims of environmental pollution and contamination, stimulating subsequent lawsuits. These lawsuits, in addition to a wave of public protest, produced a turning point in environmental legislation. The government enacted the Basic Law on Pollution Control in 1967 and amended it in 1970 to make it more effective. At the 64th Extraordinary Diet (national legislature) Session in 1971, this "Pollution Diet" passed or revised fourteen environmental protection laws and established the Environmental Agency (*kankyocho*) (Gresser, Fujikura, and Morishima

1981). At the time, these laws were reputed to be the strictest in the world. They introduced many innovative systems of environmental governance, including shifting power to local government and imposing pollution control regimes upon factories (Imura and Schreurs 2005). These reforms rapidly reduced the most toxic and visible forms of air and water pollution (Broadbent 2002).

The sudden rise in oil prices in 1973, known as the oil shock, brought about a regression in environmental legislation in the late 1970s and the 1980s. Conservative politicians of the ruling Liberal Democratic Party (LDP) criticized environmental legislation as a barrier to economic recovery. Moreover, due to environmental regulation, the quality of air and water improved and media coverage on environmental pollution decreased. In general, citizens' concerns shifted to the economy.

Although extreme pollution-related disease decreased during this period, the types and varieties of environmental problems continued to increase. These included airport noise, bullet train noise and vibrations, pollutions related to household garbage and noise from neighbors, acid rain, forest degradation, and dioxin from the growing number of trash incinerators built in response to Japan's limited landfill space. Local protest movements against such problems continued to simmer. Over the decades, environmental movements were important vehicles for awakening citizens to their civic responsibilities and political capacities, expanding the role of civil society and contributing to the historic regime change of 2009 (Hasegawa 2004; Hasegawa 2010; Schreurs 2004).

The 1992 Earth Summit in Rio de Janeiro shifted media coverage and citizens' concerns back to environmental issues. Under this new global framework, with the decline of Cold War tensions and increasing of varieties of environmental problems, the Japanese government replaced the Basic Law on Pollution Control with the Basic Law for Environment in 1993. The new law stressed the concept of sustainability, the role of local governments, and the partnership of citizens and nongovernmental organizations (NGOs) with governments on environmental regulations and policy-making processes.

In 1996, the government passed an environmental impact assessment (EIA) act. This act was very controversial. The Environmental Agency had tried from its start in 1971 to pass an EIA law but the ruling LDP politicians, officials of MITI (Ministry of International Trade and Industry), and leaders of Keidanren (the Federation of Economic Organizations) opposed the measure, fearing it would prevent more large-scale development projects. By 1996, however, most such projects were being built overseas, not within Japan, and these officials finally capitulated to the rising public environmental concern.

In December 1997, the Japanese government hosted the Kyoto Conference on the prevention of global warming. The conference agreed upon the Kyoto Protocol, the first legal worldwide framework for climate change protection. This conference promoted a shift in media coverage and citizens' concerns toward climate change issues. Climate change protection became the new focal point of environmental issues. In 1998, to meet the protocol target of a 6 percent decrease of greenhouse gas (GHG) emissions from the 1990 level, the Japanese government passed the Global Warming Protection Law.

In 2001, under the reorganization of government ministries, the Environmental Agency was promoted to become the Ministry of Environment. This promotion and the increase of the ministry's tasks was another sign of rising social expectations for environmental regulation (Hasegawa, Shinohara, and Broadbent 2007). Despite these changes, the Japanese government did not pass formal laws to reduce Japan's GHG emissions. The Ministry of Environment, backed by environmental NGOs, lawyers, and scientists, pushed for national laws such as cap and trade or carbon tax to reduce national GHG emissions. But the Ministry of Economy, Trade and Industry (METI, formerly MITI) and the Keidanren defended voluntary action plans for each economic sector and strongly opposed a strict cap-and-trade system or carbon-tax system.

In 2009, after victory in the general election, the Democratic Party of Japan set up its Cabinet. This represented a huge political change in Japan, as it was only the second time since 1955 that the long-dominant LDP had lost control of the Cabinet. Newly elected prime minister Yukio Hatoyama declared an aggressive new goal of achieving a 25 percent decrease in GHG emissions from their 1990 level by 2020.

How this new government handles this problem may determine the future of Japanese environmental policy and regulation.

Environmental Law in South Korea

South Korea experienced very rapid economic growth beginning in the 1960s. This fast growth created serious environmental problems, such as air and water pollution. To address these environmental problems, environmental policies and laws have been adopted ex post facto, or retroactively. In the 1990s, with the development of a strong environmental movement, popular demands improved the environmental law system (Ku 2010). Though the development of environmental law contributed to reducing environmental problems, the efficacy and integration of these laws remain controversial.

The Park Chung-hee administration launched the first Five Year Economic Development Plan in 1962 and legislated the Pollution Prevention Act in 1963 in order to address environmental pollution. This act, however, did not have the proper articles to enact proactive environmental policy. As the government's focus was on rapid economic development, it did not organize the environmental administration system effectively and failed to implement the law sufficiently. As heavy chemical industries developed in the 1970s, they created serious air, water, and soil contamination in industrial sites such as Ulsan and Onsan. To respond to these environmental problems, in 1977 the government replaced the Environmental Pollution Prevention Act with the Environmental Conservation Act.

In the 1980 constitutional law, the right to a clean environmental was first legislated. Although operating under an authoritarian system, the environmental article showed progress, at least within that field. The establishment of the Environmental Agency in 1980 also improved the administration of environmental law. Since the 1980s, new laws put urban pollution and the destruction of nature on the public agenda alongside industrial development.

In 1990, in order to respond to complex environmental problems more systematically, the government replaced the Environmental Conservation Act with various new laws, such as the Framework Convention on Environmental Policy, the Clean Water Conservation Act, and the Clean Air Conservation Act. It changed the Environmental Agency to the Ministry of Environment (MOE) in 1990, making it more influential. Furthermore, laws for nature conservation, such as the Natural Environment Conservation Act and the Environmental Impact Assessment Act, were legislated. In the 1990s, the environmental administration system was extended and professionalized. As a result, the MOE currently implements forty-six environmental laws.

Environmental laws were not well implemented until the 1980s, and beginning in the 1990s they have been enacted more quickly in response to increased public awareness and environmental (Cho 1999). The 1991 Nakdong River incident, involving water contamination by phenol leakage, was a catalyst of this improvement. The empowerment of environmental organizations has helped to improve systems of public participation, especially in the area of EIAs.

In spite of the progress and professionalization of environmental law and administration, South Korea still faces environmental problems such as urban air pollution, water quality, waste management, nature conservation, and climate change. In addition, environmental conflicts among civil society, government, and the business sector continue because the South Korean government and business sector still implement large construction projects, destroying ecologically vulnerable sites such as tidal flats and river basins.

In environmental conflicts, lawyers perform important roles to preserve the environment. Environmentalists and pro-environment lawyers took legal action against the government to stop large-scale development projects such as the Seamangeum reclamation project and four large river projects (Lee and Park 2009). The results of these cases have differed greatly. In some cases, environmentalists won the first hearing in some cases, though they were defeated during the second and third. Conversely, sometimes environmentalists and government officials cooperated in preserving environment. For example, environmental NGOs cooperated with the MOE in legislating four acts for large river water quality improvements in the early 2000s.

South Korean environmental laws have also had problems concerning ad hoc legislation and a fragmented law system. Furthermore, environmental laws are not strong enough to fully address the pollution and destruction caused by economic development (Koh 2008; Kim 2010). Cooperation of civil society, government, and the business sector is essential to improve environmental legal and administration system in South Korea.

Environmental Law in Taiwan (Republic of China)

The Taiwanese law system is based largely on the German civil law system, in which laws are codified and not determined by judges. Taiwan's legal structure includes six codes: the Constitution, the Civil Code, the Code of Civil Procedures, the Criminal Code, the Code of Criminal Procedures, and Administrative laws. After the KMT (Kuomintang, or the Nationalist Party) regime retreated to Taiwan in 1949 when it lost the civil war to the Communist Party, law systems have diverged between Taiwan (the Republic of China) and China (the People's Republic of China). Between 1949 and 1987, the KMT-led central government declared martial law in Taiwan, suppressing basic civil legal rights. The civil justice system was subordinate to the military justice system on politically sensitive issues. Martial law and authoritarian regulations also diminished the autonomy of the legal profession and legal system. After martial law was lifted in 1987 under the trend of political democratization, legal reforms were initiated and proliferated.

During its pursuit of economic growth starting in the 1960s, the KMT government did not regulate pollution abatement. As a result, environmental consciousness and social discontent grew rapidly. In 1980s, many environmental protests were initiated due to pollution produced by private businesses and state-owned or -protected enterprises. Since the late 1980s, when membership-based environmental organizations such as the Taiwan Environmental Protection Union burgeoned, the character of the environmental movement changed and expanded to include ecological issues such as wildlife and forest resource preservation. This environmental awareness led to the proliferation of environmental regulations and political reform. Social movement scholars often regard the emergence of environmental movement in Taiwan as one of the major sources of Taiwan's democratization (Tang and Tang 2000). As an island that has limited land and natural resources, lacks international recognition and support, and is vulnerable to the impact of climate change, the enactment of environmental law to improve its self-sustainability and connection to the international community has become a major task for Taiwan in the twenty-first century.

Like many other developing countries, Taiwanese environmental law emerged in response to environmental challenges accompanying its economic growth. Not until the mid-1970s, when rapid industrial development brought about environmental degradation and raised citizens' environmental concerns, did environmental law appear in Taiwan's legal system. Before the mid-1970s, environmental regulations were only enacted to keep watch over pollution produced by small-scale and family-operated factories. This changed with the enactment of the Water Pollution Control Act (1974) and the Air Pollution Control Act (1975). These regulations, however, did not specify the procedures authorities should take and often were not enforced.

Between 1986 and 1987, the Lukang community initiated a series of mass demonstrations against the construction of a titanium dioxide plant by the DuPont Corporation. Environmental organizations also protested against nuclear reactors planned by state-owned electricity plants. In response, the Taiwanese government passed the Guidelines for Environmental Policy at the Current Stage in October 1987, seeking to balance environmental protection and economic development. The guidelines state that "if there is a severe negative impact on the environment in the course of economic development, priority consideration shall be given to environmental protection" (Arrigo, Lin, and Lin 1996).

Between the late 1980s and early 1990s, existing acts were modernized and amended, and more acts were enacted to mediate specific pollution. Major environmental regulations included the Solid Waste Act, Water Pollution Act, Air Pollution Act, Soil and Groundwater Remediation Act, Recycling Law, Public Nuisance Dispute Resolution Act, Environmental Impact Assessment Act, and Toxic Substances Act. This sudden proliferation of environmental laws, however, did not come with effective enforcement. Formed in 1987, the Taiwan Environmental Protection Administration (TEPA) is responsible for drafting and enforcing environmental laws. TEPA, however, is not a cabinet-level government unit, a fact that impedes its capacity to implement integrated environmental policies.

In addition to laws for pollution control, laws for conservation have also been gradually enacted. The Wildlife Conservation Act, which has been administered by the Council of Agriculture, was promulgated in 1989 and amended in 1994 to protect endangered species. In response to increasing concerns over the impact of climate change, in June 2009 the Legislative Yuan passed the Renewable Energy Act, aimed at advancing the development of renewable energy. It also amended the Energy Management Act to regulate energy consumption.

In 2002, environmental law attained a higher, constitution-like status by the enactment of the Basic Environmental Act. This act incorporates the concepts of "environment first" and sustainable development. It clearly

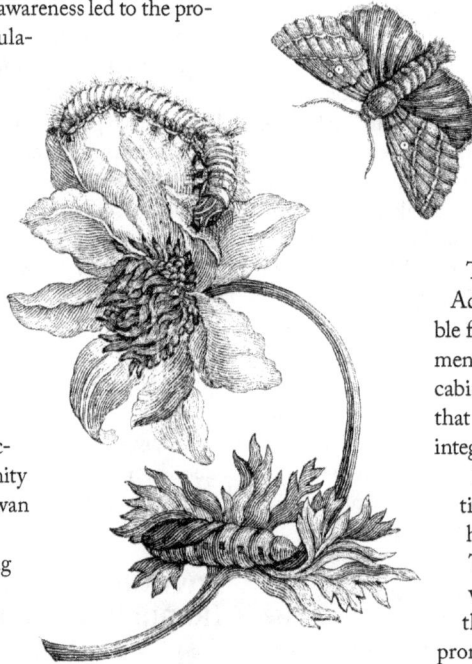

states that "in the event that economic, technological or social development has a seriously negative impact on the environment or there is concern of endangering the environment, the protection of the environment shall prevail." It adopted concepts such as civil participation, collecting fees from beneficiaries or users, setting appropriate lawyer fees paid by the defendant agency, and returning detection and appraisal fees and other litigation costs to plaintiffs. In May 2010, the Environmental Education Act was passed, making Taiwan one of few countries that legally require public officials and students to complete environmental education courses each year.

Taiwanese lawyers played a significant role in amending national environmental laws and ameliorating an unjust political regime through litigation strategies. They have been less influential in international negotiations and regional agreement due to the controversial national status of Taiwan. Following Taiwan's withdrawal from the United Nations in 1971, China attained the UN seat representing the legitimate status of government of China. Since that time, because of China's opposition, Taiwan has been unable to participate in most international negotiations, such as the Kyoto Protocol. The Taiwanese legal profession, therefore, has been excluded from participation in most international negotiations.

One major controversy about environmental law was the lack of transparency and civil participation in the legislative and policy-formation process. Before democratization, civil participation was suppressed by the KMT government. The affected citizens and their opinions were often ignored during law and policy making. Environmental groups had long sought to increase the opportunity to express concerns and participate in decision making. But it was not until the enactment of the Wildlife Conservation Act of 1994 that experts and interest groups, among others, acquired the legal status to participate in policy discussion. In that year, environmental activists also proposed more democratic forms of civil participation during policy debate on the construction of the Fourth Nuclear Power Plant. In 1994 the residents of Yenliao voted to reject the nuclear reactors in a nonlegally binding referendum, with 96.2 percent voting against the construction. The Association for Promotion of a Referendum on the Fourth Nuclear Power Plant also advocated a national referendum on this issue. As a result, in 2000 the plant construction project was temporarily suspended under the Democratic Progressive Party's administration. This suspension, however, was lifted in 2001 due to pressure from the industry and legislature.

Similar concerns about administrative and institutional failure also occurred in the Public Nuisance Disputes Mediation Act and the Environmental Impact Assessment Act (Ho and Su 2008; Jou and Liaw 2006). The Environmental Impact Assessment Act requires authorities to establish a review committee that is composed of not less than two-thirds scholars and experts. Environmentalists and legal experts criticize the EIA process for tending to be symbolic and invalid. The process falls short of ideal in multiple ways: affected local people usually are not informed of the EIA, time pressure and indecisive scientific evidence cast doubt on the assessment, and the opinions of environmental experts and town people usually do not influence development projects. Disputes over the validity of EIA in governmental development projects have frequently occurred. For example, in March 2010 the Supreme Administrative Court upheld a construction project to expand the Central Taiwan Science Park in Taichung County, which had attained initial conditional EIA approval. The court decided that the EIA review procedure was defective in that citizens' right to participation was largely ignored or prevented. TEPA, however, refused to order suspension of the construction or criticize any administrative conduct. This event has increased the tensions between environmental groups and TEPA.

Although many environmental laws are enacted, the government often fails or is reluctant to enforce them, making them simply tokens. Due to development-based policy ideology, the Executive Yuan and Legislative Yuan have been inefficient in deliberating environmental laws. Several environmental bills and regulations are still under discussion and pending in the Legislative Yuan. For example, the Greenhouse Gas Reduction Act submitted in 2006 is still stalled due to debates over its impact on industry.

Under development ideology, the government and industry favored voluntary reduction rather than regulatory measures in the three National Energy Conferences held in 1998, 2005, and 2009. Controversy continues over whether to adopt a carbon-trading system in the Greenhouse Gas Reduction Act. Environmental organizations; legal experts considered the mechanism ineffective and proposed to create carbon taxes instead. To mitigate and adapt to the impacts of climate change, legislation put into effect by the Greenhouse Gas Reduction Act and relevant regulations are crucial in providing the legal basis for developing and implementing the necessary national measures.

Environmental Law in China

Since the beginning of the economic reform in the late 1970s, China has witnessed a stunning economic boom with an aggregate GDP growth rate of 10 percent per year. Three decades later, China had grown into the second-largest economy in the world. This economic miracle, however, was not cost free. Severe environmental deterioration emerged and persisted. China's high-speed economic development strategy relied heavily on intensive labor and exploited natural resources. Within these thirty years, China became one of the biggest pollution producers and one of the worst-polluted countries in the world (Vermeer 1998).

The deteriorating environment increasingly threatened public health, compromised economic growth, triggered social unrest, and even disturbed diplomatic relations. The World Bank (1997) estimated that air pollution–related deaths accounted for 21 percent of China's mortality, and that water and air pollution was costing China 8 percent of its GDP annually in direct damage. In 2003, the Chinese government admitted that the number of environmental disputes had risen 25 percent annually since 1997 and more than 500,000 cases were reported in 2003 (Yang 2005). The impacts of China's environmental degradation have spread well beyond its borders and become increasingly menacing to its neighbors. Infamous examples include acid rain caused by sulfur dioxide from China that hit South Korea and Japan in the late 1990s and sandstorms that hit South Korea and Japan in the early 2000s.

China launched its first piece of environmental legislation in the 1970s. The 1978 amendment to the Chinese Constitution proclaimed "the state protects environment and natural resources. It prevents and controls pollution and other public hazards." This amendment was more the result of diplomatic efforts than environmental concerns, however. During and after China's return to the United Nations in the early 1970s, China attempted to enhance its diplomatic presence and influence through intensive involvement in the international environmental regime. Since 1972, China has actively participated in international environmental talks and ratified forty-two international environmental treaties, covering issues such as biodiversity, hazardous waste, nuclear pollution, fishery resources, ozone layer, and climate change. Environmental diplomacy indeed improved China's diplomatic position, but when combined with the growing pressure from environmental problems, it also changed the Chinese leadership's attitude toward environmental welfare and boosted domestic legislation on environmental protection (Economy 2005).

A 1982 amendment to the Chinese Constitution further clarified that the state must protect and improve the environment of its people and its ecosystem. China had already introduced its first Environmental Protection Law (for trial implementation) in 1979, amending and improving it in 1989. In the 1980s, China enacted the Marine Environment Protection Law (1982), Law on Water and Soil Conservation (1982), Law on Prevention and Control of Water Pollution (1984), Forestry Law (1984), Grassland Law (1985), Law on Mineral Resources (1986), and Law on the Protection of Wildlife (1989). In the 1990s, China enacted the Law on Prevention and Control of Environmental Pollution by Solid Waste (1996) and the Law on Prevention and Control of Pollution from Environmental Noise (1997). In the 2000s, China enacted the Law on Prevention and Control of Atmospheric Pollution (2000), Law on Desert Prevention and Transformation (2002), Law on Environmental Impact Assessments (2003), Law on Promotion Cleaner Production (2003), Law on Prevention and Control of Radioactive Pollution (2003), Renewable Energy Law (2006), Law on Energy Conservation (2008), and Law on Promoting Circulation Economy (2009). Since the 1970s, China has promulgated or revised nineteen environment-related laws, more than sixty regulations, and more than one thousand industry standards.

Besides the environmental legal framework, China also built an administrative apparatus to enforce environmental protection. The National Environmental Protection Agency (NEPA) was established in 1988 under the Ministry of Urban and Rural Construction and Environmental Protection. Ten years later, NEPA was upgraded to State Environmental Protection Administration (SEPA) and achieved independent status within the State Council. SEPA was finally upgraded to a full ministry in 2004, indicating the increasing seriousness of the central government's effort to address environmental problems. After three decades of promulgating law, building organization, and making policy, China has created one of the most comprehensive environmental protection legal frameworks in the developing world (World Bank 2001).

Although China has successfully built an impressive legal framework on environmental protection, the framework itself has not always produced desired results (Jahiel 1998). Main factors undermining the effectiveness of Chinese environmental legislation include the legislative principle of "preferring vague over precise," the domination of administrative branches in legislative negotiation, the insufficient authority of environmental enforcement, and the lack of abiding by the laws (Shu 2009). China still has a long way to go before its environmental legal framework and administrative apparatus can really work in protecting its environment from further deterioration (Shu 2009).

Assessment

Japan, South Korea, Taiwan, and China each produced a body of environmental law that addressed the problems of industrial pollution and other forms of environmental protection with varying degrees of effectiveness. The greatest study has been directed to Japan, and shows that the laws effectively reduced severe air and water pollution that was the source of human illness. The other three governments passed a host of laws as well, but further evaluation is needed to determine their effectiveness. In all cases, social tensions induced by local industrial pollution became an important spur to the reduction of such pollution. These tensions became very public, creating pressure for the governments to enact laws that addressed the problems. In China, the political system muted the public expression of these tensions, but the government passed a series of environmental laws nonetheless. China, however, is still in the midst of a rapid growth stage, the like of which created such intense pollution in the other three societies. It is difficult to gauge the effectiveness of China's environmental laws, but many accounts attest to the continuation of severe problems.

Comparison between these four countries shows that, while the growth/environment dilemma arises from identical causes (i.e., the rapid growth of a manufacturing industry unrestrained and eager to dispose of its wastes in the cheapest way possible), it causes different results within each domestic political system. The tensions between victims, polluters, and government proceed through different political processes, producing different legal or regulatory vehicles and degrees of improvement. For example, in Japan, the environmental movements emerged twenty years after the new democratic Constitution of 1945 and could use many avenues to pressure the government. In Taiwan and Korea, the environmental movements emerged during authoritarian regimes and had to proceed cautiously until those regimes ended. Currently in China, the weakness of local citizen "watchdog" groups may help account

for the continuing severity of industrial pollution, despite the presence of formal law.

Jeffrey BROADBENT
University of Minnesota

Koichi HASEGAWA
University of Tohoku, Japan

Dowan KU
Environment and Society Research Institute, South Korea

Taehyun PARK
Kangwon University, South Korea

Yu-Ju CHIEN
University of Minnesota

Jun JIN
Tsinghua University, China

See also in the *Berkshire Encyclopedia of Sustainability* Development, Sustainable—Overview of Laws and Commissions; Environmental Law (several articles: China; India and Pakistan; Pacific Island Region; Southeast Asia); Kyoto Protocol

FURTHER READINGS

Arrigo, Linda Gail; Lin, Tze-Luen; & Lin, Yvonne. (1996). Environmental conditions and environmental law in Taiwan. In Antonella Capria et al. (Eds.), *A world survey of environmental law* (pp. 765–777). Milano, Italy: Giuffre Editore.

Broadbent, Jeffrey. (1998). *Environmental politics in Japan: Networks of power and protest.* Cambridge, UK: Cambridge University Press.

Broadbent, Jeffrey. (2002). Japan's environmental regime: The political dynamics of change. In Uday Desai (Ed.), *Environmental politics and policies in the industrialized countries* (pp. 295–355). Cambridge, MA: Massachusetts Institute of Technology Press.

Cho, Hong Sik, & World Jurist Association. (1999). The development of Korean environmental law: A lesson for developing countries. Work paper; 19th Biennial Conference on the law of the world, Budapest, Hungary, and Vienna, Austria.

Economy, Elizabeth C. (2005). *The river runs black: The environmental challenge to China's future.* Ithaca, NY: Cornell University Press.

Gresser, Julian; Fujikura, Koichiro; & Morishima, Akio. (1981). *Environmental law in Japan.* Cambridge, MA: Massachusetts Institute of Technology Press.

Government of Japan, Ministry of Environment. (2010). Laws. Retrieved December 2, 2010, from http://www.env.go.jp/en/laws/

Hasegawa, Koichi. (2004). *Constructing civil society in Japan: Voices of environmental movements.* Melbourne, Australia: Trans Pacific Press.

Hasegawa, Koichi. (2010). Collaborative environmentalism in Japan. In Henk Vinken et al. (Eds.), *Civic engagement in contemporary Japan: Established and emerging repertoires* (pp. 85–100). New York: Springer.

Hasegawa, Koichi; Shinohara, Chika; & Broadbent, Jeffrey. (2007). The effects of "social expectation" on the development of civil society in Japan. *Journal of Civil Society, 3*(2), 179–203.

Ho, Ming-Sho. (2010). Environmental movement in democratizing Taiwan (1980–2004): A political opportunity structure perspective. New York: Springer.

Ho, Ming-Sho, & Su, Feng-San. (2008). Control by containment: The politics of institutionalizing pollution disputes in Taiwan. *Environment & Planning, 40,* 2402–2418.

Imura, Hidefumi, & Schreurs, Miranda A. (Eds.). (2005). *Environmental policy in Japan.* Northampton, MA: Edward Elgar.

Jahiel, Abigail. (1998). The organization of environmental protection in China. *The China Quarterly, 156,* 757–787.

Jin, Jun. (2010). Institutionalized official hostility and protest leader logic: A case study of a long-term Chinese peasants' collective protest at Dahe Dam. In J. B. Broadbent and Vicky Brockman (Eds.), *East Asian Social Movements: Power, Protest and Change in a Dynamic Region.* New York: Springer.

Jou, Jin-Juh, & Liaw, Shu-Liang. (2006). A study on establishment of EIA system in the Taiwan region. *Journal of Environmental Assessment Policy & Management, 8,* 479–494.

Kim, Hong Kyun. (2010). *Environmental law.* Seoul, South Korea: Hongmoonsa.

Koh, Moon-Hyun. (2008). Development of Korean environmental law and its desirable amendment direction. *Journal of Korean Comparative Public Law Association, 9*(3).

Ku, Do-Wan. (2010). The Korean environmental movement: Green politics through social movement. In J. B. Broadbent and Vicky Brockman (Eds.), *East Asian Social Movements: Power, Protest and Change in a Dynamic Region.* New York: Springer.

Lee, Wong-Yung, & Park, Tae-Hyun. (2009). The problems of the 4-rivers renewal project in light of the principle of representative democracy. *Journal of the Korea Planners Association, 44*(7).

People's Republic of China, Ministry of Environmental Protection. (2010). Laws. Retrieved December 2, 2010, from http://english.mep.gov.cn/Policies_Regulations/laws/

Republic of China (Taiwan), Environmental Protection Administration. (2010). Environmental law library. Retrieved December 2, 2010, from http://law.epa.gov.tw/en/

Republic of Korea, Ministry of Environment. (2010). Environmental laws. Retrieved December 2, 2010, from http://eng.me.go.kr/content.do?method=moveContent&menuCode=law_law

Schreurs, Miranda A. (2002). *Environmental politics in Japan, Germany, and the United States.* Cambridge, UK: Cambridge University Press.

Shu, Min. (2009). Zhongguo Huanjing Lifa de Shenshi Yu Jiantao [A review of the quality of China's environmental legislation]. *Zhongguo Dizhi Daxue Xuebao(Shehui Kexue Ban)* [*Journal of China University of Geosciences (Social Sciences Edition)*], *9*(5), 10–15.

Tang, Ching-Ping, & Tang, Shui-Yan. (2000). Democratizing bureaucracy: The political economy of environmental impact assessment and air pollution prevention fees in Taiwan. *Comparative Politics, 33,* 81–99.

Ui, Jun (Ed.). (1992). *Industrial pollution in Japan.* Tokyo: United Nations University Press.

Vermeer, Eduard B. (1998). Industrial pollution in China and remedial policies. *The China Quarterly, 156,* 952–985.

The World Bank. (2001). China: Air, land, and water—Environmental priorities for a new millennium. Washington, D.C.: Author.

Yang, Guobin. (2005). Environmental NGOs and institutional dynamics in China. *The China Quarterly, 181,* 46–66.

Environmental Law—Europe

Roughly 60 percent of Europe's population of over 800 million is governed by the European Union (EU). The EU's dual legal treaties address sustainable development and environmental protection. The EU can establish binding regulations for all member states without ratification by their individual governments, but most EU environmental law takes the form of a directive, where there is room for maneuvering and for the application of different regulatory traditions of members.

Nearly 500 million of Europe's total population of over 800 million people live in the European Union (EU), an organization of twenty-seven European states, making it the world's third-largest population after China and India. The EU is not only a regional but also a so-called supranational organization. This means that the EU can adopt legislation that is binding and directly applicable to all individuals and entities within its member states without ratification or any other type of approval by national parliaments or governments. The EU is not a state, however. It does not have a general competence in all matters related to the life of its citizens, but it "shall act only within the limits of the competences conferred upon it by the Member States in the Treaties to attain the objectives set out therein. Competences not conferred upon the Union in the Treaties remain with the Member States" (TEU 1992, Article 5, para. 2).

Today the EU has a dual legal basis: the Treaty on European Union (TEU) and the Treaty on the Functioning of the European Union (TFEU), which have emerged from earlier treaties as modified by the so-called Lisbon Treaty, signed on 13 December 2007 and entered into force in on 1 December 2009. Historically, the EU goes back to the establishment of the European Coal and Steel Community (established in 1951), the European Economic Community (EEC), and the European Atomic Energy Community (both established in 1957). From 1967 onward, they were referred to as the European Communities (on the basis of the Merger Treaty, signed in 1965). With the Maastricht Treaty (signed in 1992, entered into force in 1993), the European Economic Community was renamed the European Community. Initially the EU was established formally without a separate legal personality. Only after a series of treaty amendments came into effect (Amsterdam Treaty signed in 1997, entered into force 1999; Nice Treaty signed in 2001, entered into force 2003; and Lisbon Treaty) has the EU itself, as successor of the European Communities, been equipped with a legal personality (TEU 1992, Article 47): "The Union shall replace and succeed the European Community" (Article 1, para. 3).

First established by six member states (Belgium, France, Italy, Luxembourg, the Netherlands, and West Germany), the EU has been enlarged several times: Denmark, Ireland, and the United Kingdom joined in 1973; Greece joined in 1981, followed by Spain and Portugal in 1986; in 1995, Austria, Sweden, and Finland became member states. Ten member states—Cyprus, the Czech Republic, Estonia, Hungary, Latvia, Lithuania, Malta, Poland, Slovenia, and Slovakia—followed in 2004; and Romania and Bulgaria became member states in 2007.

EU Law and National Environmental Law

As has been pointed out in the TEU, the EU shall act only within the limits of the competences conferred upon it by the member states. The TFEU distinguishes between exclusive, shared, and supporting competences of the EU. In the field of environmental law, the EU enjoys shared competences, in particular on the basis of TFEU Articles 191–193. The EU may exercise these competences subject to the principles of subsidiarity (TEU 1992, Article 5, para. 3) and proportionality (Article 5, para. 4).

Two levels of EU law have to be distinguished. First, the treaties can be labeled as primary legislation in that they can be characterized as the constitutional law of the European Union. Second, legislation and other legal acts adopted on the basis of these treaties are labeled secondary legislation; most important are regulations and directives. According to TFEU Article 288, a regulation "shall have general application. It shall be binding in its entirety and directly applicable in all Member States" (para. 2). In contrast, a directive "shall be binding, as to the result to be achieved, upon each Member State to which it is addressed, but shall leave to the national authorities the choice of form and methods" (para. 3). In addition, there are decisions that are binding upon those to whom they are addressed (para. 4) as well as nonbinding recommendations and opinions (para. 5).

Both primary and secondary EU legislation enjoy supremacy over national law. It has been confirmed many times by the Court of Justice of the European Union, which ensures that the law is observed in the application of the treaties (TEU 1992, Article 19). In the case of a conflict between EU law and the law of a member state, EU enjoys precedence, so that the law of a member state may not be applied.

History of EU Environmental Law

In the early years of European integration (1958–1972), the European Economic Community (EEC) Treaty did not include any specific reference to environmental protection. Environment-related directives were not adopted in pursuit of a European environmental policy but rather to facilitate the establishment of the common market envisaged by the founding treaties. It was not until 1972 that the EU Paris Summit emphasized the importance of a Community environmental policy and called upon Community institutions to establish a program of action to this end. In the following years, the Community made use of its competences in the field of approximation and harmonization of laws as well as the so-called flexibility clause, permitting Community action in areas not expressly covered by the (then) EEC Treaty.

A much broader Community environmental policy was developed on the basis of the first major amendment to the EEC Treaty, the Single European Act, which was signed in 1986 and entered into force in 1987. The inclusion of Articles 130(r) to 130(t) into the EEC Treaty allowed the Community to adopt measures "to preserve, protect and improve the quality of the environment, to contribute toward protecting human health, and to ensure a prudent and rational utilization of natural resources." Since the Single European Act limited Community competence in

this field by establishing the principle of subsidiarity, the Community could only intervene in environmental matters when measures adopted could be better attained at the Community level than at the level of the individual member states. This limitation notwithstanding, the Single European Act marked the development of a stronger role for environmental protection at the European level.

The Treaty of Maastricht (1992/1993) marks the consolidation of the treaty basis of European environmental law. For the first time, the protection of the environment was included among the objectives of the (then) EC Treaty. According to EC Treaty Article 2, the Community shall have as its task, "to promote throughout the Community a harmonious and balanced development of economic activities, sustainable and non-inflationary growth respecting the environment." As stipulated in EC Treaty Article 3, the policies of the Community shall include "a policy in the sphere of the environment."

Further progress was made with the Treaty of Amsterdam (1997/1999) strengthening the environmental policy objective toward a "high level of protection and improvement of the quality of the environment" (EC Treaty Article 2). In addition, the provisions on the approximation of laws were optimized toward better protection of the environment, allowing for stricter national provisions subject to certain (procedural) conditions.

The Treaty of Nice and the Treaty of Lisbon largely reaffirmed these developments. Environmental protection and sustainable development continue to occupy a prominent place in the objectives of the European Union. Also, the integration principle continues to apply, and TFEU Article 194, paragraph 2, envisages another specialized environmental integration principle for the EU's energy policy. The inclusion of climate change is a modification that serves as an example of a regional or worldwide environmental problem that falls within the scope of EU environmental policy (TFEU Article 191, para. 1).

Objectives and Principles of EU Environmental Law

The preamble of the Treaty on European Union not only refers to sustainable development but also to environmental protection. TEU Article 3, paragraph 3, reiterates the EU's commitment to sustainable development and a high level of protection and improvement of the quality of the environment. This applies to both economic and technological development. It is noteworthy that TEU Article 3, paragraph 5, encourages the EU, "in its relations with the wider world" to contribute to "the sustainable development of the Earth." This external dimension is further specified by TEU Article 21. According to this article, the EU defines and pursues common policies and actions to "foster the sustainable economic, social and environmental development of developing countries" (TEU Article 21(2)(d)) and to "help develop international measures to preserve and improve the quality of the environment and the sustainable management of global natural resources, in order to ensure sustainable development" (TEU Article 21(2)(f)). While environmental protection and sustainable development thus play a prominent role, the question remains how these objectives can be weighed and balanced in case of conflicts.

TFEU Article 11, which ensures that environmental protection requirements are taken into account when defining and implementing EU policies, shows a strong movement toward the integration of environmental objectives into other policy sectors and thus a strong indication for a prioritized treatment of the environment aiming at sustainable development. The environmental protection requirements include all the policy objectives referred to in TFEU Article 191(1) as well as the principles mentioned in TFEU Article 191(2).

The integration principle can be read as only ensuring that environmental protection is at least taken into consideration if other policy areas are concerned even though it does not enjoy priority. One possible approach to resolving potential conflicts between objectives such as the internal market on the one hand and environmental protection on the other hand is to apply the principle of proportionality in the process of integrating environmental concerns. An argument against prioritized environmental protection is that there are also other policy objectives that seem to enjoy a similar degree of attention. Reference may be made here to TFEU Article 13, which states: "In formulating and implementing the Union's agriculture, fisheries, transport, internal market, research and technological development, and space policies, the Union and the Member States shall . . . pay full regard to the welfare requirements of animals." Articles 11 and 13 nevertheless assume an anthropocentric approach to environmental protection due to the prominent role of the principle of sustainable development in Article 11.

TFEU Article 191(1) lists four policy objectives applicable to EU policy on the environment: protection of the environment, protection of human health, prudent utilization of natural resources, and international cooperation for environmental protection. While these policy objectives largely seem to be self-explanatory, a few comments may be made. The first concerns the question of whether or not reference to the environment includes a territorial limitation to the geographical scope of the EU. In the pre-Maastricht period, this argument was often presented to limit the competence of the Community in the field of environmental policy. Since Maastricht, due to the reference to international cooperation, it can easily be argued that the EU is competent to address environmental problems of a regional or global scope. It is noteworthy that

the Lisbon Treaty explicitly asks for "combating climate change" among the objectives of international cooperation. This is a confirmation of the EU's well-developed climate change policy and sends a political signal to both member states and partners of the EU.

As far as natural resources are concerned, this can be read as a reference to Principle 2 of the Declaration of the United Nations Conference on the Human Environment of 1972, the so-called Stockholm Declaration, which includes in the natural resources of the Earth such things as air, water, land, flora, fauna, and rare ecosystems, thus supporting a broad interpretation of the notion of natural resources.

Article 191(2) TFEU explicitly states five principles upon which EU environmental policy shall be based: high level of protection principle, precautionary principle, prevention principle, source principle, and polluter pays principle.

The high level of protection principle simply underlines that within the EU's process of law making, it is not possible to simply adopt the lowest common denominator. Even though it is not necessary to attain the highest level of protection of the environment, there must be a tendency to a high level of protection that is recognizable either in the preamble of a legislative act or otherwise in the operative part of such an act.

The precautionary principle was first introduced into EU law by the Maastricht Treaty in 1992. Its origins can be traced back to national legislation in a number of European states, some of which weren't members of the European Community at that time, including Sweden, Switzerland, and the Federal Republic of Germany. Precautionary action has generally been recognized as a core principle in EU law. In its "Communication on the Precautionary Principle," issued in February 2000, the European Commission stated: "Recourse to the precautionary principle presupposes that potentially dangerous effects deriving from a phenomenon, product or process have been identified, and that scientific evaluation does not allow the risk to be determined with sufficient certainty. . . . Decision-makers need to be aware of the degree of uncertainty. . . . Decision-makers faced with an unacceptable risk, scientific uncertainty and public concerns have a duty to find answers" (Europa 2005). The most basic understanding of the precautionary principle is that the legislator cannot refer to scientific uncertainty as an excuse for inaction. While this seems to be the common opinion of most international agreements that take up the precautionary principle, EU law has gone beyond this basic viewpoint. It operates as a license to take action, without indicating at which level such action should be taken and what kind of action should be taken; it provides guidance in case of serious or irreversible environmental risk. It is doubtful whether the principle can even be read as a duty imposed upon the EU to take action for responding to a given environmental risk in light of possibly conflicting with other principles of EU law, such as the already mentioned principles of subsidiarity and proportionality. In the EU context the precautionary principle can be read as *in dubio pro natura* (when in doubt, favor life).

The third principle included in TFEU Article 191(2) is the prevention principle, which basically means that the EU has to take preventive action if necessary. It allows action to be taken in favor of the environment at an early stage and calls for measures to prevent damage from occurring at all. A good example is the directive on packaging and packaging waste (Directive 94/62 [OJ 1994 L 365/10]) that states that the best means of preventing the creation of packaging waste is to reduce the volume of packaging.

The source principle requires the EU to take action at the source of environmental damage or pollution. Damage should not be prevented by using end-of-pipe technologies (which remove already formed contaminants from air, water, etc.), but environmental damage should be rectified at its source. By way of example reference may be made to the Water Directive (Directive 76/464 [OJ 1976 L 129/23), which does not focus on cleaning up polluted water but sets emissions standards for blacklisted substances.

The polluter pays principle was already implemented by the European Community before it was incorporated into the TFEU. The principle requires the EU to internalize environmental costs and to use economic instruments that guarantee the polluter bares the cost of pollution. Early examples are the EC Council Recommendation 75/436/EURATOM, ECSC, EEC of 3 March 1975 regarding Cost Allocation and Action by Public Authorities on Environmental Matters, and a number of EC Environment Action Programmes. In essence the EU can ensure the polluter pays principle by laying down specific standards or by creating a system of environmental liability. This should confirm that persons who are responsible for pollution in fact pay the costs thereof.

The Making of EU Environmental Law

In EU environmental law, the general law makes procedures of the TFEU apply in principle. The procedures for law making are laid down in TFEU Articles 289 and 294. This first requires an initiative by the European Commission, which submits its proposal to the European Parliament and the Council. The European Parliament then adopts its position at first reading and communicates it to the Council. If the Council approves the Parliament's position, the act shall be adopted in the words corresponding to the Parliament's position. Should the Council not approve the European Parliament's position, it adopts its own position at the first reading and communicates it to the Parliament who can then approve the Council's position, reject the Council's position (nonadoption of the proposed act), or propose amendments to the Council's position by a majority of its component members. The Council, in response, can either adopt these amendments by a qualified majority or refer the matter to the so-called Conciliation Committee. If a compromise is reached here, the act is adopted; if not, the act is assumed to be dead. In principle, according to TFEU Article 192, this procedure applies to all environmental law making in the European Union with the exception of matters listed in TFEU Article 192(2). In these cases, the Council must act unanimously after consulting the European Parliament, the Economic and Social Committee, and the Committee of the Regions. Among others, this affects provisions primarily of a physical nature, matters related to town and country planning, quantitative water management and land use, and measures significantly affecting the choice between different energy sources and the general structure of a member state's energy supply. It is noteworthy that eco-taxation is obviously covered by this provision and thus subject to the special decision-making procedure.

To mention fishery policy, which is an exclusive competence of the EU, the most important measures taken by the EU relate to the setting of fishing quotas. Apart from TFEU Article 43, which foresees a particular power for the Council in this field, TFEU Article 218, which deals with agreements between the EU and third countries or international organizations, has to be taken into account.

Reference should also be made to the Energy Title (Title XXI), newly introduced by the Treaty of Lisbon. The new TFEU Article 194, among others, includes as a policy objective that the EU "promote energy efficiency and energy saving and the development of new and renewable forms of energy." Legal basis for pertinent action is provided by Article 194(2). While the scope of the Energy Title is limited by reference to the internal market and undistorted conditions of competition, it is a meaningful complement to the general environmental powers of the EU. External energy environment policy remains within the ambit of TFEU Article 192.

The EU has adopted several different legislative acts in the field of environmental protection. The following incomplete list may simply serve as a sample:

- Directive 2008/98/EC of the European Parliament and of the Council on Waste and Repealing Certain Directives (OJ 2008 L 312/3)
- Directive 2000/60/EC of the European Parliament and of the Council Establishing a Framework for Community Action in the Field of Water Policy (OJ 2000 L 327/1)
- Directive 98/83 EC on the Quality of Water Intended for Human Consumption (OJ 1998 L 330/32)
- Directive 2006/113/EC of the European Parliament and of the Council on the Quality Required of Shellfish Waters (OJ 2006 L 376/14)
- Directive 2006/44/EC of the European Parliament and of the Council on the Quality of Fresh Waters Needing Protection or Improvement in order to Support Fish Life (OJ 2006 L 264/20)

- Directive 2008/1/EC of the European Parliament and of the Council Concerning Integrated Pollution Prevention and Control (OJ 2008 L 24/8)
- Directive 2005/35/EC of the European Parliament and of the Council on Ship-Source Pollution and on the Introduction of Penalties for Infringements (OJ 2005 L 255/11)
- Directive 92/43/EEC on the Conservation of Natural Habitats and of Wild Fauna and Flora (OJ 1992 L 206/7)
- Directive 2009/147/EC of the European Parliament and of the Council on the Conservation of Wild Birds (OJ 2010 L 20/7)
- Directive 2003/87/EC of the European Parliament and of the Council Establishing a Scheme for Greenhouse Gas Emission Allowance Trading within the Community and Amending Council Directive 96/61/EC (OJ 2003 L 275/32)

Implementation and Enforcement

Generally speaking, EU law is implemented by member states. Apart from competition policy, the EU has very limited administrative powers. Even in the case of generally and directly applicable regulation, the implementation of an act remains in the hands of member states. They are responsible for the implementation of environmental impact assessments, for licensing procedures, and other types of administrative acts to be taken.

In the case of directives, which are binding upon member states but leave the choice of form and matters to the national authorities, the national legislator must first adopt implementing legislation and then take administrative action. Since most of EU environmental law takes the form of a directive, there is room for maneuvering and for the application of different regulatory traditions of member states. Thus, civil law countries are in a position to apply traditional licensing systems, whereas common law countries can continue to favor incentive-based regulation. This notwithstanding, there have been complaints that the EU has not always respected these different regulatory traditions, particularly in the field of water law. While it is difficult to access the validity of such criticism in the overall context of EU environmental law, it is true that the regulatory traditions of member states cannot be fully respected in all cases if the objectives of the Treaty are to be met; examples include EU measures adopted in the field of environmental impact assessment, environmental information, and participation of citizens in environmental decision making.

The Court of Justice of the European Union has contributed actively not only to European integration as a whole but also to the implementation of European environmental law. Member states have not always liked these decisions,

in particular the doctrine of direct effect. Under certain circumstances, this doctrine can be implemented directly in member states even if the time limit for a decision's implementation has expired, its content is clear and unambiguous, and it does not disadvantage individual citizens. Further work on both the implementation and integration of environmental law remains a challenge for the twenty-seven member states of the EU, whose future depends, as does the world's, on finding sustainable solutions to economic growth, technology development, and resource management.

Thilo MARAUHN and Ayse Martina BOEHRINGER
University of Giessen

See also in the *Berkshire Encyclopedia of Sustainability* Development, Sustainable—Overview of Laws and Commissions; Enforcement; European Union Greenhouse Gas Emission Trading Scheme; Polluter Pays Principle; Precautionary Principle; Registration, Evaluation, Authorisation, and Restriction of Chemicals; Restriction of Hazardous Substances Directive; United Nations—Overview of Conventions and Agreements

FURTHER READINGS

Backes, Chris W., & Vershuren, Jonathan M. (1998). The precautionary principle in international, European, and Dutch wildlife law. *Colorado Journal of International Environmental Law and Policy, 9*(1), 43–70.

Burns, William C., & Mosedale, C. Thomas D. (1997). European implementation of CITES and the proposal for a council regulation (EC) on the protection of species of wild fauna and flora. *The Georgetown International Environmental Law Review, 9*, 389–433.

Dross, Miriam, & Bloch, Felix. (2004). The reform of the EU Common Fisheries Policy—A step towards greater precaution in the conservation of fishery resources. *Environmental Law Network International Review, 1/2004*, 17–25.

Europa. (2005). The precautionary principle. Retrieved December 7, 2010, from http://europa.eu/legislation_summaries/consumers/consumer_safety/l32042_en.htm

Gunst, Andreas. (2005). Impact of European law on the validity and tenure of national support schemes for power generation from renewable energy sources. *Journal of Energy and Natural Resources Law, 23*, 95–119.

Jans, Jan H., & Vedder, Hans. H. (2008). *European environmental law* (3rd ed.). Groningen, The Netherlands: Europa Law.

Kallis, Giorgos, & Butler, David. (2001). The EU Water Framework Directive: Measures and implications. *Water Policy, 3*(2), 125–142.

Lanham, Heather A. (2005). The effect of EU enlargement on the environment: A look at Malta. *Colorado Journal of International Environmental Law and Policy, 16*, 467–494.

Markus, Till. (2010). Making environmental principles work under the common fisheries policy. *European Energy and Environmental Law Review, 19*(2), 132–144.

Treaty on European Union (TEU). (1992). Retrieved December 1, 2010, from http://eur-lex.europa.eu/en/treaties/dat/11992M/htm/11992M.html#0000000001

Treaty on the Functioning of the European Union (TFEU). (2008). Retrieved December 1, 2010, from http://eur-lex.europa.eu/LexUriServ/LexUriServ.do?uri=OJ:C:2008:115:0047:0199:EN:PDF

Vedder, Hans. (2010). The Treaty of Lisbon and European law and policy. *Journal of Environmental Law, 22*, 285–299.

Environmental Law—India and Pakistan

India and Pakistan have a long and complicated history—one often punctuated by conflict. There are, however, some commonalities between the nations in environmental law: a British common law heritage, strong judiciaries, weak executive enforcement, and public interest litigation. While India's more activist courts have issued several extensive decisions in favor of environmental protection, the Pakistani courts' pro-environment views have yet to be institutionalized.

India and Pakistan are the second and sixth most populous nations in the world, respectively. India alone has 1.15 billion people. The two were ruled jointly under the British before the Partition of 1947 divided them into India and East and West Pakistan; East Pakistan split off in 1971 to become Bangladesh. India and Pakistan have fought several wars, particularly over the borders of Kashmir. Both now possess nuclear weapons. Seasonal monsoons and large rivers flowing out of the Himalayas dominate the environmental geography of both nations.

India

India is a common law country. British and American precedents are widely cited, and English is the language of the bar and bench. Its three main environmental laws are the Water Act of 1974, the Air Act of 1981, and the Environmental Protection Act of 1986.

Agencies and Legislation

India's environmental laws are administered jointly by a weak and understaffed Central Pollution Control Board; State Pollution Control Boards (SPCBs) of varying strengths, capacities, and effectiveness; and the central government's Ministry of Environment (MOE). The MOE has the power to issue environmental clearances—allowing a development project to go forward, for example, despite its noncompliance with environmental laws or regulations.

Article 21 of the Indian Constitution guarantees the right to life, which the courts have interpreted as including the right to a healthy environment. The constitution also enables any citizen or group to bring an interlocutory appeal directly to the High Court of each state or to the Supreme Court if a constitutional question is raised.

Most environmental cases, especially between 1980 and 2000, have been brought by a small band of public interest litigators led by Supreme Court advocate M. C. Mehta. Since 2000, however, the courts have become markedly less hospitable to public interest litigation (PIL). In several recent cases, judges have dismissed PIL petitions as frivolous or motivated by personal gain.

2010 Overhaul of Environmental Institutions

In 2010, India's central government launched the first major overhaul of environmental governance and management since 1986. It proposed, and Parliament enacted, the National Green Tribunal Bill, creating a kind of "supreme court" of environmental law. Also in 2010, the MOE proposed a new institution for environmental management, compliance, and enforcement, to be called the National Environment Protection Authority (NEPA). Among other innovations, NEPA will institute a civil administrative process to impose sanctions on polluters. This would be housed within the new NEPA and, ideally, staffed with a cadre of young, trained professionals, including lawyers. The courts have been too reluctant to punish polluters and have even denied SPCBs the power to impose penalties by finding ambiguities in the Environmental Protection Act. The draft NEPA bill, however, still fails to address the SPCBs' lack of power to punish polluters.

The Supreme Court's Activist Role

The Supreme Court of India is undoubtedly the most activist court in the world, which has led it to issue sweeping decisions in favor of environmental protection. In the Ganges water pollution case, a bench of the Supreme Court, while directing that several tanneries be closed down for discharging untreated effluents into the Ganges river, held that "we are conscious that closure of tanneries may bring unemployment (and) loss of revenue, but life, health and ecology have greater importance to the people" (*M. C. Mehta v. Union of India*, 1988).

The justices appear to have exceeded their constitutional boundaries (and customary separation of powers) in at least two areas, however. In the so-called Delhi Pollution case (*M. C. Mehta v. Union of India*, 2002), the Court preempted executive authority over air pollution and ordered all bus companies in the capital city of Delhi to power their buses with compressed natural gas (CNG) rather than petroleum or diesel fuel. In *T. N. Godavarman Thirumulkpad v. Union of India*, instituted in 1995, the Supreme Court took on the subject of forest cover and found itself issuing orders dealing with the rights of forest dwellers, employment in the wood products and timber industries, and the respective powers of federal and state forestry officials. The case is on a "continuing mandamus," meaning that the case remains open for court orders and actions relating to it; the Court has issued new orders flowing from the case virtually every week since 1995.

Judicial Approval of Development Projects

The Supreme Court's assumption of executive power in these cases contrasts with the judiciary's invariable approval of, or deference to, the executive regarding *all* large infrastructure projects. Notwithstanding the occasional court defense of clean air, water, and forests, and protection of people's access to common or protected spaces, there seems to be an inherent pro-development bias in the High Courts and the Supreme Court.

In the cases of the Tehri (*TBVSS v. Uttar Pradesh*, 1992) and Narmada (*Narmada Bachao Andolan v. Union of India*, 2000) dams and the Dahanu power plant (*Dahanu Taluka Environment Protection Group v. Bombay Suburban Electricity Supply Company, Ltd.*, 1991), the respective judges emphasized that it is not the job of the Court to interfere in these development activities because they raised scientific and technical issues and policy matters, which are best left to the executive agencies. The views expressed by judges in all environmental litigation concerning infrastructure projects have supported the government's assertion that it must carry out its development activities, such as dams and power plants, in the national interest.

In these cases, the judges seem complicit with the executive branch in subordinating environment to development. For example, in the Tehri Dam case, the government's own expert committee had identified several violations of the conditions that the MOE imposed on the project before granting an environmental clearance, but the majority judgment allowed the government to construct the dam anyway. Similarly, in the Dahanu case, the Supreme Court did not follow the MOE's Appraisal Committee report, which declared that Dahanu was unsuitable for the construction of a thermal power plant as it did not meet environmental guidelines. In the Narmada Dam case, the dissent urged that construction of the dam should not be allowed because it violated environmental guidelines, and the government had not provided for rehabilitation and resettlement of the project-affected people. But the majority judgment allowed the construction of the dam and found the government's report on rehabilitation and resettlement measures sufficient.

Reexamination and Retreat

With the Supreme Court finally beginning to wonder whether it has overstepped its constitutional mandate, Indian lawyers and scholars ought to re-examine the most flagrant example of such judicial activism, namely Godavarman, which has affected all forest cover, all forest dwellers, and the timber and wood products industries throughout India for more than fifteen years. While the concern for forest conservation provided the initial justification for judicial intervention, it has led the Supreme Court to effectively take over the day-to-day governance of many aspects of Indian forests, far beyond anything that may be justified constitutionally. The outcomes for the forests have been mixed, and the jurisprudence is of questionable quality, highlighting the dangers of judicial overreach.

Pakistan

Pakistan possesses a legal framework for environmental protection but lacks enforcement capacity. Given this gap, the judiciary has encouraged public interest environmental litigation. Judges have convened commissions to resolve scientific questions and formulate environmental policy, but they lack the capacity to bring about systematic change.

The World Bank estimates that environmental degradation costs 6 percent of Pakistan's gross domestic product (GDP) per year (World Bank 2006, 6). Preserving freshwater resources is the country's most serious challenge. While 90 percent of Pakistanis have access to clean water, only 58 percent utilize improved sanitation facilities. Urban concentrations of particulate matter (PM) are amongst the world's highest and lead to 22,700 premature deaths every year (World Bank 2006, 40). Pakistan gets most of its electricity from natural gas (50 percent) and hydropower (30 percent). It relies heavily on fossil fuels for transportation, although the government promotes compressed natural gas (CNG) as an alternative.

Legal System and History

Since its independence from Great Britain in 1947, Pakistan has alternated between periods of civilian and military rule. The country has four provinces— Punjab, Sindh, Balochistan, and North West Frontier Province—as well as the Federally Administered Tribal Area, all of which possess significant autonomy under the 1973 Constitution.

Pakistan inherited a common law legal system from Britain with a judicial system similar to other Commonwealth nations. The president appoints Supreme Court justices upon consultation with the chief justice. Historically the judiciary has been reluctant to confront political and military elites, but on 3 November 2007, General Parvez Musharraf declared a state of emergency and sacked several justices, including the chief justice, Iftikhar Muhammad Chaudhry. The legal profession rallied around the justices and demanded their reinstatement. Since then, the Court has become aggressively political, even stripping influential politicians of immunity for past crimes.

Environmental Legislation

Many of Pakistan's environmental laws date back to the colonial era and focus on exploiting resources rather than protecting ecosystems. The first general environmental law was the 1983 Environmental Protection Ordinance. In 1997 Parliament passed the Pakistan Environmental Protection Act (PEPA), which requires an environmental impact assessment (EIA) for any project likely to cause an "adverse environmental effect."

The National Environmental Quality Standards (NEQS) sets limits on the emission of smoke, carbon monoxide, noise, and other forms of pollution from motor vehicles. The Pakistan Environmental Protection Agency (EPA) is also in the process of establishing air-, water-, and land-quality standards.

Many natural resource issues fall under the constitutional jurisdiction of provincial legislatures. PEPA does not automatically override other statutes, making it difficult to enforce. Furthermore, there is no legal obligation on federal and provincial governments to coordinate their environmental policies.

Environmental Agencies

The prime minister serves as chairman of the Pakistan Environmental Protection Council (PEPC), along with the federal Minister of Environment, provincial environmental ministers, and various representatives from trade and environmental groups. PEPC supervises enforcement of PEPA and approves comprehensive environmental policies.

The EPA reviews EIAs, prepares NEQS, and establishes protected areas in environmentally sensitive regions, but it lacks the funding and scientific capacity to adequately enforce laws and design standards. In 2005, its federal staff numbered only fifty-two. Each province has its own EPA, although they tend to suffer even greater resource constraints.

PEPA also created "environmental magistrates" to hear minor cases and environmental tribunals with exclusive jurisdiction over serious crimes. Decisions can be appealed to the high courts. While their caseload has risen slowly, the tribunals are actively seeking a larger role in environmental adjudication.

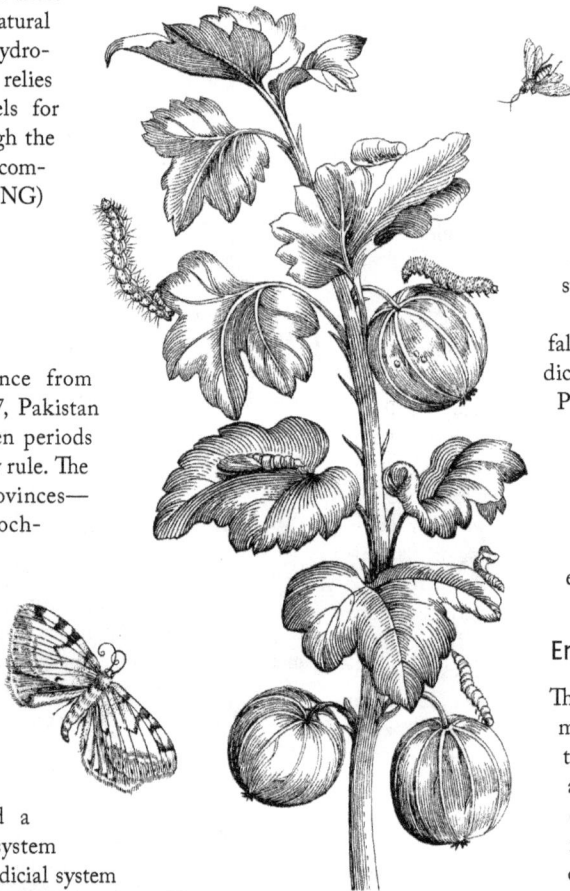

Public Interest Environmental Litigation

Under Article 184(3) of the Constitution, the Supreme Court has original jurisdiction over petitions to enforce fundamental rights. Furthermore, Article 2A requires that all laws conform to Islamic law, which allows citizens to seek substantive justice from the courts. To encourage such PIL, the Supreme Court waives standing requirements and fees.

Environmental PIL began relatively modestly. Judges generally allowed officials to remedy a problem before intervening, but in 1994, Dr. Parvez Hassan, a partner at Hassan and Hassan, helped residents file a complaint against a proposed grid station. In *Shehla Zia v. WAPDA*, the Supreme Court read the right to a clean and healthy environment into the constitutional right to life (Article 9), as well as a customary international law of "right to the human environment." It also adopted the precautionary principle to anticipate any harm that might come from electromagnetic radiation.

After *Shehla Zia*, the judiciary became a major force in environmental policy making. Some environmental attorneys and nongovernmental organizations (NGOs), such as Syed Mansoor Ali Shah, Ahmad Rafay Alam, and the Lahore Conservation Society, have become innovators in bringing environmental issues to the court's attention. The judiciary itself often engages in a "rolling review" of PEPA implementation. The Supreme Court can even initiate PIL *suo moto* (on the court's cognizance). In March 2010, in *Lahore Conservation Society v. Government of Punjab*, the chief justice ordered a halt to logging around a canal after reading a letter in a newspaper.

Pakistani environmental PIL frequently uses commissions composed of government officials, businessmen, and environmentalists to resolve scientific questions and design policies. In 2003, in *Syed Ali Mansoor Shah v. Government of Punjab*, the Lahore High Court established the Lahore Clean Air Commission in response to a petition against vehicular emissions. It recommended introducing Euro II CNG buses, phasing out two-stroke rickshaws, and setting ambient air quality and vehicle emission standards within three years.

Unsustainable Judicialization

Unfortunately, courts lack the technical capacity to formulate long-term environmental policy. Furthermore, by assuming such a pronounced role, judges might inadvertently atrophy the capacity of executive agencies to address environmental problems. For example, in *suo moto* cases, the provincial EPAs are reluctant to take any action for fear that it might lead to contempt of court proceedings.

Currently, the judiciary's policy preferences seem aligned with those of environmentalists, but pro-environment attitudes are not institutionalized. While the membership of the commissions is intended to represent diverse stakeholders, PIL minimizes formal adversarial processes, which could undermine the rights of weaker parties. This is especially worrying considering Pakistani judicial independence is relatively young.

International and Regional Issues

While Pakistan relies upon the Indus basin for much its cultivable land, the Indus River's sources are located in India. Given their history of conflict, Pakistan viewed this as a serious security challenge. In 1960, India and Pakistan agreed upon the Indus Water Treaty, which partitioned the Indus River system's resources. Despite occasional tensions, the treaty remains intact, but it does not cover transboundary pollution. Furthermore, the Permanent Indus Commission lacks enforcement powers.

In the 2004 Islamabad Declaration, South Asian Association for Regional Cooperation (SAARC) announced its intention to create a regional environment treaty. The most recent SAARC Summit in April 2010 focused on climate change. Thus far, however, SAARC has been reluctant to mediate transboundary environmental disputes amongst its members.

Convergence or Divergence?

Despite the long-standing hostility between India and Pakistan, these South Asian neighbors share similar approaches to environmental law. In both, strong judiciaries encouraged PIL to compensate for weak executive enforcement. In fact, Parvez Hassan has cited M. C. Mehta's litigation and Indian jurisprudence as models for Pakistan.

But in other ways, both India and Pakistan might be taking different paths. While India's Supreme Court seems to be reexamining the wisdom of PIL, Pakistan's seems even more confident of its authority to issue *suo moto* orders (the Lahore Conservation Society case may well become its Godavarman). It remains to be seen whether these developments represent the end of the convergence of South Asian environmental law or merely a temporary divergence.

Armin ROSENCRANZ
Stanford University

Dominic J. Nardi Jr.
University of Michigan

See also in the *Berkshire Encyclopedia of Sustainability* Bhopal Disaster; Environmental Law (several articles:

China; East Asia; Russia and Central Asia; Southeast Asia); International Law; Transboundary Water Law

Further Readings

Alam, Ahmad Rafay. (2006). *Public interest litigation and the role of the judiciary*. Islamabad, Pakistan: Paper presented at the International Judicial Conference: Justice for All, Islamabad, Pakistan, 11–14 August 2006. Retrieved May 22, 2010, from http://www.supreme-court.gov.pk/web/subsites/scp50/Articles/17/2.pdf

Bhatnagar, Manav. (2009). Reconsidering the Indus Water Treaty. *Tulane Environmental Law Journal, 22,* 271–313.

Divan, Shyam, & Rosencranz, Armin. (2002). *Environmental law and policy in India: Cases, materials, and statutes.* Oxford, UK: Oxford University Press.

Hassan, Parvez, & Hassan, Jawad. (2009). Pakistan. In Louis J. Kotzé & Alexander R. Paterson (Eds.), *The role of the judiciary in environmental governance: Comparative perspectives* (pp. 381–410). The Hague, The Netherlands: Wolters Kluwer Law & Business.

Lau, Martin. (2007). Access to environmental justice: Karachi's urban poor and the law. In Andrew Harding (Ed.), *Access to environmental justice: A comparative study* (pp. 177–204). Leiden, The Netherlands: BRILL.

Lele, Sharachchandra; Dubash, Navroz; & Dixit, Shantanu. (2010). A structure for environment governance: A perspective. *Economic and Political Weekly, 45*(6), 13–15.

Nardi, Dominic J. (2008). Greening environmental rights: Separating law and morality in environmental public interest litigation in Pakistan. *Environmental Law Reporter, 38,* 10029–10038.

Razzaque, Jona. (2004). *Public interest environmental litigation in India, Pakistan, and Bangladesh.* The Hague, The Netherlands: Kluwer International Law.

Rosencranz, Armin, & Sahu, Geetanjoy. (2009). National Green Tribunal Bill, 2009: Proposals for improvement. *Economic and Political Weekly, 44*(48), 8–10.

Rosencranz, Armin; Boenig, Edward; & Dutta, Brinda. (2007). The Godavarman Case: The Indian Supreme court's breach of constitutional boundaries in managing India's forests. *Environmental Law Reporter, 37,* 10032–10042.

Rosencranz, Armin, & Jackson, Michael. (2003). The Delhi pollution case and the limits of judicial power. *Columbia Journal of Environmental Law, 28,* 223–254.

World Bank. (2006). *Pakistan: Strategic country environmental assessment.* Washington, DC: The World Bank.

Court Cases

Dahanu Taluka Environment Protection Group v. Bombay Suburban Electricity Supply Company, Ltd., 1991

Lahore Conservation Society v. Government of Punjab, 2010

M. C. Mehta v. Union of India (Kanpur Tanneries), 1988

M. C. Mehta v. Union of India, 2002

Narmada Bachao Andolan v. Union of India, 2000

Shehla Zia v. WAPDA, PLD 1994 SC 693

Syed Ali Mansoor Shah v. Government of Punjab, 2003

Tehri Bandh Virodhi Sangharsh Samiti (TBVSS) v. Uttar Pradesh, 1992

T. N. Godavarman Thirumulpad v. Union of India, 1995 (continuing mandamus)

Environmental Law—Pacific Island Region

The Pacific island region encompasses a huge expanse of ocean and twenty-two countries and territories of diverse cultures, societies, and legal systems. Natural resources, which are often regulated by the customary practices and laws of the region's indigenous peoples, are important to the economies of these nations. Environmental law must reconcile written law and customary law, but it will be effective only if and when enforced by the government.

Environmental law in the Pacific island region, mirroring Pacific life itself, is a mixture of the ancient and the modern. Customary laws governing the use of land and marine resources that have been in place for many centuries exist alongside modern systems of environmental regulation enacted by Pacific governments. The countries of this vast region participate actively in international environmental fora and maintain their own system of regional environmental treaties and institutions.

Introduction to Regional Legal Systems

The twenty-two countries and territories of the Pacific island region (PICTs) control a vast expanse of more than 38 million square kilometers, or about four times the area of the United States of America. Only 2 percent of this area is land, scattered over thousands of large and small islands. For instance, the Federated States of Micronesia's Exclusive Economic Zone (EEZ)—the area of seabed stretching 200 nautical miles from the nation's shores—is larger than the land area of Argentina; the country's EEZ is 4,000 times the size of its landmass. (See Figure 1 on page 101). Within this region of island nations there is a diverse array of societies and cultures, as well as a variety of legal systems. (See Table 1 on page 100).

Fifteen of the twenty-two PICTs are either independent countries or governed in "free association" with New Zealand or the United States. Free association refers to a treaty-based arrangement wherein an otherwise independent country cedes specified sovereign powers, such as rights to exclude strategic interests of third countries from being established within the territory of the freely associated state, to another country in return for benefits such as preferential migration status or increased levels of aid. The remaining seven remain dependent territories governed by the United States, France, New Zealand, or the United Kingdom. Samoa was the first PICT to gain independence in 1962; the most recent is the Republic of Palau in 1994.

The legal systems of each independent Pacific island country tend to be adapted versions of those of their former colonizing nation. Over time these countries are integrating many elements specific to their own needs and priorities into their legal systems, with environmental law being an area of much innovation in this regard.

A significant aspect of environmental law in the Pacific island region is the continuing role played by customary law, and the coexistence of customary law with the formal laws enacted by governments. (Customary law can be defined as traditional common practice that has become part of the accepted and expected conduct and is treated as a legal requirement; there are more than 1,200 language groups in the Pacific Island region so an exact definition of the term is very difficult.) Most Pacific island societies have maintained customary legal arrangements for many centuries, although the vibrancy of custom differs from place to place, as does the impact upon custom caused by many decades of colonial rule.

TABLE 1. Pacific Island Countries and Territories (2010)

Name of Pacific Island Country or Territory	Political Status (Year of Independence or Autonomy)	Legal System	Population	Land Area (km²)
American Samoa	Territory of United States	United States	66,432	199
Cook Islands	Free association with New Zealand (1965)	Parliamentary democracy	19,569	240
Federated States of Micronesia	Free association with United States (1986)	Presidential democracy	107,154	702
Republic of Fiji	Independent (1970)	Military	957,780	18,274
French Polynesia	French overseas collectivity	France	264,000	4,167
Territory of Guam	Unincorporated territory of United States	United States	178,000	541
Republic of Kiribati	Independent (1979)	Parliamentary democracy	99,482	811
Republic of Marshall Islands	Free association with United States (1986)	Presidential democracy	65,859	181
Republic of Nauru	Independent (1968)	Parliamentary democracy	14,264	21
New Caledonia	French overseas collectivity	France	249,000	18,575
Niue	Free association with New Zealand (1974)	Parliamentary democracy	1,354	260
Commonwealth of the Northern Mariana Islands	Commonwealth in political union with the United States (1986)	United States	48,317	464
Republic of Palau	Free association with United States (1994)	Presidential democracy	20,879	459
Papua New Guinea	Independent (1975)	Parliamentary democracy	6,064,515	462,840
Pitcairn Islands	British overseas territory	Parliamentary democracy	51	47
Samoa	Independent (1962)	Parliamentary democracy	179,000	2831
Solomon Islands	Independent (1978)	Parliamentary democracy	523,000	28,896
Tokelau	Territory of New Zealand	New Zealand	1,416	10
Kingdom of Tonga	Independent (1970)	Parliamentary democracy	122,580	747
Tuvalu	Independent (1978)	Parliamentary democracy	12,375	26
Republic of Vanuatu	Independent (1980)	Parliamentary democracy	221,552	12,189
Wallis and Futuna Islands	French overseas collectivity	France	15,289	264

Source: Author.

Figure 1. Map of the Exclusive Economic Zones (EEZs) of the Pacific Island Region

The highlighted EEZs (which stretch 200 nautical miles from a nation's or territory's coastline) show the nations and territories in peril of indundation in the event of sea level rise: the Federated States of Micronesia, Papua New Guinea, French Polynesia, and the Cook Islands.

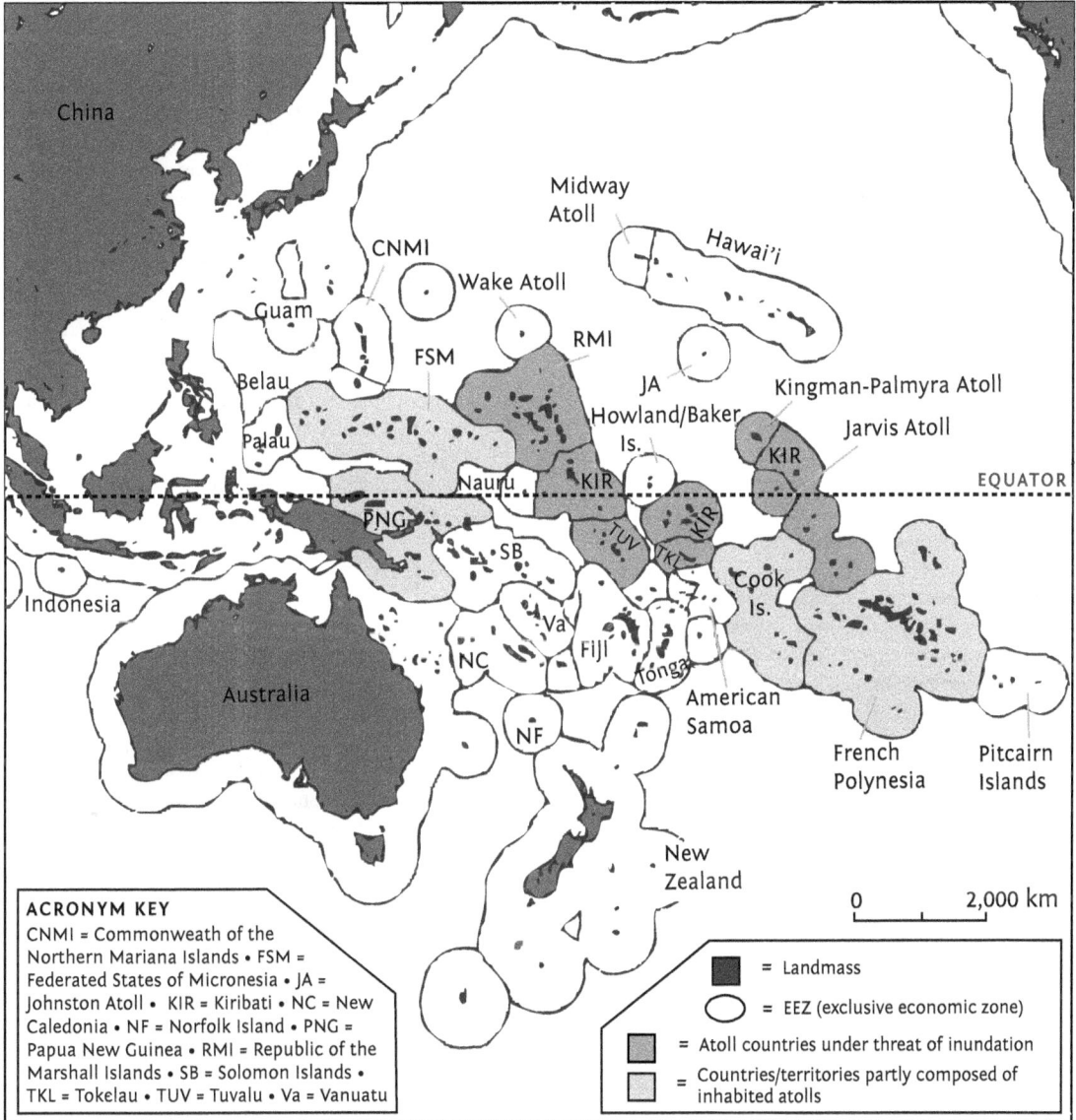

Source: US Geological Survey, adapted by Berkshire Publishing. Retrieved December 9, 2010, from http://walrus.wr.usgs.gov/research/projects/pac_eez_minerals.html

Customary law is important in understanding Pacific environmental law because the regulation of land and natural resources are always subjects of indigenous customary legal systems in PICTs as elsewhere. According to traditional fisheries experts, the "Pacific island region probably contains the world's greatest concentration of still-functioning traditional community-based systems for managing coastal-marine fisheries and other resources" (Ruddle 1998, 105).

The Role of Environmental Law

The demands of life on small islands require the adoption of sustainable modes of living, and these in turn require effective systems of environmental law. The environmental history of the Pacific island region provides clear examples of this. In the precolonial period some island societies, such as those of the Rapanui of Easter Island, suffered terminal decline due to their own unsustainable use of the environment. More recently, the growth of modern industries such as fisheries, mining, and plantation agriculture has led to widespread environmental degradation in PICTs, thus requiring the implementation of modern systems of environmental law.

All PICTs have enacted a suite of environmental laws empowering their governments to implement environmental regulatory controls that are, at least on paper, broadly comparable to those in countries such as Australia and the United States. The earliest of these was enacted in the 1960s, a few more in the 1970s, and since the mid-1980s there have been many additions to the compendium of Pacific island environmental legislation.

Co-Management Approaches

Initially, much environmental legislation was transplanted from countries outside the region without much adaptation for the specific needs of PICTs. More recently, particularly since the beginning of the twenty-first century, PICT lawmakers have sought to amend or redraft their environmental laws to adjust requirements for their own specific priorities, economies, and cultures.

Examples of newer Pacific-specific laws include Vanuatu's Environmental Management and Conservation Act of 2002, Part 2 of which allows for the registration of conservation areas, but only upon the application of the customary owners whose land would be subject to the conservation measures. Similarly, the interaction of Samoa's Village Fono Act of 1990 and Fisheries Act of 1988 enables traditional village decision makers to set their own fisheries laws, which are then recognized and enforceable through national law.

Approaches for the sustainable use of PICT natural resources, wherein governments and traditional rural communities cooperate in matters of environmental regulation, are becoming widespread through the region. These so-called co-management strategies are proving to be more effective than the governments' previous attempts to exclude customary landowners from their traditional resource management role.

Waste, Pollution, and EIAs

All PICTs struggle with meeting the challenge of effective waste management due to scarcity of land and the increasing volume of imported goods and materials. The environmental impact assessment (EIA) is a cornerstone of environmental law systems in many jurisdictions, and PICTs are no exception in this regard. The aim of an EIA is assessing new development projects, prohibiting those that pose unacceptable risks or costs, and ensuring that those allowed to proceed are undertaken in a manner that minimizes unnecessary environmental impacts. Examples of laws regulating waste, pollution, and environmental impact assessment in PICTs include Niue's Environment Act 2003, Fiji's Environment Management Act 2005, and the Cook Islands Environment Act 2003.

The State of Pohnpei in the Federated States of Micronesia has a suite of environmental laws and institutions originally adapted from United States models, but in recent times Pohnpeian lawmakers have increasingly given careful consideration to the adaptation of laws to suit local needs and priorities. A good example is State Law No. 6L-66-06; section 17 creates a predisposal fee for all imports: US$100 for each shipping container and US$100 for each motor vehicle. This money is paid into a fund to be used for public environmental awareness and cleanup programs. The inclusion of motor vehicles illustrates a well-targeted regulatory action addressing one of Pohnpei's particularly problematic waste streams: Pohnpei receives a relatively large number of imported second-hand vehicles that have a short useful life span in Pohnpei's harsh coastal environment and are costly to dispose of in an environmentally sound manner.

Fisheries

Fisheries and marine resources are centrally important in most PICTs, and so laws regulating both oceanic and coastal fishing activities operate in all jurisdictions. The Pacific island region has the world's largest tuna fishery, and the income derived from commercial fishing licenses is crucial to many PICTs, as is the sustainable management of fisheries for the benefit of future generations. Examples of laws regulating Pacific fisheries include Tonga's Fisheries Regulation Act, the Palau's Fisheries Management Act, and Nauru's Fisheries Act. As outlined below, much PICT oceanic fisheries regulatory activity is undertaken on a cooperative basis under regional agreements and treaties.

Papua New Guinea

The country of Papua New Guinea (PNG), while usually considered to be part of the Pacific island region, is unique in many respects. PNG is by far the largest and most populous country in the region and has remarkable cultural diversity; the island of New Guinea (which also includes the Indonesian province of West Papua) is home to over 1,100 language groups, or around one in eight of the world's languages. PNG's cultural diversity is matched by its biological diversity because it is the location of the world's third-largest tropical rain forest, as well as being a hot spot for marine biodiversity.

Unfortunately PNG struggles with the challenge of effective and sustainable environmental regulation. PNG is reliant upon income from its mining and logging industries, and there has historically been a combination of lax regulation of mining and logging in PNG along with frequent instances of corrupt practices that allow illegal logging and excessive pollution from mines to continue unabated.

On paper PNG has an impressive suite of environmental legislation. Unfortunately the implementation of these laws is at best haphazard. The poor standards of governance by PNG's executive branch are to some degree balanced by the independence of the PNG judiciary, which is often called upon by rural landowners asserting their legal rights to due process and environmental quality against mining and timber companies, as well as ineffectual PNG government agencies. A recent landmark case illustrating this is *Ramu Nico Management v. Tarsie*. In this case a group of landowners from the Rai Coast area of Madang Province in PNG successfully sought a temporary injunction to prevent a nickel mine from constructing and operating a deep sea tailings disposal system to manage waste. Joined as defendants with the company were the PNG Mineral Resources Authority and the PNG Department of Environment and Conservation. As of October 2010, the court had not yet decided whether to grant a permanent injunction, but public discussion of the case was successfully raising public awareness of the problems of inadequate disposal of mining waste.

International and Regional Environmental Law

PICTs identify as a regional grouping for many purposes, including those relating to environmental protection and natural resource management. The key regional organization for environmental matters is the Secretariat of the Pacific Regional Environment Programme (SPREP). SPREP's programs include regional coordination and capacity building in the areas of multilateral treaty negotiations, waste, pollution, and biodiversity conservation.

There are several other supranational Pacific island regional agencies with roles relating to environmental management:

- Pacific Islands Forum Fisheries Agency
- Secretariat for the Pacific Community
- Pacific Islands Applied Geoscience Commission
- Pacific Islands Forum Secretariat

Since the 1970s, PICTs have developed numerous international treaties addressing various aspects of environmental protection and ensuring regional cooperation toward that goal:

- Convention on the Conservation of Nature in the South Pacific (1976)
- Nauru Agreement Concerning Cooperation in the Management of Fisheries of Common Interest (1982)
- South Pacific Nuclear Free Zone Treaty (1985)
- Convention for the Protection of the Natural Resources and the Environment of the South Pacific Region (1986)
- Protocol for the Prevention of Pollution of the South Pacific Region by Dumping (1986)
- Convention for the Prohibition of Fishing with Long Driftnets in the South Pacific (1989)
- Niue Treaty on Cooperation in Fisheries Surveillance and Law Enforcement in the South Pacific Region (1992)
- Convention to Ban the Importation into Forum Island Countries of Hazardous and Radioactive Wastes and to Control the Transboundary Movement and Management of Hazardous Wastes within the South Pacific Region (1995)
- Convention on the Conservation and Management of Highly Migratory Fish Stocks in the Western and Central Pacific Ocean (2000)
- Convention on the Conservation and Management of High Seas Fishery Resources in the South Pacific Ocean (2009)

In addition, PICTs participate in international environmental law at a global level. SPREP often plays an important role in assisting PICTs with coordination in relation to their participation in multilateral environmental treaty negotiations. The Association of Small Island States (AOSIS), a group that includes Caribbean nations as well as PICTs, frequently plays a similar role. By working together, small-island developing states are able to be heard more effectively at international treaty negotiations. The original proposal for the treaty that eventually became the Kyoto Protocol was first proposed by AOSIS at the first Conference of the Parties of the UN Framework Convention on Climate Change (UNFCCC COP 1).

Current Issues and Future Challenges

There are two recurring issues regarding the effective implementation of Pacific island environmental law. The first of these is the relationship between governmental laws and agencies and customary laws and institutions. There is widespread agreement that each has important roles to play in the sustainable management of Pacific island environments, but defining these roles and achieving a cooperative relationship between them has proved difficult in the past and is likely to remain so. An illustration of this is the Fiji Locally Managed Marine Areas network (FLMMA), a network established in 2002 linking approximately one hundred village-based marine protected areas. FLMMA has achieved significant successes in conserving resources, but to date civil society organizations have been more closely involved in it than government agencies, and it has no basis in law. FLMMA is dealing with these issues in cooperation with government; draft legal provisions have been discussed as of October 2010, but no law has been passed.

The second issue is the lack of effective action undertaken by Pacific governments to enforce the environmental laws that have been enacted. This lack of enforcement is in part a result of the first issue; Pacific government agencies are at times reluctant to step into areas of social control traditionally dealt with by customary laws and institutions. Another major factor that results in an absence of environmental-law enforcement is that Pacific environmental agencies lack adequate resources, such as sufficient staff numbers, technical knowledge and equipment, and financial resources. This is a very common deficiency of environmental regulatory agencies throughout the developing world.

In the future, the impacts of climate change will be the most significant challenge faced by those seeking to apply law and policy for the protection of the environment in the Pacific island region. Climate change is already impacting Pacific island environments in the form of rising sea levels, inundated freshwater ecosystems, and degraded coral reefs. Climate change presents an unprecedented threat to PICTs and makes the important task of finding ways to

effectively protect Pacific island environments an absolute imperative.

Justin Gregory ROSE
University of the South Pacific

See also in the *Berkshire Encyclopedia of Sustainability* Climate Change Mitigation; Convention for the Prohibition of Fishing with Long Drift Nets in the South Pacific; Customary International Law; Environmental Law (several articles: Australia and New Zealand, Southeast Asia; United States and Canada); Fishing and Whaling Legislation; Law of the Sea; Natural Resources Law; Waste Shipment Law

FURTHER READINGS

Boer, Ben. (1996). *Environmental law in the South Pacific: Consolidated report of the reviews of environmental law in the Cook Islands, Federated States of Micronesia, Kingdom of Tonga, Republic of the Marshall Islands and Solomon Islands.* Gland, Switzerland and Cambridge, UK: International Union for the Conservation of Nature.
Boer, Ben; Ramsay, Ross; & Rothwell, Donald R. (1998). *International environmental law in the Asia Pacific.* The Hague, The Netherlands: Kluwer.
Cordonnery, Lawrence. (2003). Environmental law issues in the South Pacific and the quest for sustainable development and good governance. In Anita Jowitt & Tess Newton Cain (Eds.), *Passage of change: Law, society and governance in the Pacific.* Canberra, Australia: Pandanus.
Corrin Care, Jennifer; Newton, Tess; & Paterson, Don. (1999). *Introduction to South Pacific law.* London: Cavendish.
Fa'asili, Ueta. (1999). The use of village by-laws in marine conservation and fisheries management. (Secretariat of the Pacific community information paper No. 17). Noumea, New Caledonia: SPC.
Graham, Tom, & Idechong, Noah. (1998). Reconciling customary and constitutional law: Managing marine resources in Palau, Micronesia. *Ocean & Coastal Management, 40*, 143–164.
Johannes, Bob. (2002). The renaissance of community-based marine resource management in Oceania. *Annual Review of Ecological Systems, 33*, 317–340.
Lawrence, Peter. (1994). Regional strategies for the implementation of environmental conventions: Lessons from the South Pacific. *Australian Yearbook of International Law*, pp. 203–229.
Ntumy, Michael. (Ed.). (1995). *South Pacific islands legal systems.* Honolulu: University of Hawaii Press.
Pacific Islands Legal Information Institute (PacLII). (n.d.). Homepage. Retrieved August 26, 2010 from http://www.paclii.org
Ramu Nico Management (MCC) Ltd v. Tarsie [2010] PGSC 5; SC1056 (8 June 2010).
Ruddle, Kenneth. (1998). The context of policy design for existing community-based fisheries management systems in the Pacific Islands. *Ocean & coastal management, 40*, 105–126.
Secretariat of the Pacific Regional Environment Programme. (2010). Homepage. Retrieved August 26, 2010 from www.sprep.org
Rose, Justin. (2008). Community-based biodiversity conservation in the Pacific: Cautionary lessons in regionalizing environmental governance. In Michael Jeffery, Jeremy Firestone, & Karen Bubna-Litic (Eds.), *Biodiversity conservation, law and livelihoods: Bridging the north–south divide.* Cambridge, UK: Cambridge University Press.

Environmental Law—Russia and Central Asia

Russia and Central Asia are vast areas, rich in natural resources. Management of these resources has often been a struggle, balancing the good of the environment with the possibility of economic and industrial development. In light of the shared history between these nations, it is crucial that the Central Asian republics and Russia work together to form policies and regulations promoting sustainable development and environmental protection.

For most of the twentieth century, Russia and the countries that compose Central Asia—Kazakhstan, Kyrgyzstan, Tajikistan, Turkmenistan, and Uzbekistan—were all a part of the Soviet Union. This common national heritage provides these countries with a shared legislative background that continues to influence their policies as independent states. During the Soviet era, there was widespread natural resource exploitation that impacted the environment across the region. Since establishing independence, environmental laws have been enacted to varying degrees by all these nations, with emphasis placed primarily on natural resource management.

Russia

Even after the disintegration of the Soviet Union in December 1991, Russia remains the largest country in the world with an area of over 17 million square kilometers. It is rich in natural resources such as coal, oil, gas, chemicals, and metals that provide 80 percent of the country's budgetary income. The most exploited natural resources are forests, which cover 69 percent of the land; minerals, especially oil and gas; and fish resources. In many instances, however, this abundance of natural resources is not easily accessible and requires large investments in infrastructure. For example, of the forested lands, only 45 percent are located in accessible, developed areas. Areas in the far east, southeast, and the Ural Mountains are all exploited. This occurs in addition to the widely spread practices of illegal fishing, illegal hunting, and degradation of habitats.

Pollution

Air pollution remains another urgent problem, despite the fall in economic activities that are the main sources of pollution. Concentration of harmful substances in the air is very high, affecting 69 percent of cities (Ministry of Natural Resources 2006). High levels of pollution are primarily due to noncompliance with environmental regulations by industrial facilities, low production discipline, lack of investment into cleaner industrial technologies, and lax state control (Ministry of Natural Resources 2006). At the same time, emissions of greenhouse gases (GHGs) are less than 30 percent of 1990 levels (Roshydromet 2006); however, this is mainly due to falling production levels.

Russia's main rivers, such as the Volga, Don, Ob, and Enisei, are recognized as highly polluted. Abandoned industrial sites are another source of pollution. On average, only 40 percent of the waste produced is treated, and the rest is stockpiled in open waste sites (Ministry of Natural Resources 2006).

With the growing scarcity of fossil fuel energy resources, Russia is intending to give priority to nuclear energy, hydroelectric energy, and renewable energy resources (Ministry of Energy 2010). This would require special legal regulation.

Legislation

In response to environmental and natural resource problems from market economy models introduced in the early

1990s, environmental legislation was subjected to serious changes. Especially noticeable were the changes to ownership rights. With privatization of industrial facilities and lands came the adoption of new legal rules connected with the responsibilities of private businesses, their financial obligations, and the need to develop a mechanism of public environmental rights protection. Rapid changes in environmental legislation were caused by both the unstable economic situation and an unclear understanding of how to harmonize practiced Soviet models of natural resources use and environmental protection with the market economy.

Many of the laws initially adopted have been repealed or replaced by new laws. In 2006, the Forest Code replaced the 1997 Forest Code, which had replaced the Fundamentals of the Forest Legislation of 1993. The same fate came of the water legislation with the twice-adopted Water Code (1995 and 2006), land use legislation with the twice-adopted Land Code (1991 and 2001), and the Federal Law on Environmental Protection (1991 and 2002). If not replaced by new acts, others, such as the Law on Wildlife (1995), Law on Air Protection (1999), Law on Minerals (1992), and Law on Specially Protected Areas (1995), were amended many times, sometimes with provisions that were not environmentally favorable.

These replacements and amendments were necessitated primarily because of a lack of strategic political view about what kinds of legal rules were needed, covert and open lobbying by economic interests, and ignorance in public and scientific opinion. As a result environmental legislation moved toward removing administrative involvement and control.

The 2004 amendments to the 1995 Water Code weakened the regulations of water-protected zones to allow building and other development activities. A new Water Code, adopted in 2006, replaced the administrative regulators with civil regulators, and permits for water use were replaced by water use contracts. Auctions and competition were widely practiced in establishing the procedures for granting natural resources rights. This approach is also used in other natural resources laws. Forest fires during summer 2010 demonstrated the country's lack of preparation due to the Forest Code of 2006, which had dismantled the state system of forest protection. These unfavorable changes to environmental policies occurred not from concern about the environment but instead from the economic interests connected to the environment.

New acts have supplemented the more traditional legislation from the Soviet Union that separately addressed each type of natural resource with a different code. Legislation now addresses environmental problems including waste management, industrial safety, nuclear energy development, and environmental impact assessments (EIAs). Global climate change and increasing shortages in traditional energy resources accelerated development of a new area of environmental law: energy law. Currently, environmental legislation is encompassed by over thirty federal laws and hundreds of regional regulatory acts that concern issues such as environmental pollution, natural resources use and protection, specially protected areas, and environmental security. Among more recently adopted legislation are federal laws on fishing (2004); hunting (2009); and the state nuclear energy corporation, Rosatom (2007). In 2010 the federal legislature (the State Duma) considered a draft law on the handling of radioactive waste.

The laws on environmental pollution—the Law on Environmental Protection (2002), the Law on Air Protection (1999), the Water Code (2006), and the Law on Handling of Wastes (1998)—are based on such tools as setting standards, permitting impacts, EIAs, and ecological expertise. These laws also introduced the Institute of Public Environmental Rights. According to the Russian Constitution and environmental legislation, the public has the right to a favorable environment, access to true information about the state of the environment, and compensation for environmental damage caused by environmental pollution. These public rights are not frequently defended due to legal uncertainties, apathy of the people toward their environmental rights, and complications connected with evidence and proofs. The only legal area that is well-developed is access to information. Under the Law on Hydrometeorology (1998), individuals can freely request information on the state of the environment and pollution from state authorities. The types of information accessible are quite limited, however, and only include data obtained by environmental monitoring authorities. The Laws on State Secrets (1993) and on Commercial Secrets (2004) further narrow the publicly accessible information.

Regulation and Compliance

Legal environmental regulation under the Constitution of the Russian Federation (RF) falls within the joint jurisdiction of the RF and the federal regions (Article 72). This means that both the federal and regional levels of government can regulate environmental issues. There are eighty-three regions that are members of the RF. Federal environmental legislation plays a superior role to regional legislation. Regions regulate only issues specifically given to them, such as when adopting regulations on bathing in water bodies under the Water Code, or developing sand, gravel, and other common minerals under the Law on Minerals. At the May 2010 meeting of the State Council on Ecology, the RF president indicated that codification, strengthening environmental standards, reestablishing a nonbudgetary ecological fund (dismantled in 2000), and removing abandoned industrial sites were priorities for further environmental legislation.

Implementation, including control of compliance, is vested with numerous state authorities. Centralization of state governance dominates this area. Federal authorities that, under the Constitution, administer federal property have practically all the power in regulating natural resources use. This is because all land belongs to the RF, with the exception of some private land and certain small water bodies and trees on that land. The federal authorities also regulate and control all polluting activities, although they often delegate certain powers to the RF regions, including those connected with federal ownership governance. The Ministry of Natural Resources and Ecology plays the principal role at the federal level. Its agencies and services include the Federal Service of Control Over Natural Resources, Federal Agency of Minerals Use, Federal Agency of Water Resources, and Federal Agency of Hydrometeorology. The other relevant authorities include the Federal Forest Service (forest use and protection); Federal Service for Ecological, Technological, and Nuclear Control (permitting of emissions, industrial security, and safety of nuclear material use); Federal Service of Human Well-being; Ministry of Health (air, soil, and water quality standards); and Federal Fisheries Agency (fishing regulations).

International Cooperation

Russia actively participates in international cooperation and is a party to most global and regional international forums on biodiversity, wildlife protection, air pollution, industrial safety, among others. Russian climate legislation is heavily influenced by multilateral climate change agreements. In 2009 the president approved the Climate Doctrine, which outlined areas of action, though it did not establish mandatory rules. Also in 2009, the government adopted the Energy Strategy, in place until 2030, which outlines measures to raise energy efficiency. Governmental action on climate change is often connected with the Kyoto Protocol, which sets binding targets for all ratifying industrialized nations to reduce GHG emissions from their 1990 levels by the end of 2012.

Central Asia

The five Central Asia Republics (CARs)—Kazakhstan, Kyrgyzstan, Tajikistan, Turkmenistan, and Uzbekistan—have inherited severe environmental problems from intensive exploitation of natural resources during the Soviet era. One of the most telling examples of this is the devastating degradation of the Aral Sea, its ecosystem, and its surrounding areas as a result of massive water diversions for irrigated agriculture, predominantly cotton monoculture, beginning in the 1960s.

As of 2010, Central Asian economies continue to depend on extraction of raw materials and irrigated agriculture. The countries' economies mainly rely on the primary export of a small handful of dominant commodities: oil and ferrous metals (Kazakhstan); nonferrous metals (Kyrgyzstan); aluminum and cotton (Tajikistan); gas, oil, and cotton (Turkmenistan); and gold and cotton (Uzbekistan). These dominating subsectors are polluting and resource-use intensive (EEA and ETUC 2007).

In addition, global climate change poses serious threats to the region's environmental, ecological, and socioeconomic systems (Perelet 2007).

Central Asia is home to almost 60 million people. All countries in the region, except Kazakhstan, are experiencing a steady population growth, especially in rural areas. Currently, 60 percent of the Central Asian population lives in rural areas, and almost half of the rural population lives in poverty, directly or indirectly depending on natural resources to sustain their livelihood (World Bank 2010). The countries' economies and the daily lives of their citizens therefore rely heavily on the availability and quality of land, water, and energy resources, as well as on seasonal climate and weather conditions. Given the interdependency of natural resource use and management within the region, inherited from the Soviet epoch, transboundary cooperation between the countries is crucial.

Environmental Policies, Legislations, and Institutions

In the civil law system of the CARs, environmental requirements are mostly prescribed in constitutions, specialized laws on environmental protection, and a wide range of laws and bylaws regulating public health and the use and protection of land, water, air, minerals, forest, and wildlife. In institutional terms, the ministries or state committees of the environment are the lead governmental

agencies responsible for environmental matters. Other related agencies include, but are not limited to, the ministries of health, agriculture, water resources, emergency, and safety control.

The CARs identified their environmental priorities and objectives in national environmental protection plans. They also linked environmental concerns to broader sustainable development goals through poverty reduction strategies such as the 2006 Poverty Reduction Strategy in Tajikistan, the 2006 Concept of Transition to Sustainable Development for the Period 2007–2024 of Kazakhstan, and the Welfare Improvement Strategy of the Republic of Uzbekistan for 2008–2010. The countries cooperate on a wide range of environmental matters. At the subregional level, for example, they composed the 2006 Framework Convention on Environmental Protection for Sustainable Development in Central Asia. They also work together at the regional level under the aegis of Commonwealth of Independent States and the UN Economic Commission for Europe. Examples include the 1992 Agreement on Interaction in the Field of Ecology and the Environmental Protection, to which all CARs are parties, and the 1992 Convention on the Protection and Use of Trans-boundary Watercourses and International Lakes, to which Kazakhstan and Uzbekistan are parties. The CARs also cooperate at the global level as they are all parties to the 1992 UN Framework Convention on Climate Change and many others.

Land Management and Protection

Central Asian economies continue to depend on arable lands as the main productive resource, especially for cotton and wheat monocultures inherited from the Soviet epoch. In recent years, however, awareness about the interlinked problems of economic development and environmental degradation has increased. The CARs have initiated agrarian and land reforms to increase investment and agriculture production along with sustainable resources use. Some countries, such as Kazakhstan and Kyrgyzstan, enabled the privatization of agricultural lands and shifted from the large agricultural enterprises, or collective and state farms, that dominated in the Soviet time to individualized of farming. Others, such as Tajikistan and Uzbekistan, preferred to keep lands in state ownership.

Issues within land management still include the mounting problems of soil salinity, erosion, and contamination. More than half the irrigated lands in the region are salinized and/or waterlogged as a result of unsustainable agricultural practices, such as overgrazing, overcropping, and lack of appropriate soil fertility management (ADB 2008). Over 88 percent of irrigated soils in Kyrgyzstan and 97 percent of agricultural lands in Tajikistan are eroded, and 80 percent

of land area in Turkmenistan and Uzbekistan is affected by desertification (UNESCAP 2007). Soil contamination from the widespread use of fertilizers, pesticides, and agricultural chemicals also remains a significant problem across the region. This is especially true in Uzbekistan, whose fertilizer use amounts to more than three-quarters of the total fertilizer used in Central Asia, mainly for its cotton industry (EEA and ETUC 2007). Although the problems of land degradation and desertification are addressed in land codes of the countries, overall sustainable agroenvironmental policy is still to be developed.

At an international level, the CARs joined the UN Convention to Combat Desertification, which initiated a Sub-regional Action Programme for the CARs in 2003. Regionally, the countries also cooperate under the Central Asian Countries Initiative on Land Management (ADB 2008) and the Central Asian Sub-regional Training Program for Sustainable Land Management.

Water Management and Protection

The problems of water quantity and quality are a major concern and among the most contentious cross-border issues in Central Asia. In terms of water quantity, Turkmenistan and Uzbekistan are ranked among the ten countries with the least-secure water supplies in the world in the Water Security Risks Index (Maplecroft 2010). This was calculated by measuring access to improved drinking water and sanitation, the availability of renewable water, the reliance on external supplies, the relationship between available water and supply demands, and the water dependency of each country's economy. Kyrgyzstan and Tajikistan, although rich in water resources, also face the regional problems of melting glaciers, inadequate access to clean water and sanitation, and water use inefficiency. The United Nations Environment Programme's (UNEP) 2005 Global International Waters Assessment forecasts that by 2050 the glaciers on the mountains of Central Asia may reduce by one-third in area and volume if the current rate of 0.8–1.0 percent decrease per year continues. According to the World Health Organization (WHO) and the United Nations Children's Fund (UNICEF), 10–39 percent of the rural population in Central Asia has no access to improved sources of drinking water (WHO and UNICEF 2010). Progress has also been slow in improving water use efficiency, especially in irrigation, which accounts for over 90 percent of water withdrawals in Central Asia.

In terms of water quality, many surface and groundwater sources across the region are polluted. Agricultural discharge (collector-drainage waters and livestock), industrial, and municipal wastes are the major sources of water pollution (UNEP 2006). The situation is especially acute in the lowlands of Kazakhstan, Turkmenistan, and

Uzbekistan, resulting in increased illness (e.g., kidney disease, oncological and acute infectious diseases), and adult and child mortality rates (UNECE 2010c). Since 1990, there has been a reduction in polluted industrial waste releases, but water contamination is increasing due to reduced effectiveness in the management of irrigation (UNEP 2006).

Given the interdependency of water and other related resources, there is an emerging consensus within the region that integrated water resources management (IWRM) offers a promising path toward sustainable water resource development. Some principles of IWRM, including the provisions on environmental flows, have been incorporated into the 2003 Water Code of Kazakhstan and the 2005 Water Code of Kyrgyzstan. Other countries in the region are in the process of preparing national IWRM plans and are undertaking water use and protection reforms. National programs to ensure access to basic water needs in rural areas are also widely implemented.

Ensuring effective and peaceful management of transboundary water resources is a high priority in Central Asia. The CARs have signed a variety of bilateral and multilateral agreements and established an institutional framework to address transboundary water management issues at the regional level. Despite these legal developments, a complex web of the region's water-related problems, comprised of water allocation controversies, competition between irrigation and hydropower, water quality deterioration, and the danger of river contamination by toxic radioactive wastes, is still to be resolved.

Air Quality Management and Protection

Air pollution remains a serious problem in both urban and rural environments. The major sources of air pollution are thermal power stations, especially those using cheap, low-quality coal. Kazakhstan, which relies on coal as a major energy source, is therefore responsible for 44 percent of air pollutants in Central Asia (UNEP 2006). Although air pollution from point sources declined to some extent in the 1990s as a result of economic recession, pollution from diffuse sources has increased 65–70 percent in urban areas. This was mainly the result of growth and the poor conditions of road transport, namely the age of the vehicles,

poor vehicle maintenance, and variable fuel quality (EEA and ETUC 2007). Pollution is exacerbated by the concentrations of particulate matter from desertification, desert dust, and the dried Aral Sea bed (OECD 2007a).

To address air pollution problems at the national level, the CARs adopted laws on ambient air protection, which mostly reaffirmed or slightly revised Soviet ambient environmental standards, utilizing maximum allowable concentrations (MACs). In practice, as evidence from Uzbekistan suggests, a large number of pollutants that are covered by emission standards are not actually monitored by facilities because of the difficulty in measuring and regulating small quantities (UNECE 2010c). Environmental dimensions have also been introduced in the countries' transport strategies.

The CARs strive to address the significant transboundary threats caused by air pollution through existing bilateral and multilateral arrangements. For example, in 1994 Tajikistan and Uzbekistan signed an agreement to improve the ecological situation in the negatively impacted zone of the Tajik aluminum plant. At a wider regional scale, Kazakhstan, Tajikistan, Kyrgyzstan, and Turkmenistan are the parties to the United Nations Economic Commission for Europe's (UNECE) Convention on Long-Range Trans-boundary Air Pollution.

Energy and the Environment

It has gradually been recognized that the current use of fossil fuels should be coupled with the development of more environmentally friendly energy alternatives such as solar, wind, geothermal, and small-scale hydropower. Presently, the proportion of electricity produced using nonfossil fuels varies from zero in Turkmenistan to about 15 percent in Kazakhstan and Uzbekistan, and more than 90 percent in Tajikistan and Kyrgyzstan (EEA and ETUC 2007, 24–25). Despite the current lack of renewables as an active part of their energy program, Kazakhstan, Uzbekistan, and Turkmenistan have great potential for their development. Regulatory frameworks to support the development of renewable energy, however, are largely absent or inadequate. Only Kazakhstan (2009) and Kyrgyzstan (2008) have adopted laws on renewable energy sources. Currently, the United Nations Development Programme (UNDP) is assisting Turkmenistan

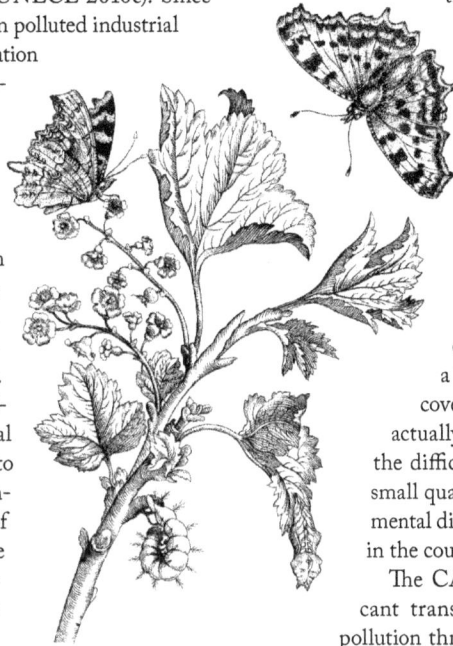

in introducing legislation on renewable energy. The development of extensive nonfossil-fuel potential in Tajikistan and Kyrgyzstan remains problematic due to the countries' focus on large-scale hydropower development, which might generate negative transboundary environmental impacts and is already causing increased tensions between these countries and their downstream neighbors, who view such developments as a threat to their water security.

The CARs also participate in the UN Framework Convention on Climate Change (UNFCCC), an international policy response to climate change, as non-Annex I (developing) countries. This is with the exception of Kazakhstan, which has upgraded its status to become an Annex I (developed) country for the purpose of the Kyoto Protocol. The countries established a legislative and regulative framework to meet their commitments and conduct studies concerning greenhouse gas emissions inventories, vulnerability, and mitigation (Perelet 2007).

Environmental Liability and Citizen Enforcement

Environmental legislation in the CARs is backed up by the mechanisms of civil, administrative, and criminal enforcement. The administrative and criminal codes of the countries contain specific chapters on misconduct in the field of environment. The most common punitive action is financial, through fees and fines. All countries, except Turkmenistan, have specialized units responsible for compliance monitoring and administrative enforcement (OECD 2007b).

As in the Soviet era, citizens still seek to redress violations through governmental agencies. Currently, however, a number of instruments at the national, regional, and global levels are available for individuals and the public. Individuals, groups, and the populace as a whole can enforce their environmental rights in domestic courts and submit individual complaints to compliance committees of international conventions. The implementation of the 1998 Aarhus Convention on Access to Information, Public Participation in Decision-Making, and Access to Justice in Environmental Matters, to which Kazakhstan, Kyrgyzstan, Tajikistan, and Turkmenistan are parties, is illustrative in this respect. The Kazakhstan nongovernmental organization (NGO) Green Salvation submitted to the compliance committee of the convention three of four communications alleging noncompliance by Kazakhstan to its obligations under the convention. The compliance committee has supported the communications, and subsequently the convention's Meeting of the Parties (MOP) recommended a range of actions in order to bring the Kazakh government into compliance with the convention. As a step to implement the MOP's decision, Kazakhstan developed a strategy and

adopted a new environmental code and several regulations, including provisions on access to information.

Facing the Future

Since the dissolution of the Soviet Union, many efforts have been made to improve a legal framework for natural resource use and environmental protection in Russia and Central Asia. Progress varies across the countries and policy areas, and significant problems remain in implementing regulatory provisions.

Stronger environmental cooperation between the CARs is essential if the complex web of water, energy, food, and environmental issues is to be resolved. Currently, the CARs have taken steps to strengthen the existing institutional structure and better coordinate their efforts to support effective dialogue between them. In addition, a significant step forward could be made if all countries joined the 2006 Framework Convention on Environmental Protection for Sustainable Development in Central Asia, which lays down a framework to further strengthen regional environmental cooperation. To date, the convention has been signed by Kyrgyzstan, Tajikistan, and Turkmenistan, and has not been entered into force. Overall, more focus on implementation and compliance with regulatory provisions at national, regional, and international levels should be a priority for the CARs in order to ensure more effective protection of the region's fragile resources.

Irina KRASNOVA
Moscow State Academy of Law

Dinara ZIGANSHINA
University of Dundee

Bakhtiyor R. MUKHAMMADIEV
United States Embassy, Tashkent

Note: the United States Government would like it to be known that "the views expressed in this article are solely those of the authors and do not represent the views of the United States Government."

See also in the *Berkshire Encyclopedia of Sustainability* Development, Sustainable—Overview of Laws and Commissions; Enforcement; Environmental Law—Europe; International Law; Natural Resources Law; Water Security

FURTHER READINGS

Asian Development Bank (ADB). (2008). Land degradation in Central Asia. Retrieved November 16, 2010, from http://www.adb.org/Documents/CACILM/Land-Degradation-CentralAsia.pdf
Constitution of the Russian Federation (adopted 12 December 1993, entered into force 25 December 1993). Retrieved November 29, 2010, from http://www.constitution.ru/en/10003000-01.htm

European Environmental Bureau (EEA) & European Trade Union Confederation (ETUC). (2007). *Sustainable consumption and production in South East Europe and Eastern Europe, Caucasus and Central Asia*. Copenhagen: EEA/UNEP.

Food and Agriculture Organization of the United Nations (FAO). (2005). EarthTrends data tables: Freshwater resources 2005. Retrieved November 16, 2010, from http://earthtrends.wri.org/pdf_library/data_tables/wat2_2005.pdf

Maplecroft. (2010). Water security risk index 2010. Retrieved August 9, 2010, from http://www.maplecroft.com/about/news/water-security.html

Ministry of Energy of the Russian Federation. (2010). Energy strategy of Russia for the period up to 2030, approved 13 November 2009. Retrieved November 16, 2010, from http://energystrategy.ru/projects/docs/ES-2030_(Eng).pdf

Ministry of Natural Resources, Russia. (2006). Report on the state of the environment.

Organisation for Economic Co-operation and Development (OECD). (2007a). *Policies for a better environment: Progress in Eastern Europe, Caucasus and Central Asia*. Brussels, Belgium: OECD

Organisation for Economic Co-operation and Development (OECD). (2007b). *Progress in modernising environmental regulation and compliance assurance in Eastern Europe, Caucasus, and Central Asia*. Brussels, Belgium: OECD.

Perelet, Renat. (2007). *Central Asia: Background paper on climate change* (Human Development Report Office Occasional Paper No. 2007/11). New York: UNDP.

Roshydromet [Federal Service for Hydrometeorology and Environmental Monitoring]. (2006). Annual review. Retrieved November 29, 2010, from http://meteo.ru/english/publish/review-2006.pdf

Severskiy, I., et al. (2005). *Global international waters assessment: Aral Sea* (GIWA Regional assessment 24). Kalmar, Sweden: University of Kalmar / United Nations Environment Programme (UNEP).

United Nations Economic Commission for Europe (UNECE). (2004). *Environmental performance review of Tajikistan*. New York and Geneva: United Nations.

United Nations Economic Commission for Europe (UNECE). (2010a). *Environmental performance review of Kazakhstan: Second Review, October 2008*. New York and Geneva: United Nations.

United Nations Economic Commission for Europe (UNECE). (2010b). *Environmental performance review of Kyrgyzstan: Second Review, October 2009*. New York and Geneva: United Nations.

United Nations Economic Commission for Europe (UNECE). (2010c). *Environmental performance review of Uzbekistan: Second Review, April 2010*. New York and Geneva: United Nations.

United Nations Economic and Social Commission for Asia and the Pacific (UNESCAP). (2007). *Assessment of progress on mitigating and reversing desertification and land degradation processes, and implications for land management in the changing context of the ESCAP region with special reference to the Asia Pacific countries*. Jakarta, Indonesia: UNESCAP.

United Nations Environment Programme (UNEP). (2006). *Appraisal reports on priority ecological problems in Central Asia*. Ashgabad, Turkmenistan: UNEP.

United Nations Environment Programme (UNEP). (2009). *Turkmenistan—The state of the environment (draft)*. Ashgabad, Turkmenistan: UNEP.

World Bank. (2010). Data by country. Retrieved November 29, 2010, from http://data.worldbank.org

World Health Organization (WHO) & United Nations Children's Fund (UNICEF). (2010). *Progress on sanitation and drinking-water: 2010 Update*. Geneva: WHO/UNICEF.

Environmental Law– South America

A strong focus on environmental protection, especially as linked to human rights, has become a prominent part of legislation around the world. Various countries in South America, including Argentina, Brazil, Chile, Colombia, and Venezuela, have all committed to guidelines and legal requirements for environmental protection. Their continued efforts and presence in the international community will help to strengthen the global environmental protection movement.

The enforcement of sustainable development through various pieces of legislation has evolved across the globe, including South America. Agreements, controversies, and legislative developments have all contributed to the field of environmental law in South America. These factors have largely resulted in the creation of firm guidelines for environmental protection, as well as specific legislation addressing the myriad environmental issues faced by nations throughout South America. The importance of environmental protection can clearly be seen in the constitutions of countries such as Argentina, Brazil, Chile, Colombia, and Venezuela, among others, where the environment is protected as a branch of human rights.

Argentina

Argentina is a federal system based on continental law. This means that it is founded on the superiority of a federal core of written legislation, rather than judicial precedents as is common law. Written law, both federal and provincial, must be applied on a case-by-case basis. Consequently, tribunals can decide on their own understanding, even when they contradict Supreme Court decisions, and their judgments will eventually be modified. Though there have not been many opportunities to apply the new directives

judicially, Argentina might have problems standardizing the application of environmental norms and reacting quickly to environmental situations where timing is essential.

Since the 1972 UN Conference on Human Environment in Stockholm, the need to protect the environment as a condition for human well-being has been acknowledged and developed by the international community. In 1994, Argentina introduced in its federal Constitution the right to a healthy environment, that is, an environment where both unpolluted nature (e.g., clean soil, air, water) and fulfilled socioeconomic needs coexist in harmony. The laws that supplement the Constitution, however, do not include concrete definitions for sustainable development principles. As opposed to European environmental legislation, such as European Parliament Directive 2004/35/CE on environmental liability, which specifically defines environmental damage and creates strict parameters to determine both liabilities and remedies, Argentina's definition of environmental damage is vague and broad, giving rise to a large range of interpretation and uncertainty. Progress made in the realm of environmental protection led to the amendment of the Argentine Constitution, but only recently has jurisprudence grown and the Supreme Court become deeply involved.

Industrial development and the evidence of climate change led to the broadening of environmental law. After the 1994 constitutional reform, eighteen international treaties were ratified, and eleven substantial environmental laws and regulations were enacted, including the Protocol for the Environmental Protection of the Antarctic Territory, the International Treaty on Substances that Affect the Ozone Layer, and the General Law on the Protection of the Argentine Environment, its Waters and Native Forests.

These laws have provided environmental principles generating diverse obligations. Some examples include conducting environmental impact assessments (EIAs) prior to performing any activity that may adversely affect the environment, implementing environmental insurance policies and mandatory regulations related to the handling of hazardous materials and waste, and requiring company disclosure of its compliance with environmental regulations.

One of the most controversial regulations is the strict liability regime applied to environmental contamination. Civil environmental liability is a noncontractual, objective liability that imposes the responsibility of remediating any damages upon the owner of a potentially dangerous object or practice, unless the damage was caused by a third, unrelated party or the consequences of such damage were inevitable. Criminal liability may also apply to directors, managers, statutory auditors, and other key employees. Regulatory aspects and environmental risk management have become important factors in preventing liabilities.

Although there have been very few judicial precedents displaying trends on environmental protection, this may be changing. For example, in 2006 the Supreme Court made a judgment on the polluted Matanza-Riachuelo River Basin—perhaps the greatest environmental contamination area in Argentina—taking a clear stance that might set environmental criteria for future cases. The case, *Mendoza, Beatriz S. y otros c. Estado Nacional y otros (Fallos 329:2316)*, addressed the more than fifteen thousand industrial subjects polluting one of the most populated areas in Argentina. The court required the state and forty-four enterprises to take action; the latter had to provide information on the materials they poured into the river while the former was impelled to create a plan to clean the basin, starting with EIAs and the creation of a registry for polluting agents.

In order to ensure future generations a healthy environment, Argentina's challenge seems to reside in broadening its legislation as well as strengthening the enforcement of environmental regulations through more specific legislation and a firm commitment from all the parties involved.

Brazil

In Brazil, environmental protection is reflected in the Brazilian Constitution of 1988, which dedicated a special chapter to environmental issues, providing general guidance for environmental policies in the country. The Constitution established the right to an ecologically balanced environment and imposed on both public authorities and the Brazilian people the duty to defend and preserve the environment for future generations. This focus on environmental protection was new; previous constitutions did not specifically address environmental protection, though there were some provisions concerning the environment.

One of the key events in Brazilian environmental law history was the enactment of Federal Law No. 6938 of 31 August 1981. This statute formally established a national environmental policy; prior to 1981, only a loose collection of separate rules had existed. Among the important innovations brought by the 1981 legislation were the establishment of strict liability for polluters (i.e., responsibility regardless of knowledge, fault, or degree of intent) and of the role of federal and state district attorneys in suing polluters for environmental harm. The powers of the district attorneys were further strengthened by the Public Civil Action Law (Federal Law No. 7347 of 24 July 1985), which is similar to American class action law, and the Consumer Code (Federal Law No. 8078 of 11 September 1990), which provided the classification for diffuse rights, rendering the provisions of environmental legislation more effective. The Public Civil Action Law also grants district attorneys and other environmental authorities the possibility of executing consent agreements with polluting individuals.

Consent agreement is a negotiated agreement usually reached between district attorneys and offenders in order to cease certain practices and/or provide the appropriate remediation of the environmental damage. Alternative sanctions are also a possibility in consent agreements (i.e., instead of paying a fine, offenders may provide equipment to environmental authorities). This measure appears to be very effective in protecting the environment. In addition, Federal Law No. 9605 of 12 February 1998 focused on environmental crimes and administrative infractions, framing a number of activities as a crime or infraction against the environment and providing district attorneys, environmental protection agencies, courts, and the Brazilian public an instrument to identify which sanctions must be applied to environmentally harmful activities.

In the agribusiness sector, the Forestry Code has shown great potential in the area of environmental protection. Brazilian rural properties are subject to the provisions of the Forestry Code (Federal Law No. 4771/65). Among other provisions, the Forestry Code creates permanent preservation areas where no production activity can be conducted. Furthermore, the code also provides percentages of land on individual properties to be preserved for environmental purposes. The Forestry Code and its provisions have caused debates between farmers and environmentalists and currently can be considered the main focus of discussion in the realm of Brazilian environmental law.

Brazil has always played a major role on the international environmental stage, and its engagement in the worldwide concern about the environment has a well-established background. Its concern was evident in the country's proactive participation in the UN Environment and Development Conference, held in Rio de Janeiro in June 1992. Because of its size, its rapidly growing economy, and the fact that a vast share of its territory is covered by forest, Brazil has been and will likely continue to be a key player in the ongoing climate negotiations.

Chile

In 1980, Chile's political Constitution, for the first time, recognized the importance of protecting the environment as part of the state's duty to promote welfare. The Constitution guarantees all people the "right to live in an environment free of pollution." It adds, "the State is duty bound to assure that such rights not be affected and to care for the conservation of nature."

The constitutionally guaranteed right to a pollution-free environment potentially conflicts with other constitutional rights, such as the right to engage in economic activity or the right to property. One example is the mining industry, where the production process may have environmental consequences. In this regard, the Constitution provides that a basic constitutional right may be limited for environmental reasons only by law (i.e., not by any hierarchically inferior norm), and then only to the extent that the limitation does not affect the essence of the right.

Law No. 19300 on General Environmental Guidelines (LBGMA is its Spanish acronym), which had been passed by Congress in January 1994, was published in the *Official Gazette* on 9 March 1994. This body of law filled a very important gap in the legal order of the country, resulting in a structured environmental regulatory system. This law governs a series of conflictive interests, based on the premise that no activity, regardless of how legitimate it may be, can be developed at the cost of harming the environment.

The LBGMA law does not intend to cover all matters related to the environment, and special laws are required to govern areas that have particular complexity. Rather this law, as its name indicates, is comprised of a set of general guidelines. It created a framework, wherein an ordering process of existing and future environmental legislation takes place.

The LBGMA law governs, on a quite exhaustive basis, the environmental impact assessment systems of public and private investment projects or activities, notwithstanding the regulations that must be dictated for the system to become effective. Projects or activities indicated by the law may only be executed or modified with the prior assessment of their environmental impact. Additionally, all environmental permits or rulings, which according to the current legislation may be issued by state agencies, are granted through the environmental impact assessment system (SEIA is its Spanish acronym).

The law also creates a system integrating all of the sectoral environmental requirements. This is known as a "single-window" system, where all procedures are received by a single institution. Such a system is materialized via the coordination exercised by the relevant Regional Environmental Commission (COREMA is its Spanish acronym) or by the National Commission for the Environment (CONAMA is its Spanish acronym), where applicable. A resolution certifies whether the project or activity complies with all applicable environmental regulations and additionally indicates the conditions under which the specific permits will be granted during project implementation, including prospective research and restoration works. If the assessment is favorable, no state agency may deny the relevant environmental authorizations; on the other hand, if the ruling is negative, such state agencies must deny them. Relevant environmental resolutions handed down by COREMA or CONAMA are based on the opinion that the respective state agencies have on the environmental acceptability, resulting from the revision they make of the relevant EIA documents. Such assessments are conducted through an environmental impact statement (DIA is its Spanish acronym) or by an environmental impact study (EIA is its Spanish acronym).

Chile has made a great progress in its environmental legislation, especially with the introduction of the Superintendency of the Environment and the Environmental Assessment Agency, two institutions that will raise the standards of environmental protection in that country.

Colombia

The Colombian legal system is based on civil law, which has written, codified laws as the foundation for all legal matters, as opposed to the dependence on judicial precedents in the common law system. The Colombian Constitution is developed through laws enacted by Congress and regulated through presidential decrees and the resolutions of ministries and other agencies. Under the Colombian Constitution and the law, natural resources must be utilized without harming the cultural, social, and economic integrity of the indigenous and Afro-Colombian communities. Decisions regarding environmental matters require prior consultation with representatives of these communities.

The Colombian focus on environmental issues began in the 1970s, after the 1972 Stockholm Conference. The Natural Resources Code was enacted in 1974, resulting in a system of national parks and protected areas; a system for permits; and concessions to oversee the organized use of water sources and the disposal of waste, discharges, and emissions. This code is divided into two large sections, and when it was originally enacted, it was a catch-all of environment regulation. The first section is divided into four subsections: definitions, mechanisms of environmental policy, international environmental problems, and environmental preservation regulations. The second section addresses property and the use of natural resources. In Latin America, the 1974 Code was the first of its kind to be issued (González Villa 2006). In addition to the code, the 1991 Constitution provided that all persons are entitled to a healthy environment and that the state must prevent damages to the environment and pursue legal action when damages have been caused.

Law 99/1993 created the Ministry of the Environment to protect the environment and required environmental licenses for projects or activities that could materially affect the environment. This ministry was then merged with another to create the Environmental, Housing and Territorial Development Ministry. Under current regulations, there are three main environmental authorities. The first is the Environmental, Housing and Territorial Development Ministry, which defines the policies and regulations concerning renewable natural resources and the environment in order to guarantee sustainable development. Second are the Regional Autonomous and Sustainable Development Corporations, known as the CARs, which are in charge of managing, within the area of their jurisdiction, the environment and the renewable natural resources to sustain development. Territorial entities integrating the different CARs are determined on the basis of their geographic characteristics, such as the formation of a geopolitical, biogeographical, or hydrogeographical unit, or having the same ecosystems. Third are the Great Urban Centers for municipalities, districts, and metropolitan areas with more than 1 million inhabitants. These have the faculty to grant licenses, concessions, permits, and authorizations, the issuance of which is attributed to the relevant CAR. A law allowing civil and class actions also provides incentive to sue when damages to the environment are caused by private parties or by the state.

One of the major legal discussions in Colombia is the burden of proof in environmental damages. In civil law, the aggrieved party must prove the existence of a damage, determine who caused the damage, and demonstrate that the person or party was actually at fault for causing that damage. Environmental regulation has been moving toward more objective criteria, where negligence is assumed to exist by law if damage has been caused to the environment (Law 1333/2009, Art. 5, Para. 1). Another discussion is the compensation for environmental damages. Current regulation provides the guidelines to value damages as a result of harm to the environment.

Colombia is included within the list of megadiverse countries, and it has to balance the country's development with the protection of its resources. One example of this conflict is a 2010 amendment to the Mining Code as it prohibited mining in *páramos* (high elevation areas above the tree line but below the permanent snow line) because these areas are essential for Colombia's water supply (Procuraduría General de la Nación 2008). Another example is a general complaint that major infrastructure projects are unnecessarily delayed by environmental authorities (*Diario La República* 2010).

Venezuela

The Bolivarian Republic of Venezuela has a civil law legal system. As a consequence, all legal regulations, including environmental issues, are governed by the principles set forth in the Constitution and laws of Venezuela. Matters concerning the environment are mainly regulated by the Venezuelan Constitution, which recognizes the existence of environmental rights and establishes general principles to govern activities that may cause damage to the environment. Several laws, such as the Organic Law of the Environment (OLE) and the Criminal Law of the Environment, regulate the activities that may damage the environment as well as the sanctions applicable to individuals or legal entities in the event of breach of environmental regulations.

Environmental matters are further regulated by the Ministry of the Popular Power for the Environment (MARN is its Spanish acronym), which was established by the OLE. MARN is the competent body to authorize, on a case-by-case basis, the performance of activities that are potentially damaging to the environment, as long as such activities produce benefits for the country and cause only reparable damages.

Additionally, there are several other laws and regulations concerning specific issues regarding the conservation of the environment, such as the regulations for the use of land and water and the disposal of waste and hazardous materials. One example of such a law is the 2007 Waters Law, which set forth the manner in which natural water resources, such as rivers and lakes, may be used for commercial and industrial activities.

Venezuela has also played an active role in international environmental issues. In 2009, Venezuela executed five cooperation agreements and several bilateral agreements regarding the use of water, environmental regulations, productive reforestation, and territorial occupation. Also, Venezuela actively participated in the Fifteenth Conference of the Parties of the UN Framework Convention on Climate Change, which took place in 2009 in Copenhagen, Denmark.

Environmental regulations in Venezuela have existed for over two decades. For example, MARN has recognized that two of the key aspects for improving the enforcement of environmental regulations in Venezuela are the environmental education of the population and the better distribution of the population within the territory. Unfortunately, these education campaigns and urban planning projects have not reached the majority of the population.

Continuing Improvement

Many South American countries have significant legal instruments to protect and monitor the environment adequately. Countries including Argentina, Brazil, Chile, Colombia, and Venezuela are also concerned with the development of further instruments, some of them very strict, to ensure environmental protection. Recent developments in environmental legislation point to a trend of more stringent requirements and more aggressive and systematic enforcement actions. The enforcement of such laws and regulations, however, still must be improved; enforcement may be even more effective if it results from both domestic and international efforts.

Renata Campetti AMARAL
Baker & McKenzie, São Paulo

Alejandra BUGNA
Baker & McKenzie, Buenos Aires

Gustavo BORUCHOWICZ
Baker & McKenzie, Buenos Aires

Alessandro De Franceschi DA CRUZ
Baker & McKenzie, Porto Alegre, Brazil

Antonio ORTUZAR, Jr.
Baker & McKenzie, Santiago

María Eugenia REYES
Baker & McKenzie, Caracas

María Victoria ROMERO
Baker & McKenzie, Caracas

Cristina RUEDA
Baker & McKenzie, Bogotá

See also in the *Berkshire Encyclopedia of Sustainability* Development, Sustainable—Overview of Laws and Commissions; Environmental Law—Central America and the Caribbean; Environmental Law, Soft vs. Hard; International Law; National Environmental Policy Act; United Nations—Overview of Conventions and Agreements

FURTHER READINGS

Amado Gutiérrez, Luis. (2006). *La gestión penal del ambiente: El sector privado y la experiencia a diez años* [Criminal management of the environment: The private sector and ten years of experience]. Caracas, Venezuela: Publicaciones UCAB.

Argentinean Secretariat of Environment and Sustainable Development. (2010). Homepage. Retrieved September 22, 2010, from http://www.ambiente.gov.ar/

Ball, Philip. (2000). *Life's matrix: A biography of water.* Berkeley: University of California Press.

De Benedectis, Leonardo. (2005). La responsabilidad ambiental en la Unión Europea: Análisis comparativo de la directiva 2004/35 CE y la normativa argentina [Environmental liability in the European Union: Comparative analysis of the Directive CE 2004/35 and the Argentinean legislation]. *Revista de Derecho Ambiental, 3.*

de Bessa Antunes, Paulo. (2008). *Direito ambiental* [Environmental law]. Rio de Janeiro: Lumen Juris.

Brazil Ministry of the Environment. (2010). Homepage. Retrieved September 22, 2010, from http://www.mma.gov.br/sitio/

Brazil Ministry of Science and Technology. (2010). Homepage. Retrieved September 22, 2010, from http://www.mct.gov.br/index.php/content/view/77650.html

Conesa Fernandez-Vitora, Vicen. (2010). Guia metodologica para la evaluacion del impacto ambiental [Methodology guide for environmental impact assessment (4th ed.)]. Madrid, Spain: Mundi-prensa.

Diario La República [Journal of the Republic]. (2010, March 23). Proyectos frenados por licencias ambientales [Environmental licenses halt projects]. Retrieved November 27, 2010, from http://www.larepublica.com.co/archivos/RSE/2010-03-25/proyectos-frenados-por-licencias-ambientales_96331.php

European Parliament. (2004). Directive 2004/35/CE on environmental liability. Retrieved September 22, 2010, from http://eur-lex.europa.eu/LexUriServ/LexUriServ.do?uri=CELEX:32004L0035:en:NOT

Flores Garnica, José Germán. (2006). Impacto ambiental de incendios forestales [Environmental impact of forest fires]. México City, Mexico: Mundi-Prensa.

Gonzalez Velasco, Jaime. (2009). *Energías renovables* [Renewable energy]. Barcelona, Spain: Reverté.

González Villa, Julio Enrique. (2006). Derecho ambiental Colombiano [Colombian environmental law]. Bogotá: Universidad del Externado de Colombia

González Villa, Julio Enrique. (2007). La indemnización dentro de los procesos de acciones populares por daños al ambiente [Compensations in class-action law suits for environmental damages]. In *El Daño Ambiental: Vol. 1* [Environmental Damage]. Bogotá: Universidad del Externado de Colombia.

Gore, Al. (2009). *Our choice: A plan to solve the climate crisis.* Emmaus, PA: Rodale Books.

Government of Chile. (2010). National Commission for the Environment. Retrieved September 22, 2010, from http://www.conama.cl

Macías Gómez, Luis Fernando. (1998). *Introducción al derecho ambiental* [Introduction to environmental law]. Bogotá, Columbia: Legis Editores S.A.

Milaré, Édis. (2007). *Direito do ambiente: A gestão ambiental em foco* [Law of the environment: Environmental management in focus]. São Paulo, Brazil: Revista dos Tribunais.

Mollar, Marcos Nelio. (2009). La protección internacional del medio ambiente como derecho humano [The international protection of the environment as a human right]. *Revista de Derecho Ambiental, 19.*

Morato Leite, José Rubens, & de Araújo Ayala, Patryck. (2010). *Dano ambiental: Do individual ao coletivo extrapatrimonial— Teoria e prática* [Environmental damage: From the individual to the collective extrapatrimonial—Theory and practice]. São Paulo, Brazil: Revista dos Tribunais.

Procuradoría General de la Nación [Attorney General's Office]. (2008). Situación de los páramos en Colombia frente a la actividad antrópica y el cambio climático [The situation of Colombian *páramos* vis-à-vis anthropic activity and climate change]. Retrieved November 27, 2010, from http://www.humboldt.org.co/chmcolombia/download/libro4.pdf

Rodas Monsalve, Julio César. (2001). *Constitución y derecho ambiental: Principios y acciones constitucionales para la defensa del ambiente* [The Constitution and environmental law: Constitutional principles and actions for protecting the environment]. Bogotá, Colombia: Cargraphics.

Torrente Bayona, César, & Acosta Irreño, Óscar David. (1996). Marco jurídico del derecho ambiental en Colombia [Legal frame of environmental law in Colombia]. Bogotá: Ministry of the Environment of Colombia and Bogotá Chamber of Commerce.

Universidad Externado de Colombia. (2005–2007). *Lecturas sobre derecho del medio ambiente* [Readings on environmental law]. Bogotá: Universidad Externado de Colombia.

Venezuelan Ministry of the People's Power for Environment. (2010). Homepage. Retrieved September 22, 2010, from http://www.minamb.gob.ve

Yarrow, Joanna. (2009). *Eco-Logical: Join the debate!* London: Duncan Baird Publishers.

Zapata Lugo, José Vicente. (1997). *Desarrollo sostenible: Marco para la ley internacional sobre el medio ambiente—Legislación y lineamientos internacionales* [Sustainable development: Framework for international law on the environment—Legislation and international guidelines]. Bogotá, Colombia: Ediciones Librería del Profesional.

Environmental Law— Southeast Asia

The eleven nations in Southeast Asia have undergone rapid development in the past fifty years, which has resulted too often in unchecked pollution and exploitation of natural resources. Most have established governmental departments for the environment, and environmental legislation has been enacted in most countries, with variable success. The Association for Southeast Asian Nations also endorses cooperative activities to address many regional environmental issues.

Southeast Asia's geographic diversity makes it home to some of the most important ecosystems in the world. Since the 1960s, however, much of the region has undergone rapid industrialization, leading to pollution and resource exploitation, but enforcement of environmental laws still suffers from corruption and insufficient public interest litigation. Rather than discuss all eleven countries in Southeast Asia, this article will instead focus on those that readers will most likely encounter through the practice or study of comparative environmental law. Information on the other countries can be found in the Further Readings listed below.

Indonesia

The highest source of law in Indonesia is the 1945 Constitution. General authority to regulate environmental matters has been delegated to the State Minister of Environment. The Regional Autonomy Law of 1999 (amended in 2004), however, grants regional governments broader authority to manage certain matters as specified in the Regional Autonomy regulations, including mining, environmental matters, environmental quality standards, forestry, and local area planning.

Recently the national parliament (*Dewan Perwakilan Rakyat,* or People's Representative Council) passed a new Environmental Protection and Management Law (Environmental Law No. 32 of 2009), which replaced the previous law (No. 23 of 1997). The law mandates that any business or activity that has an environmental or social impact must prepare and maintain Environmental Impact Analysis (AMDAL) documents, which consist of an environmental impact assessment (ANDAL), an environmental management plan (RKL), and an environmental monitoring plan (RPL). If the AMDAL documents are not required, the proponent of such business/activities must still prepare environmental management effort (UKL) and environmental control effort (UPL) documents.

The AMDAL or UKL/UPL documents must be submitted to the relevant environmental offices for approval or any recommendations. Once granted, they must be submitted to the environment minister, governor, or regent/mayor as appropriate to obtain an environmental permit. An environmental permit is a prerequisite to any relevant business/activities permits. It can be revoked if, for instance, the permit holder does not satisfy the obligations in the AMDAL or UKL/UPL, or upon the order of the State Administrative Court.

Under the environmental law, all environmental permit holders must set aside funds to be used as a type of environmental bond. The funds must be deposited in a government bank as stipulated by the environment minister, governor, or regent/mayor. The law also requires the proponent of activities that have high environmental risks to carry out periodic environmental audits. Any central or local government official who grants an environmental permit without following the proper procedures is subject to penalties under the statute.

This environmental law grants third parties and individual persons the right to file reports on alleged environmental pollution/damage to the relevant environmental officer. Local communities and environmental nongovernmental organizations (NGOs) also have the right to file class action suits if the community suffers a loss caused by the environmental pollution/damage. The community may recover pecuniary compensation for such losses, while environmental NGOs can only seek remediation of the pollution/damage. Persons or NGOs working on behalf of the right to a proper and healthy environment by legal means will not be liable to any criminal charges or civil claims.

Myanmar (Burma)

Myanmar (formerly Burma) has been ruled by the military since 1962. In 1988, the military cracked down on prodemocracy protests and formed a new military junta, which rejected the former government's socialist policies. In 1994, private businesses were allowed to operate, which led to a rush for the country's natural resources, particularly forestry, gems, and fisheries. Less than twenty years later, many forests are already empty, and commercial fisheries have polluted the rivers.

For a long time, the Myanmar government took little action with regard to environmental law; the country still lacks a general environmental framework. But in 2008, category-four Cyclone Nargis struck the country, killing over 138,000 people and destroying thousands of homes. The damage was exacerbated by deforestation and pollution in waterways, which forced the junta to recognize the importance of environmental protection. It has since required universities to teach environmental studies and law courses. Even so, the country lacks lawyers who study or practice environmental law. There are also no environmental law NGOs.

Myanmar does not have a separate ministry dedicated to environmental protection. Its National Commission for Environmental Affairs (NCEA) is based in the Ministry of Foreign Affairs. The NCEA is not geared toward law enforcement or handling environmental conflicts; rather it grew out of the government's participation in international environmental conferences.

Under the new 2008 Constitution, the Union government, not the states, will have jurisdiction over environmental protection. The constitutional principles state that the government shall protect the natural environment, although, given the military's control over the legal system, the constitution will most likely not be enforceable in court.

The Philippines

Under the 1987 Constitution, the Philippines has three independent branches of government: a presidential executive, a bicameral legislature, and a judiciary led by the Supreme Court. Furthermore, local government units (LGUs), such as provinces, cities, and *barangay* (villages), operate with a wide degree of autonomy. Laws define rights and obligations of persons, corporations, and government, although court decisions also set binding precedents.

In its Declaration of Principles, section 16 of the Constitution mandates the state to "protect and advance the right of the people to a balanced and healthful ecology in accord with the rhythm and harmony of nature." In 1993, the Supreme Court held that this was an immediately demandable right, without need for enabling legislation (*Oposa v. Factoran*). This right is complemented by several provisions on the right to health, public participation, access to information, social justice, and respect for indigenous peoples' rights.

Environmental laws passed by Congress over the last two decades encompass the whole range of environmental issues, including clean air and water, waste management, and protected areas and wildlife management. Since 2008, new legislation has focused on climate change and disaster risk management. Other trends in national environmental law and policy include increasing the role of LGUs, wider public participation in decision making, and an ecosystem/integrated approach to addressing environmental issues.

The Supreme Court has been a key catalyst in enhancing environmental justice. In *Oposa,* the Court recognized the right of future generations to demand action to conserve natural resources for their (future) benefit. In the 2008 case of *Metro Manila Development Authority v. Concerned Residents of Manila Bay,* the Supreme Court went as far as ordering the responsible agencies to clean up Manila Bay to a specific standard, in the process creating an advisory

committee composed of leading environmental experts to ensure compliance until the environmental standard is met. In 2000, the Court upheld the constitutionality of the Indigenous Peoples Rights Act, which recognized the right of indigenous peoples to decide on resource extractive activities within their ancestral domains (*Cruz v. National Commission on Indigenous Peoples*).

In 2007, the Supreme Court designated 117 trial courts to hear environmental cases. In 2010, it promulgated special rules for environmental cases, which introduced two new special civil actions:

- The writ of *kalikasan* (nature) allows NGOs to sue on behalf of affected parties and obtain an environmental protection order.
- The writ of continuing mandamus compels agencies or officials to perform their duty until the environmental objective is achieved.

The Integrated Bar of the Philippines (the official national organization of lawyers) has also organized on behalf of environmental justice. It has created a National Environmental Action Team to provide legal services in environmental cases. Its current efforts include filing actions to compel LGUs to comply with requirements on waste management and natural resource conservation. Public-interest environmental law practice is vibrant in the Philippines. The leading legal NGOs are Tanggol Kalikasan (Defend Nature) and the Environmental Legal Assistance Center. Filipino lawyers also play important roles in international negotiations and implementation of multilateral environmental agreements (MEAs).

The Philippines has played a key role in negotiating multilateral environmental agreements—for example, speaking on behalf of the Group of 77 (an intergovernmental group of developing nations) and China and facilitating the committee formulating proposals for reducing emissions from deforestation and forest degradation under the UN Framework Convention on Climate Change.

Singapore

Singapore inherited a common law system and parliamentary democracy from Great Britain. This tiny island state has progressed from third world to first world in just a few decades, whilst cleaning up its environment. It prides itself as a "City in a Garden." Its air and water quality are consistently well within World Health Organization standards. Much of this success is due to effective and visionary leadership. The same political party that won the first election has governed the state since independence in 1959.

Singapore's environmental management policies were, at the outset, integrated with the economic policies. Cleaning up, greening, and protecting the environment were indeed a major part of Singapore's strategies for success since, as stated by its first prime minister, Lee Kuan Yew, "in wooing investors, even trees matter." An excellent public housing system was developed, which today houses 85 percent of the population, most of whom own their apartment on ninety-nine-year leases. The city is now 100 percent sewered, which has contributed substantially in the reduction of water pollution. Singapore overcame its water shortage through careful planning and sound investments in water technology, and it has become a leader in effective water management and governance.

Singapore has also pioneered innovative measures including environmental taxation to control pollution and to reduce the use of motor vehicles. It was one of the first countries to implement the polluter pays principle and introduce congestion road pricing (i.e., electronic toll collection to discourage traffic during peak periods). It also requires all owners of motor vehicles to first purchase a Certificate of Entitlement (COE) before the vehicle can be used on the road. COEs last only ten years and can cost as much as the price of the vehicle. The Income Tax Act grants a 100 percent allowance on capital expenditures for the installation of pollution-control or energy-efficiency equipment. Perhaps most famously, littering—which courts have construed as a strict liability offense—incurs a fine of S$1,000 or a Corrective Work Order (in which the offender must clean up a specific location).

While much of Singapore's natural landscape was converted for development, the government also established nature reserves, national parks, and bird sanctuaries to increase green areas and enhance biodiversity. Singapore is a responsible party to many international conventions, including the Convention on Biological Diversity (CBD). It is now taking steps to reintroduce native plant species and has initiated the Cities Biodiversity Index to measure the biodiversity of cities, which will be presented for endorsement by the CBD parties at the tenth Conference of the Parties (COP 10) of the CBD in Nagoya, Japan, in October 2010.

Singapore has fostered a very livable environment through effective environmental laws. These include the Environmental Protection and Management Act; the Environmental Public Health Act; Hazardous Waste (Import, Export and Transit) Act; Endangered Species (Import and Export) Act; Parks and Trees Act; Sewerage and Drainage Act and the Prevention of Pollution from the Sea Act; as well as subsidiary regulations and soft laws, such as various Codes of Practice and Guidelines.

Thailand

While never colonized, Thailand patterned its legal system on European civil law. The country is a parliamentary democracy, albeit subject to heavy military and business influence. The judiciary is divided into justice, administrative, and military courts. The 1997 Constitution separated the judiciary from the Ministry of Justice and created a Constitutional Court. After a military coup in 2006, that constitution was replaced by a new one in 2007, but this did not change the structure of the judiciary.

The Enhancement and Conservation of National Environmental Quality Act of 1992 established a National Environmental Board (NEB) and an Environmental Fund. The NEB advises the government on policy and prescribes environmental quality standards. The fund provides grants or loans for pollution abatement technologies to local governments or businesses.

In 2005, the Supreme Court of Justice created a separate environmental division with thirteen justices to reduce backlog in environmental adjudication. The court has adopted the precautionary principle and waives court fees for indigents. The judiciary also created an environmental Court of Appeal and is expected to introduce lower-level environmental courts soon. These courts do not handle environmental suits seeking judicial review, which is the exclusive purview of separate Administrative or Constitutional Courts.

The 2007 Constitution plays a crucial role in promoting an awareness of people's rights to participate with the government or communities in preservation and management of natural resources. Most importantly, Section 67 ensures the protection of environment by prohibiting any project likely to have a serious environmental impact, unless (1) an environmental impact assessment (EIA) and health impact assessment (HIA) have been undertaken, (2) a public hearing has been held, and (3) an independent advisory body, comprised of environmental and health experts from private organizations and educational institutions, has provided comments.

On 2 December 2009, the Supreme Administrative Court ordered the suspension of operating permits for seventy-six investment projects in the Map Ta Phut industrial estate in Rayong Province, on the grounds of failure to comply with EIA and HIA requirements under Section 67 of the Constitution. The case has received much public attention since then, particularly from international companies that have investment projects in Map Ta Phut. Although the regulation that defines the scope of projects likely to have serious environmental impacts has not yet been adopted, this case marked a significant step in the development of Thai environmental law enforcement.

Environmental law and regulations of Thailand have been progressively developed since an issuance of the Enhancement and Conservation of National Environmental Quality Act, and many regulations establishing water and air quality standards have been adopted under it. In addition, the enforcement of environmental law in Thailand has been strengthened in the recent years, as observed in the Map Ta Phut case. Apart from the laws as mentioned, various provisions regarding the protection of the environment in Thailand can be found under the Factory Act and the regulations adopted thereunder, such as the Notification of the Ministry of Industry Concerning the Management of Industrial Waste and Unused Materials. Moreover, there are a number of notifications of the Ministry of Industry that require factory operators to comply with requirements of protecting environmental quality, such as the Notification of Ministry of Industry Requiring Industrial Factories to Install Additional Equipment for Wastewater and Air Emission Control.

Vietnam

According to Vietnam's 1992 Constitution, all branches are accountable to the National Assembly, which is dominated by the Communist

Party. The Ministry for Natural Resources and Environment (MNRE) handles national terrestrial environmental issues, while the Provincial People's Committees, the executive arm of local government, exercise responsibility for environmental protection within localities under their jurisdiction.

The 2005 Law on Environmental Protection requires developers to prepare an EIA for projects that utilize the land or cause an adverse impact in natural areas. The law also requires individuals or organizations managing or transporting hazardous wastes to obtain a permit; however, it does not determine liability for previously contaminated lands. While individuals and NGOs can bring suits or administrative complaints for infringements of their rights and lawful interests under the law, they generally cannot bring third-party suits.

Land use and property rights have become particularly contentious. In 2003, the National Assembly passed the Law on Land, which reaffirms that all land is the property of the state. Individuals, however, can lease land and obtain a Land Use Registration Certificate in order to protect their interests. Land users must resolve any claims in the civil people's courts; this requirement has led to a backlog of land cases. Indeed, the number of land complaints sent to MNRE nearly tripled from 2004 to 2007, mostly regarding inadequate compensation for takings.

Vietnam's environmental legal framework has progressed considerably since the country began its economic reforms in the early 1990s. In addition to the aforementioned legislation, Vietnam has also recently passed or significantly revised its Law on Water Resources, the 2004 Forest Protection and Development Law, a number of regulations relating to fines for environmental violations, and an environmental protection fund. The government has increasingly tried to decentralize responsibility for environmental protection, which occasionally leads to inconsistent policy implementation. Unfortunately, enforcement remains a critical challenge; over the past five years, Vietnam has become a regional hub for trade in illegal timber and wildlife.

Association of Southeast Asian Nations (ASEAN)

Established by five founding members—Indonesia, Malaysia, the Philippines, Singapore, and Thailand—under the 1967 Bangkok Declaration, ASEAN has since admitted Brunei Darussalam, Cambodia, Laos, Myanmar, and Vietnam. It has also established the ASEAN Plus Three (namely China, Japan, and South Korea) and several "dialogue partners" to enhance its cooperative activities, including those relating to the environment (ASEAN Charter, Article 44). The countries include China, the European Union (EU), India, Japan, New Zealand, South Korea, Russia, the United States, Pakistan, Australia, and Canada. Non-ASEAN member states and relevant intergovernmental organizations may appoint and accredit ambassadors to ASEAN (ASEAN Charter, Article 46). It enjoys observer status in the United Nations.

Since the environment was put on the agenda in 1978, ASEAN has developed numerous environmental instruments, comprising hard (e.g., ASEAN Agreement on Transboundary Haze Pollution [AATHP], 2002) and soft laws (e.g., ASEAN Declaration on Heritage Parks, 2003, and ASEAN Declaration on Environmental Sustainability, 2007). Some of these hard and soft laws have been implemented by ASEAN member states. For example some member states have passed legislation to implement the AATHP, and all ASEAN member states have designated ASEAN Heritage Parks in their respective countries. The scope of its environmental law is comprehensive and straddles the three mutually reinforcing "pillars" or "communities," namely, the ASEAN political-security, economic, and sociocultural communities, with the environment under the third pillar. Certain transboundary issues, such as pandemics (e.g., avian flu) and climate change, however, are under the first pillar so that ASEAN can give its highest priority and mobilize its security measures. Since 2000, transboundary environmental challenges in ASEAN have proven to be anything but static. Their impacts on ecosystems and human security are wide-ranging; a case at hand is climate change and the disasters it could inflict, such as the collapse of fisheries and a rise in sea level, causing Southeast Asia's many island states to disappear or become diminished.

Apart from the general programs, strategies, plans of action, and blueprints, the main sectoral areas include nature and natural resources, forestry, transboundary pollution, water resources management, energy and climate change, and zoonotic diseases. With the ASEAN Charter put into force in December 2008, there is a renewed spirit to work toward timely implementation of 1997's ASEAN Vision 2020, which, inter alia, envisions "a clean and green ASEAN with fully established mechanisms for sustainable development to ensure the protection of the region's environment, the sustainability of its natural resources, and the high quality of life of its peoples" by 2015 instead of 2020. The report card of ASEAN environmental management is uneven however; there are some successes and some failures. For example, the AATHP is in force, whereas the ASEAN Agreement on the Conservation of Nature and Natural Reserves (1985) is not. While all ASEAN member states have designated at least one ASEAN Heritage Park in their country, in some instances, the implementation in regard to management is still in the process of being effectively managed.

Southeast Asia's diversity has produced a wide range of environmental laws with varying levels of effectiveness. Singapore began serious environmental protection first and has successfully employed market incentives to induce compliance. Some of the more industrialized states, such as Thailand and Malaysia, have developed sufficient environmental legislation and bureaucracies, although enforcement is occasionally weak. Some countries in the region, such as Cambodia, Laos, and East Timor, have only just begun to develop environmental protection institutions. Generally, public interest environmental litigation does not play a large role in enforcing environmental laws, with the exception of the Philippines and increasingly Thailand. Overall, the region is moving toward convergence as environmental protection takes a higher priority, particularly since trends like global warming could threaten the region's island nations.

Dominic J. Nardi Jr.
University of Michigan

Sansanee DHANASARNSOMBAT
ENHESA Inc., United States

James KHO
Ateneo de Manila University School of Government

KOH Kheng-Lian
National University of Singapore

LYE Lin Heng
National University of Singapore

Chit Chit MYINT
SEEgreen, Myanmar (Burma)

Deny SIDHARTA
Soemadipradja & Taher, Indonesia

See also in the *Berkshire Encyclopedia of Sustainability* Environmental Law (several articles: China; East Asia; India and Pakistan; Pacific Island Region); Environmental Law, Soft vs. Hard; Transboundary Water Law

FURTHER READINGS

Asian Environmental Compliance and Enforcement Network (AECEN). (2010). Homepage. Retrieved June 30, 2010, from http://www.aecen.org

Association of Southeast Asian Nations (ASEAN). (1997, December 15). ASEAN Vision 2020. Retrieved September 12, 2010, from http://www.aseansec.org/1814.htm

Bryant, Raymond L. (1997). *The political ecology of forestry in Burma 1824–1994.* Honolulu: University of Hawaii Press.

Charter of the Association of Southeast Asian Nations, adopted 20 November 2007.

Craig, Donna G., & Robinson, Nicholas A. (2004). *Capacity building for environmental law in the Asian and Pacific Region: Approaches and resources.* Manila, The Philippines: Asian Development Bank.

Fahn, James. (2003). *A land on fire: The environmental consequences of the Southeast Asian boom.* Boulder, CO: Westview Press.

Gatmaitan, Dante. (2003). The illusion of intergenerational equity: *Oposa v. Factoran* as Pyrrhic victory. *Georgetown International Environmental Law Review, 15,* 457.

Gollin, Karin L., & Kho, James L. (Eds.). (2009). *After the romance: Communities and environmental governance in the Philippines.* Manila, The Philippines: Ateneo de Manila University Press.

Harding, Andrew. (Ed.). (2007). *Access to environmental justice: A comparative study.* Leiden, The Netherlands: BRILL.

Hirsch, Philip, & Warren, Carol. (Eds.). (1998). *The politics of environment in Southeast Asia: Resources and resistance.* London: Routledge.

Koh, Kheng Lian. (Ed.). (2009). *ASEAN environmental law, policy and governance: Selected documents* (Vols. I & II). Singapore: World Scientific Publishing Co.

Koh, Tommy; Manalo, R. G.; & Woon, Walter. (Eds.). (2009). *The making of the ASEAN Charter.* Singapore: World Scientific Publishing.

Lye, Lin Heng. (2008). A fine city in a garden—Environmental law and governance in Singapore. *Singapore Journal of Legal Studies,* 68–117.

National University of Singapore. Asia-Pacific Centre for Environmental Law (APCEL). Retrieved June 27, 2010, from http://law.nus.edu.sg/apcel

Nardi, Dominic J. (2008). Do Indonesian judges need scientific credibility? *Indonesia v. Newmont* and a proposal on the use of scientific evidence in Indonesian courts. *Georgetown International Environmental Law Review, 21,* 113.

Nguitragool, Paruedee. (2010). *Environmental cooperation in Southeast Asia: ASEAN's regime for trans-boundary haze pollution.* London: Routledge.

Tiwari, S. (Ed.). (2010). *ASEAN: Life after the charter.* Singapore: ISEAS.

World Bank. (2010). *Socialist Republic of Vietnam: Forest law enforcement and governance.* Washington, DC: World Bank.

Environmental Law—United States and Canada

Divergent histories have led Canadian and US governments to adopt differing laws to protect the environment despite geographic similarities, a common heritage, and a deep cultural attachment to their natural environment. In Canada the federal government negotiates laws and regulations regarding shared resources among the provinces, whereas the US federal government sets standards but allows individual states to interpret, implement, and enforce federal laws and goals.

In the mid-seventeenth century, after the last French and Indian War, every North American east of the Alleghenies was a subject of the British Crown. Since then, two states have emerged from these settlements, which would otherwise have become a single transplanted Anglo-American culture: one by revolution (the United States) and one by evolution (Canada). Both shared the same lush landscape and biodiversity, both had native populations that roamed freely over the undemarcated territory, and both were peopled primarily by English, Irish, Scottish, and Welsh immigrants. Both were settlement colonies meant to have permanent populations rather than exploitation colonies conquered for their resources, but both are resource rich and consequently became independent states largely because of this fact.

The legal systems of both nations are constitutional, both are democracies, and both have roots in the "common law" tradition. The air and waters (most notably the Great Lakes) shared by the nations make transboundary cooperation in environmental protection a necessary priority. But they also have differences in how they regulate use of the environment, and neither is at the forefront of sustainability in the twenty-first century.

Canadian Environmental Law and Policy

This article uses the dialectic between revolution and evolution to explain Canadian environmental law through its sources: constitutional, administrative, statute, and judge-made common law.

Constitutional Law in Canada

In the United States, violent revolution and the country's initial small-state status in a world of superpowers required that the individual states transcend their separate-but-equal status for a more centralized federal system. This gave the fledging US government a monopoly on interstate commerce and international relations, and an advantage in the balance of power with its constituent states, which was further centralized after the Civil War with the end of slavery. Canada, without the pressure of intense external or internal conflict—and in its slower and more nonviolent evolution toward statehood—was much more dependent on its provinces holding the balance of power in the consolidation of the nation through the process of negotiation.

The dialectic between revolution and evolution is demonstrated in the differences between the Constitution of the United States and the Canadian Constitution Act of 1867. In the United States, the revolution was fought within the context of the Articles of Confederation, which were based on the prominence of the states in the politics and policy of a set of equal, although united, colonies. The framers of the Constitution abandoned this loose confederation as unworkable within the context of a young state trying to survive in an eighteenth-century world of European hegemony. In Canada, the voluntary confederation of separate colonies was both the goal and the result of negotiations that resulted in the 1867 British North American Act, which then established a constitutional structure that remained unamended until 1982.

Specifically, Canada evolved to its independence and its constitutional status in two phases, one in 1867 and one in 1982. The Constitution Act of 1867 divides the powers of the state into provincial concerns for property, justice, and civil rights, and federal concern for the more universal imperatives defined in terms of peace, order, and good government (POGG). The primary jurisdiction of the provinces over civil rights—which meant minority rights for French Catholics in majority-English provinces and for the minority Protestant English in Quebec—was matched by their monopoly control over property (s.92(13)), which gave them jurisdiction over land, natural resources, and all uses of the environment. To the degree that the most basic environmental pollution and conservation decisions involve land use, the provinces have considerable power to regulate for or against a sustainable future. And because of the traditions of settlement colonies and their predisposition toward development, it was the use of the land and the development of the economy through its resource base that has primarily occupied Canadians. Provincial control over mines, minerals, forests, and hydropower (s.109) therefore grants them preeminence over the regulation of both the extraction of goods from nature and the use of environmental media as sinks, which were both considered necessary to Canada's economic progress. While the provinces have no power over anything out of their territorial jurisdiction, the large geographic size of most of the provinces is able to contain many environmental media that in the United States would trigger interstate commerce regulations and federal jurisdiction.

The independent powers of the Canadian federal government in areas like criminal law (s.91(27)), taxation (s.91(3)), and federal undertakings or public works (s.91(29), 92(10)), gives it some control over interprovincial environmental concerns. But its constitutional authority over navigation (s.91(10)), seacoasts, and fisheries (s.91(12)), as well as rivers, harbors, and canals (s.108), and its general police power within POGG, is most often used to establish federal or national jurisdiction in environmental law. Even if one contended that the federal government has historically been more focused on preservation and concern for future generations, its lack of definitive supremacy, even in the area of international relations and Canada's contribution to international law and the environment, defeats its intentions. The provinces seek and gain at least consultation and more often than not participation, even for matters of international concern, as has been demonstrated in the efforts of the federal government pertaining to climate change. Any preeminence the federal government might have had for a national or international policy was trumped by provincial action, when, for example, British Columbia passed its own carbon tax, and Ontario and Quebec instituted independent cap-and-trade systems.

In addition to the original British North American / Constitution Act of 1867, the Canadian Constitution was amended in 1982, which made Canada more autonomous from the United Kingdom and introduced the Charter of Rights and Freedoms, which is administered by the federal government and the federal supreme court. This second round of constitutionalism has had two prominent effects on the regulation of the environment. First, it has solidified the practice of administrative consensus building between the federal government and the provinces, which has made Canadian federalism even more dependent on cooperation between national and local governments for the success of environmental policy. Second, it has created a national rights regime that may have ramifications for the future of a sustainable environment.

Administrative Law in Canada

In addition to the stated constitutional powers of each level of the Canadian federal system, there are "concurrent" powers, which constitutionally require the cooperation of federal and provincial rule makers in the control of, for example, water and air pollution or the export of resources and electrical power. Here, like the Article VI powers of federal supremacy in the United States, the Canadian doctrine of paramountcy gives Ottawa the advantage in conflicts with the provinces, but on a much more conditional basis.

Because of the evolutionary nature of Canadian political history, the provinces continue to hold disproportionate administrative power, making negotiation between federal and provincial authorities the norm even for some interprovincial and international matters. In Canada, federalism is an effort of equals to negotiate a point of equilibrium on issues of national importance. Unlike the US administrative practice of cooperative federalism, where the federal government sets national policy on the environment and the states implement that policy, in Canada a system of consensus federalism requires that the federal government play referee between provincial and federal interests, mitigating conflicting regional interests in order to achieve a coordinated national policy.

Statute Law in Canada

Any major effort to change Canadian environmental law requires that the federal and provincial governments cooperate. The most critical issues require a federal-provincial conference where the premiers and the prime minister meet to discuss the issue before parliamentary legislation. Even less serious matters usually require consultation as an effort to empower "consensus federalism."

The most prominent piece of environmental legislation on the federal level is the Canadian Environmental Protection Act (CEPA), which is a comprehensive environmental risk law that places federal regulation on the introduction of toxic and hazardous material into the national environment. In addition, the Federal Fisheries Act grants the Canadian government the power to regulate coastal waters for wildlife preservation and pollution prevention.

Major pollution control law, however, including all existing permit systems for land, air, and water regulation, has been legislated through the provinces. For example, Ontario's Environmental Protection Act includes a permit control system for air emissions and rules for solid waste management, all contaminant spills, and the cleanup of environmental sites. Ontario also has legislation for environmental assessment, water resources, mining and resource extraction, pesticides, and even its own Environmental Bill of Rights. Since most pollution and other sustainability dilemmas involve land use and property rights, the provincial legislatures play a role even when the federal government takes the lead.

Judge-Made Common Law in Canada

Common-law countries like Canada began with a well-developed tort system that handled environmental problems as private legal matters between plaintiffs and defendants. Before there was any regulatory legislation to treat environmental quality as a collective good, the courts, based on British precedent in *Rylands v. Fletcher* (1886), used liability and nuisance law to allow those harmed by pollution to sue for monetary compensation, if not injunctive relief. When this was no longer deemed reasonable given the collective nature of environmental goods, the federal and provincial

courts each took jurisdiction. Division of labor was along the constitutional lines already explained, but when the distribution of power in a particular instance is unclear, the federal supreme court steps in. This is demonstrated in *R. v. Crown Zellerbach Canada Ltd.* (1 S.C.R. 401 (1988)), where the supreme court validated the Ocean Dumping Control Act as a manifestation of federal POGG powers, while tempering federal paramountcy by saying that the act does not apply to provincial waters.

United States Environmental Law and Policy

The US Constitution, unlike more recently drafted national constitutions, does not explicitly address the putative right to a healthy environment. This remains true despite decades of debate about whether such a right should be subject to constitutional guarantee. The first meaningful attempt to enshrine environmental rights in the US Constitution came in 1968 when Senator Gaylord Nelson (D-WI) proposed a constitutional amendment that read, "Every person has the inalienable right to a decent environment. The United States and every State shall guarantee this right" (H.R.J. Res. 1321, 90th Cong. (1968)). Although this and similar subsequent attempts to include environmental rights in the US Constitution failed, Senator Nelson's proposed amendment did much to raise awareness about then-looming environmental issues.

The absence of a federal constitutional right does not mean that there are no environmental rights under US law. First, many states guarantee some version of environmental rights in their state constitutions. Second, a host of federal legislative enactments create environmental rights akin to a constitutional right to a healthy environment. These laws were promulgated pursuant to the Constitution's Commerce Clause, which states that the US Congress shall have the power "to regulate Commerce with foreign Nations, and among the several States, and with the Indian Tribes" (Art. I, Sec. 8(3)). Although not obviously directed at environmental laws, the Commerce Clause has been read alongside the Necessary and Proper Clause which gives Congress the power "to make all Laws which shall be necessary and proper for carrying into Execution the foregoing Powers, and all other Powers vested by this Constitution in the Government of the United States, or in any Department or Officer thereof" (Art. I, Sec. 8). Read together, the Commerce Clause and the Necessary and Proper Clause have been interpreted to reach not only interstate commerce but also intrastate activities that have a substantial relation to interstate commerce and therefore affect interstate commerce (*United States v. Lopez*, 514 US 549 (1995)). Many environmental impacts like those related to the production, handling, and disposal of industrial wastes fall into one or both categories. As a result, Congress has a relatively wide reach vis-à-vis environmental lawmaking. At its outer limits, this expansive federal power over environmental decision making is the subject of intense political controversy, particularly when those statutes purport to limit landowner choices about property development.

Statutory Enactments in the United States

In the late 1960s, Congress began using its Commerce Clause power to enact statutes targeting activities that cause pollution or otherwise threaten the environment. In general, these statutory enactments focus on two aspects of environmental protection: 1) incorporating environmental concerns into the planning process; and 2) directives and controls on private activities, particularly industrial activities. The National Environmental Policy Act (NEPA, 42 U.S.C. §§4321-4349) is the most significant example of the former, while the Clean Air Act (CAA, 42 U.S.C. §§7401-7671(q)), the Clean Water Act (CWA, 33 U.S.C. §§1251-1387), and the Resource Conservation and Recovery Act (RCRA, 42 U.S.C. §§6901-6992k) are examples of the latter. Congress also created federal agencies with authority in the environmental area, including the Environmental Protection Agency (EPA), the Council on Environmental Quality (CEQ), the National Forest Service, the National Marine Fisheries Service (NMFS), and the Bureau of Land Management (BLM). These expert agencies work under delegated legislative authority to develop and implement regulatory programs intended to meet the goals identified in congressional environmental legislation.

Federal Environmental Planning Statutes in the United States

NEPA, enacted in 1969, recognized "the profound impact of man's activity on . . . the natural environment . . ." (42 U.S.C. § 4331(a) (2006)). Additionally, NEPA announced "a national policy which will encourage productive and enjoyable harmony between man and his environment; [and] to promote efforts which will prevent or eliminate damage to the environment . . ." (42 U.S.C. §4321). To that end, NEPA explicitly commits the federal government to "1. fulfill the responsibilities of each generation as trustee of the environment for succeeding generations; [and] 2. assure for all Americans safe, healthful, productive, and esthetically and culturally pleasing surroundings . . ." (42 U.S.C. §4331(b)).The government does this by conducting an environmental assessment (EA) or producing an environmental impact statement (EIS) whenever "a major Federal action significantly affecting the quality of the human environment" is contemplated (42 U.S.C.

§4332(C)). These documents include the environmental impact of the proposed action as well as possible alternatives to the proposed action.

NEPA's focus on environmental impacts as part of the planning process has been adopted in over eighty countries and has been incorporated into numerous international conventions. In 2009, the International Court of Justice declared that the requirement that major actions be preceded by an environmental impact assessment had become customary international law (Case Concerning Pulp Mills on the River Uruguay (*Argentina v. Uruguay*), Judgment of 20 April 2010, para. 204).

Overall, NEPA requires that the federal government consider the environmental consequences of its actions *before* making major decisions. NEPA has, however, some significant limitations that hinder its ability to protect the environment and ensure sustainable decision making. First, and most significantly, despite the sweeping statutory language, the Supreme Court concluded that NEPA imposed only procedural requirements on federal agencies (*Robertson v. Methow Valley Citizens Council*, 490 US 332, 350 (1989)). Thus, the Supreme Court interpreted NEPA's mandate narrowly—merely requiring that agencies identify and consider environmental impacts, not that they mitigate or minimize them.

A second key limitation to NEPA's reach is that the statute applies only to federal agencies. Thus activities proceeding without federal funding, and not in need of a federal permit, remain unaffected. Many states have similar state environmental impact assessment (SEPA) laws, but gaps remain, particularly when funding for an activity is wholly private. Because land use is traditionally a state and local function, this significantly limits the federal government's ability to require comprehensive environmental planning and sustainable development.

More recent congressional enactments, like the Toxic Release Inventory (TRI) contained in the Emergency Planning and Community Right to Know Act (EPCRA, 42 U.S.C. §§11001-11050) have mandated information disclosure and transparency, putting US law on a trajectory similar to emerging international norms, which tend to focus on participation and access to information. Other statutes, like the Endangered Species Act (ESA, 16 U.S.C. §§1531-1544) combine planning and substantive elements requiring interagency consultation before the federal government takes or permits any action likely to jeopardize animals listed as endangered or threatened.

Substantive (US) Federal Environmental Statutes

The major substantive environmental statutes focus on restricting pollution stemming from economic activities and set standards for handling the wastes that are generated as side products of that activity. Federal standards apply just about any time pollutants are released into the air or water, and whenever hazardous wastes are generated, transported, or disposed of within the United States. (The major exception is water pollution from nonpoint sources like runoff from agricultural fields or parking lots.) These statutes require federal agencies to adopt standards based on human health, with varying degrees of consideration of the costs involved in meeting those standards. To achieve those standards, these statutes direct federal agencies to specify technologies and processes that anyone generating these wastes must adopt, or outcomes per regulated pollutant that those generators must achieve. These requirements are then laid out in permits that those generating the pollution are required to obtain.

In general, these substantive federal environmental statutes tend to identify broadly worded goals, delegating the task of developing programs to implement and enforce those goals to expert federal agencies. The agencies then draft rules, monitor regulated activity, and enforce regulations. Unless a statute contains its own procedural requirements, these agency activities are governed by the Federal Administrative Procedure Act (APA, 5 U. S.C. §§551-559). In addition to this role, many federal environmental programs are administered by states under a program of cooperative federalism. Under Section 110 of the Clean Air Act (42 U.S.C. §7410), for example, after the federal government sets acceptable air quality standards, states can develop implementation plans to achieve those standards within state borders. Once the federal government approves a state implementation plan (SIP), the primary enforcement authority asses from the federal government to the state. States differ from each other, and from the federal government, in the way they interpret, implement, and enforce these federal laws—sometimes resulting in uneven environmental protection. Cooperative federalism contemplates such variation, so long as states meet a minimal standard identified in the SIP.

One important check on this federal and state discretion is the citizen suit provision contained in most environmental statutes. Citizen suit provisions allow concerned citizens to act as private attorneys general and sue in federal court to enforce environmental statutes. A citizen suit can be brought either against the government to demand that it take a nondiscretionary duty mandated by an environmental statute, or against a private individual or entity believed to be in violation of a permit or other statutory requirement. These statutes thus provide for citizen enforcement of environmental standards, should the government fail to do so.

Successful citizen suit litigants can typically recover their court costs and attorneys' fees from the opposing party—a critical provision, as most private citizens would otherwise be unable to bring such suits.

Sustainability

Because of the size differences in the two nations (the United States has 310 million people, while Canada has slightly less than 34 million), as well as the fundamental differences in their legislative structures, there are obvious differences in the way the two nations approach sustainability issues. But they also share a common heritage and a deep cultural attachment to their natural environment. This attachment is rooted in the key role that many resource industries play in the national economies of both countries, and in an abiding pride in and attachment to the beauty of their natural endowments. Thus, for both Canada and the United States, sustainability impulses stem from the twin desires to manage resources for future consumption as well as to preserve those resources for future generations.

Sustainability in Canada

Law for sustainability in Canada, as elsewhere in North America, is retarded by property law, market-based assumptions about regulation, and the consensus nature of Canadian politics. The law professor Stepan Wood argues that "sustainability in Canada . . . will likely only arise if people are prepared to choose fundamentally different goals for their society, including a fundamentally different economic model in which maintenance of ecological integrity is a precondition to all development. Environmental law is ultimately a means to an end, not an end in itself" (Wood, Tanner, and Richardson, 62). The consensus nature of Canadian politics as well as its legacy as a resource-rich settlement colony has exacerbated the reluctance to change, which has resulted in more than twenty

different Canadian sustainability strategies, many with overlapping means, ends, and jurisdiction.

If one additionally argues that anticipatory policy is the best environmental sustainability law, then change requires centralization and authoritative national policy. The federal government nearly did this with CEPA to anticipate risk in the environment and regulate it *ex ante*, and it may be able to do this again with a combination of its acknowledged POGG powers and the Charter of Rights and Freedoms in support of sustainability. While the Charter does not contain any specific environmental rights, it creates a federal system of national rights that the court has already confirmed are applicable to all Canadians (*R. v. Hape*, SCC 26 (2007)), and, when properly circumscribed, transcendent of provincial law (*R. v. Hydro-Québec*, 217 SC, NR 24 (1997)). It is this universal system of Canadian rights that, in addition to negotiation and consensus, may someday provide a national "means" for the legal assurance of a sustainable environment in Canada.

Sustainability in the United States

Because the US approach to environmental law regulates industry-by-industry, pollutant-by-pollutant, and media-by-media, overall systemic planning can be very difficult. For example, air emissions restrictions may simply result in increased water pollution or land disposal, rather than genuine pollution reduction. Problems stemming from the fragmented nature of environmental law are compounded by the lack of national land use planning. Even where federal law does control land use, most notably in national forests and federally owned lands, the relevant agencies are required to promote economically valuable uses like grazing, logging, and mining, with conservation and habitat or ecosystem preservation a secondary priority. Conflicts with property rights (as in the case of wetlands preservation and endangered species habitat protection) raise significant constitutional questions that often limit the ability of environmental agencies to make the most environmentally sound choices.

While a more comprehensive approach might be desirable, the United States is unlikely to abandon its incremental and piecemeal approach in favor of new legislation any time soon. That leaves agencies in the position of creatively interpreting their existing authority in order to respond to new environmental threats—like climate change—as well as to account for developing notions of environmental justice and intergenerational equity.

Cooperation

The controversial North American Free Trade Agreement (NAFTA) of 1994, the central trade agreement between Canada, the United States, and Mexico, has had numerous effects on the economies and the environments of the three nations; critics contend that NAFTA has failed to create jobs, while others contend that the drive for more industrialized development leads to more fossil fuel use and pollution. NAFTA, however, took the significant step (unique among international trade agreements at the time) of creating an explicit link between the environment and commerce of Canada and the United States with its environmental side agreement, the North American Agreement on Environmental Cooperation, which created a North American Commission for Environmental Cooperation (CEC), which is overseen by a public advisory committee (Gallagher 2009).

There are currently more than thirty governmental agreements between the United States and Canada. The obvious point of cooperation between the two nations is the Great Lakes region, home to 30 percent of Canadians and 10 percent of Americans. With the five lakes and the surrounding watershed providing drinking water to 33 million people, the need for transboundary cooperation in environmental protection of the waters and the air shared by both nations is abundantly clear. Again, however, evolution in Canada has made the social conventions of a settlement colony the foundation of its difficulty with a transition to a sustainable regulatory structure. The revolutionary context of US origins has made the fight for sustainability not one of slowly eroding conventions but the clash of minority arguments from principle based in environmental values against the principles of private property, independence, and the sense that small government is best. Both nations have adjustments to make and much to learn from one another.

John Martin GILLROY
Lehigh University

Rebecca M. BRATSPIES
City University of New York School of Law

See also in the *Berkshire Encyclopedia of Sustainability* Clean Air Act; Clean Water Act; Endangered Species Act; Free Trade; Land Use—Regulation and Zoning; Love Canal; National Environmental Policy Act; Natural Resources Law; Nuisance Law; Real Property Law; Tort Law; Trail Smelter Arbitration (*United States v. Canada*); Transboundary Water Law

FURTHER READINGS

Boyd, David R. (2003). *Unnatural law: Rethinking Canadian environmental law and policy.* Vancouver, Canada: UBC Press.

Bratspies, Rebecca M. (forthcoming 2011). Human rights and environmental regulation. *New York University Journal of Environmental Law.*

Bratspies, Rebecca M. (2008). Reconciling the irreconcilable: Progress toward sustainable development. In Russell A. Miller & Rebecca M.

Bratspies (Eds.), *Progress in international law* (pp. 813–834). Leiden, The Netherlands and Boston: Martinus Nijhoff.

Bratspies, Rebecca M., & Miller, Russell A. (Eds.). (2006). *Transboundary harm in international law: Lessons from the Trail Smelter Arbitration.* Cambridge, UK: Cambridge University Press.

Center for Progressive Reform. (2007). CPR for the environment: Breathing new life into the nation's major environmental statutes. Retrieved November 20, 2010, from http://www.progressivereform.org/articles/CPR_701.pdf

Dernbach, John C. (2009). *Agenda for a sustainable America.* Washington, DC: Environmental Law Institute.

Environment Canada and the US Environmental Protection Agency. (2003). Our Great Lakes. Retrieved November 20, 2010, from http://binational.net/ourgreatlakes/ourgreatlakes.pdf

Flournoy, Alyson C., & Driesen, David M. (2010). *Beyond environmental law: Policy proposals for a better environmental future.* Cambridge, UK: Cambridge University Press.

Gallagher, Kevin P. (2009, November). NAFTA and the environment: Lessons from Mexico and beyond. In Kevin P. Gallagher, Timothy A. Wise & Enrique Dussel Peters (Eds.), *The future of North American trade policy: Lessons from NAFTA. Pardee Center Task Force Report* (pp. 61–69). Retrieved November 20, 2010, from http://www.bu.edu/pardee/task-force-report-nafta/

Gerrard, Michael B., & Foster, Sheila R. (Eds.). (2008). *The law of environmental justice: Theories and procedures to address disproportionate risks* (2nd ed.). Chicago: American Bar Association.

Gillroy, John Martin. (1999). Canadian and American environmental federalism: A game-theoretic analysis. *Policy Studies Journal, 27*(2), 360–388.

Hughes, Elaine L.; Lucas, Alastair R.; & Tilleman, William A., II. (2003). *Environmental law and policy* (3rd ed.). Toronto: Emond Montgomery.

Kysar, Douglas A. (2009). *Regulating from nowhere: Environmental law and the search for objectivity.* New Haven, CT: Yale University Press.

Wood, Stepan; Tanner, Georgia; & Richardson, Benjamin J. (forthcoming). What ever happened to Canadian environmental law? *Ecology Law Quarterly, 37*(4).

COURT CASES

Case Concerning Pulp Mills on the River Uruguay (*Argentina v. Uruguay*), Judgment of 20 April 2010, para. 204.

R. v. Crown Zellerbach Canada Ltd. (Her Majesty The Queen v. Crown Zellerbach Canada Ltd.), 1 S.C.R. 401 (1988).

R. v. Hape (Lawrence Richard Hape v. Her Majesty The Queen), SCC 26 (2007).

R. v. Hydro-Québec (Her Majesty The Queen v. Hydro-Québec), 217 SC, NR 24 (1997).

Robertson v. Methow Valley Citizens Council, 490 US 332, 350 (1989).

United States v. Lopez, 514 US 549 (1995).

Intergenerational Equity

The idea of sustainability is anchored in part by the belief that earlier generations have moral obligations to subsequent generations. The common understanding of equity among individuals cannot address these obligations fully, and the issue is further complicated because future people cannot be present when important decisions affecting their well-being are made. This suggests that some moral obligations are owed to society as a whole.

The concept of sustainability clearly addresses the relationship between the present and the future, with the apparent implication that people of the present have moral obligations to people in the future. This core, normative meaning is given several labels including "intergenerational equity," "intertemporal justice," and "rights of future generations." All of these terms emphasize the complex relationship between current actions and policies and the rights of future generations.

Many historic cultures have carefully planned their bequest to the future, but it has only been recognized in the last century that choices made by earlier generations might seriously alter the environment of the future and threaten the quality of life of future people. The growth of technological power accompanying the Industrial Revolution has enabled modern humans to affect their environment more pervasively and violently, releasing gases that warm the atmosphere, and destroying complex forest ecosystems for development. While many of these actions have supported economic growth and social development, they also impose risks on the future. How should such risks affect decisions in the present? The challenge to "live sustainably" or to "develop sustainably" can be understood as a moral commitment to being "fair" to future generations (WCED 1987; Tremmel 2009).

Four Questions

There are disagreements among scholars about how to capture the essence of justice and equity in general, and the application of these concepts to the future creates special puzzles and issues. Addressing intergenerational equity requires addressing four sub-problems: (1) the trade-offs problem, (2) the ignorance problem, (3) the distance problem, and (4) the valuation problem (Norton 2005).

1. Intergenerational Trade-Offs

One question is whether members of any generation should seriously worry about their successors, since history shows a long-term pattern of economic and social development that, over time, has led to more wealth and higher standards of living. Assuming this pattern will continue, it can be asked, Why should early generations sacrifice consumption to save for the future if people of the future will be richer and happier than we are? (Solow 1993). The growth of technological power, however, raises the question: Is it possible that an earlier generation might undertake risks that doom the future? If so, would that earlier generation be held responsible for a huge moral insult to humanity?

Assuming positive answers to these latter questions are plausible, it seems that technologically advanced societies do face a moral challenge. How should a society trade off the current benefits of rapid development against risks that such developments might injure future people? In moral reasoning about obligations among contemporaries, equity can be conceived as impartiality, and impartiality can then be tested against our intuition of reciprocity. Actions consented to by all parties affected can then be accepted as fair even when there are quibbles about the exact conditions of fairness. Unfortunately, this useful moral touchstone is unavailable when many of the affected parties are not yet born: they cannot be represented in negotiations leading to a "contract" acceptable to all parties.

Intergenerational moral judgments thus suffer from *asymmetry of consequences*: people of any present generation can affect the well-being of future people, but not vice versa (except in the case of overlapping generations). This asymmetry, since it undermines the useful moral test of consent of the affected parties, apparently requires some substantive, generation-independent criterion for what counts as a harm, what counts as a benefit, and some way of calibrating such criteria to apply across multiple generations. The trade-offs problem, then, seems insoluble without addressing the fourth sub-problem, valuation.

2. The Ignorance Problem

Many moral problems require a careful examination of the complex impacts of current actions, but the asymmetry of intergenerational moral relations also puts into question the usual understanding of what we need to know to be fair to individuals. For example, in modern democracies, we assume that if the desires of the majority of citizens are known, it is usually justifiable to try to achieve these goals. To expand this solution to problems with multigenerational impacts, however, we would need to know the preferences of future people. Values and preferences change over time, and making decisions today based only on the preferences of contemporary people would be to paternalistically impose current values on the future. Again, the asymmetry of intergenerational morality seems to undermine our usual moral reasoning.

The asymmetry also creates another confusing and difficult form of ignorance: ignorance of the identity of future individuals. In the ethics of contemporary relations, we usually assume the "person-regarding principle" (PRP), the theory that all moral harms must affect some identifiable person (Parfit 1984). For example, if an individual dumps toxins in a stream, the harmed party will be the downstream users and others indirectly affected by damages to those users. But if someone stores dangerous radioactive waste in a way that will threaten those living one hundred years from now, the individuals who are harmed are not present and not even able to be identified and described as individuals.

If it is assumed that the person-regarding principle applies to intratemporal moral relations, however, a paradox arises. Suppose that a given generation, facing alternative pathways into the future, chooses to maximize immediate gratification and does not worry about using resources wisely. When compared to a society that chooses

to husband resources for the use of future persons, one would assume the policies of the former society are morally inferior. As the actions and policies followed in the two scenarios play out, however, different persons will meet, and different individuals will be born from matings in the two scenarios. Applying PRP, the persons who are actually born on the profligate scenario are not harmed, but benefited—they get the gift of life. If sustainable policies had been pursued instead, the alternate individuals who might have existed cannot be harmed because they might never exist. Perhaps intergenerational fairness cannot be analyzed in terms of fairness to individuals.

Since the asymmetry involved in intergenerational morality apparently requires a divergence from the individualistic morality of the PRP, some theorists have recognized obligations to collectives of unidentifiable individuals, such as "the generation alive in 2200," as is proposed by legal scholar Edith Brown Weiss (1988). Brown Weiss proposed that earlier generations have both rights and obligations regarding the "common patrimony of natural and cultural resources of our planet," with the rights to use these resources accruing to present individuals even as those rights also impose an obligation to protect the common patrimony. Sidestepping the question of individualism associated with the use of "rights" language, Brown Weiss, following Edmund Burke (1790), proposes that society be understood as a partnership between those who have lived in the past, the present, and the future. She says, "The planetary rights proposed here for future generations are not rights possessed by individuals. Rather they are generational rights which can only be usefully conceived at a group level" (Brown Weiss 1988, 96). This reasoning leads her to invoke the analogy of a trust: each generation receives the patrimony of nature and culture from previous generations and "holds [it] in trust for future generations" (Brown Weiss 1988, 2).

Peter Brown (1994) has further developed the idea of intergenerational trusts, arguing that humans are universally obligated to act as stewards of resources for future generations, protecting and restoring natural systems when damaged. This model is conceptually helpful because, in law, a trust might be written to provide benefits for all generations of offspring of a couple, and managers of that trust can be faulted if they fail to protect the family assets for individuals not yet born and not yet identifiable.

Another conceptualization, developed by some American environmentalists, begins by noting the reference to "posterity" in the Preamble to the US Constitution, arguing that constitutional protections for resources, such as biodiversity, being consistent with that declaration, should be formalized as constitutional amendments to protect the rights of posterity (Schlickheisen 1994).

3. The Distance Problem and Time Preference

The problems of trade-offs and ignorance are exacerbated as one considers longer frames of time. In fact, because generations overlap, if one restricts one's ethical purview only to the present and perhaps one subsequent generation, the problems of trade-offs and ignorance are minimized. Policies can be justified over two generations because younger individuals are constantly coming of age, and parents presumably can speak and consent at least tentatively for their younger children. So understanding intergenerational equity seems also to raise questions about the temporal distance to which our moral obligations extend. Prior to the development of powerful technologies, it might have been argued that all morality could be a relation between parents and children; one generation tries to pass on undamaged resources to the next generation and leaves obligations regarding the next generation. This reasoning, however, seems less cogent as the world faces global climate change determined by choices made today that will affect many future generations in an accelerating manner.

When economists face the distance problem, they typically introduce discounting, a practice whereby the effects of a decision today are temporally weighted toward the present: effects in the present count 100 percent of positive and negative impacts, while impacts felt in later years are reduced by a chosen percentage each year (Lind 1982; Frederick, Loewenstein, and O'Donoghue 2002). A high discount rate thus expresses a strong time preference for the present over the future, and suggests that impacts on the distant future should have negligible effect on current decisions. While it is clear that most individuals, most of the time, do express a preference to enjoy benefits sooner and to delay costs, it is less clear that such a practice can be justified as a matter of social policy (Page 1977). Some authors, then, argue for a "social discount rate" close to zero, even as we expect individuals to discount future impacts (Stern 2006). The growing realization that the impacts of climate change resulting from slow-changing variables like carbon dioxide in the atmosphere may have huge and increasing impacts on future generations has thus sparked a high-stakes debate that seems to imply that current policies must be evaluated for their impacts on the distant future (Stern 2006; Nordhaus 2007).

4. The Valuation Problem

The previous three problems in understanding intergenerational equity would be alleviated if we had a time-sensitive means of comparing values across time. Economists have suggested one approach to cross-generational value comparisons, sometimes referred to as *weak sustainability*. According to this view, which equates individual well-being with the ability to fulfill one's preferences, we can conceive sustainability as an injunction to act so as to not decrease the opportunities of future people to attain at least the same level of welfare or preference satisfaction as earlier generations (Solow 1993). Because they measure per capita income for people alive at a given time, economists suggest that sustainability can be achieved simply by protecting the capital base of the society, since wealth allows the development of technologies that can fulfill preferences more and more efficiently. According to this weak sustainability view, as long as a society maintains its capital base (including money, technologies, and natural resources valued together), it is sustainable.

This approach to intergenerational equity, however, seems to beg important questions. First, if the value of capital resources is discounted across time, the calculations involved will be presentist in implications, so this proposal does not satisfactorily answer moral aspects of the distance question. Second, on this view, as long as a society does not decline in measurable economic wealth, it is impossible to harm future people, whereas most environmentalists would argue that a future world of rich people who have destroyed most of the world's biological diversity and natural beauty could be worse off, even if they are wealthier than prior generations who enjoyed the richness of life on earth (Norton and Toman 1997).

While economists have thus provided a general conception of intergenerational equity, they do so in a way that assumes certain questions are answered, though many others think these same questions remain open. For example, ecologists have observed that concentration on efficiently developing wealth can result in reductions in the resilience of ecological systems (Gunderson and Holling 2002; Walker and Salt 2006). Resilience and other ecological features are thus treated as "natural capital," with the implication that increases in economic wealth can actually

destabilize natural systems as more and more natural capital is transformed into products and waste.

The economic view can be countered with an alternative view, normative sustainability, which challenges the economists' conception of value as preference-fulfillment, arguing instead that communities with a multigenerational perspective must identify what they believe is valuable enough to perpetuate for the future. On this view, which combines well with the trust doctrine of Brown Weiss and Brown, each generation must engage the question, What in our society, culture, and environment is valuable enough that it should be protected for the future?

Sustainability and Future Generations

Normative sustainability thus adds to the economic goal of protecting the wealth of the society the goal of protecting the community's cherished values—including love of nature and natural systems—as a trust for future generations, a trust that will bind earlier generations with later ones in an ongoing chain identifying and perpetuating the values of a society understood as a partnership of ongoing generations. This rich idea of the moral relations among generations is the core idea anchoring the concepts of sustainability and sustainable development in concern for the future.

Bryan G. NORTON
Georgia Institute of Technology

See also in the *Berkshire Encyclopedia of Sustainability* Biotechnology Legislation; Development, Sustainable—Overview of Laws and Commissions; Environmental Law, Soft vs. Hard; Justice, Environmental; Nanotechnology Legislation; Precautionary Principle; Principle-Based Regulation; Weak vs. Strong Sustainability Debate; World Constitutionalism

FURTHER READINGS

Becker, Carl. (1934). Progress. In Edwin R. A. Seligman & Alvin Johnson (Eds.), *Encyclopaedia of the Social Sciences* (Vol. 12, pp. 214–246). London: Macmillan.

Brown, Peter G. (1994). *Restoring the public trust*. Boston: Beacon Press.

Brown Weiss, Edith. (1988). *In fairness to future generations: International law, common patrimony, and intergenerational equity*. Tokyo: United Nations University.

Burke, Edmund. (1955). *Reflections on the Revolution in France*. Indianapolis, IN: Bobbs-Merrill. (Original work published 1790)

Bury, John B. (1928). *The idea of progress: An inquiry into its origin and growth*. London: Macmillan.

Foundation for the Rights of Future Generations. (2010). Homepage. Retrieved August 3, 2010, from http://www.intergenerationaljustice.org/

Frederick, Shane; Loewenstein, George; & O'Donoghue, Ted. (2002). Time discounting and time preference: A critical review. *Journal of Economic Literature, 40*(2), 351–401.

Gunderson, Lance H., & Holling, C. S. (2002). *Panarchy: Understanding transformations in human and natural systems*. Washington, DC: Island Press.

Lind, Robert. (1982). *Discounting for time and risk in energy policy*. Washington, DC: Resources for the Future.

Nordhaus, William D. (2007). A review of the *Stern Review on the Economics of Climate Change. Journal of Economic Literature, 45*(3), 686–702.

Norton, Bryan G. (1982). Environmental ethics and the rights of future generations. *Environmental Ethics, 4*(4), 319–337.

Norton, Bryan G. (2005). *Sustainability: A philosophy of adaptive ecosystem management*. Chicago: University of Chicago Press.

Norton, Bryan G., & Toman, Michael. (1997). Sustainability: Ecological and economic perspectives. *Land Economics, 73*(4), 553–568.

Page, Talbot. (1977). *Conservation and economic efficiency: An approach to materials policy*. Baltimore: Johns Hopkins University Press.

Parfit, Derek. (1984). *Reasons and persons*. Oxford, UK: Oxford University Press.

Partridge, Ernest. (Ed.). (1981). *Responsibilities to future generations*. Buffalo, NY: Prometheus.

Schlickheisen, Rodger. (1994). Protecting biodiversity for future generations: An argument for a constitutional amendment. *Tulane Environmental Law Review Journal, 8*, 181–221.

Sikora, R. I., & Barry, Brian. (Eds.). (1978). *Obligations to future generations*. Philadelphia: Temple University Press.

Solow, Robert M. (1993). Sustainability: An economist's perspective. In Robert Dorfman & Nancy Dorfman (Eds.), *Economics of the environment: Selected readings* (3rd ed., pp. 179–187). New York: Norton.

Stern, Nicholas. (2006). *The economics of climate change*. London: HM Treasury.

Tremmel, Joerg Chet. (2009). *A theory of intergenerational justice*. London: Earthscan.

Walker, Brian, & Salt, David. (2006). *Resilience thinking*. Washington, DC: Island Press.

World Commission on Environment and Development (WCED). (1987). *Our common future*. Oxford, UK: Oxford University Press.

International Law

International law has been evolving for centuries to provide a framework for international and transnational activities. Like other areas of the law, its purpose is to allow participants to deal with each other with some level of predictability and thus to reduce misunderstandings and to avoid conflicts and confrontations. International environmental laws are especially important, since environmental issues do not obey national boundaries.

International law, with its primary goal of providing a structure for dealings among international and transnational governments, is a more primitive system of law than the domestic legal systems found in advanced nations. It does not have a legislative body with the capacity to enact laws binding on all nations, an executive branch or a military or police force that can enforce the laws that do exist, or judicial tribunals that have broad jurisdiction or the power to issue binding and enforceable decrees in many circumstances. Although early versions of such bodies can be found in the United Nations and in emerging regional organizations, the process of constructing institutions that both enjoy widespread support and can meet the challenges presented by a deeply divided world is just beginning.

Some have argued that international law is not really law because a superior body cannot enforce it. But most commentators contend that because most countries follow international law most of the time, and because those countries that violate its norms do frequently suffer consequences, it should be viewed as a system of law.

International law is less developed than other systems of law because larger and more powerful nations do not always accept that it is advantageous to subordinate their self-interest to an international or multinational rule, while smaller nations will see the benefit of an international structure that protects the weak against the powerful. The

foundations of international law, however, have always been reciprocity and enlightened self-interest. In an era of storm surges and rising sea levels, of depleted resources and endangered species, international cooperation on environmental matters—and the rule of law—has never been more important or necessary. This overview of international law, which examines its sources, practices, and the history of how it emerged in the modern (and divided) world, puts into broad context the challenges nations and states face as they develop international frameworks to address a sustainable future.

Sources of International Law

The primary sources of international law are treaties—bilateral and multilateral—and "customary international law," which emerges from the actual practices of states and is undertaken with an understanding that these practices are required by law (*opinio juris sive necessitatis*). The "practices" of states are usually found in actions taken by a country, but they can sometimes be discovered in the statements their diplomats or leaders issue or in their votes at international organizations or diplomatic conferences. To become "custom," a practice must have the widespread (but not necessarily universal) support of countries concerned with the issue and must usually have continued for a period of time long enough to signify understanding and acquiescence. Occasionally a regional custom can emerge, if the countries of a certain part of the world order their affairs in a certain manner.

In recent years, it has become accepted that some principles of customary international law are so important that they are called "peremptory norms" or *jus cogens* (commanding law) and that no country is permitted to depart from these principles. Among these norms are the prohibitions on aggression, genocide, crimes against humanity, slavery, extrajudicial murder, prolonged arbitrary detention, torture, and racial discrimination. The International Law Commission (ILC) adds to the list of prohibitions any act that results in "a serious breach of an international obligation of essential importance for the safeguarding and preservation of the human environment, such as those prohibiting massive pollution of the atmosphere or of the seas" (ILC 1996).

Although most historical summaries of the development of international law focus on its growth in Europe and the West, the reality is more complex. Practices governing interactions among nations and peoples also developed in Asia and elsewhere, and these norms have been merging with those that came to be accepted in the West. The growing recognition that groups, as well as individuals, have human rights protected under international law is an example of a non-Western contribution to international law.

Emergence of Modern International Law

Most scholars explain that "modern" international law emerged in Europe at the time of the Renaissance and Enlightenment through the Peace of Westphalia, which ended the Thirty Years War (1618–1648) and gave formal recognition to the sovereign state system. This treaty-based system was designed, in part, to allow Catholic and Protestant states to coexist in Europe. International law became necessary to confirm the boundaries among these states and to bring some order to their dealings with each other. Countries accepted the doctrine of *pacta sunt servanda* (treaties are to be observed), now a fundamental principle of international law, and established some machinery for the settlement of disputes. During the years that followed, citizen participation in government grew in England and then in France through the French Revolution. As monarchies crumbled, individuals, corporations, nongovernmental organizations, and international organizations emerged as part of the international legal system.

The Final Act of the Congress of Vienna (1815), signed by Austria, France, Great Britain, Portugal, Prussia, Russia, and Sweden, which formally ended the Napoleonic Wars, was another significant event, because it created a system of political and economic cooperation in Europe and also articulated governing norms of international law. Among the principles that emerged from this Congress was a set of rules governing diplomatic protocol, a condemnation of the slave trade, the principle of free navigation (not only for the riparian states but for all states) on the major rivers of Europe, and the neutrality of Switzerland. Treaties, both bilateral and multilateral, began to

cover a wide range of topics, supplementing and sometimes replacing custom as a source of law.

During the period of colonial expansion that took place in the last half of the nineteenth century, the concepts of international law that had been utilized in Europe and the West were introduced into Asia by the Western powers. Western international law was then even more primitive than it is today. No global institutions existed, and only a few special-purpose regional organizations had been created. Some topics—such as diplomatic immunity—were fairly well defined, and consensus had also been reached on the important goals of stopping piracy and slavery.

War was still viewed by many as an acceptable instrument of foreign policy, but the dramatic increase in destructive weaponry resulting from the Industrial Revolution caused many to realize that some constraints were needed on the use of force. Major international meetings were called, the most significant being the 1899 and 1907 Hague Conferences, which were designed to codify the laws of armed conflict and establish limits on certain types of military activities. The growth of daily newspapers in the industrialized countries had the effect of allowing common citizens to participate more fully in policy decisions, and led, in many countries, to a democratization of international politics.

Many described the nature of the evolving international legal system as one of consent—or "positivism"—wherein only those norms agreed upon by states could be enforced against them. But perhaps because of the theocracies that had governed many parts of Europe in previous centuries, the Canon law that had developed during that period, and the religious fervor that still burned brightly for many people, others contended that certain inherent principles also governed nations. Tension emerged between this "natural law" formula as the basis of international law and the perspective of "positivism" promoted by others, and this tension still exists today.

The Dutch diplomat Hugo de Groot (1583–1645), who wrote four hundred years ago under the Latin name Grotius, is often called the father or founder of international law because he tried to reconcile natural and positive law. His analysis of the laws of war, the law of the sea, and the protection owed to diplomats laid the framework for modern thinking on these topics. He believed that a "law of nature" could be deduced by logical reasoning, rather than by resort to divine sources, and thus tried to formulate a law that could be acceptable to all, conceivably even to "infidels."

Another continuing issue has been whether international law is incorporated into national legal systems, and is thus part of the law applied by national courts (monism), or whether it is a separate and distinct legal system governing nations but not accessible by normal citizens in disputes in domestic courts (dualism).

Continuing Challenges of a Divided World

After World War I, the League of Nations was established and served to promote dialogue and negotiations, but its efforts to stop the continuing imperialistic activities of some nations were unsuccessful and the world again engaged in massive slaughters in World War II. The 1928 Kellogg-Briand Pact, which outlawed the recourse to war, did not stop warfare, but it at least has required countries to come up with some justification for armed conflict, with "self-defense" being the most common excuse. Because wars so often are fought over natural resources such as water access—the civil war in Darfur, Sudan, being one example—international law relating to conflict is intimately connected to environmental issues.

The United Nations was established in 1945, and the nations of the world have entered into numerous additional bilateral and multilateral treaties since then on subjects ranging from economic affairs to endangered species to human rights to arms control. The UN Security Council, with 15 members, including 5 permanent members (China, France, Russia, the United Kingdom, and the United States) that can veto any resolution, has the responsibility to deal with threats to the peace and breaches of the peace. The General Assembly, now with 192 members, serves as a forum for discussion and annually enacts a wide range of resolutions addressing global problems. The International Court of Justice (ICJ) sits in The Hague, the Netherlands, and decides cases brought to it by governments, but it has yet to rule on more than a few explicitly environmental cases. Numerous more-specialized tribunals have also been created.

Regional organizations have emerged in almost all areas of the world, with the European Union and other European organizations being particularly effective in addressing regional issues, reducing tensions among nations, and working toward environmental protection. Many in the developing world still view international law as dominated by the West and by the rich and powerful countries. Efforts are continuing to find ways to restructure the United Nations to reflect the world's diversity more fairly and to allow it to operate more efficiently.

The international legal system is still a work in progress. As the world becomes increasingly interdependent, and environmental issues become ever more pressing, international law will become more important and more complex. Countries remain reluctant to give up essential elements of sovereignty and autonomy. But as transnational problems present themselves, transnational solutions will continue to be devised. Through this incremental process, international law will continue to grow.

Jon M. VAN DYKE
University of Hawaii

See also in the *Berkshire Encyclopedia of Sustainability* Armed Conflict and the Environment; Customary International Law; Enforcement; Environmental Law, Soft vs. Hard; International Court of Justice; Law of the Sea; Principle-Based Regulation; Transboundary Water Law; United Nations—Overview of Conventions and Agreements; Weak vs. Strong Sustainability Debate; World Constitutionalism

FURTHER READINGS

Anand, Ram Prakash. (1982). *Origin and development of the law of the sea: History of international law revisited.* The Hague, The Netherlands: Martinus Nijhoff.

Buergenthal, Thomas, & Murphy, Sean D. (2002). *Public international law.* St. Paul, MN: West Group.

Henkin, Louis. (1979). *How nations behave.* New York: Columbia University Press.

International Law Commission. (1996). Draft Articles on State Responsibility, Report of the International Law Commission on the Work of its Forty-Eighth Session, art. 19(3)(d), at 125, 131, UN Doc. A/51/10 (1996).

Janis, Mark W. (2003). *An introduction to international law.* New York: Aspen Publishers.

Lawrence, Thomas Joseph. (1895). *The principles of international law.* London: MacMillan.

Levi, Werner. (1991). *Contemporary international law: A concise introduction.* Boulder, CO: Westview Press.

McIntyre, Owen J. (1998). Environmental protection of international rivers: Case concerning the Gabcikovo–Nagymaros project (Hungary/Slovakia). *Journal of Environmental Law, 10,* 79–91.

Nussbaum, Arthur. (1954). *A concise history of the law of nations.* New York: MacMillan.

Paust, Jordan J.; Fitzpatrick, Joan M.; & Van Dyke, Jon M. (2005). *International law and litigation in the US* Second ed. St. Paul, MN: West Group.

Investment Law, Energy

Countries worldwide have sovereignty over their natural resources and may develop them according to their own environmental laws and regulations. International law recognizes the need for modern investment treaties—such as the North American Free Trade Agreement and the Energy Charter Treaty—that include provisions affecting the energy industry and its sustainability. Assessing how such treaties will impact the foreign investment climate in participating states remains a challenge for the future.

It is widely accepted that foreign investment is critical for sustainable development, and more so with respect to the oil and gas industry, a capital-intensive industry with a long gestation period (Elder 1991; Ginther, Denters, and de Waart 1995; Vale Columbia Centre and WAIPA 2010). Although international law recognizes national sovereignty over natural resources, international law places limitations on the exercise of such sovereign rights in a situation where it causes harm to other states or when it is pursued in an unsustainable manner (Cameron 2010). Consequently, the emergence of sustainability laws has had an impact on worldwide energy investments (Sands 1995).

The development and use of oil, gas, and nuclear energy are subject to specific international regulation. Other sources of energy—coal and renewable sources such as wind, solar, and geothermal—are scarcely regulated by international instruments. Because the effects of their operations are thought to be confined within national borders, they constitute an insignificant percentage of the global energy mix, and/or they cause relatively less damage to the environment as to attract much international attention. The development and use of oil, gas, and nuclear energy pose more serious environmental, health, social, and cultural consequences; they may result in oil spills, pollution

and degradation of the environment, displacement of local communities, or accidents (Smith and RMMLF 2010; Park 2002; Gao 1998; Horbach 1999).

The North American Free Trade Agreement (NAFTA) and the Energy Charter Treaty (ECT), two multilateral trade and investment treaties, have direct relevance to the energy sector and how it might be developed in a sustainable manner. Other relevant international instruments include the Law of the Sea Convention 1982, Climate Change Convention 1992, the Convention on Biodiversity 1992, the United Nations Framework Convention on Climate Change (UNFCC) 1997, the Kyoto Protocol 1997, and the increasing network of bilateral investment treaties (Cameron 2010; Vandevelde 2010). This article focuses only on NAFTA and the Energy Charter Treaty because, generally speaking, the key provisions on investment in both treaties are similar to those contained in most other investment treaties, and, more specifically, both contain explicit provisions on sustainability. Additionally, the ECT deals exclusively with the energy sector, and NAFTA contains a chapter on energy.

Historical Background and Objectives

After fourteen months of negotiations, the leaders of the United States, Canada, and Mexico signed NAFTA on 7 October 1992, and the treaty came into effect on 1 January 1994. NAFTA was built upon the Canada-United States Free Trade Agreement of 1989. Before the NAFTA agreement came into effect, however, a Supplementary Agreement was reached in August 1993, upon the insistence of President Clinton, to address concerns over protection of the environment and workers' rights, neither of which were sufficiently addressed in the original NAFTA. The

Supplemental Agreement is a comprehensive trade and investment agreement that affects all aspects of doing business in Canada, Mexico, and the United States. It seeks to eliminate barriers (such as tariffs) to the free flow of goods and services, removes restrictions to investment, and strengthens intellectual property rights among the three countries. It was envisaged by the contracting states as an effort toward establishing a free trade area in the North American continent (similar to the European Union and the European Free Trade area) so as to enhance the competitiveness of the region in global trade and investment (Smith and Cluchey 1994). For the Canadian government, the main objectives for signing NAFTA were to get Canadian goods, services, and capital access to Mexico on an equal footing with the United States, and to make Canada attractive to foreign investors wishing to invest in the North American market (Saunders 1994). From the United States' perspective, NAFTA would help provide closer and more stable sources of energy supplies from Canada and Mexico and reduce its over reliance on the more unstable Middle Eastern oil (Smith and Cluchey 1994).

The ECT is the result of a political initiative in Europe in the early 1990s following the end of the Cold War and the disintegration of the Soviet Union. The then Dutch prime minister initiated the process by suggesting the creation of a European energy community and urged the development of the European Energy Charter, a nonbinding political declaration signed in The Hague in 1991 by fifty-six states, including the European Community and Australia, where ratification is still in progress. The Charter "represents a political commitment to cooperate in the energy sector, based on the principles of development of open and efficient energy markets" (Corell 2005). The participants to the Charter did acknowledge the need for a binding international legal framework for effective cooperation in the sector, and so negotiations for the ECT started in late 1991. The ECT and the Protocol on Energy Efficiency and Related Environmental Aspects (PEEREA) were signed in Lisbon on 17 December 1994 and came into force on 16 April 1998. Although the United States and Canada participated in the negotiations, they did not sign the treaty. As the name suggests, the ECT is a sectoral agreement; it deals solely with the energy industry and covers issues of trade, investment, transit, and environment.

The main goals of the initial negotiation parties were to help the Eastern European countries transition to market economies by injecting Western investment into their energy sector, which would help in ensuring security of energy supplies to western Europe. In this regard, the ECT "plays an important role as part of an international effort to build a legal foundation for energy security, based on the principles of open, competitive markets and sustainable development" (Energy Charter Secretariat n.d.). For the Eastern European and resource countries, "the main attraction of the treaty was to appear attractive, to be seen to play the rules of the global economy, reduce their political risk perception and not to be left out of possibly significant energy policy dialogue" (Wälde 2004). Overall, the "fundamental aim of the ECT is to strengthen the rule of law on energy issues by creating a level playing field of rules to be observed by all participating governments, thereby mitigating risks associated with energy-related investment and trade" (Energy Charter Secretariat n.d.). To date, the ECT has been signed by fifty-four members while twenty-four countries act as observers.

Energy Investment

With regard to energy, NAFTA Article 602 states that the agreement "applies to measures relating to energy and basic

petrochemical goods originating in the territories of the Parties and to measures relating to investment and to the cross-border trade in services associated with such goods." With respect to the Mexican energy sector, NAFTA falls short of achieving the objective of creating a common energy market and the liberalization of the sector. Due to historical and constitutional reasons, limitations are placed on foreign involvement in Mexico's energy sector, and these policies are reflected in NAFTA. Chapter 6, Annex 602.3 reserves to the Mexican state or its state entities all activities relating to exploration and exploitation of oil and gas, ownership and operation of pipelines, all foreign trade, transportation, storage, and distribution of Mexican crude oil and natural gas. Thus, NAFTA may have less impact on energy trade and investment in Mexico than it does in the United States and Canada, which "are bound to permit the free flow of energy goods and investments and of services throughout the energy sector" in accordance with the agreement (Herman 1997). This has the effect of constraining the ability of future Canadian governments from reverting to the old nationalistic and protectionist energy policy of the 1980s as reflected in the National Energy Programme of 1980 (Saunders 1994). Even with regard to Mexico, there are possibilities for foreign investment in the nonbasic petrochemicals and certain aspects of electricity generation sectors, which are not subject to the constitutional restriction on investment (Saunders 1994). Energy investment under NAFTA chapter 6 is reinforced by chapter 11, which is the most important chapter because it defines the rights and obligations of investors and the state parties. Similar to other investment treaties, including the ECT (Part III, Articles 10–17), NAFTA chapter 11 provides for a definition of protected "investment" and "investors," and the standard of treatment to be accorded such investments and investors from other member states. The standards of treatment include national and most-favored-nation treatment, fair and equitable treatment, full protection, and security. Other provisions that address more specific situations include conditions on expropriation of covered investment, guarantees on rights of free transfer of payments related to an investment, prohibition on performance requirements, and provisions intended to promote transparency or access to courts. These substantive provisions are backed by investor-state or state-state dispute resolution provisions. The first provision vests in the foreign investor a direct action (through international arbitration) against the host state for alleged violation of the investor's substantive rights, and the second includes a dispute settlement mechanism between the two state parties concerning the interpretation or application of the treaty (Vandevelde 2010; Konoplyanik and Wälde 2006). Over the years, several cases have been brought by foreign investors seeking to challenge measures adopted by host states that were alleged to not conform to their international investment treaty obligations under the applicable treaty (Vandevelde 2010; Salacuse 2010).

Sustainable Development

Both NAFTA and the ECT contain provisions on sustainability. In its preamble, the NAFTA state parties signal their support to promote sustainable development. In order to achieve this objective, the treaty permits each contracting state to take appropriate measures to ensure that investment activity in its territories is implemented in a manner consistent with environmental protection, provided such measures are consistent with the overall objectives of NAFTA. Furthermore, as specified by Article 1114(2), "it is inappropriate to encourage investment by relaxing domestic health, safety, or environmental measures."

In addition, the NAFTA Side Agreement on Environmental Cooperation provides for sanctions for lax enforcement of domestic environmental laws and standards. The provisions are to ensure that trade and investment activities in the member states' territories are conducted in a sustainable manner by preventing a "race to the bottom" approach by member states. Thus the Side Agreement (Article 1) expresses the willingness of the parties to promote certain conditions:

- sustainable development based on cooperation and mutually supportive environmental and economic policies
- enhanced compliance with and enforcement of environmental requirements
- transparency and public participation in developing environmental norms
- economically effective environmental measures

Under the Side Agreement, members of the public, including nongovernmental organizations (NGOs), are allowed to challenge a state party if it fails to effectively enforce its environmental laws or regulations. The Side Agreement establishes the Commission for Environmental Cooperation (CEC), the institutional framework to receive petitions from members of the public and, if necessary, investigate the claims and prepare a factual record, which might be published by the Council. (The Council is the CEC's governing body, composed of high-level environmental authorities from Canada, Mexico, and the United States.) The process has been utilized by many individuals and organizations with varying degrees of success. Hence, it has been described as a "'spotlighting' instrument intended to enhance governmental accountability and transparency" (Markell 2010; Knox 2010).

Similarly, Article 19 of the ECT enjoins member states to "strive to take precautionary measures to prevent or minimize environmental degradation" and to "take account of environmental considerations throughout the formulation and implementation of their energy policies." The treaty also requires that the member states take specific actions relating to the following:

- the promotion of market-based price reform and fuller reflection of environmental costs and benefits
- the encouragement of international cooperation
- information sharing on environmentally sound and economically efficient energy policies
- the promotion of environmental impact assessment activities and monitoring
- the promotion of public awareness on relevant environmental programs
- the research and development of energy efficient and environmentally sound technologies, including the transfer of technology

Although these are soft law and not legally binding obligations, they may have indirect legal implications, such as "justifying regulatory measures subject to the scrutiny of the investment protection regime" (Wälde 2001). Furthermore, the Protocol on Energy Efficiency and Related Environmental Aspects (PEEREA) requires member states to formulate policy principles aimed at improving energy efficiency, reducing negative environmental impact, and fostering international cooperation between member states. The implementation of the PEEREA would provide transition economies with good practices and an opportunity to share experiences and policy advice on energy efficiency issues with their Western counterparts.

Impact and Current Challenges

According to the United States government, NAFTA has achieved its core goals of expanding trade and investment between the three countries. It asserts that "from 1993 to 2007, trade among the NAFTA nations more than tripled, from $297 billion to $930 billion" and that "business investment in the United States has risen by 117 percent since 1993, compared to 45 percent increase between 1979 and 1993" (Office of the United States Trade Representative 2008). With respect to the energy sector, the business and legal climate in Canada and Mexico have become more hospitable to foreign energy-related investment as a result of NAFTA (Smith and Cluchey 1994). Concerning sustainable development, it has been noted that the NAFTA regime "has had its greatest success as a regional effort to promote sustainable development. It has contributed to stronger environmental protections, especially in Mexico," and it has formed a basis for subsequent United States Free Trade Agreements to include environmental protection provisions (Knox 2010). But concerns over the

fairness or neutrality of the process, the slow pace of the procedure, and the apparently "toothless" character of the mechanisms have marred the success of the Side Agreement on Environment (Markell 2010; Knox 2010). Furthermore, one of the strongest challenges facing NAFTA, the ECT, and other investment treaties relates to how to reconcile the obligations of the state parties toward foreign investors and the needs for regulatory autonomy in the areas of environmental protection and human rights. The absence of clear guidelines in the investment treaties on how to resolve such potential conflicts poses a serious legal and policy challenge to state parties and foreign investors who have to rely on the interpretative decisions of arbitral tribunals (Kingsbury and Schill 2010; Vandevelde 2009).

Some general conclusions can be drawn from this overview of energy investment law. First, although every country has sovereignty over its natural resources and the right to develop them in accordance with its environmental laws and regulations, modern investment treaties such as NAFTA and the ECT may constrain a member-state's discretion. Second, modern investment treaties vest substantive and procedural rights in foreign investors to challenge egregious host-state measures before international tribunals in a manner never before known under general international law. Third, it is not yet settled how to strike a proper balance between energy investment and sustainable development, hence the uncertainty in the legal relationship between foreign investors and host states. Finally, it is difficult to assess the extent to which modern investment treaties, such as NAFTA and the ECT, have contributed to improving the investment climate in the energy sector of the state parties.

Peter CAMERON and Abba KOLO
University of Dundee

See also in the *Berkshire Encyclopedia of Sustainability* Climate Change Disclosure—Legal Framework; Climate Change Mitigation; Development, Sustainable—Overview of Laws and Commissions; Energy Conservation Initiatives; Environmental Law—United States and Canada; Environmental Law, Soft vs. Hard; Free Trade; Investment Law, Foreign; Green Taxes; Utilities Regulation

FURTHER READINGS

Cameron, Peter. (2010). *International energy investment law: The pursuit of stability.* Oxford, UK: Oxford University Press.
Corell, Hans. (2006). Introduction to the Energy Charter Treaty. In Clarisse Ribeiro (Ed.), *Investment arbitration and the Energy Charter Treaty* (pp. 1-3). Huntington, NY: JurisNet.
Elder, P. S. (1991). Sustainability. *McGill Law Journal, 36,* 831–834.
Energy Charter Secretariat. (n.d.) About the charter. Retrieved November 23, 2010, from http://www.encharter.org/index.php?id=7
Gao, Zhiguo. (1998). Environmental regulation of oil and gas in the twentieth century and beyond: An introduction and overview. In Zhiguo Gao (Ed.), *Environmental regulation of oil and gas* (pp. 3–58). London: Kluwer Law International.

Ginther, Konrad; Denters, Erik; & de Waart, P. J. I. M. (1995). *Sustainable development and good governance.* Dordrecht, The Netherlands: M. Nijhoff.

Herman, Lawrence L. (1997). NAFTA and the ECT: Divergent approaches with a core of harmony. *Journal of Energy and Natural Resources Law, 15*, 129–133.

Horbach, Nathalie. (1999). Lacunae of international nuclear liability agreements. In Nathalie Horbach (Ed.), *Contemporary developments in nuclear energy law* (p. 43). London: Kluwer Law International.

Kingsbury, Benedict, & Schill, Stephan. (2010). Public law concepts to balance investors' rights with state regulatory actions in the public interest – the concept of proportionality. In Stephan Schill (Ed.), *International investment law and comparative public law* (pp. 75–104). Oxford, UK: Oxford University Press.

Knox, John H. (2010). The neglected lessons of the NAFTA environmental regime. *Wake Forest Law Review, 45*, 391–424.

Konoplyanik, Andrei, & Wälde, Thomas. (2006). Energy Charter Treaty and its role in international energy. *Journal of Energy and Natural Resources Law, 24*(4), 523–558.

Markell, David. (2010). The role of spotlighting procedures in promoting citizen participation, transparency, and accountability. *Wake Forest Law Review, 45*, 425–467.

Office of the United States Trade Representative. (2008). NAFTA facts. Retrieved November 23, 2010, from http://www.ustr.gov

Park, Patricia. (2002). *Energy law and the environment.* London: Taylor & Francis.

Salacuse, Jeswald W. (2010). *The law of investment treaties.* Oxford, UK: Oxford University Press.

Sands, Philippe. (1995). International law in the field of sustainable development: Emerging legal principles. In Winfried Lang (Ed.), *Sustainable development and international law* (pp. 53–66). London: Graham & Trotman / M. Nijhoff.

Saunders, J. Owen. (1994). GATT, NAFTA and the North American energy trade: A Canadian perspective. *Journal of Energy and Natural Resources Law, 12*, 4–9.

Smith, Ernest E. & Cluchey, David P. (1994). GATT, NAFTA and the trade in energy: A US perspective. *Journal of Energy and Natural Resources Law, 12*, 27–58.

Smith, Ernest E., & Rocky Mountain Mineral Law Foundation (RMMLF). (2010). *International petroleum transactions* (3rd ed.). Denver, CO: Rocky Mountain Mineral Law Foundation.

Vale Columbia Centre & World Association of Investment Promotion Agencies (WAIPA). (2010). Investment promotion agencies and sustainable FDI: Moving towards the fourth generation of investment promotion. Retrieved November 23, 2010, from http://www.vcc.columbia.edu/files/vale/content/IPASurvey.pdf

Vandevelde, Kenneth. (2009). A comparison of the 2004 and 1994 US model BITs. In Karl Sauvant (Ed.), *Yearbook on international investment law & policy 2008–2009* (pp. 283–315). Oxford, UK: Oxford University Press.

Vandevelde, Kenneth. (2010). *Bilateral investment treaties.* Oxford, UK: Oxford University Press.

Wälde, Thomas. (2001). International disciplines on national environmental regulation: With particular focus on multilateral investment treaties. In Permanent Court of Arbitration (Ed.), *International investments and protection of the environment* (pp. 29–47). The Hague, The Netherlands: Kluwer Law International.

Wälde, Thomas. (2004). The Energy Charter Treaty: Expanding the liberalization of energy industries. Unpublished paper on file with the authors.

Investment Law, Foreign

As multinational corporations seek to reduce costs, they increasingly turn to developing countries in order to conduct business. The way in which that business is conducted can have substantial impacts on the environment and human rights of communities within host states. The proper legal management of foreign investment can help to promote sustainable development by setting standards that protect the environment and human health.

Foreign investment law, policies, and practices impact a diverse range of areas well beyond the field of investment, reaching into issues such as environmental protection, human rights, and economic development. For this reason, foreign investment inflows, and the international legal framework regulating their protection, can have both positive and negative consequences for the states in which foreign investors operate, termed *host states*. In particular, foreign investment and international investment law can have profound implications for sustainable development policies.

Foreign Investment and Sustainable Development

The relationship between foreign investment activities and the sustainability objectives of host states is complex, involving the potential for substantial economic benefits and increased standards of living, but also the risk of detrimental social and environmental effects.

Foreign Direct Investment Inflows

The term *foreign investment* encompasses both foreign direct investment and foreign portfolio investment. Foreign direct investment is defined by the UN Conference on Trade and Development (UNCTAD) as

> investment involving a long-term relationship and reflecting a lasting interest and control by a resident entity in one economy (foreign direct investor or parent enterprise) in an enterprise resident in an economy other than that of the foreign direct investor (FDI enterprise or affiliate enterprise or foreign affiliate). FDI implies that the investor exerts a significant degree of influence on the management of the enterprise resident in the other economy. Such investment involves both the initial transaction between the two entities and all subsequent transactions between them and among foreign affiliates, both incorporated and unincorporated. (UNCTAD 2008)

Foreign portfolio investment is described as including:

> a variety of instruments which are traded (or tradeable) in organized and other financial markets: bonds, equities and money market instruments. The International Monetary Fund even includes derivatives or secondary instruments, such as options, in the category of FPI. The channels of cross-border investments are also varied: securities are acquired and sold by retail investors, commercial banks, investment trusts (mutual funds, country and regional funds, pension funds and hedge funds). (UNCTAD 1999)

Global flows of foreign capital continued to increase at exponential rates from 2000 until the global financial crisis that engulfed financial markets in 2008–2009 and slowed growth (UNCTAD 2009). UNCTAD reports indicate that global foreign direct investment reached an estimated $897 billion in 2005, a 29 percent increase on 2004 figures. The upward trend continued, with 2006 experiencing a

38 percent increase overall on 2005, reaching $1,306 billion in global foreign direct investment inflows, followed by the high point of $1,979 billion in 2007 (UNCTAD 2008). Despite the global impact of the financial crisis, however, all regional groupings of developing economies—namely Africa, Latin America, and Asia—have continued to record increases in foreign direct investment inflows (UNCTAD 2008; UNCTAD 2009). Global levels of foreign capital inflows are expected to resume their upward trend in 2011 (UNCTAD 2009).

These figures do not mean that foreign direct investment distribution among states is equal; many developing countries do not have the necessary funds to promote the desired levels of development. Addressing inequalities in the funding of development is a key component of the Millennium Development Goals as set out in the UN Millennium Declaration (2000). This was also a key issue for the International Conference on Financing for Development in Monterrey, Mexico, in March 2002, which produced the Monterrey Consensus, a document that sought to address financing for development through a comprehensive, cross-institutional, and partnership-emphasizing approach.

Foreign investment inflows can potentially involve substantial benefits for host states. Increased levels of capital in the economy; the initiation of new infrastructure projects; increased employment levels; increased economic growth rates; and the introduction of new, safer, and more efficient technologies can generate wealth and increase standards of living in host states (Hunter, Salzman, and Zaelke 2002, 1268–1274). There are also many reasons for multinational corporations to engage in foreign direct investment. Generally, decisions to expand into foreign investment are made to lower costs or to generate further profits through expansion into new markets. The reduction of costs might be achieved through low-cost production processes, cheaper labor, an abundance of inexpensive raw materials, tax incentives, or the avoidance of import/export tariffs (Hunter, Salzman, and Zaelke 2002, 1269).

Foreign Investment Practices: Controversies

There is a more controversial side, however, to foreign investment inflows. Significant causes of concern include the means by which such costs-savings are made and the consequences of these activities for host states, particularly for local communities. The concern surrounds whether these lower costs, and the consequential increase in the level of foreign investment, are achieved at the expense of the social fabric or environmental conditions of the local community (Zarsky 1999; Neumayer 2001). Are the production processes cheaper because the environmental standards are lower or because the true environmental costs are not reflected in the prices? Is the actual cost of repairing environmental damage from corporate activities an externality imposed on the local community? Is the cost of labor cheaper because there are no worker protection measures in place? In the midst of fierce competition to attract foreign investment, will states lower their domestic environmental and health standards, effectively engaging in what is called a regulatory "race to the bottom," so as to further reduce the costs of doing business and thus become more attractive to potential foreign investors? (Hunter, Salzman, and Zaelke 2002, 1269–1274; Zarsky 1999; Neumayer 2001, 41–67). In summary, what are the environmental politico-legal consequences of interstate competition for foreign investment? (Esty and Geradin 1998).

These questions raise the specter of "pollution havens" and "regulatory chill." The pollution haven theory is based on the premise that in order to remain competitive in the market for foreign investment, states will set unacceptably low environmental standards, or set adequate standards but not enforce them, essentially causing the unraveling of environmental restrictions—hence the description "race to the bottom" (Zarsky 1999; Neumayer 2001). The hypothesis is that multinational corporations that cannot continue environmentally damaging practices in developed states as a result of increasingly restrictive environmental protection standards will be able to export those practices to developing states with low environmental protection measures, producing so-called pollution havens.

The regulatory chill, or "political drag," argument puts forward the idea that the fear of a loss of competitiveness in international markets, as well as capital flight from states with high environmental standards, has led policy

makers to refrain from raising environmental standards and tightening regulations. The theory does not require there to be any actual movement of investment dollars to states offering pollution havens, only the existence of the fear that there might be capital flight (Neumayer 2001; Esty and Geradin 1998). A version of the regulatory chill theory also affects international investment disputes. The argument is that the threat of investor claims against the host state may preclude the strengthening of environmental regulation. It has been suggested that the fear of facing investor claims not only encompasses the potential for large damages awards, but is also driven by the substantial costs involved in defending arbitral proceedings (Tienhaara 2009). Indeed, commentators have pointed to a number of incidents as examples of investment dispute–related regulatory chill, including the withdrawal of Canadian legislation banning a fuel additive on environmental and health grounds following the commencement of investor-state arbitration; the abandonment of highly restrictive tobacco legislation following threatened investor claims; and the non-implementation of new forestry legislation in Indonesia prohibiting the operation of open-cast mining in designated areas following discussions with foreign-owned mining corporations (Tienhaara 2009).

International Investment Agreements

Foreign investment is governed by different legal instruments at individual, national, and international levels. At the individual level, an investor may enter into contracts with the host state that governs the operation of the investment. Nationally, states often implement domestic legislation regulating the conditions under which foreign investment is permitted. Internationally, foreign investment is protected by a network of bilateral investment treaties and investment provisions within free trade agreements, such as chapter 11 of the North American Free Trade Agreement (NAFTA). These international investment protection agreements now number approximately three thousand (Newcombe and Paradell 2009) and are the dominant mechanism through which investment protection is pursued at the international level. Such treaties also contain the central tenets of international investment law.

Background of International Investment Agreements

Prior to the development of bilateral investment treaties, foreign investment disputes fell within an area of customary international law known as the diplomatic protection of aliens. In the wake of a wave of postcolonial nationalizations and the advent of the so-called New International Economic Order in the mid-twentieth century, capital-exporting states developed bilateral investment treaties as a more effective mechanism to protect foreign investment. The first bilateral investment treaty was entered into in 1959 between Germany and Pakistan.

The particular scope of foreign investment protection contained within each bilateral investment treaty varies, yet they all possess core protection guarantees, such as adherence to the national treatment standard, most-favored-nation treatment requirements, fair and equitable treatment, and guarantees against uncompensated expropriation of the investment. The national treatment standard provides that foreign investors and their investments are to be "accorded treatment no less favorable than that which the host state accords to its own investors" (Dolzer and Schreuer 2008). Guarantees of most-favored-nation status entail extending to investors of signatory states any privilege or benefit that has been granted to a third state (Newcombe and Paradell 2009). Key components of the fair and equitable treatment standard are the legitimate expectations of the investor regarding the regulatory framework of the host state, the maintenance of a stable legal and business environment, and following due process (Newcombe and Paradell 2009; McLachlan, Shore, and Weiniger 2007).

International law also permits expropriation of foreign-owned property, but only if the expropriation is for a public purpose, if it is nondiscriminatory and is not of an arbitrary nature, and if compensation is paid. Direct expropriation of an investment is not difficult to identify as it involves the seizure of physical assets. More subtle forms, however, are inherently less identifiable as compensable action. The various manifestations are characterized by a diminution

in property rights or interference with property interests without a formal transfer of ownership. This category of indirect expropriation, together with other claims such as alleged breaches of the fair and equitable treatment standard, is increasingly forming the basis for challenges by the investor to public welfare regulation in the host state, such as environmental protection measures, health and safety requirements, and social policy initiatives. This trend has significant implications for the implementation of domestic sustainability programs within host states, as such challenges have the potential to limit policy options and preclude the introduction of new regulatory approaches.

Legal Challenges

Over the last decade, there has been an increasing number of disputes between investors and host states concerning the treatment given to investments by government bodies. These disputes have often involved allegations of breaches of bilateral investment treaties or investment provisions within free trade agreements. The majority of such treaties contain dispute-settlement clauses permitting an investor to require that the host state resolve the dispute before an international arbitral tribunal, a system known as investor–state arbitration. This system is a decentralized dispute-settlement mechanism comprising ad hoc arbitral panels. There is no permanent dispute-settlement body and no appellate facility. Most investment treaties, however, specify a particular set of procedural rules to govern the establishment and operation of individual tribunals, such as the rules for the International Centre for the Settlement of Investment Disputes (ICSID) and the UN Commission on International Trade Law (UNCITRAL). These rules can have significant implications for the management of hearings as they determine procedures on the appointment of arbitrators, the ability of third parties to submit amicus curiae briefs, and whether there is public access to the documents and hearings. These restrictions have drawn criticism, largely on the basis that the lack of transparency surrounding the proceedings and the commercial model adopted are inappropriate for investor–state arbitration given that public interest issues are necessarily implicated in disputes involving the state (Tienhaara 2009; Van Harten 2007).

Considerable controversy has also surrounded the potential impact that international investment law and the system of investor–state arbitration can have on the domestic sustainability programs of host states. This concern has been generated by recent investor challenges to the introduction of new regulation designed to meet the environmental, health, social, economic, or human rights needs of host states. For example, investors have brought claims against states that have established affirmative action employment policies, created regulations protecting groundwater from contamination with harmful chemicals, restricted mining on lands of indigenous cultural significance, taken emergency financial measures, prohibited the use of potent pesticides, and banned fuel additives to protect human health and the environment (*Methanex Corporation v. United States*, 2005; *Glamis Gold v. United States*, 2009; *Sempra Energy International v. Argentina*, 2007; *Dow Agro Sciences LLC v. Canada*, filed 2009; *Ethyl Corporation v. Canada*, 1999; *Foresti v. South Africa*, filed 2007). Investors in these cases claimed that the new regulatory measures detrimentally affected the value of their investments and therefore breached the applicable investment treaty. When such claims are successful, host states can be required to pay large compensation awards to investors. For these reasons, it has been argued that international investment law and investor–state arbitration can impinge on host state policy creation, including on domestic sustainable development programs.

Sustainable Finance

In contrast to the circumstances surrounding investor–state arbitration, there is a more positive form of interaction between foreign investment practices, law, and sustainability objectives. New trends in corporate behavior have emerged over the last decade that may influence foreign investment practices and the substantive development of international investment law. The adoption of voluntary codes setting standards for environmental corporate conduct, the integration of corporate social responsibility programs, the establishment of ethical investment funds, and the emergence of the sustainable finance movement all reflect an increasing shift in emphasis toward accommodating public concerns about the role of multinational corporations in socially and environmentally harmful practices (Assadourian 2006; McBarnet 2007; Jeucken 2004). *Sustainable finance* is the term coined to describe the process of integrating environmental and social criteria into investment and financial decision making. As attention has turned to the wider effects of corporate practices, companies needed to respond to pressure from consumers, nongovernmental organizations, shareholders, and other stakeholders to improve their social and environmental performance.

This shift in the expectations of corporate conduct has also had an impact within the investment sector, leading to a different emphasis in more recent bilateral investment treaties, termed *new generation BITs* (Newcombe 2007). Traditionally, bilateral investment treaties have not referred to public interest issues or the policy needs of the host state, focusing solely on investment protection and promotion. In contrast, several recent international investment agreements, such as the US-Uruguay Bilateral Investment Treaty, contain express references to sustainable development, protection of the environment, and the health and safety of the public in the host state (Newcombe 2007). These initiatives perhaps point to a future in which an enhanced level of awareness of sustainability issues can be developed within international investment law and investor–state arbitration.

Kate MILES
University of Sydney

See also in the *Berkshire Encyclopedia of Sustainability* Development, Sustainable—Overview of Laws and Commissions; Fair Trade; Free Trade; International Law; Investment Law, Energy

FURTHER READING

Assadourian, Erik. (2006). Transforming corporations. In the Worldwatch Institute (Ed.), *State of the world 2006* (p. 171). New York: W. W. Norton & Company.

Cordonier Segger, Marie-Claire; Gehring, Markus; & Newcombe, Andrew. (Eds.). (forthcoming). *Sustainable development in international investment law*. Montreal: Centre for International Sustainable Development Law.

Dolzer, Rudolf, & Schreuer, Christoph. (2008). *Principles of international investment law*. New York: Oxford University Press.

Esty, Daniel C., & Geradin, Damien. (1998). Environmental protection and international competitiveness: A conceptual framework. *Journal of World Trade, 32*(3), 5–46.

Hunter, David; Salzman, James; & Zaelke, Durwood. (2002). *International environmental law and policy* (2nd ed.). New York: Foundation Press.

Jeucken, Marcel. (2004). *Sustainability in finance: Banking on the planet.* Delft, The Netherlands: Eburon Academic Publishers.

McBarnet, Doreen. (2007). Corporate social responsibility beyond law, through law, for law: The new corporate accountability. In Doreen McBarnet, Aurora Voiculescu & Tom Campbell (Eds.), *The new corporate accountability: Corporate social responsibility and the law* (p. 9). Cambridge, UK: Cambridge University Press.

McLachlan, Campbell; Shore, Laurence; & Weiniger, Matthew. (2007). *International investment arbitration: Substantive principles.* Oxford, UK: Oxford International Arbitration Series.

Neumayer, Eric. (2001). *Greening trade and investment: Environmental protection without protectionism.* London: Earthscan Publications Ltd.

Newcombe, Andrew. (2007). Sustainable development and investment treaty law. *The Journal of World Investment & Trade, 8*, 357–408.

Newcombe, Andrew, & Paradell, Lluís. (2009). *Law and practice of investment treaties: Standards of treatment.* Alphen aan den Rijn, The Netherlands: Wolters Kluwer.

Tienhaara, Kyla. (2009). *The expropriation of environmental governance: Protecting foreign investors at the expense of public policy.* New York: Cambridge University Press.

United Nations Conference on Trade and Development (UNCTAD). (1999). Foreign portfolio investment (FPI) and foreign direct investment (FDI): Characteristics, similarities, complementarities and differences, policy implications and development impact. Retrieved January 16, 2008, from http://www.unctad.org/en/docs/c2em6d2&c1.en.pdf

United Nations Conference on Trade and Development (UNCTAD). (2007). *World investment report 2007: Transnational corporations, extractive industries and development.* Retrieved March 2, 2008, from http://www.unctad.org/en/docs/wir2007_en.pdf

United Nations Conference on Trade and Development (UNCTAD). (2008). Foreign direct investment: Statistics. Retrieved January 16, 2008, from http://unctadstat.unctad.org/ReportFolders/reportFolders.aspx?sRF_ActivePath=P,5,27&sRF_Expanded=,P,5,27&sCS_ChosenLang=en

United Nations Conference on Trade and Development (UNCTAD). (2009). *World investment report 2009: Transnational corporations, agricultural production and development.* Retrieved January 20, 2010, from http://www.unctad.org/en/docs/wir2009_en.pdf

United Nations Millenium Declaration. (2000). United Nations General Assembly Res. 55/2, Doc. A/55/L.2.

Van Harten, Gus. (2007). *Investment treaty arbitration and public law.* Oxford, UK: Oxford University Press.

Zarsky, Lyuba. (1999). Havens, halos and spaghetti: Untangling the evidence about foreign direct investment and the environment. In *Foreign Direct Investment and the Environment* (pp. 47–73). Paris: Organisation for Economic Co-operation and Development.

COURT CASES

Dow Agro Sciences LLC v. Government of Canada, Notice of Arbitration (31 March 2009).

Ethyl Corporation v. Canada, Jurisdiction Phase, 38 ILM 708 (1999).

Glamis Gold Ltd v. United States of America, Award (June 2009).

Methanex Corporation v. United States of America, 44 ILM 1345 (2005).

Piero Foresti and others v. Republic of South Africa, ICSID Case No. ARB(AF)/07/1

S. D. Myers, Inc. v. Canada, Partial Award (Decision on the Merits) (November 2000).

Sempra Energy International v. Argentina, Award, ICSID Case No. ARB/02/16 (2007).

Law of the Sea

A number of UN conventions and other treaties establish the legal regimes that govern the use of the oceans. Because of the ecological sensitivity of the seas and oceans of the world, most agreements are influenced by environmental law although they regulate other activities. Although these laws are designed to be able to be adapted to emerging challenges, they are having difficulty responding to current human pressures on the oceans.

The Law of the Sea is one of the oldest areas of international law. The oceans cover more than 70 percent of the planet's surface, and their importance both for exploitable living resources and for navigation is reflected in a number of important legal treatises written on this issue over the centuries. In modern times the best-known defense of the freedom of navigation, *De mare liberum*, was written in 1608 by the Dutch jurist Hugo Grotius to defend the rights of the Dutch East India Company to navigate the oceans freely. This was more than a century after the Papal Bull and the 1494 Treaty of Tordesillas purported to divide the newly discovered lands and oceans outside Europe between Spain and Portugal.

In the latter half of the twentieth century, a number of important attempts were made to develop a comprehensive legal regime for the oceans. In 1958 in The Hague, the United Nations Conference on the Law of the Sea (known as UNCLOS I) concluded four conventions, which covered the legal regimes of the territorial sea and contiguous zone, the continental shelf, the high seas, and fisheries. As sophisticated as these treaties were, they failed to address a number of key issues, such as the permissible width of the territorial sea, which up until then had been generally been accepted as three nautical miles (often dubbed the "cannon shot rule," although this may not the basis of the width criterion). Although they entered into force, these conventions were never ratified by a large number of States, and in 1960, a second and unsuccessful attempt (known as UNCLOS II) was made to solve outstanding issues. In the 1970s, inspired by a famous speech by the Maltese ambassador Arvid Pardo, in which he claimed that the international seabed and its resources should be the "common heritage of mankind," the United Nations General Assembly agreed to a conference to develop a comprehensive legal regime for the oceans.

The 1982 UN Law of the Sea Convention

The result was a process that started in 1974 and lasted for nine years, until December 1982 when in Montego Bay, Jamaica, the 1982 UN Convention on the Law of the Sea (LOSC) was finally concluded. It was described by the final conference chairman, Tommy Koh of Singapore, as "a constitution for the oceans." The Third United Nations Conference on the Law of the Sea (UNCLOS III) was a protracted and historic process, which evolved its own innovative decision-making procedure based on consensus and a "package deal" approach to the finalization of a comprehensive treaty regime (in which no reservations were permitted, so concessions were made by some parties in exchange for different concessions by others).

The Convention itself comprises 320 articles with nine annexes. It developed new legal concepts, such as the 200 nautical mile (nm) exclusive economic zone, archipelagic status for island states, the special status of the deep sea bed as the common heritage of mankind, and the definition of the outer edge of the continental shelf as beyond 200 nm. It created new institutions to regulate these concepts—an International Seabed Authority (ISA), a Commission on the Limits of the Continental Shelf (CLCS), and an

International Tribunal on the Law of the Sea (ITLOS), to act an important new part of the comprehensive compulsory dispute settlement system that it established. It also contained mechanisms—called legislation by reference—whereby key provisions, such as environmental standards, could be updated by other treaty regimes, such as the shipping conventions administered by the International Maritime Organization.

The Convention also introduced important new environmental obligations. Customary international law had traditionally had problems reconciling freedom of the seas with restrictions on the rights to pollute the oceans. The 1982 Convention requires unequivocally that all states "have the obligation to protect and preserve the marine environment" and to take proactive measures to "prevent, reduce, and control pollution of the marine environment," including those steps necessary to "protect and preserve rare or fragile ecosystems as well as the habitat of depleted, threatened or endangered species and other forms of marine life."

The Implementation Agreements of 1994 and 1995

Despite this massive achievement, the treaty languished for more than a decade without coming into force because a number of developed countries—led by the United States—objected to the provisions relating to the regime for seabed mining. In a breakthrough pioneered by the UN secretary general, in 1994 the General Assembly agreed an Implementation Agreement, which modified the way that some of the more controversial provisions would be applied. This compromise allowed the Convention to come into force in November 1994.

A year later, a second Implementation Agreement was agreed relating to the legal regime of straddling fish stocks and highly migratory fish stocks. This issue had been called the "unfinished agenda" of the 1982 treaty, and the negotiation of the Agreement had been mandated by the 1992 UN Conference on Environment and Development

(UNCED). The 1995 UN Fish Stocks Agreement incorporates modern thinking on capture fisheries management, such as the use of the precautionary principle and the ecosystem approach to fisheries.

Sectoral and Regional Conventions

Although the 1982 Convention provides the overarching framework for the law of the sea, the majority of detailed regulatory issues are covered by a wealth other treaty regimes that concern the regulation of fisheries at a species and regional level, the management of coastal areas under the regional seas conventions mostly administered by the UN Environment Programme (UNEP), and marine pollution from shipping.

Although there are a myriad of international fisheries treaty regimes, and records of bilateral regimes date back to the nineteenth century, most are creations of the post–World War II years, the majority negotiated under the auspices of the UN Food and Agriculture Organization (FAO). These are not environmental law agreements, but the evolution of international environmental law has introduced new concepts into the practice of many of these bodies. Early fisheries treaties focused on the needs of human exploitation, using concepts such as maximum sustainable yield (defined in human consumption terms). The recognition by biologists—still not shared by many fishers—that fishery resources are finite resources that require systematic conservation and management has been given a further boost by the growing adoption of the precautionary principle now endorsed by FAO for all capture fishery operations. Equally important has been the recognition that fish exist within a marine ecosystem and that sustainable exploitation requires an understanding of, and respect for, the parameters and constraints of that ecosystem. These concepts are reflected the 1995 UN Fish Stocks Agreement and a number of other new fisheries agreements. This agreement

was quickly followed by the finalization within FAO of a non-binding Code of Conduct for Responsible Fishing, followed by a series of International Plans of Action, including one that sets out an agenda for the control of Illegal, Unregulated and Unreported (IUU) Fishing.

In addition to bilateral fisheries agreements, there are a number of Regional Fisheries Bodies set up by treaty, some of them purely advisory and others with management responsibilities. The latter are known as Regional Fisheries Management Organizations (RFMOs), and they cover key species, such as tuna. There is also a web of general fisheries treaty bodies but with major geographical gaps. A treaty setting up an RFMO to cover the South Pacific was concluded in 2009, and another is being negotiated for the North Pacific. There are other gaps in the South Atlantic and central Pacific.

More than 140 countries participate in thirteen Regional Seas programs established under the auspices of the UNEP regional seas program, covering the Black Sea, the wider Caribbean, east Asian Seas, eastern Africa, south Asian Seas, ROPME Sea Area (the Persian Gulf), Mediterranean, northeast Pacific, northwest Pacific, the Red Sea and Gulf of Aden, southeast Pacific, Pacific, and western Africa. Six of these programs are directly administered by UNEP. All of the Regional Seas programs have developed action plans and most also have developed specific legal frameworks with conventions and protocols. In addition there are a number of partner program of regional seas treaties, which are not under the UNEP umbrella. These regional treaty regimes include those for the Antarctic, the Baltic, the Caspian, and the North-East Atlantic.

Regulation of Shipping and Marine Pollution

The International Maritime Organization (IMO) provides a key forum for the regulation of shipping issues, including pollution from ships. The IMO functions by consensus, and national delegations are often drawn from industry as well as government and nongovernmental organizations. The regulatory authority for tankers—like vessels of all kinds—is the nation whose flag the vessel flies (the flag state). Many of the nations with the largest number of vessels are open registry states or flags of convenience. Although the LOSC does give port states authority to apprehend vessels for acts of pollution in breach of "applicable international rules and standards," in general for a treaty regime to apply to its vessels, the flag state must become a party to the treaty, so the challenge has been to impose stricter standards on vessel owners in a way in which they are likely to agree to them. IMO has done this through the gradual introduction of new technology into the construction of tankers, such as divided hulls with so-called "Load on Top" systems that allow tankers to

filter oil from ballast water, separate ballast water tanks, and even double hulls to lessen the risk of oil leaks from impacts.

The 1973/78 MARPOL Convention (the International Convention for the Prevention of Pollution from Ships) provides the main regulatory regime for pollution from vessels of all sorts, including oil tankers, and was extended to noxious liquid substances, packaged waste, sewage, garbage, and to air pollution. This gradualist approach has been reinforced by the fact that the detailed standards set by the MARPOL annexes are adopted and amended by the IMO Marine Environment Protection Committee (MEPC) and subject to acceptance by two-thirds of the parties, constituting at least 50 percent of the tonnage of the world merchant fleet. MARPOL requirements, and also those of the London Convention regulating dumping at sea (discussed below), are incorporated by reference into the 1982 LOSC, and those provisions that are in force may now be argued to be binding on all parties to the 1982 Convention; since they can be considered part of customary law, they are therefore binding on all nations. Incorporation by reference is an important means of introducing dynamism into the overarching framework of the 1982 Convention so as to keep it up to date. When the Convention text uses phrases such as "applicable international rules and standards established by the competent international organization," it is recognizing that over time these organizations will develop new rules and standards that, by reference, become part of the applicable regime of the 1982 Convention.

London Convention

The 1972 London Convention regulating dumping at sea has also taken a gradualist approach. If dumping takes place on the high seas, the only bodies that can regulate this activity are the flag states and the states whose ports the vessel sails from or returns to. The 1972 Convention adopted what has now become a common approach in environmental agreements—a listing system. It initially listed substances that could not be dumped in the ocean, as well as substances that could be dumped only with a permit. As public support for the elimination of dumping in the oceans has grown, the regulatory structure, which requires signatory states to enforce obligations against any vessels loading in their ports and their flag vessels anywhere in the world, has progressively tightened its regime. The initial approach of listing banned substances has been entirely replaced by what is called a "negative listing" approach. Negative listing is an important application of the precautionary principle. It reverses the presumption that any nonlisted substances may be dumped. Under the negative list, only listed substances may be dumped and everything else is prohibited. By the use of this approach, the parties to the

1972 London Dumping Convention have effectively ended the ocean dumping of waste, and for this reason in 1990 it was renamed the London Convention. In 1996, a protocol was concluded with the 1972 Convention that reflects the precautionary approach as well as the negative listing methodology. In 2006, the Convention was amended to envisage sub–ocean floor storage of CO_2, which results from carbon and capture and storage.

Contemporary Threats to the Marine Environment

In the 1970s, much attention was given to the exploitation of so-called manganese nodules, which contain a range of valuable minerals but are found in the deepest parts of the ocean floor. In the last twenty years, however, oceanographic research has revealed the existence of new types of deep sea resources. These include "black smokers," volcanic vents that are rich in valuable minerals such as gold and copper and are surrounded by life forms, which live in ecosystems with water temperatures above 300°C and which are sulfur rather than carbon based. In addition, ancient cold water corals and cold seeps have been discovered, each with their own unique ecosystems.

Threats to marine resources are principally posed by humankind. Marine pollution from land-based sources constitutes the single most important threat, together with discharges from vessels and non-sustainable fishing. The growing intensity of human activities in the ocean, such as shipping, the laying of submarine cables, as well as growing fishing practices put major pressures on the marine environment. The great challenge is to develop legal regimes regulating human activities, which cover not only national zones also areas beyond national jurisdiction.

David FREESTONE
The George Washington University Law School

See also in the *Berkshire Encyclopedia of Sustainability* Common Heritage of Mankind Principle; Convention for the Prevention of Pollution From Ships; Convention for the Prohibition of Fishing with Long Drift Nets in the South Pacific; Convention for the Safety of Life at Sea; Convention on Civil Liability for Oil Pollution; Customary International Law; Fishing and Whaling Legislation; International Law; Transboundary Water Law; United Nations—Overview of Conventions and Agreements

FURTHER READINGS

Agreement for the Implementation of the Provisions of the United Nations Convention on the Law of the Sea of 10 December 1982 relating to the Conservation and Management of Straddling Fish Stocks and Highly Migratory Fish Stocks. Adopted 4 August 1995 at New York. Entered into force 11 December 2001. 2167 UNTS 3.

Agreement to Promote Compliance with International Conservation and Management Measures by Fishing Vessels on the High Seas, done at Rome on 24 November 1993. Entered into force 24 April 2003. (1994). Reprinted in *International Legal Materials, 33*, 968–980.

Anderson, David. (2008). *Modern law of the sea: Selected essays.* Leiden, Netherlands: Martinus Nijhoff Publishers.

Churchill, Robin Rolf, & Lowe, Alan Vaughan. (1999). *The law of the sea* (3rd ed.). Manchester, UK: Manchester University Press.

Code of Conduct for Responsible Fisheries, Rome, 31 October 1995. (1995). *11 International Organizations and the Law of the Sea: Documentary Yearbook 700.* The Hague: Netherlands Institute for the Law of the Sea (NILOS)/Kluwer Law International.

Feenstra, Robert. (Ed.). (2009). *Hugo Grotius Mare Liberum 1609–2009: Original Latin text and English translation.* Leiden, Netherlands; Boston: Martinus Nijhoff Publishers.

Freestone, David, & Makuch, Zen. (1996). The new international environmental law of fisheries: The 1995 Straddling Stocks Agreement. *Yearbook of International Environmental Law, 7*, 3–49.

Freestone, David; Barnes, Richard; & Ong, David M. (Eds.). (2006). *The law of the sea: progress and prospects.* New York: Oxford University Press.

O'Connell, D. P. (1981). *The international law of the sea* (2 vols.). Oxford, UK: Oxford University Press.

Rothwell, Donald R., & Stephens, Tim. (2010). *The international law of the sea.* Oxford, UK: Hart Publishing.

Natural Resources Law

Natural resources law performs three basic functions: it specifies the parts of nature that can be owned and the basic terms of use rights, it facilitates resource-related transactions, and it provides mechanisms to coordinate uses and resolve inevitable disputes. Within these functions, a key question for lawmakers is whether a part of nature is identified as a discrete resource or an attribute of land ownership.

Natural resources law is the body of legal rules that encourages and controls uses of nature, particularly the parts of nature that people find valuable. Most societies have rules prescribing who can use nature, where, and in what ways. When markets play a dominant role, a society's legal system tends to include more complex laws that go beyond defining use rights in nature to regulating commercial transactions. Similarly, a society concerned about environmental degradation will have rules limiting resource-related activities to reduce environmental harms. In such societies, natural resources law may have multiple aims: to encourage and facilitate uses of nature, to promote fairness among citizens, and to ensure that human activities do not unduly pollute or degrade the natural environment.

In order to understand natural resources law, it is important to identify its main elements and basic functions. As lawmakers craft laws, they have certain options to meet their particular circumstances and needs. The United States has detailed, varied bodies of natural resources law among its fifty individual states. Although the laws of other nations can vary considerably from US laws, the underlying functions of natural resources law are basically the same everywhere. In some manner, lawmakers in all nations must devise rules that perform these basic functions. As such, one can identify similarities among legal systems and among the laws governing specific natural resources.

Basic Functions

Broadly speaking, natural resources law performs three basic tasks. First, it specifies the parts of nature that can be owned and defines or prescribes the terms of the legal rights (use rights) that users acquire. Many uses of nature involve the extraction and consumption of parts of nature. Other uses—recreational activities and nondamaging uses of a land surface such as hiking and recreational boating—are mostly nonconsumptive. Valuable parts of nature can lie beneath, on, or above the surface. Resources that people consume can be either naturally renewable (plants, animals, some energy sources) or nonrenewable (most minerals and fossil fuels). Laws setting the terms of resource-use rights typically prescribe what can be used and in what ways, specify the duration of use rights and their transferability, address the inevitable conflicts among resource users, and impose cleanup or restoration obligations once a resource-use activity ends. Natural resources law also includes rules that allocate use rights—that is, rules specifying how governments make ownership rights in nature initially available to first users.

The second basic task of natural resources law is to facilitate resource-related transactions. Resource-use rights often arise in private transactions—licenses, leases, sales, conveyances, and the like. Typically, private parties enjoy considerable freedom in how they structure such transactions (as do governments when they are engaged in similar commercial transactions). Natural resources law can assist such transactions, thereby making markets more regular and efficient. One way it does so is by prescribing rules of contract or deed interpretation that govern a transaction unless the parties choose otherwise. The law, for instance, may provide definitions for commonly used terms (for example, mineral rights, mining claims, water rights, and hunting easements). It may prescribe widely accepted royalty arrangements and presumptions governing the duration of use rights (for example, the rule that a particular use right lasts only so long as its owner makes continued use of it). In such instances, the law fills in the gaps in incomplete contracts and incorporates customary understandings into private transactions. If private parties desire, they can usually reject these legal conventions and deviate from customary practices to define terms as they see fit. In some instances, lawmakers insist that contracts or deeds include specific terms designed to foster some public policy, without regard for the wishes of the parties. For example, laws governing oil and gas leases may insist that all leases require lessees to clean up well sites when pumping ends.

The third major task for natural resources law—one that is gaining in importance—is to facilitate the emergence of governance regimes by which resource users (and perhaps other people) coordinate resource uses and resolve disputes. For instance, irrigators in many jurisdictions are empowered to form irrigation or water-conservancy entities, which can orchestrate water uses over large areas. Similarly, owners of land parcels above a particular oil and gas field might be empowered to form joint-management entities to facilitate drilling and recovery methods (termed pooling and unitization arrangements in the United States). Looking ahead, natural resources law might well include more provisions that are aimed at encouraging resource users to work in concert for joint benefit.

What Comes with Land?

A key task for lawmakers is to prescribe which parts of nature can be owned and to set the basic terms of use rights. A particular part of nature could be viewed as a discrete resource such as a right to divert and use water, a right to cut trees, a right to hunt, or a right to graze livestock in an area. Alternatively, a right to use part of nature could be viewed as an attribute of land ownership, meaning that the legal right to use the resource is one of the entitlements held by the owner of the land that includes the resource. Lawmakers regularly employ both of these alternatives—treating a resource as part of the land and treating it as a discrete resource that one acquires separately. Thus, in surveying the law of a jurisdiction, it is useful to learn which parts of nature belong to the landowner and which parts are discrete assets.

Landownership almost always includes rights to use the soil, to harvest most or all plants, to grow crops, and to engage in some range of surface-use activities. Even on these basic points, however, legal systems vary. In colonial America for instance, English law withheld certain tall trees from private owners, reserving the trees for use by the Crown as ship masts. Nature protection laws in many countries today (e.g., Great Britain) similarly protect particular forests and even specific trees.

Beyond such uses of soil and vegetation, there is less agreement among legal systems on the parts of nature that attach to land. Landownership, for instance, may or may not include rights to extract minerals on or beneath the surface—that is, rights to remove coal, metals, oil and gas, and building stone. When minerals are excluded from landownership, then either the government retains the minerals for state exploitation or they are separately allocated as discrete resources. Jurisdictions take a variety of approaches on this critical issue of mineral ownership. A landowner, for instance, may have rights to engage in "hard rock" mining (removing coal, stone, and metals) but have no right to remove oil and gas. Laws can draw even finer distinctions. British law, for instance, long provided that gold and silver remained the property of the Crown, no matter where it was located. Landowners had the right to obtain all other minerals. Similar variations arise with respect to water, a critical resource in much of the world. Landowners may or may not have rights to use water that flows over, adjacent to, or beneath their lands. In the United States, this issue is largely governed by the laws of the individual states. Laws in the eastern part of the country tend to empower landowners to use both surface and groundwater, with rights shared among landowners. Laws in the western part of the country more often treat water as a discrete resource and include separate rules governing who can gain water rights and how these rights can be obtained.

Similar legal variations exist with wildlife. Lawmakers must consider the following questions: Does an owner of land own the wildlife located on it? (In the United States, the answer to this question is no, but in Great Britain, for

example, the answer if yes.) Typically, if a landowner owns the wildlife located on the land, the rights end when a wild animal migrates. Alternatively, does the legal system view rights to use wildlife, which are often tightly controlled by species, season, and location, as separate resources allocated apart from land? Similar issues arise over uses of air space, access to light and wind, and uses of caves. All such rights may or may not be included in the bundle of rights held by landowners.

On several of these issues, lawmakers sometimes distinguish between the ownership of a physical resource in place and a legal right to use or capture the resource. For instance, American states provide that water in lakes and rivers remains public property; landowners only acquire rights to use it. In American law governing oil and gas, some states assert that landowners own underlying oil and gas in place. Other states assert that oil and gas are not owned until these resources are physically captured; what a landowner acquires, when gaining land, is simply the right to use the land surface to drill and extract. At first glance, these two approaches appear quite different: either landowners own the oil and gas or they do not. In practice, the two approaches produce similar results. All landowners own the oil and gas they pump from wells on their land. Accordingly, a landowner who owns oil and gas in place may lose their rights to a neighbor's well. On the other hand, a landowner who possesses only a right to drill is not disadvantaged. The landowner still has the right to capture and retain as much oil and gas as possible. Thus, the distinction has only minor significance.

Natural resource regimes also vary in terms of a landowner's ability to exclude people from land. Landowners typically can halt interferences with their own activities, or at least significant interferences; this is perhaps the key component of owning nature. On the other hand, landowners may or may not have power to exclude outsiders from crossing or otherwise using their lands in ways that cause no interference. Thus, private land may remain open to public hikers without the landowner's consent. In many societies, the public holds expansive rights to use unenclosed private lands for hunting, foraging, travel, and livestock grazing. In these societies, resource-related activities are sometimes viewed as use rights available for either all members of the public or residents of a local village.

As lawmakers prescribe the rights that attach to landownership, they typically must deal with spillover effects or externalities. They must consider the ways actions by one landowner can harm other resource users. For instance, natural resources law typically prescribes whether a landowner can excavate in ways that physically threaten neighboring lands. Similarly, it prescribes the freedom a landowner has to divert surface waters and otherwise alter natural drainage. It may also prescribe rules on vegetative cover by banning certain unwanted species, requiring mowing or other weed control, or regulating forest or pasture management.

Whenever lawmakers treat a part of nature as a discrete resource, they confront a practical challenge. Nature's parts are ecologically intermingled; they do not exist as neatly shaped packages. It is up to lawmakers to define the physical boundaries of the discrete resource, a task that necessarily requires line-drawing. For instance, a jurisdiction that views water as a discrete resource must somehow fragment the continuous hydrologic cycle. Rainfall absorbed by plants presumably belongs to the landowner. But can a landowner capture water on a rooftop cistern system; does that water belong to the landowner, or must the landowner acquire a separate resource right to collect it? Similarly, can a landowner capture and retain diffuse surface waters before they reach a stream? What about water from naturally recurring

springs or water that is hydrologically disconnected from any stream that would otherwise go unused? When water is scarce, lawmakers are obligated to supply answers. Similar questions arise when the law views subsurface minerals as discrete assets. Which minerals are included with land, and which are not? Is peat a mineral or part of the soil? What about minerals that protrude from the land surface? What about minerals embedded in low-grade ore formations?

Such issues inevitably arise whenever lawmakers decide to define a part of nature as a discrete resource. (They also arise when a landowner voluntarily severs a resource and conveys it separately.) The challenge that lawmakers face is easily stated: the more embedded a resource is in ecological processes, the harder it is to draw lines between the land and the discrete resource. Line-drawing is regularly required when a legal system allows a person to acquire a resource by being the first to seize it. For instance, mineral rights might go to the first person to discover a mineral deposit, but what are the legal boundaries of the mineral deposit? Where does the mineral deposit end, and where do the rights of the landowner begin? Does the new mineral owner gain ancillary rights to use the land surface (for example, cutting timber needed to support mining shafts)?

Using Land

Once the law has defined the physical elements that are considered part of land, it must then explain how the owner can use the land. This subject is an aspect of property or land-use law; yet it is also a component of natural resources law, given that so many resources are included in the landowner's bundle of rights.

A few specific issues on this topic were identified in the previous section. Can a landowner alter natural drainage or remove vegetation? Can an owner farm in ways that erode soil or harm rare wildlife species? Adding complexity is the physical reality that actions by one landowner can readily disrupt other lands and land uses. Disputes among neighboring landowners are common and often involve variations on a basic fact pattern: one landowner favors an intensive land use (perhaps generating noise, vibrations, odors, or traffic) while another landowner plans a more sensitive one. Such disputes today sometimes involve renewable energy sources, as landowners regularly tap solar and wind energy sources, and their efforts are harmed when neighbors interfere with the light or wind. Another common fact pattern in disputes arises when actions of a landowner clash with uses of a discrete, separately owned resource or when owners of two discrete-use rights disrupt one another.

In some way, the law must resolve such disputes. Legal rules can be clear and precise, granting one party superior rights. They can also feature vague principles or values that courts must apply to resolve the conflicts. Generally speaking, lawmakers tend to use one or more of a relatively small number of approaches to resolve disputes among neighboring users. One common legal approach is simply to favor the land or resource user who came first in time. A second approach is to evaluate competing activities and to give preference to the one that is, in some sense, more reasonable or socially beneficial. A third approach, which is not always possible, is to divide the resource in question into fair shares—for instance, allowing owners of land above an aquifer to share the underground water in proportion to the sizes of their landholdings. A fourth approach considers whether one or the other party to a dispute might mitigate or end the conflict by making reasonable adjustments or accommodations in its activities. For instance, a court may consider whether one party can reduce its resource use through conservation measures. If a party can mitigate the conflict or accommodate the needs of the other side, then the law may insist that it do so.

A fifth, older approach for resolving disputes among users—a once-popular approach that was typically pushed aside with the coming of industrialization—is to resolve disputes by using nature as the baseline of legitimate resource use. That is, lawmakers might prescribe rights in land and discrete resources so that owners must use what they own without materially altering the natural incidents of lands owned by others. In the United States two centuries ago, courts typically ruled that landowners were entitled to enjoy the "natural incidents" of their lands, including wind, water, and light. A neighbor who materially disrupted these natural incidents acted wrongly. Thus, water law allowed landowners to use river water so long as they did not diminish the natural quantity or quality of the water flow. This legal approach favored sensitive, agrarian land uses over the newer, polluting industrial uses. Not surprisingly, the nature-as-a-baseline approach was often pushed aside so that polluting factories and railroads could arise and so that urban landowners could block air and light with their tall buildings.

A sixth, final approach that is often used to resolve disputes differs from the others. Instead of crafting laws that directly resolve disputes, lawmakers can create mechanisms or processes by which the competing users resolve disputes on their own through a type of governance mechanism. As noted above in "Basic Functions," natural resources law might authorize resource owners to form private or quasi-public entities with powers to adjudicate disputes, perhaps even averting the disputes in advance by limiting who can do what. Such arrangements can encourage resource users to work in concert, recognizing and resolving competing needs without resort to courts. Another aim could be to facilitate shared-management arrangements that are more economically efficient or that produce better environmental outcomes. Thus, owners of land around a lake might be empowered to create a lake-management entity to resolve disputes relating to uses of the lake and shorelines. Owners of land in grazing districts might be encouraged to form grazing-management bodies to resolve disputes and, perhaps, going further, to arrange joint-grazing activities on larger spatial scales. Over time, lawmakers might well see increasing benefits in this approach to resolving disputes, given the costs, delays, and unpredictability of the other methods listed in this section.

Allocating Discrete Resources

Once a part of nature is defined as a discrete resource, not part of the land, a legal system must make the resource available to potential users in some manner. This is the allocation function of natural resources law. A resource could be retained for use by the public (for instance, rights to use a river for travel or fishing). The rights could be allocated to some subset of the public (for example, to inhabitants of a particular village). Alternatively, the resource could be offered to individuals or businesses through one of many possible allocation methods.

One longstanding allocation method is to make a resource available to whomever is first to occupy or start using the resource. This first-in-time method has a long history. It is an easy allocation method in that no elaborate government structure is required to implement it. It is also typically favored by the first people to arrive in a geographic region since it favors them over later arrivals.

As a method of allocation, first-in-time raises predictable issues whenever it is employed. What action must a person take to qualify as first? A well-known American court ruling raised this issue in a dispute over a dead fox. Was a hunter considered first in time when he spotted the fox and pursued it closely, or was a person first only when he actually physically seized the fox? (The court decided it was the latter.) In western US water law, the rule gradually developed that a person was first to capture a water flow only if the person physically diverted the water from the stream and applied it to a beneficial use; mere diversion was not enough, nor did a water right evolve if the use was not beneficial. In mining law, a person was first to find a valuable mineral deposit only if the person properly staked out the claim, filed papers on it, and could show that the deposit was valuable.

A second issue that arises under first-in-time schemes has to do with the timing of the capture when the action required to complete the work of capture takes time, as is often the case. How is timing determined when the work of capture takes months or years, as it might when diverting water for miles and applying it to an irrigation or mining effort? Does the timing of the capture date back to the first step in the process, or is the timing of capture dated only when all work is complete? In western US water law, the rule soon emerged that a diversion of water related back in time to the first step in the diversion process, at least so long as the capturer used reasonable diligence to complete the needed work.

A third, related issue under first-in-time schemes has to do with the legal protections a capturer enjoys against interference by others. Mining codes in the American West typically gave prospectors protection against interference on all lands they physically occupied. More generally, lawmakers banned what they deemed unfair competition. As a policy matter, lawmakers who are trying to encourage resource discovery and exploitation typically must offer prospectors and other potential resource owners some degree of protection against interference. If they do not, the danger of disruption can discourage people from undertaking the search process.

Allocation of a resource based on first-in-time, or what might be termed historic use, is by no means free of moral or social objection. One complaint is that government essentially gives the resource away for free with no income for taxpayers. A second complaint is that resource users who are first on the scene are not, for that reason alone, particularly deserving or morally superior. A first-in-time rule can reward industry and initiative, but the reward can easily be excessive, particularly when the first occupiers can hoard a resource. Later generations can be particularly disadvantaged. At the global level, in terms of planetary resources, the disadvantage can fall on countries that are later to develop.

This moral complaint has arisen in disputes over ocean resources and, more recently, in clashes over rights to pollute the planet's atmosphere. Developed countries typically claim that reductions in emissions, required to mitigate climate change, should begin from historic patterns of use. This policy position implicitly accepts the existing allocation scheme under which countries first to develop captured disproportionate shares of the planet's absorption capacity. An alternative approach is to allocate Earth's capacity on a per capita basis—an equal share for each person on the planet—without regard for prior patterns of pollution. Such an approach would require that reductions be made disproportionately by countries with above-average pollution levels per person. A per-capita allocation scheme would withdraw the advantage gained by countries that were first in time to industrialize.

Lawmakers devising natural resource regimes have a wide variety of other methods to use when allocating resources to initial users. An obvious method is either by sale at the highest prices the market will bear or by auction. Another approach is to allocate a resource based on how the resource will be used or on characteristics of the prospective user. Thus a resource could be made available by permit only to people who will use it in the public interest, however it is defined. Alternatively, a resource could be offered based on the personal abilities or characteristics of users. Thus, marine resources are sometimes allocated to subsistence fishers, particularly communities that retain traditional patterns of harvesting. Rights to plant gardens could be allocated to low-income applicants. Rights to engage in demanding recreational activities (for example, river rafting and mountain climbing) could be allocated based on demonstrated individual skill. Many resource-allocation schemes favor local users in an effort to stabilize and protect local economies. In some jurisdictions, lawmakers bundle discrete resources and allocate them as a package when the resources are best used together. For instance, a right to graze cattle in a semiarid area may be bundled with a right to use water for that purpose.

Rights to Use Discrete Resources

As lawmakers prescribe rules governing discrete natural resources, the main challenge they face is to prescribe the contours of each use right— what it covers, how the resource can be used, and how the terms of one resource right fit together with other resource and landowner entitlements. The numerous issues that fall into this category are often related to the physical features or attributes of particular resources. Sometimes lawmakers favor strict rules of priority as a means of clarifying rights and avoiding disputes. Thus, mineral law in the United States has typically provided that owners of subsurface minerals have priority when their excavation methods disrupt uses of the land surface; such owners can use the land surface, even destroy it, when such use is reasonably necessary to excavate and remove minerals. Oil and gas lessees similarly can make reasonable use of the land surface unless limited by the terms of a lease. Holders of mineral rights do face limits on their actions, limits that have slowly grown in recent decades. For instance, they typically can use the land surface only to exploit minerals on that land, not to aid in the exploitation of minerals on other lands. Also, they may be required to compensate surface owners for the damage they cause.

The many conflicts among resource users have given rise to rich, complex bodies of law, commonly tailored to the specific needs and consequences of using particular resources. Thus, irrigators in arid lands may have rights to cross adjacent lands to convey water to the places where they will use the water. Public users of waterways may possess rights to enter private lands along a river to avoid waterway obstructions. American Indian tribes with reserved rights to fish at traditional fishing sites may have, as ancillary entitlements, rights to dry the fish before transporting them. Holders of specific grazing rights may have the legal ability to construct fences and watering facilities. Further, the definition of a resource-use right in many resource settings somehow must prescribe the extent or intensity of the permissible use. For instance, a right to harvest trees in a region would need to specify what trees can be removed, where they can be removed, in what ways they can be removed, and with what damage to soils, water, and other trees. A right to graze livestock would specify the numbers and types of animals that can be grazed, where the grazing can occur, and whether the landowner (which could be a government agency) can order changes in grazing levels due to drought.

Duration and Transfer of Rights

Two key issues when defining resource-use rights have to do with their duration—how long they last—and whether the owner of a use right can sell or otherwise transfer it. Land ownership is typically (although not always) understood as perpetual, and landowners can transfer land at will. In the case of discrete natural resources, the law is more varied. Discrete-use rights in nature are rarely perpetual in duration. Often a use right includes a built-in term limit (for instance, a set number of years). Alternatively, the use right may last until the resource is fully exploited or so long as the use right remains valuable to the owner. In many instances, a resource-use right ends when its owner abandons it (it is typically not possible to abandon land). A use right can also be forfeited for simple nonuse or lost by failure to comply with an express duty to exploit the resource. For instance, oil and gas leases in the United States typically extend indefinitely beyond an original term of years "so long as" the lessee continues to extract petroleum in paying quantities. Once production ends—and unless the parties agree otherwise—the lease right terminates. As these examples illustrate, the duration of a use right is often linked to another major definitional element of the right: a use-it-or-lose-it obligation that compels the holder to exploit the resource. (Landowners sometimes face similar duties—they too can lose their rights if they leave land unused—though such duties of continuous use are far less common with land than with discrete natural resources.)

As for the ability of resource owners to transfer what they own, laws sometimes distinguish between resource-use rights of a *commercial* nature, which are transferable, and those of a more *personal* or familial nature, which may not be transferable. Thus, a right to log a forest commercially may be transferable whereas a right given to a neighbor to enter land and collect firewood might not be. Some resource-use rights become attached by law to a parcel of land when the resource-use right is intended to benefit uses of that specific land. In a simple case, a right-of-way to cross land may benefit adjacent land that is otherwise landlocked. In such an instance, the discrete-use right (in this illustration, the right-of-way) most likely cannot be transferred except when the benefitted land itself is being transferred.

Markets in resources flourish when resources are freely transferable. Free transfer, however, can easily clash with the desires of lawmakers to insist that resources be used in ways that achieve public-policy goals. Governments may decide to allocate resources based on a calculation of public interest or based on the identities of the recipients. They may allocate water to support a local farming community; they may allocate fishing rights to subsistence fishers; or they may decide that only working farmers can own farmland. These policy preferences can be frustrated if recipients of the use rights can promptly transfer their rights to other users or other uses. To avoid that danger, thereby protecting the policy goals underlying the allocation scheme, lawmakers often impose limits on subsequent transfer of the use right. They may allow transfer only to a person or to a type of use that is consistent with the original allocation mechanism. In the American West, transfers of water rights are often subject to governmental approval to ensure that new uses are socially beneficial. Lawmakers may further limit transfers so as to protect local farming communities. The problem with such restrictions on transfer is that they interfere with the market's ability to reallocate resources. When the market cannot reallocate, then a state must develop some other reallocation method (for instance, using eminent domain to condemn existing uses,

thus freeing the resource for reallocation by government, or, if the problem is understood in advance, only allocating use rights that are limited in duration or subject to termination under specific circumstances). The power of a resource owner to transfer the resource is thus intertwined with other defining elements of the use right.

Government Regulation

The power of government to regulate resource uses is interwoven with constitutional limits on the powers of various governments, federalism issues that coordinate governance activities by multiple levels of government, and limits on regulatory action designed to protect private property. Private property is a valuable institution that is capable of fostering economic enterprise and growth and adding stability to social, economic, and political orders. At the same time, private property derives from the exercise of governmental powers (that is, private property is inherently a creation of law). And private property is easily used by owners to oppress or subjugate other people and to degrade the lands and waters upon which these people depend. Particularly in the United States, these conflicting realities have been difficult to comprehend because of widespread assumptions that private property somehow arises outside of law or existed before the emergence of governance systems. Adding to the intellectual and ideological clashes are the economic realities that holders of valuable land and resource rights tend to defend their current rights tenaciously when lawmakers, out to promote the public good, propose changes in the laws that define their rights. Similarly, established resource users (for example, irrigators) can tenaciously defend their activities even when they cause ecological harm, which is viewed by the public as unacceptable. Whether lawmakers can promote the public interest by legally refining private rights depends upon governance structures and, importantly, on the strength and vigor of a jurisdiction's democracy.

Many legal regimes have routinely allowed resource users to walk away from their operations, leaving nature to remedy scars and to absorb pollution. Increasingly, lawmakers have begun to insist that resource users clean up the worst contamination and restore lands to ecological conditions resembling their pre-extraction conditions. Oil and gas producers typically must fill in wells so as to diminish the dangers of groundwater contamination. Restoration duties are also being imposed in private transactions. Private leases and contracts governing resource activities now often require not just removal of equipment but affirmative measures to return land to specified conditions.

Natural resources law significantly affects how people use nature, particularly resource activities driven by market forces. Lawmakers can aid the quest for sustainability by reconsidering and revising the elements of natural resources law in ways that stimulate or insist upon resource uses that are consistent with the elements of sustainability. They can usefully refine the elements of resource use rights so as to prohibit ecologically degrading actions and require that resource users restore natural areas when resource extraction ends. They can improve resource allocation and reallocation methods so that patterns of resource use promote the common good. And they can better embed resources into landscape governance regimes, which, in effect, integrate multiple resource uses so as to reduce conflicts and accommodate shifting natural conditions and public values. Well-designed laws would provide frames in which market forces can operate, leading to patterns of resource use more consistent both with development aims and with the healthy functioning of landscapes.

Eric T. FREYFOGLE
University of Illinois College of Law

See also in the *Berkshire Encyclopedia of Sustainability* Environmental Dispute Resolution; Environmental Law—Europe; Environmental Law—United States and Canada; Land Use—Regulation and Zoning; Nuisance Law; Ocean Zoning; Real Property Law; Soil Conservation Legislation; Transboundary Water Law

FURTHER READINGS

Bean, Michael J., & Rowland, Melanie J. (1997). *The evolution of national wildlife law* (3rd ed.). Westport, CT: Praeger.

Boelens, Rutgerd; Getches, David; & Gil, Armondao Guevara. (2010). *Out of the mainstream: Water rights, politics and identity.* London: Earthscan.

Burke, Barlow, & Beck, Robert. (2009). *The law and regulation of mining: Minerals to energy.* Durham, NC: Carolina Academic Press.

Coggins, George Cameron; Wilkinson, Charles F.; Leshy, John D.; & Fischman, Robert L. (2007). *Federal public land and resources law* (6th ed.). New York: Foundation Press.

Daintith, Terence. (2010). *Finders keepers? How the law of capture shaped the world oil industry.* Washington, DC: RFF Press.

Dellapenna, Joseph W., & Gupta, Jouetta. (2009). *The evolution of the law and politics of water.* Dordrecht, The Netherlands: Springer.

Fischman, Robert. (2003). *The national wildlife refuges: Coordinating a conservation system through law.* Washington, DC: Island Press.

Fisher, Douglas. (2010). *The law and governance of water resources.* Cheltenham, UK: Edward Elgar.

Freyfogle, Eric T., & Goble, Dale D. (2009). *Wildlife law: A primer.* Washington, DC: Island Press.

Hu, Desheng. (2006). *Water rights: An international and comparative study.* London: IWA Publishing.

Knight, Richard L., & Bates, Sarah F. (Eds.). (1995). *A new century for natural resources management.* Washington, DC: Island Press.

Knight, Richard L., & White, Courtney. (2009). *Conservation for a new generation: Redefining natural resources management.* Washington, DC: Island Press.

Larson, Anne M., et al. (2010). *Forests for people: Community rights and forest tenure reform.* London: Earthscan.

MacDonnell, Lawrence J., & Bates, Sarah F. (Eds.). (2010). *The evolution of natural resources law and policy.* Chicago: ABA Publishing.

MacDonnell, Lawrence J., & Bates, Sarah F. (Eds.). (1993). *Natural resources policy and law: Trends and directions.* Washington, DC: Island Press.

Maxwell, Richard C.; Martin, Patrick H.; & Kramer, Bruce M. (2007). *Oil and gas law* (8th ed.). New York: Foundation Press.

McHarg, Aileen, et al. (Eds.) (2010). *Property and the law in energy and natural resources.* Oxford, UK: Oxford University Press.

Raymond, Leigh. (2003). *Private rights in public resources.* Washington, DC: RFF Press.

Reeve, Rosalind. (2004). *Policing international trade in endangered species: The CITES treaty and compliance.* London: Royal Institute of International Affairs.

Schrijver, Nico. (2008). *Sovereignty over natural resources: Balancing rights and duties.* Cambridge, UK: Cambridge University Press.

Tarlock, A. Dan; Corbridge, James N., Jr.; & Getches, David H. (2009). *Water resource management: A casebook in law and public policy* (6th ed). New York: Foundation Press.

Nanotechnology Legislation

The rapid development of nanotechnology has the potential to impact society on a level similar to the Industrial Revolution. Legal systems around the world struggle to adapt to the combination of scientific uncertainty and growing concerns about potentially adverse impacts of nanomaterials to human health and the environment. Nano-specific mandatory legal provisions are emerging in a number of developed countries.

The term *nanotechnology* commonly refers to the branch of science and engineering devoted to designing, producing, and using structures, devices, and systems by manipulating atoms and molecules at the nanoscale level, approximately one-billionth of a meter. The products of these efforts are commonly called *nanomaterials* (NM). The hopes and fears associated with nontechnology are unique. This technology is likely to have a profound impact on all sectors of the economy, including agriculture and food, energy production and efficiency, the automotive industry, cosmetics, medical appliances and drugs, household appliances, computers, and weapons.

Estimates and forecasts of future nanotechnology markets vary tremendously. Experts predict that their value will increase from an estimated $11 billion in 2009 to between $26 billion and $3 trillion by 2015 (BCC Research 2010). The latter estimate is based on calculations including the entire value of nanotechnology-impacted products, as opposed to the value of nanotechnology-based components alone. For example, if a car uses nanotechnology-enhanced paint, the entire value of the car is integrated into the estimate rather than estimating the value of the paint alone. Thus, the lower estimate is likely to provide a more accurate picture of the short- to mid-term future of nanotechnology.

Nanotechnology promoters stress the potentially beneficial applications of these new technologies while many scientific institutions and citizen organizations across the world have underscored the need to carefully assess their possible health and environmental risks. Nanotechnology is unusual in several respects that simultaneously enhance its potential benefits and risks and complicate consideration of potential regulations. Determining how to regulate nanotechnology is further complicated by the potential flow of nanomaterials through international trade channels as both products and wastes.

Because nanotechnology is a novel and rapidly developing field, existing legal systems around the world are struggling to adapt. As David Rejeski, director of the Woodrow Wilson Center for Scholars Project on Emerging Nanotechnologies, notes, "most countries are taking a wait-and-see approach, assuming that existing regulations will deal with nanotechnology, even if new materials emerge with radically different properties" (Abbott, Marchant, and Sylvester 2006, 10519). A number of countries, however, have begun to review and adapt their national regulatory systems to include nano-specific provisions.

Difficulties of Nanotechnology Regulation

Simply creating legal definitions of nano-related terms has been a contentious matter. A large number of working definitions of terms such as *nanotechnology* and *nanomaterial* have been developed, often for specific purposes. Various legal definitions, for example, have recently been included in pieces of European Union legislation and are currently being developed by regulators around the Western world. The absence of generally accepted legal definitions plays a significant role in delaying the creation of a nano-specific regulatory framework.

The balance between supporting innovation and preventing potential environmental and human health risks is at the heart of the ongoing debate about nanotechnology regulation. The debate also includes ethical aspects, such as concerns about human enhancement (the use of technology to enhance human bodies and minds, for example, via cybernetic body parts, neuroimplants, human "germline" engineering, or brain stimulation technologies to alleviate suffering or to control moods), privacy, and security, mostly arising from the future convergence of nanotechnology with other emerging fields, such as biotechnologies, cognitive science, and information technologies. More general issues concerning public access to information and societal oversight of scientific development are also debated in the context of nanotechnology regulation. All of these questions play a key role in shaping the development of nanotechnology regulation.

The debate around nanotechnologies and their regulation is spreading throughout society. It now routinely consists of active involvement and contributions from all sectors, including academic and scientific institutions; government and regulatory agencies, both as innovation promoters and risk regulators; and diverse industry sectors, such as NMs manufacturers, retailers, insurance companies, and water treatment professionals. Additionally, the debate involves all branches of civil society, from trade unions, concerned about their members' exposure to new and poorly understood hazards, to health and environmental nongovernmental organizations (NGOs) and consumer organizations.

Nanotechnology Regulation Development

The development of a legal framework for nanotechnology is evolving gradually from instruments designed mainly to support innovation and spur growth of the nanotechnology industry to more comprehensive approaches, aiming to capture some of the more complex issues of nano-related human health and environmental hazards.

Support for Innovation

As nanoscience advanced and discoveries in the field applied to the manufacture of products, the potential contributions of nanotechnology to future economic growth brought increasing government attention. In the late 1990s and early 2000s, governments around the world began to identify nanotechnology as a critical technology for the future and devised specific innovation support plans, such as the 2001 US National Nanotechnology Initiative.

In many other countries and regions, similar plans were developed between 2000 and 2009. The European Union implemented publicly funded research programs in 2002 in the context of its Sixth Framework Program; China began coordination and investment support plans in 2004; and in 2009, after years of coordinated research programs, Russia set up a public company called RUSNANO to develop a Russian nanotechnology industry through investment in infrastructure and venture capital. As of 2010, most of these plans remained operational.

These plans are based on a combination of measures designed to stimulate fundamental research as well as potential product development. Measures usually include financial support for research and development activities, investments in start-up companies, and coordination measures for nanotechnology activities of government organizations, academia, and industry. Following a general trend, a number of these plans have now evolved to include considerations of environmental and human health risks.

Voluntary Approaches

In the second half of the 2000s, scientific studies pointing to serious environmental and health hazards from certain NMs (the most famous being a study demonstrating that certain carbon nanotubes behaved like asbestos fibers in the lungs of mice) as well as reports coming from prestigious scientific institutions, international organizations such as the UN Educational Scientific and Cultural Organization (UNESCO), and from civil society warranted a precautionary approach to NMs. At the same time, the availability of nanoproducts in commercial markets increased, with little specific oversight. Governments, principally among the Organisation for Economic Co-operation and Development (OECD) member states, were faced with the question of whether their legal framework was adequate to address the challenges raised by NMs.

While governments undertook efforts to increase basic nanotechnology knowledge of the potential toxicity mechanisms of NMs, most remained reluctant to modify their regulatory framework. Most OECD governments believed that their legal frameworks were well suited for current challenges, or that they required only minor technical modifications. This position was reinforced by the systemic difficulties governments faced in trying to design legal provisions in the context of a considerable scientific knowledge gap and heavy competition to lead the "nano race."

Armed with only rigid legal frameworks requiring a very high level of scientific certainty to effectively prevent human health or environmental impacts, governments turned to voluntary instruments such as general guidelines, codes of conduct, and loose certification systems. Such instruments included invitations from the Japanese

Ministry of Trade and Industry and the Ministry of the Environment to the manufacturers of NMs to implement voluntary safety measures, enhance communication with users, and provide information on test data and management methods. Other countries, such as Germany and the United Kingdom, set up voluntary surveys to identify the quantities of NMs being produced or used. A retailer organization in Switzerland introduced a voluntary code of conduct for nanotechnology in consumer products. Under this code, participants commit to applying the precautionary principle and to providing maximum levels of transparency for consumers. Most of these voluntary schemes, in particular the information-gathering schemes, did not deliver the expected results and led to the consideration of specific nanoregulation for NMs in a number of countries.

Nano-Specific Regulation

Although most countries around the world are still struggling to identify how to adapt their regulatory frameworks to nanotechnology, major players such as the European Union, Canada, and the United States are enacting mandatory nano-specific provisions and inserting them into their legal frameworks.

After introducing specific nanoprovisions in the revision of its cosmetics regulations (e.g., premarketing notifications and labeling), the European Union is currently discussing inclusion of similar nano-specific provisions in various regulations such as the Novel Food Directive, Food Packaging Directive, Restriction of Hazardous Substances (ROHS) / Waste Electric and Electronic Equipment (WEEE) directives, and Biocide Directive. In parallel, the European Union is also investigating the necessary adaptation of its Registration, Evaluation and Authorisation of Chemicals (REACH) regulations. The European Union is likely to introduce specific nanoprovisions in the revision process scheduled for 2012.

In Canada, the establishment of the first mandatory information-gathering scheme accompanies discussions on revising chemical regulation in order to adapt it to NMs. European Union member states such as France and Italy are preparing similar information-gathering statutes. In the United States, the Environmental Protection Agency (EPA) is using the Toxic Substances Control Act (TSCA)

to regulate NMs on a case-by-case basis. The EPA currently favors the use of Significant New Use Rules (SNURs) to regulate certain NMs, such as carbon nanotubes and nanosilver, with the declared intention of requiring a notification on every NM in commerce. In the meantime, a number of US states, such as California, Massachusetts, and South Carolina, are also enacting provisions to regulate NMs.

International Initiatives

Many countries are exploring various ways of regulating NMs at local, national, and regional levels. Concerns about market disruptions, such as those experienced with genetically modified organism (GMO) technologies, led OECD countries to initiate international coordination processes. In 2006, the OECD created two working parties: the Working Party on Manufactured Nanomaterials (WPMN) to promote international cooperation on human health and environmental safety issues, and the Working Party on Nanotechnology (WPN) to advise on emerging policy-relevant issues in science, technology, and innovation.

The Strategic Approach to International Chemical Management (SAICM), a global, multistakeholder process that promotes chemical safety around the world, nominated nanotechnology and NMs as one of four emerging issues in 2009. In this context, awareness-raising workshops have been organized throughout 2010 in each of the UN regions, to be followed by capacity-building workshops in 2011. Other international organizations, such as the Food and Agriculture Organization (FAO) and World Health Organization (WHO), also started to take up the issue, organizing conferences and meetings in early 2010.

Future of Nanotechnology Regulation

The question of whether to regulate NMs, as well as how to do so effectively, is heavily linked to our limited scientific understanding of these materials and their potential risks. New NMs, such as three-dimensional systems that could self-assemble or be used to target drug delivery to specific parts of the body, are expected to be on the market in the next three to ten years. The reduced time between scientific

discovery and market entry further complicates the matter. Current legislation and policies attempt to regulate existing materials and provide adequate regulation of the future generation of NMs while encouraging innovation.

This situation led to a number of controversies, reminiscent of the controversies that arose at the early stage of GMO development. Promoters of NMs claim that they are necessary to solve a range of global crises relating to energy, water, and food, while critics point to the large number of futile, unregulated applications currently on the market, such as odorless socks, that use inappropriately assessed, potentially hazardous technology, subject to unresolved ethical, scientific, biological, legal, and social issues. Nanotechnology is a rapidly evolving field, even in terms of its very definition. Ultimately, the way we create, or fail to create, a balanced regulatory framework could serve as a blueprint for how other new technologies are utilized to benefit humanity while avoiding negative health and environmental impacts and adequately addressing ethical and social issues.

David AZOULAY
Center for International Environmental Law

See also in the *Berkshire Encyclopedia of Sustainability* Biotechnology Legislation; Chemicals Legislation and Policy; Genetically Modified Organisms Legislation; Precautionary Principle; Registration, Evaluation, Authorisation, and Restriction of Chemicals; Restriction of Hazardous Substances Directive

FURTHER READINGS

Abbott, Kenneth W.; Marchant, Gary E.; & Sylvester, Douglas J. (2006). A framework convention for nanotechnology? *Environmental Law Reporter, 36*(12), 10931–10942. Retrieved November 18, 2010, from http://ssrn.com/abstract=946777

BCC Research. (2010, July), A realistic market assessment. Retrieved November 18, 2010, from http://www.bccresearch.com/report/NAN031D.html

Breggin, Linda K., & Carothers, Leslie. (2006). Governing uncertainty: The nanotechnology environmental, health, and safety challenge. Retrieved September 27, 2010, from http://www.eli.org/pdf/research/nanotech/nanocolumbiaarticel%20final.pdf

Breggin, Linda K.; Falkner, Robert; Jaspers, Nico; Pendergrass, John; & Porter, Read. (2009). Securing the promises of nanotechnology: Towards transatlantic regulatory cooperation. Retrieved September 27, 2010, from http://eprints.lse.ac.uk/25425/1/Securing_the_promise_of_technologies_towards_transatlantic_regulatory_cooperation(LSERO).pdf

Brown, Simon. (2009). The new deficit model. *Nature Nanotechnology, 4*, 609–611.

The Center for International Environmental Law (CIEL). (2009). Addressing nanomaterials as an issue of global concern. Retrieved September 27, 2010, from http://www.ciel.org/Publications/CIEL_NanoStudy_May09.pdf

Commission of the European Communities. (2008). Regulatory aspect of nanomaterials. Retrieved September 27, 2010, from http://eur-lex.europa.eu/LexUriServ/LexUriServ.do?uri=COM:2008:0366:FIN:EN:PDF

Foss Hansen, Steffen; Maynard, Andrew; Baun, Anders; & Tickner, Joel A. (2008). Late lessons from early warnings for nanotechnology. *Nature Nanotechnology, 3*, 444–447.

Friends of the Earth Australia. (2008). Discussion paper on nanotechnology standardization and nomenclatures issues. Retrieved September 27, 2010, from http://www.ecostandard.org/downloads_a/2008-10-06_foea_nanotechnology.pdf

Invernizzi, Noela, & Foladori, Guillermo. (2010). Nanotechnology implications for labor. *Nanotechnology Law and Business, 7*(1), 68–78.

Kimbrell, George A. (2009). Governance of nanotechnology and nanomaterials: Principles, regulations and renegotiating the social contract. *Journal of Law, Medicine and Ethics, 37*(4), 706–723.

Lövestam, Göran, et al. (2010). JRC reference report: Consideration on a definition of nanomaterial for regulatory purpose. Retrieved September 27, 2010, from http://ec.europa.eu/dgs/jrc/downloads/jrc_reference_report_201007_nanomaterials.pdf

Mantovani, Elvio; Porcari, Andrea; Meili, Christoph; & Widmer, Markus. (2009). FramingNano report: Mapping study on regulation and governance of nanotechnologies. Retrieved September 27, 2010, from http://www.framingnano.eu/images/stories/FramingNanoMappingStudyFinal.pdf

Marchant, Gary E., & Sylvester, Douglas J. (2006). Transnational models for regulation of nanotechnology. *Journal of Law, Medicine and Ethics, 34*(4), 714–725.

Roco, Mihail C., & Bainbridge, William S. (Eds.). (2001). *Societal implications of nanoscience and nanotechnology*. Dordrecht, The Netherlands: Kluwer Academic Publishers.

Royal Commission on Environmental Pollution (RCEP). (2008). Novel material in the environment: The case of nanotechnology. Retrieved September 27, 2010, from http://www.official-documents.gov.uk/document/cm74/7468/7468.pdf

Schaper, Marcus. (2006). Nanotechnology and the lessons (not) learnt from the transatlantic biotechnology dispute [Abstract]. Retrieved September 27, 2010, from http://www.allacademic.com/meta/p_mla_apa_research_citation/0/9/8/9/3/p98930_index.html

Swiss Re Center for Global Dialogue. (2005). Nanotechnology: "Small size—large impact?" Retrieved September 27, 2010, from http://media.cgd.swissre.com/documents/nanotechnology_report.pdf

Tullis, Terry K. (2004). Current intellectual property issues in nanotechnology. *UCLA Journal of Law and Technology Notes*, 12. Retrieved September 27, 2010, from http://www.lawtechjournal.com/notes/2004/12_040809_tullis.php

United Nations Educational, Scientific and Cultural Organization (UNESCO). (2006a). The ethics and politics of nanotechnology. Retrieved September 27, 2010, from http://unesdoc.unesco.org/images/0014/001459/145951e.pdf

United Nations Education, Scientific and Cultural Organization (UNESCO). (2006b). Outline of a policy advice on nanotechnologies and ethics. Retrieved September 27, 2010, from http://www.unesco.org/new/fileadmin/MULTIMEDIA/HQ/SHS/pdf/NanoPolAdvice_Outline_Apr06.pdf

Nuisance Law

The word nuisance, largely French in origin, simply means harm. Nuisance law, both public and private, attempts to create balance between the rights of landowners and the rights of others by limiting the uses of land and providing recourse for landowners when their rights are impeded. Nuisance law can help to promote sustainability by defining and prohibiting the harmful ecological impact of certain land uses.

Nuisance, as a legal concept or principle, refers to an activity or person that causes harm, particularly harm that violates rights. The principal form of nuisance—private nuisance—is a central component of the law of land ownership. It instructs landowners to use their property in such a way as to cause no legal harm to other landowners or to the public. Through this instruction, nuisance law sets an overall limit on the uses of private land. At the same time, nuisance provides a legal remedy for owners and users of land who are disrupted in their use and enjoyment of that land. Thus nuisance is also a source of landowner rights; it is the body of law that protects landowners against certain interferences when using and enjoying their lands. Supplementing private nuisance law is a related law, termed public nuisance. It prohibits and provides remedies for certain harms against the public.

The Definition of Private Rights

Nuisance is most often introduced as a basic limit on how an owner of land can use it: the owner must avoid engaging in land uses that qualify as a nuisance because of their ill effects on other landowners. In this light, nuisance is a form of land-use control and is studied along with more precise land-use limits, based on statutes and regulations. Yet, as noted, nuisance can also be understood as a protection of private rights in land. As a legal matter, the rights of land ownership are defined by the remedies made available to landowners to protect their rights; without a remedy there is no legal right. For landowners, trespass law provides one legal remedy. It gives landowners the power to halt direct, physical invasions of their lands. Nuisance expands this legal protection. It provides a remedy when land-use activities are disrupted substantially in ways that either do not involve physical invasions or in which the invasion is not direct and immediate.

Private nuisance, then, protects a landowner against indirect or invisible invasions, such as those caused by light, noise, dust, vibrations, odors, or chemical pollutants. It can also protect against nearby land uses that pose manifest dangers, such as open mining pits or exposed industrial or construction hazards. The term has been applied to land uses that attract potentially dangerous guests or tenants, such as halfway houses or prisons, as well as to land uses that are simply so visually unappealing or that entail unwanted images (e.g., pornography) as to be deemed harmful. Generations ago, and again more recently, the term has been applied to structures that block sunlight (e.g., reaching solar panels) or wind (providing ventilation or powering turbines). Livestock operations, tanneries, distillers, mining tailings, and even mortuaries have been frequent targets of nuisance suits. Typically a nuisance is a continuing land use; a factory, for instance, that continues to emit water pollution. It can, however, be a one-time event (e.g., an oil spill) when the event is caused by negligence or arises from an inherently hazardous activity.

In many settings, nuisance law is called upon to resolve disputes between two or more landowners whose land uses clash. It is the law's task to decide which land use to permit and which to limit—or alternatively, to allow both land uses to continue and leave the parties to resolve the dispute on their own. Disputes of this type highlight how the property rights of landowners necessarily contain two elements: the right to use land with some degree of intensity and the right to be protected against interference with one's activities. The law must reconcile these conflicting rights. If the law allows noisy, polluting, dangerous land uses—thereby expanding the right to use—then it must necessarily reduce the protections that landowners enjoy against harms caused by neighbors.

This interplay of the right to use land and the right to halt interferences illustrates an inaccuracy in the popular image of land ownership as a bundle of discrete rights, larger or smaller in size. The right to use land and the right to halt interferences are reciprocal rights; an increase in one right can only come with a decrease in the other. Plainly, lines must be drawn between the two rights, requiring important choices about the types of land uses society will favor.

Defining Harm and Offering Remedies

To say that a landowner needs to avoid causing harm really says little until the term *harm* is defined. Over time, the vague term has received widely differing applications, and its continued evolution seems inevitable.

On the eve of the Industrial Revolution, Anglo-American law purported to ban all harm-causing land uses other than those that were trivial. With the coming of industrialization and the rise of cities, landowners sought to use lands with greater intensity. Land-use conflicts increased. Courts responded favorably to industrialization and urbanization by curtailing the protections landowners enjoyed against interferences by their new noisy or polluting neighbors. This dominant legal change entailed a revision to the do-no-harm rule, such that landowners thereafter could complain about interferences only when the harm they suffered was substantial; if the harm was not substantial, they simply had to tolerate it. Landowners also had to show, in order to prevail, that the imposition of this substantial harm was in some way unreasonable. Again, if the harm-creating activity seemed reasonable under the circumstances and values of the new industrial age, then the affected landowners had no remedy. These more relaxed land-use limits helped facilitate railroads, textile mills, mines, and stockyards. They also necessarily withdrew legal protections for more sensitive land uses and permitted greater ecological degradation.

Over the generations, lawmakers assessing the harmfulness of land uses have tended to base their determinations on particular factors or characteristics (Klein 2007; Nagle 2008; Bone 1986). Often they look to whether a contested land use is common or usual in the surrounding area. They consider the economic and social utility of the land use: the more useful it is, the less likely it will be deemed harmful. Courts often consider whether, in a dispute between two landowners, one of them could diminish the clash by making accommodations to the other. Also quite relevant is priority in time: if two land uses seem equally reasonable, the law tends to favor the one that began operating first. On the eve of industrialization, this last factor was often decisive. Harm often arose only when two conflicting land uses stood side by side; either land use alone could operate without difficulty. The tendency of courts (so far as we can tell from fragmentary records) was to conclude that the later land use created the harm. As industrialization proceeded, priority in time was given less weight, likely because the more intensive industrial land uses, which courts wanted to encourage, often came later. Priority in time, though, never became irrelevant and might well be rising in importance.

Scholars and lawmakers have had little success defining nuisance with precision due to the myriad facts that seem relevant in particular land-use settings. The tendency has been to compile a list of relevant factors and to use them when assessing disputes. Nuisance law, then, remains vague in general content. Thus people applying the various factors possess considerable discretion.

The issue of whether a given activity amounts to a nuisance—that is, whether an activity imposes substantial harm on a private landowner under unreasonable circumstances—is intertwined with another issue, also important: the selection of a remedy for the injured landowner. The longstanding rule was that a nuisance invades a landowner's property rights and that the law should stand ready to halt the invasion by issuing an injunction. That is, an injunction was essentially

automatic once a determination of nuisance was made. The landowner could also recover monetary damages for past harm. In recent decades, courts have increasingly backed away from this linkage of right and remedy. They have done so in response to cases in which a landowner is clearly being harmed, substantially and unreasonably, but the harm comes from an activity that appears socially or economically valuable. In such a case, an injunction could halt a valuable land use, imposing costs on a defendant landowner that could greatly exceed the economic benefit of the injunction to the plaintiff.

Is it wise to halt an activity that has public value when the cost of halting it exceeds the economic harm suffered by the plaintiff? Some courts have answered "no" to this question. In doing so, they have effectually separated the issues of landowner right and legal remedy. Under certain circumstances, they will offer an injured landowner a monetary award that compensates for the harm—past and future—even as they allow the harm to continue. Typically this occurs only when the economic effect of an injunction on the landowner causing the harm exceeds by a considerable margin the economic effect of the nuisance itself.

When an injunction is issued, the plaintiff who obtains the injunction typically can negotiate with the defendant landowner, possibly leading to an agreement that allows the nuisance to continue upon payment of money to the plaintiff. When this happens, the defendant could pay a dollar amount much greater than the plaintiff's actual economic losses. To some observers, such an outcome seems unjust; the law, in effect, is empowering the plaintiff landowner to extract an unfair, disproportionate gain. Others defend the practice and outcome. In practice, landowners who obtain injunctions typically seem disinclined to give up their injunctive rights in return for money. Because negotiation is rare, whichever outcome the law prescribes—either an injunction or money damages—tends to be final.

When nuisance law includes an automatic injunction it more completely protects a landowner's use and enjoyment of land. Landowners cannot, against their will, be forced to accept payment in exchange for allowing a neighbor to invade their rights. Such a legal approach is commonly termed a property law. When the law limits an injured landowner to monetary damages for the harm, withholding an injunction, it is termed a liability rule. A vast scholarly literature has arisen debating the relative merits of property and liability rules, chiefly in terms of their relative economic efficiency.

Decision Making and Clarity

As explained, nuisance effectively limits how landowners can use their lands: they must avoid land uses that harm other landowners substantially and unreasonably.

In the case of many types of land-use nuisances, legislative and regulatory bodies have supplemented this vague limit by prescribing more precise land-use rules, specifying which land uses are permitted in which places. Some of these take the form of public health or environmental laws. Others are land-use or zoning ordinances. Many go beyond proscribing actions that would amount to a nuisance in an effort to create and sustain high-quality landscapes. Precise land-use rules are particularly important in countries that rely little, if at all, on the general principle of do-no-harm.

Such statutes and regulations must fit together with the broader, common law prohibition of nuisances. The questions are these: If a particular land use is barred by statute or regulation, is the land use automatically deemed a nuisance? Alternatively, if a statute or regulation allows a specific land use in a given location, is that activity then immune from the claim that it is a nuisance?

The general rule is that legislative and regulatory provisions are highly relevant in deciding whether an activity is a nuisance, but not dispositive. A land use can comply with all zoning and health laws and still, because of its location or manner of operation, amount to a nuisance. A violation of a land-use or health law can provide evidence that a land use is unreasonable where it is taking place, but the plaintiff in a nuisance action still must prove substantial harm and show that, under the circumstances, the harm is unreasonable.

This overlap between the vague common law prohibition of nuisances and the more precise land-use and public health laws raises an important policy question: Is it better for the law to be vague or is it better to draw a more precise line between actions that are permissible and those that are not? A vague rule fails to provide clear notice of what is permitted. On the other hand, a vague rule can be applied to the full array of harm-causing activities, whether or not they were anticipated. It can protect against novel land uses and novel types of harm. A detailed rule provides clearer notice, both to potential plaintiffs and defendants, thereby facilitating dispute resolution. But clear legal rules can have unanticipated effects and miss unexpected harms, as it is impossible to take into account all relevant factors and circumstances affecting the propriety of a given land use in a given place.

On this issue of vagueness or flexibility versus clarity, many observers have drawn upon economic thought to speak in favor of clarity. The argument is that markets and bargaining flourish when people know with certainty who owns what and who can do what. When rules are clear, parties can buy, sell, and otherwise propose deals to avoid or resolve land-use disputes. When rules are vague, such negotiating is allegedly less likely. One difficulty with applying this wisdom is that harm-causing land uses can have ill effects that spread widely, affecting even landowners not involved in negotiations. Moreover, the public as a whole often has legitimate interests in how land is used. The greater the public interest, the less freedom individual landowners should have, through negotiation, to allow harmful activities to continue.

Less attention has been given to another way of reducing the costs of vagueness. Litigation over a nuisance is typically costly and time consuming. It is particularly challenging when suits involve multiple plaintiffs and defendants. As a result, nuisance suits are relatively rare. The costs and delays of litigation could be reduced by creating new dispute-resolution mechanisms that operate more quickly and less formally, with less reliance on lawyers and rules of evidence.

Public Nuisance

Private nuisance, as noted, is a remedy available for private landowners whose use and enjoyment of land have been disrupted. Public nuisance—a related but distinct body of law—offers protection for citizens and communities against activities that cause public harm. The basic idea is the same: a remedy exists to halt activities that impose substantial harm. Public nuisance actions are usually brought by government lawyers on behalf of a government body with jurisdiction over the place where the alleged nuisance is taking place. A private citizen can also bring an action in public nuisance, although a private plaintiff usually must show special injury. The plaintiff must be harmed in a way different or more severe than the general citizen body. Bodily injury typically suffices to satisfy this special-injury standing requirement. In some settings, economic injury can also suffice. For instance, an oil spill could qualify as a public nuisance, harming the public generally. Citizens whose economic livelihood is directly affected by the spill (e.g., fishers) could recover damages for economic losses not suffered by citizens generally. As in the case of private nuisance, this common law doctrine is intermingled with public health and safety rules. An action that complies with extensive regulation is unlikely to be viewed as a public nuisance. Violations of statutes and regulations provide evidence that an activity causes public harm.

Public nuisance actions have often addressed specific categories of unwanted land uses—houses of prostitution, gambling, or distilleries. A variety of structures, including poorly maintained bridges and buildings, mines, and waste piles, can qualify as public nuisances because of dangers they pose, even if only to trespassers. In most jurisdictions, blockages of public roads or other travel corridors (e.g., navigable waterways) are viewed as public nuisances. Travelers whose routes are blocked typically remain able, under long-standing precedent, to remove the blockage physically as a form of self-help.

Nuisance and Ecological Harm

In recent years, many scholars and conservation organizations have taken interest in using nuisance law, both private and public, to halt land uses that cause pollution or other ecological degradation. Water pollution, often of groundwater, has spawned many nuisance suits. In many settings (involving, for instance, dust, soot, or visible gases) it is unclear whether the interference a landowner suffers is direct, physical, and visible, thus making a trespass action appropriate, or whether it is indirect or relatively invisible so that a private nuisance action is appropriate. The distinction is important. A trespass action can be brought without any need to show substantial harm or unreasonableness; the physical invasion is itself enough. Landowners thus try, when possible, to have an interference viewed as a trespass rather than a nuisance.

The core element of nuisance law—the idea of harm—is sufficiently flexible such that no real legal change is needed to apply nuisance to novel types of degradation. A court could conclude that a wide array of activities—soil erosion, excessive drainage, leaching from mining sites, blockages of solar panels or wind turbines—violate the vague but powerful do-no-harm rule. In recent years, various groups have used public nuisance to challenge activities that contribute to climate change. Predictably, such cases raise difficult issues relating to causation and to whether the harm is being imposed unreasonably. Some courts are reluctant to engage issues that they view as chiefly political, or when they seem powerless to craft a remedy that would reduce the harm materially. Novel nuisance suits, however, are likely to continue as courts are pressed to use common law to

protect landowners and communities against long-term degradation.

Eric T. FREYFOGLE
University of Illinois College of Law

See also in the *Berkshire Encyclopedia of Sustainability* Civil Liability Convention for Oil Pollution Damage; Common Heritage of Mankind Principle; Customary International Law; Environmental Dispute Resolution; Enforcement; Intergenerational Equity; Land Use—Regulation and Zoning; Ocean Zoning; Real Property Law; Tort Law

FURTHER READINGS

Abate, Randall S. (2010). Public nuisance suits for the climate justice movement: The right thing and the right time. *Washington Law Review, 85*, 197–252.

Arnold, Craig Anthony. (2002). The reconstitution of property: Property as a web of interests. *Harvard Environmental Law Review, 26*, 282–364.

Bone, Robert G. (1986). Normative theory and legal doctrine in American nuisance law: 1850–1920. *Southern California Law Review, 59*, 1104–1226.

Freyfogle, Eric T. (2003). *The land we share: Private property and the common good.* Washington, DC: Island Press.

Goldstein, Robert J. (1998). Green wood in the bundle of sticks: Fitting environmental ethics and ecology into real property law. *Boston College Environmental Affairs Law Review, 25*, 347–430.

Klein, Christine A. (2007). The new nuisance: An antidote to wetland loss, sprawl, and global warming. *Boston College Law Review, 48*, 1155–1235.

Merrill, Thomas W. (2005). Global warming as public nuisance. *Columbia Environmental Law Journal, 30*, 293–332.

Nagle, John Copeland. (2008). From swamp drainage to wetlands regulation to ecological nuisances to environmental ethics. *Case Western Reserve Law Review, 58*, 787–812.

Singer, Joseph William. (2009). *Property* (3d ed.). New York: Aspen Publishers.

Polluter Pays Principle

The polluter pays principle has become one of the most prominent standards on which worldwide environmental policy is based. The initial concept was first addressed in the 1970s; today its scope is much broader, encompassing not only pollution prevention and control but also liability for cleanup costs. In more recent years it has been extended to product impacts during the whole lifecycle.

The polluter pays principle (PPP) was first mentioned in the recommendation of the Organisation for Economic Co-operation and Development (OECD) of 26 May 1972 and reaffirmed in the recommendation of 14 November 1974. As a main function of the principle, these recommendations specify the allocation "of costs of pollution prevention and control measures to encourage rational use of scarce environmental resources and to avoid distortions in international trade and investment." The polluter should bear the expense of carrying out the measures "decided by public authorities to ensure that the environment is in an acceptable state" (OECD 1972).

In the 1972 Declaration of the United Nations Conference on the Human Environment in Stockholm, the principles did not feature, but in 1992 in Rio de Janeiro, PPP was laid down as Principle 16 of the UN Declaration on Environment and Development. This stated that national authorities should endeavor to promote the internalization of environmental costs and the use of economic instruments, taking into account the approach that the polluter should, in principle, bear the cost of pollution, with due regard to the public interest and without distorting international trade and investment.

The European Community took up the OECD recommendation in its first Environmental Action Program (1973–1976) and then in a recommendation of 3 March 1975 regarding cost allocation and action by public authorities on environmental matters. Since 1987 the principle has also been enshrined in the Treaty of the European Communities and in numerous national legislations worldwide.

Functions and Substance of PPP

Since its first appearance in 1972, the PPP is understood in a much broader sense today, not only covering pollution prevention and control measures but also covering liability, for example, costs for the cleanup of damage to the environment (OECD 1989). Also, the field of application of PPP has been extended in recent years from pollution control at the source toward control of product impacts during the whole lifecycle (known as extended producer responsibility, or EPR).

The preventive function of the PPP is based on the assumption that the polluter will reduce pollution as soon as the costs that he or she has to bear are higher than the benefits anticipated from continuing pollution. As the costs for precautionary measures also have to be paid by the potential polluter, he or she has an incentive to reduce risks and invest in appropriate risk management measures. Finally, the PPP has a curative function, which means that the polluter has to bear the cleanup costs for damage already occurred.

Since its overall objective is to make the polluter pay, the principle leads to the question of who the polluter is; this cannot be defined without knowing what pollution is.

What Is Pollution?

There are two different concepts for defining pollution: one is to establish administrative thresholds in order to define necessary preventive measures and environmental damages. If these thresholds are exceeded, there is pollution. In this view, pollution is congruent to unlawful acts. The second concept defines pollution independently from established thresholds and focuses only on the damage (or the risk of damage), that is, the environmental impact of the emission or harmful activity. As civil liability is not connected to the breach of administrative standards in most European legislations, the second concept is also more consistent with traditional legal concepts. The weakness of this approach is that PPP cannot provide an answer to the question of whether an impact is harmful or has to be considered as damage; it remains a challenge to natural and environmental sciences to define relevant criteria that then also could be implemented by legal standards. Insofar, both concepts do not necessarily contradict each other.

The polluter pays principle does not only apply if there is a "real" pollution in terms of harm or damage to private property and/or the environment. Most legal orders go beyond this interpretation: in light of the precautionary principle, environmental legislation may also provide for measures that are taken to minimize risks—even in cases where there is a lack of scientific knowledge and scientific cause–effect relationships cannot fully be established. One example is Article 3(3) of the United Nations Framework Convention on Climate Change (UNFCCC): "Where there are threats of serious or irreversible damage, lack of full scientific certainty should not be used as a reason for postponing such measures, taking into account that policies and measures to deal with climate change should be cost-effective so as to ensure global benefits at the lowest possible cost." In these cases, the responsible person (the plant operator, the producer of a product) has to bear the costs of precautionary measures according to the PPP, even though pollution has not yet occurred.

Who Is the Polluter?

The term *polluter* refers to a polluting, harmful activity. But the above-mentioned extension of the polluter pays principle has had the inevitable consequence that legislation today often defines the polluter in a more extensive way. Not only those polluters who, in a strict sense, actually "pollute" have to be considered as such, but also those who are only causing risks for the environment and where pollution has not yet occurred.

As far as polluted sites are concerned (for instance under the US Comprehensive Environmental Response, Compensation, and Liability Act, or CERCLA), the owners, operators of disposal facilities, generators of any hazardous wastes discovered at the polluted site, and transporters of the waste can all be considered polluters in this wider sense of the term. Under the German Soil Protection Act even former owners of the polluted site may be held liable under certain circumstances.

In the *Erika* oil spill case, the European Court of Justice held in 2008 that based on Article 15 of the European Union (EU) Waste Framework Directive, the producer of hydrocarbons that became waste due to the accident at sea could be held liable for the cleanup costs. (In 1999, the oil tanker *Erica* broke in two and polluted about 400 kilometers of the French coastline in Brittany.) In accordance with the polluter pays principle, however, such a producer is not liable unless he has contributed through his conduct to the risk of pollution stemming from the shipwreck.

The question of whether the "user" could also be regarded as a "polluter" is relevant, particularly in the field of product control law. Users often pay indirectly when pollution control costs are internalized in the prices of the product.

How Much Is Paid?

The polluter has to pay the costs for preventive and precautionary measures, administrative procedures and, in case of damage occurred, the costs for reinstatement. Although, from an economic point of view, the aim would be to achieve full internalization of external costs, in legal terms the responsibility of the polluter is limited by another general principle of law: the principle of proportionality. The extent to which preventive measures can be required by an operator depends on the risk at issue and the costs of the concrete measure.

A further restriction of the principle is that the polluter has to pay only the costs for his or her own pollution and not costs caused by other polluters, as the European Court of Justice held in the 1999 case (C-293/97) concerning the obligations of farmers under the European Union (EU) Council Implementation of Nitrates Directive (91/676/EEC) to reduce the concentration of nitrates in waters below a determined threshold.

There are some exceptions to this rule, for example, when the law provides for joint and several liability. This means that in cases of several polluters, the injured party can claim for total compensation against one of the polluters of his or her choice (as under CERCLA). Under several regimes of strict liability, the maximum amount for which the polluter is liable in the case of damage is limited, whereas under the general law of tort there is no such limit.

PPP and Other Environmental Principles

As we have seen, the PPP is closely linked to other environmental principles, such as the prevention and the precautionary principles. As a complementary principle to the latter, the PPP has evolved into a comprehensive principle of polluter responsibility.

One particular form of PPP is the extended producer responsibility (EPR). EPR is defined by the OECD as the extension of responsibility to a postconsumer stage of a product's lifecycle both physically and economically. The aim is to provide incentives for producers to improve product design in terms of sustainability. This principle is applied, for instance, in the European Waste Electronic and Electrical Equipment Directive (WEEE), in the End of Life Vehicles Directive, and in the Battery Directive. Also the new EU Waste Framework Directive (2008/98/EC) provides for EPR. This states that EU member states may take appropriate measures to encourage the design of products in order to reduce their environmental impacts and the generation of waste in the course of the production and subsequent use of products, and to ensure that the recovery and disposal of products that have become waste take place without endangering human health and the environment. Measures under EPR may encourage the development, production, and marketing of products that are suitable for multiple use, that are technically durable, and that are suitable for proper and safe recovery and environmentally compatible disposal. EPR is limited by technical and economic feasibility. In the United States, one type of EPR is also known as product stewardship, which is an approach that is based more on voluntarism and shared responsibility of all stakeholders involved (but the producer still has a potentially larger responsibility).

The concept of individual producer responsibility (IPR) is laid down in the WEEE Directive. The main incentive established by the directive is the allocation of costs. Under the directive every producer of electronic or electrical equipment shall be responsible for financing the operations relating to the waste from their own products. The take-back systems set up in the EU member states are organized more collectively, however; the producer is responsible for an undifferentiated mixture of devices and not only for his own products (called collective producer responsibility). Thus, there are some shortcomings in the implementation of IPR in practice.

One understanding of the PPP interprets the principle only as a policy principle with no legal impact. This interpretation is based on the fact that the principle as such is vague and therefore not legally enforceable without further concretization. By contrast, another understanding posits that vague legal concepts are not unusual in law. Since 1972 the principle has been introduced in numerous national and international legal texts and therefore is generally considered today as a legal principle, although its application in practice depends on the implementation of further instruments.

PPP in International Law

PPP is recognized in a number of international conventions (most of which have a regional character) like the Helsinki Convention on the Protection of the Baltic Sea or the Barcelona Convention for the Protection of the Mediterranean Sea against Pollution. There is not yet a unanimous opinion as to whether PPP should be considered as a general principle of law or as a rule of customary law as provided for in Article 38 of the Statute of the International Court of Justice. The fact that most nations have introduced PPP into their national legal orders indicates there is growing international acceptance for it. This along with an increasing number of international conventions that refer to it are both strong arguments in favor of the reconnaissance of PPP as a general principle of law.

General acceptance of PPP can also be observed under World Trade Organization (WTO) law and that of its predecessor, the General Agreement of Tariffs and Trade (GATT).

PPP in European Law

Since 1987 the European Community (EC) Treaty has provided that Europe's policy on the environment shall be based, among other things, on the principle that the polluter should pay (formerly Article 174, paragraph 2 of the EC Treaty; currently Article 191, paragraph 2 of the Treaty on the Functioning of the European Union, or TFEU). Without further definition of the principle, the TEEU obliges the nations to implement the PPP in their environmental policy. Although we may conclude from this that PPP has a legally binding effect, the significance of this effect is controversial. In a case dealing with the prohibition of the use of hydrochlorofluorocarbons (HCFCs), the European Court of Justice held that the objectives, principles, and criteria set out in the relevant article of the EC Treaty on the Environment (1998) have to be respected by the legislature in implementing that policy. But the court limited its own review competence in saying that review by the court must necessarily be limited to the question of whether, in adopting particular rules, the legislature committed a manifest error of appraisal regarding the conditions for the application of the relevant article of the treaty providing for PPP.

In fact, numerous directives and regulations—so-called secondary legislation—have put into force a widespread corpus of environmental law that is largely based on the PPP.

PPP in National Law

Environmental legislation across the world is increasingly recognizing PPP. In some countries (e.g., Australia), specialized environmental courts have been set up to control the enforcement of environmental legislation and PPP. In Canada, PPP is enshrined in the preamble of the Environmental Protection Act 1999; in France the Environmental Code of 2000 defines PPP in Article L.110-1 as a principle under which the costs for preventive measures as well as reduction and remedying measures have to be borne by the polluter.

In developing and emerging countries new environmental legislation is frequently inspired and set up—often with the support of multilateral or bilateral international cooperation—by modern concepts containing environmental principles such as the PPP.

Implementation and Fields of Application

To be effective, the PPP has to be implemented by concrete instruments in international and national legislation. There are a number of legal and economic instruments available to this end. These instruments can also be combined and do not exclude each other, given that full cost internalization is usually not reached by a single instrument alone.

Environmental binding standards, emission limit values, or the so-called "best available technique" approach, set up and defined by government, are still predominant tools in many countries and environmental sectors, such as air and water pollution control (e.g., in the US Clean Air Act of 1970 and the US Clean Water Act of 1977) or cleanup of contaminated sites. According to the PPP, the costs for meeting these standards (for instance the investment of "depollution" techniques) have to be paid by the plant operators.

In the last two decades, economic instruments have gained more relevance. Tradable permits try to provide operators with an incentive to invest in pollution control measures in the most efficient way. Title IV of the US Clean Air Act Amendments pursued the objective of reducing national sulfur dioxide emissions from electricity utilities by 50 percent between 1995 and 2000 during Phase I. The Kyoto Protocol has established an international trading scheme for carbon dioxide emissions, which has also been implemented into European law. It is questionable, however, whether emission trading programs have an advantage over classic command-and-control law. This particularly holds true if allowances for existing plants are distributed free of charge ("grandfathering"), as was the case in the first trading period under the European carbon dioxide emissions trading program.

Several European countries, such as Belgium and Germany, have introduced ecotax (ecological taxation) schemes in their respective tax legislation in order to promote a more environmentally friendly use of raw materials or energy. Cost recovery charges have been set up in Australia for the purpose of financing administrative activities in the fishery sector. Furthermore, new liability rules have been set up in many countries and in the European Union under the 2004 EU Environmental Liability Directive. Certain professional activities fall under a strict liability regime if environmental damage to soil, water, or natural habitats and species is caused. The responsible person then has to inform the authorities, prevent further harm, and reinstate the damaged environment.

Another instrument is the concept of property rights that seeks to give ownership to individuals of unowned natural goods.

PPP's Contribution to Sustainability

Today the polluter pays principle has become one of the most prominent standards on which environmental policy

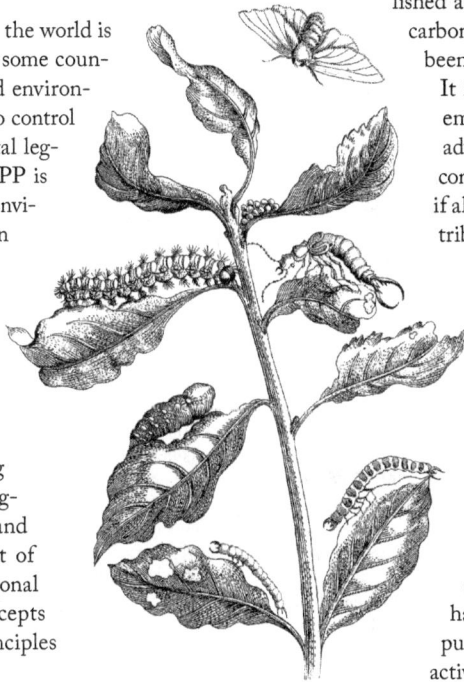

is based. It influences not only environmental policy but also environmental law on international, European, and national levels. In particular, environmental legislation in the European Union is increasingly based on PPP. The PPP has contributed considerably to the success achieved in improving air and water quality in Europe in the last thirty years.

The worldwide acceptance of PPP will probably also lead to its acceptance as a general principle of international law in the near future. Important accidents like the 2010 oil spill in the Gulf of Mexico show the constant and ever-increasing relevance of the PPP. Thus, together with the principles of prevention and precaution, the PPP will remain a core basis for sustainable development.

Gerhard ROLLER
University of Applied Sciences

See also in the *Berkshire Encyclopedia of Sustainability* Bhopal Disaster; Civil Liability Convention for Oil Pollution Damage; Clean Air Act; Clean Water Act; Convention for the Prevention of Pollution From Ships; Convention on Long-Range Transboundary Air Pollution; Convention on Persistent Organic Pollutants; Environmental Law (several articles: Australia and New Zealand; Europe; United States and Canada); Precautionary Principle; Transboundary Water Law; Waste Shipment Law

FURTHER READINGS

Beder, Sharon. (2006). *Environmental principles and policies: An interdisciplinary introduction.* London: Earthscan.

de Sadeeler, Nicolas. (2002). *Environmental principles.* Oxford, UK: Oxford University Press.

Epiney, Astrid. (2006). Environmental principles. In Richard Macrory (Ed.), *Reflections on 30 years of EU environmental law.* Groningen, The Netherlands: Europa Law Publishing.

Krämer, Ludwig. (1997). Polluter-pays-principle in community law: The interpretation of article 103r of the EEC Treaty. In Ludwig Krämer (Ed.), *Focus on European Law* (pp. 244). London: Graham & Trotman.

Mann, Ian. (2009). A comparative study of the polluter pays principle and its international normative effect on pollutive processes. Retrieved July 13, 2010, from http://www.consulegis.com/fileadmin/downloads/thomas_marx_08/Ian_Mann_paper.pdf

Renckens, Stefan. (2008). Yes, we will! Voluntarism in US e-waste governance. *RECIEL, Review of European Community & International Law, 17*(3), 286–299.

Roller, Gerhard, & Führ, Martin. (2008). Individual Producer Responsibility: A remaining challenge under the WEEE Directive. *RECIEL, Review of European Community & International Law, 17*(3), 279–285.

TREATIES / RESOLUTIONS / COURT CASES

Council of the European Communities Directive of 12 December 1991 concerning the protection of waters against pollution caused by nitrates from agricultural sources (91/676/EEC). Retrieved August 28, 2010, from http://ec.europa.eu/environment/water/water-nitrates/directiv.html

Council of the European Communities Waste Framework Directive (2008/98/EC) of 19 November 2008.

Organisation of Economic Cooperation and Development (OECD). (1972, May 26). Recommendation of the council on guiding principles concerning international economic aspects of environmental policies. Council Document no. C(72)128.

Organisation for Economic Co-operation and Development (OECD). (1974, November 14). Recommendation of the council on the implementation of the polluter-pays principle. Document no. C(74)223.

Organisation for Economic Co-operation and Development (OECD). (1989, July 7). Recommendation of the council concerning the application of the polluter-pays principle to accidental pollution. Document no. C(89)88/FINAL.

International Court of Justice. (1945). Statute of the International Court of Justice. Retrieved November 15, 2010, from http://www.icj-cij.org/documents/index.php?p1=4&p2=2&p3=0

United Nations Framework Convention on Climate Change (adopted on 9 May 1992 and entered into force 21 March 1994).

Precautionary Principle

The precautionary principle, a policy of foreseeing and preventing the potential adverse effects of future actions, is the basis of laws regulating commercial activity and natural resource management in certain regions of the globe. In the European Union, newly enacted regulation governing the marketing of chemical substances is based on the precautionary principle. In the United States, such a regulatory approach has not been widely adopted as yet.

The application of the precautionary principle as a public policy paradigm is relatively new in the regulation of commercial products, industrial processes, and natural resource management—but it is an approach that has been increasingly invoked in certain regions of the globe since the 1980s. The origin of the term *precautionary principle* is generally attributed to the German concept of *Vorsorgeprinzip*, or a "fore-caring principle," which may be translated as foreseeing the possible consequences of one's actions.

Following the extraordinary string of legislative successes in the United States in the 1970s with laws regulating air and water quality, toxic substances, and hazardous wastes, as well as the adoption of quantitative risk assessment procedures by federal and state agencies, the precautionary principle came into public discussion in the mid-1980s among European policy makers. Based on their historical tradition of precautionary approach to commercial activity, they began to use it to describe a meaningful framework for regulating new technologies and products.

Conferences, Treaties, and Law

Although the United Nations General Assembly's World Charter for Nature (1982) first introduced the idea of the precautionary principle, it was initially invoked as a legal concept at the First International Conference on the Protection of the North Sea, held in Bremen, Germany, in 1984. The term was made more explicit as a preferred policy prescription at its Second International Conference, adopted in London in 1987, which stated in Paragraph VII: "In order to protect the North Sea from possibly damaging effects of the most dangerous substances, *a precautionary approach is necessary* which may require action to control inputs of such substances even before a causal link had been established by absolute clear scientific evidence" (emphasis added).

The primacy of the precautionary principle was also embedded in the 1992 Maastricht Treaty, which led to the formation of the European Union: "[European] Union policy on the environment shall aim at a high level of protection taking into account the diversity of situations in the various regions of the Union. It shall be based on the *precautionary principle and on the principles that preventive action should be taken*, that environmental damage should as a priority be rectified at source and that the polluter should pay" (emphasis added).

At the United Nations Conference on Environment and Development ("Earth Summit") held in Rio de Janeiro in 1992, the precautionary principle was adopted as Principle 15. The conference report states, "In order to protect the environment, the *precautionary approach shall be widely applied by states according to their capabilities*. Where there are threats of serious or irreversible damage, lack of full scientific certainty shall not be used as a reason for postponing cost-effective measures to prevent environmental degradation" (emphasis added).

Finally, in February 2002, the Commission of the European Communities (CEC), while acknowledging that the Maastricht Treaty invoked but did not define the concept of precautionary principle, published a detailed "communication" document on this topic. It stated that the precautionary principle should apply not only to protecting the environment, but that "*in practice*, its scope is much wider, and specifically where preliminary objective scientific evaluation, indicates that there are reasonable grounds for concern that the potentially dangerous effects on the *environment, human, animal or plant health* may be inconsistent with the high level of protection for the Community" (emphasis in original). But the CEC document also mentioned the importance of considering risk analysis within an overall regulatory framework for the European Community. It stated that "the precautionary principle should be considered within a structured approach to the analysis of risk which comprises three elements: risk assessment, risk management, risk communication. The precautionary principle is particularly relevant to the management of risk" (CEC 2002).

Transatlantic Divide and International Applications

While widely accepted within the European Union, the precautionary principle has not been popular in the United States, especially among private sector companies and major trade associations, which have adamantly opposed the use of such an approach to regulate their commercial and industrial activities. The reason for this transatlantic divide lies in the differing ethical standards and philosophical worldviews of the two regulatory cultures.

Regulatory officials in United States have less difficulty accepting risk assessment and risk management principles for defining environmental and public health standards, such as issuing effluent discharge permits to a manufacturing plant. In contrast, European officials do not believe risk assessment procedures alone are adequate for controlling toxic substances and hazardous products in commercial transactions, especially when it comes to imported manufactured goods. European officials are more likely to suspect that a new product may come into the market without proper assessment of its impact on human health and the natural environment. The adoption of the precautionary principle as an overarching regulatory guideline has thus been more appealing to many European policy makers.

In the early 1970s, the *Vorsorgeprinzip* became the fundamental basis of German environmental law, and since then it has been referred to in judiciary and regulatory proceedings in other countries. Among these, Germany and Sweden have been foremost in applying the precautionary principle to chemical safety regulations, though to varying degrees in stringency. In Germany, for instance, a precautionary approach is regarded as follows: scientific uncertainty does not justify *not* taking regulatory action. In Sweden, on the other hand, scientific uncertainty *shifts* the burden of proof to the manufacturer of the product. The third and most stringent application of the precautionary principle is when scientific uncertainty is used as a reason to mandate that a public agency take *definitive* regulatory action.

In an important court case regarding the site of a proposed mobile telephone base station in Australia in 2006— *Telstra Corporation Limited v. Hornsby Shire Council*— the concept of precautionary principle was invoked based on a provision of environmental law adopted in New South Wales that states, "If there are threats of serious or irreversible environmental damage, lack of full scientific certainty should not be used as a reason for postponing measures to prevent environmental degradation." The law suit, however, was decided in favor of Telstra, a telecommunications firm, on the grounds that the community *did not show* sufficient basis of serious harm that would result from its exposure to radiofrequency electromagnetic radiation.

In New Zealand, the concept of the precautionary principle has been incorporated into a number of environmental and natural resources

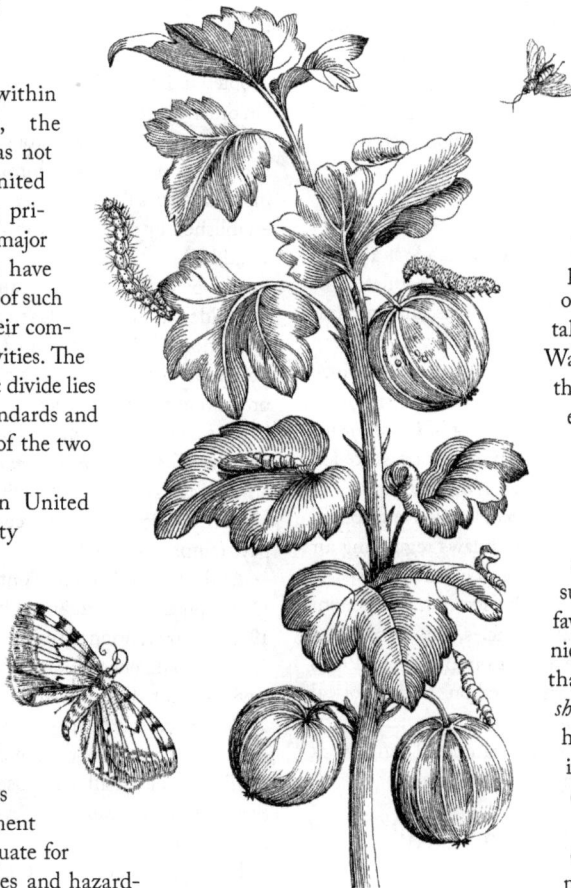

laws. Defining what may trigger precautionary action, the Resource Management Act of 1991 states that "First, novel scientific evidence will be accepted by the [Environment Court] if it is demonstrated after testing, to be more than mere conjecture or hypothesis. Second, the application of a general precautionary principle is within the Court's discretion when exercising its judgment. . . . Factors influencing the application of caution are the *reliability of the scientific evidence and the gravity of the effect* the scientific evidence tends to" (Birdsong, 1998) (emphasis added).

In June 2007, the European Union (EU) put into force a landmark regulatory framework, based on the conceptual foundation of the precautionary principle called REACH (Registration, Evaluation, Authorisation and Restriction of Chemicals). This EU directive streamlines the process by which private companies assess and manage the production, use, and marketing of chemical substances, along with providing safety information to users in their member countries. REACH requires that any manufacturer importing into or producing chemical substances of significant amount within the European Union register its product with the European Chemicals Agency based in Helsinki, Finland. Still unresolved are the extent, types, and costs of chemical safety testing that will be required of manufacturers before their existing or new products could enter the EU market.

The net result of the REACH regulatory framework shifts the burden of proof of chemical safety to the manufacturer. Under REACH'S precautionary mandate, it is now difficult for a manufacturer to introduce inadequately tested chemicals in the marketplace. Previously, the burden of proof of potential harmful impact was placed with regulatory agencies and/or the public. Thus, when REACH is fully implemented, it will have major implications for international trade in chemical substances and other manufactured products.

Application in the United States

Although the basic concept of the precautionary principle has still not taken root in the United States, a few state and local governments have begun adopting its underlying tenet in their decision-making process. For example, the Wingspread Statement on the Precautionary Principle, formulated in 1998 by a group of scientists, philosophers, lawyers, and environmental activists at the Wingspread conference center in Racine, Wisconsin, states that "when an activity raises threats of harm to human health or the environment, precautionary measures should be taken even if some cause and effect relationships are not fully established scientifically" (SEHN 2010).

As early as 1989, the Commonwealth of Massachusetts enacted the Toxic Use Reduction Act (TURA), which provided industries in the state with planning tools to voluntarily reduce their production, use, and emission of toxic substances. Such an approach does not depend on establishing the scientific certainty of the harmful effects of these substances. In 2003, the city of San Francisco passed a precautionary principle ordinance that states that "lack of scientific certainty relating to cause and effect shall not be viewed as sufficient reason for the City to postpone measures to prevent the degradation of the environment or protect the health of its citizen . . . Where there are reasonable grounds for concern, the Precautionary Principle is meant to help reduce harm" (Board of Supervisors 2003).

In an editorial published in *Environmental Health Perspectives*, Dr. Bernard D. Goldstein, a former assistant administrator for the US Environmental Protection Agency's Office of Research and Development, stated that in order to invoke the precautionary principle within a regulatory framework in the United States, one must be prepared to conduct *scientific research*: "Responsible precaution requires that we accompany proposals for precautionary actions with a research agenda to decide if the actions, once taken, are justified. The Precautionary Principle works soundly only when those who invoke it accept that the precautionary action encompasses and automatically triggers research designed to concurrently determine the wisdom of the precautionary action" (Goldstein 1999).

Outlook for the Future

As the second decade of the twenty-first century begins, the debate over whether to adopt the precautionary principle—in such diverse areas as chemical regulation, food production, and marine and wildlife management—focuses on the ways in which governments, nongovernmental organizations, and private corporations interpret, value, and support well-designed and innovative scientific research and development with regard to chemical safety and the regulation of commercial and industrial activity. And, most significantly, it depends on the ways in which we heed the original concept of the precautionary principle—foreseeing the consequences of our society's collective actions.

A. Karim AHMED
National Council for Science and the Environment

See also in the *Berkshire Encyclopedia of Sustainability* Biotechnology Legislation; Chemicals Legislation and Policy; Environmental Law—Europe; Environmental Law—United States and Canada; Polluter Pays Principle; Nanotechnology Legislation; Registration, Evaluation, Authorisation, and Restriction of Chemicals; Restriction of Hazardous Substances Directive

Further Readings

Andorno, Roberto. (2004). The precautionary principle: A new legal standard for a technological age. *Journal of International Biotechnology Law, 1*, 11–19. Retrieved November 17, 2010, from http://www.ethik.uzh.ch/ibme/team/mitarbeitende/andorno/precautionary-principle.pdf

Birdsong, Bret. (1998). Adjudicating sustainability: New Zealand's environment court and the Resource Management Act. Retrieved November 23, 2010, from http://www.fulbright.org.nz/voices/axford/docs/birdsongb.pdf

Board of Supervisors, City of San Francisco. (2003). Precautionary principle policy statement. Retrieved November 21, 2010, from http://www.greenaction.org/cancer/alert061803.shtml

Commission of the European Communities (CEC). (2002, February 2). Communication of the commission on the precautionary principle. Retrieved November 17, 2010, from http://ec.europa.eu/dgs/health_consumer/library/pub/pub07_en.pdf

Declaration of the International Conference on the Protection of the North Sea. (1984). Bremen declaration. Retrieved November 21, 2010, from http://www.seas-at-risk.org/1mages/1984%20Bremen%20Declaration.pdf

DiGangi, Joseph. (2004, September). REACH and the long arm of the chemical industry. *The Multinational Monitor, 25*(9). Retrieved November 17, 2010, from http://multinationalmonitor.org/mm2004/09012004/september04corp3.html

Goldstein, Bernard D. (1999). The precautionary principle and scientific research are not antithetical [Editorial]. *Environmental Health Perspectives, 107*(12), A594–A595. Retrieved November 17, 2010, from http://www.ncbi.nlm.nih.gov/pmc/articles/PMC1566805/pdf/envhper00517-0010.pdf

Lofstedt, Ragnar E. (2004). The swing of regulatory pendulum in Europe: From precautionary principle to (regulatory) impact analysis. *Journal of Risk and Uncertainty, 28*(3), 237–260. Retrieved November 17, 2010, from http://www.springerlink.com/content/uj172553465k2402/fulltext.pdf

Science & Environmental Health Network (SEHN). (2010). Precautionary principle. Retrieved November 21, 2010, from http://www.sehn.org/wing.html

Second International Conference on the Protection of the North Sea. (1987). London declaration. Retrieved November 22, 2010, from http://www.seas-at-risk.org/1mages/1987%20London%20Declaration.pdf

Telstra Corporation Limited v. Hornsby Shire Council. (2006). Retrieved November 21, 2010, from http://www.lawlink.nsw.gov.au/lecjudgments/2006nswlec.nsf/c45212a2bef99be-4ca256736001f37bd/fdf89ace6e00928bca25713800832056?OpenDocument

Treaty on European Union [Treaty of Maastricht], Official Journal C 191. (1992, July 29). Retrieved November 22, 1010, from http://eur-lex.europa.eu/en/treaties/dat/11992M/htm/11992M.html

United Nations Conference on Environment and Development. (1992). Rio declaration. Retrieved November 22, 2010, from http://www.unep.org/Documents.Multilingual/Default.asp?documentid=78&articleid=1163

United Nations General Assembly. (1982). World charter for nature. Retrieved November 21, 2010, from http://www.un.org/documents/ga/res/37/a37r007.htm

Real Property Law

Real property law can achieve the long-term goals of sustainability by regulating not only our relationships with each other regarding the use of land and natural resources but also our ongoing relationship with the ever-changing physical world. When property law balances environmental stewardship with the need for economic security, it becomes an important tool for attaining sustainable development.

Real property law refers to laws created by the government to protect certain interests in land or certain resources such as trees, water, oil, or minerals. When a person or group has a legally recognized interest under real property law, they have the exclusive right to possess, use, and transfer land or resources.

Sustainable development requires conscientiously managing limited environmental resources to meet ever-expanding human needs. The balance between environmental protection and human development goals (e.g., food and water security, energy production) is not always easy to achieve. By creating transparent markets for trade in land and natural resources in the context of zoning schemes for responsible land use, states can use their real property law to balance environmental management priorities with economic growth. Where communities and individuals have a legally recognized stake in land or natural resources, there is an ongoing incentive to invest in sustainable development by protecting these resources for both this generation and future ones.

There is no universal real property law, although most property law schemes provide owners with the rights to possess, use, exclude, and dispose of a particular property. Depending on whether a state wants to promote more equitable access to resources or more exclusive access for elites, states will employ different approaches to the legal administration of land and other natural resources. When states create legally cognizable property rights available to all citizens and consciously balance ecological needs with human needs, these states are more likely to experience long-term sustainable growth. In contrast, states that interfere with certain communities and individuals obtaining property rights may experience short-term growth but tend to also create preconditions for social conflict. Economic sustainability for a growing population depends on maintaining healthy lands and adequate resources.

There are generally three tools used by states to balance economic growth with environmental needs: land tenure laws, zoning, and the public trust doctrine.

Private Land Tenure and Sustainability

While restrictive zoning laws may be applied to promote environmental sustainability, governments develop land tenure laws to stimulate economic sustainability or to prevent social instability. Land tenure laws cover a variety of different types of rights over land, including private rights between two private parties, communal rights shared among a distinct community, open access rights available to everyone, and state rights assigning real property to public sector authorities. Land tenure laws describe who can use what resources and how they can be utilized. Creating property-law frameworks to secure land tenure is essential for ensuring that individuals or communities have the opportunity to protect their interest in land, develop the land, and access credit from the market by using the land as collateral. Lack of land title in some regions currently limits large-scale agricultural productivity, as individuals are less likely to invest time in cultivating tracts of land over which they have no legal interest. The stronger the

177

legal claim that a party has in relation to a property, the more likely a party will be to either add value to a property through investing in infrastructure or to protect inherent values such as the environmental integrity of a property.

The reality in most parts of the world, particularly in impoverished communities, is that individuals do not have formal, legally cognizable title to their land or resources. The government land-administration systems that should protect the interests of local communities are frequently outdated. As a result, there are ongoing conflicts over land because parties compete to secure interests in dwindling land resources. Powerful political and economic groups lobby to maintain the status quo by resisting legal reforms that improve land tenure for large numbers of land-insecure individuals.

Ownership is divided in most countries between public lands and privately held lands. Public lands may include highways, waterways, national parks, and government properties. Private land can be held in a number of different legally recognized forms. In the United States, land can be held either fee simple absolute (i.e., a form of real-property ownership that is free of any other conditions or claims against the title), or some lesser interest can be recognized. In countries such as Thailand, there are four categories of private ownership: a land title deed for ownership, a preemptive certificate allowing use of a parcel of land for a certain period of time, a certificate of utilization guaranteeing an owners right to possession, and a certificate for land acquired from the state exclusively for smallholder farming.

Some countries, such as Australia, recognize competing public and private interests in land. In a dispute over whether the Australian state or a group of aboriginals owned a set of islands off the coast of Australia (*Mabo v. Queensland*), the court concluded native title could restrict state claims to land tenure because native title had already existed prior to Australia becoming a state. Since indigenous groups are often concerned with environmentally and culturally sustaining their land for future generations, native land title may promote the goals of sustainability.

Socialist states such as China take a unique approach to land titling. Recognizing that land title is critical for stimulating economic productivity, China has introduced quasi-private rights. In 1998, China introduced "land use rights" that could be transferred between individuals and companies (Chinese Constitution 1982, Article 10, Section 4; Land Administration Law 2004, Chapter 1, Article 2). Even though "land use rights" can be considered a form of private property, ownership of Chinese land remains vested in the state and its institutions.

Given the significance of tenure and titling to community development efforts, especially in rural areas, there have been ongoing efforts to reform property laws to provide greater accessibility to land and to encourage local investment by using land as collateral for credit. In the 1990s, after several failed national attempts to provide land to smallholder farmers, the government of El Salvador launched a new land reform program with the assistance of the World Bank; its goal was to turn El Salvador into a country of property owners in hopes of stimulating small-scale development and incorporating the neediest land-poor groups into the economic and social development process. The program's overall success has been mixed. While the increase in land tenure has not raised households out of poverty, results of field research showed that households that owned even small amounts of land had better returns on their labor and were able to keep their children in school in years of economic hardship (Conning, Olinto, and Trigueros 2000, 1).

Land title alone is not enough to promote community economic sustainability. As Karol Boudreaux's 2006 case study of Langa Township in South Africa illustrates, development agencies cannot expect that granting land title alone will have a ripple effect on economic growth. The study found that while secure title spurred some limited economic activity, it did not lead to the anticipated investments into larger community projects since banks were wary of lending to individuals who worked primarily in the informal sector, and individuals were risk averse when it came to using the title to their home as collateral for loans.

Government engagement in supervising real property interests does not necessarily improve conditions of economic or social sustainability. For example, in Nigeria land title is controlled under the Land Use Act of 1978, which prohibits individuals from transferring or subleasing land without the consent of the government. The need to obtain government approval for transfer of land interests has reinforced low-level corruption, with lessors paying to obtain government approval for what otherwise would be a standard commercial property transaction. For

a businessperson to transfer land within the land use system requires fourteen government-mandated procedures and costs approximately 22 percent of the value of the land (UNCTAD 2009, 46).

Formal land tenure laws are not essential for creating conditions for community economic sustainability. In some areas, such as western Africa, customary tenure continues to govern relationships involving land (Barrows and Roth 1990). While formal land tenure (i.e., rights in real property officially recognized by state laws) may enhance opportunities for individuals to access economic resources from broader capital markets, it may also contribute in some instances to tenure insecurity by permitting local elites to acquire land that may have otherwise been assigned a different owner under the customary tenure system (i.e., rights in real property recognized under community customs and practices that may or may not be recognized by the state).

A lack of easily identifiable property rights has a greater implication for connecting communities to larger regional or global economic markets. Foreign investors are reluctant to invest in countries where they perceive a lack of secure land tenure for fear that their investment may be expropriated without compensation. As global connectivity becomes a critical component of economic sustainability, nations create laws to recognize and protect private-property rights of noncitizens. Even Cuba has guaranteed limited private-property rights (under 1995's Foreign Investment Law No. 77) in order to attract much-needed foreign direct investment. Many indigenous groups rely on having legally protected access to their ancestral lands not just to sustain their populations economically but also to maintain their communities culturally. Since indigenous groups often have particular relationships with their lands that cannot be replicated elsewhere, securing legally cognizable property rights is key to the long-term survival of many of these groups. This link between property and cultural sustainability has been recognized in international law. In 1989 the International Labour Organization recognized that "the rights of ownership and possession of the peoples concerned over the lands which they traditionally occupy [as well as] the right of the peoples concerned to use lands not exclusively occupied by them, but to which they have traditionally had access for their subsistence and traditional activities."

Zoning to Promote Environmental Sustainability

Zoning laws are regulations passed primarily by local governments to permit certain land uses in certain areas. National laws that designate geographical areas as national or provincial parks or marine protected areas serve the same function as zoning laws by restricting designated areas to certain public uses such as recreation and conservation. When carefully designed, zoning laws may contribute to sustainably managing limited resources that are being depleted due to great demand. For example in response to a flurry of large-scale tourism developments, the Thai province of Phang Nga recently passed strict zoning laws to restrict beachfront property uses for the next five years to conservation and traditional agricultural uses.

Zoning laws—especially laws designed to protect vulnerable ecosystems—may lead to conflict with communities if all human uses are prohibited in an area traditionally used by communities. For example, in central Africa, government laws creating twelve parks in the Congo basin have displaced up to 120,000 impoverished people who have customarily used the land for sustenance (Cernea and Schmidt-Soltau 2006, 1818). Some countries, such as Indonesia and Kenya, have overcome this "parks and people" problem by reaching compromises that allow communities the right to access public lands for certain products and uses in exchange for local stewardship of the land.

As the unilateral implementation of laws designed to protect public property demonstrates, environmental sustainability cannot be promoted at the exclusion of long-term economic sustainability. Conservation that ignores the rights and the needs of agricultural, fishing, and hunting-gathering groups is not sustainable in the sense that sustainability requires a balance between human needs and ecological protection. New legal characterizations based on co-management have been proposed to address simultaneously the environmental need to protect vulnerable ecosystems with the need to sustain local livelihoods. Two of these designations include the National System of Conservation Units created under the Marine Extractive Reserves in Brazil (Lei No. 9.985/Article 225) and Community Conserved Areas in Australia, which was created under the Australian government's Indigenous Protected Area Program. In both of these programs, the state has identified ecosystems containing biodiversity values, ecological services, and cultural values, and relies on communities to promote conservation of these ecosystems through the application of indigenous or customary laws and practices.

Public Trust

Real property laws generally recognize both private and public property interests. As far as public property interests, some countries recognize a "public trust" property interest in certain resources that have been historically shared. The public trust doctrine asserts that the public has a legal right to access and use certain resources, without any restriction being placed by private owners. Originally applied to the public's right to access navigable waterways without interference from private riparian owners, the doctrine has been extended to include a public interest in tidelands, lake beds, and other natural resources.

The public trust doctrine requires governments to act as a trustee to ensure rights to access and use certain resources on behalf of the public, even though the public may not own the underlying title to the property. The international community protects rights of all citizens to certain shared resources through a version of the public trust referred to as "common heritage of mankind." The seabed beyond national jurisdictions is considered to be a common heritage resource, meaning that financial benefits derived from the use of the resource by private users are broadly shared.

Implication of Real Property Law

Real property law achieves the long-term goals of sustainability by structuring not only our relationships with each other regarding the use of land and natural resources, but also our ongoing relationships with our dynamically changing physical world. Zoning mechanisms that acknowledge both environmental values and community needs can provide rational land-use planning. Likewise, land tenure mechanisms that provide previously marginalized groups with formally recognized property rights have the potential to contribute to greater social equity. Where property law balances the values of environmental stewardship with the need for economic security, the law becomes a potent tool for sustainable development.

Anastasia TELESETSKY
University of Idaho College of Law

See also in the *Berkshire Encyclopedia of Sustainability* Development, Sustainable—Overview of Laws and Commissions; Environmental Dispute Resolution; Environmental Law (several articles: Africa, Sub-Saharan; Australia and New Zealand; Central America and the Caribbean; China; United States and Canada; South America); Investment Law, Foreign; Land Use—Regulation and Zoning; Natural Resources Law; Nuisance Law; Ocean Zoning

FURTHER READINGS

Barrows, Richard, & Roth, Michael. (1990). Land tenure and investment in African agriculture: Theory and evidence. *Journal of Modern African Studies, 28*(2), 265–297.

Baslar, Kemal. (1998). *The concept of the common heritage of mankind in international law.* Leiden, The Netherlands: Martinus Nijhoff.

Bernhardt, Roger, & Bernhardt, Ann. (2005). *Real property in a nutshell.* St. Paul, MN: Thomson West.

Boudreaux, Karol. (2006, April). The effects of property titling in Langa Township, South Africa (Mercatus Policy Series, Policy Comment No. 4). Fairfax, VA: Mercatus Center, George Mason University.

Bruce, John, et al. (2006). *Land law reform: Achieving development policy objectives.* Washington, DC: World Bank.

Cernea, Michael, & Schmidt-Soltau, Kai. (2006). Poverty risks and national parks: Policy issues in resettlement. *World Development, 34*(10), 1808–1830.

Conning, Jonathan; Olinto, Pedro; & Trigueros, Alvaro. (2000). Managing economic insecurity in rural El Salvador: The role of asset ownership and labor market adjustments. Madison, WI: Broadening Access and Strengthening Input Market Systems. Retrieved November 3, 2010, from http://www.basis.wisc.edu/live/NICA%20papers/conning_olinto.pdf

Nolon, John. (2006). *Compendium of land use laws for sustainable development.* New York: Cambridge University Press.

Ubink, Janine; Hoekma, Andre; & Assies, William. (Eds.). (2009). *Legalising land rights: Local practices, state responses, and tenure security in Africa, Asia, and Latin America.* Leiden, The Netherlands: Leiden University Press.

United Nations Conference on Trade and Development (UNCTAD). (2009). *Investment policy review: Nigeria.* Retrieved August 30, 2010, from http://www.unctad.org/en/docs/diaepcb20081_en.pdf

LAWS AND COURT CASES

Government of Australia, Native Title Act 1993 (entered into force 1 January 1994).

Government of Brazil, Marine Extractive Reserves in Brazil, Lei No. 9.985/Article 225, July 2000.

Government of Cuba, Foreign Investment Law No. 77, Ley De La Inversion Extranjera, ch. 6, Gaceta Oficial de la Republica de Cuba, Extraordinary Ed. No. 3, 6 September 1995.

Government of El Salvador, Decree No. 17, Diario Official, Vol. 310, No. 40, 26 February 1991.

Government of the Peoples' Republic of China. (1982). Constitution. Retrieved August 30, 2010, from http://english.gov.cn/2005-08/05/content_20813.htm

Government of the Peoples' Republic of China. (2004). Law of the Peoples' Republic of China on Land Administration. Retrieved August 30, 2010, from http://www.fdi.gov.cn/pub/FDI_EN/Laws/GeneralLawsandRegulations/BasicLaws/P020060620320252818532.pdf

International Labour Organization Convention Concerning Indigenous and Tribal Peoples in Independent Countries, No 169, 28 ILM 1382 (adopted 27 June 1989).

Mabo v. Queensland 1988. HCA [High Court of Australia] 69; (1989) 166 CLR 186 (8 December 1988).

Silent Spring

Silent Spring (1962), written by marine biologist Rachel Carson, exposed the widespread harm of synthetic chemical pesticides. Silent Spring created public and political awareness of the danger of these chemical pesticides to fish, birds, small mammals, beneficial insects, and humans through the effects of biomagnification. Many of these pesticides were banned in the United States and, eventually, much of the world.

Silent Spring (1962) was the third and most influential book written by marine biologist and natural history writer Rachel Carson (1907–1964). The book is a specific, passionate, and well-documented exposé of the use and promotion of a new generation of synthetic pesticides created through the manipulation of molecules containing carbon and hydrogen atoms. Most notable of these pesticides, DDT (dichloro-diphenyl-tricholor-ethane) became known as the one of the most harmful pesticides produced at the time. Its misuse was one of the driving causes behind the placement of the American bald eagle on the endangered species list in the United States. Carson maintained that these chemicals were produced and applied indiscriminately to vast areas of land including farms, neighborhoods, and entire towns with little testing or consideration for people or the environment, causing cancer, liver disease, and other fatal health effects. The eventual effects of the chemicals combined with the awareness generated by *Silent Spring* caused many of the pesticides to be banned in the United States and most of the world. *Silent Spring* ushered in a new era of public environmental consciousness in the late twentieth century. It influenced and inspired many of the environmental laws passed and agencies created to regulate and monitor potentially harmful products or actions. Many existing and developing sustainable approaches to agriculture and lifestyle can be credited to the legacy of *Silent Spring*.

Beginning in the late 1930s, the chemical industry in the United States developed new, powerful pesticides by manipulating hydrocarbons and combining them with other elements such as chlorine to produce pesticides such as DDT, chlordane, heptachlor, dieldrin, aldrin, and endrin. By the mid-1940s they were available to the public; their use increased as their benefits, such as killing harmful insects that attacked agricultural fields, ornamental plants, and humans, were touted. The main thrust of Carson's argument was based on the effects of *biomagnification*, in which insects or other life destroyed by the pesticides are consumed and the effects of the poison destroy life higher on the food chain. Carson highlighted several instances where people and large mammals were sickened, killed, or produced stillborn offspring. Of particular interest was the destruction of the songbird population; many noticed a stark absence of birds and the presence of dead birds in their communities. The very title of the book, *Silent Spring*, points to an imaginary time in communities around the country where no birds would sing due to the fatal effects of the chemicals. To make her case, Rachel Carson relied on numerous scientists, physicians, and researchers and buttressed her argument with over fifty pages of sources for her research. Her examples were specific and relied on the latest research available at the time.

Reaction

The chemical industry reacted strongly and considered her argument one-sided. The industry and its sympathizers questioned her research and her reputation as a scientist, labeled her argument overly emotional and alarmist, and suggested that she did not consider the benefits of pesticides to society. One reviewer suggested that Carson wished to "rever[t] to a passive social state devoid of technology, scientific medicine, agriculture, sanitation, and education" (Darby 1962). Dr. Robert White-Stevens, industry spokesperson at the time, considered Carson not "a scientist but rather . . . a fanatic defender of the cult of the balance of nature" (White-Stevens 1972). The Monsanto Corporation published a story titled "The Desolate Year," wherein the entire landscape depicted in the story was decimated by an unchecked insect population due to the banning of chemical pesticides.

Still, the public and political impact of the book was swift. Many began to debate not whether chemical pesticides were harmful, but how harmful they actually were. In her book, Carson brought to the public's awareness that humans can do lasting and significant damage to the environment, particularly with the manufacture of substances previously unknown. In 1962 President John F. Kennedy instructed the President's Science Advisory Committee to investigate Carson's claims. In 1963, the committee released its report, largely validating Carson's claims, yet still making the case that chemical pesticides have a role in regulating pest populations. The committee's recommendations included research on the selective use of chemical pesticides and nonchemical control methods as well as the revision of "existing Federal advisory and coordinating mechanisms" to research, approve, and regulate chemical substances. "Elimination of the use of persistent toxic pesticides should be goal," was the overarching statement of the study (The President's Scientific Advisory Committee 1963).

Following this report, a cascade of significant legislative events occurred, most of them addressing the specter of environmental damage and decline. In 1963, the first congressional subcommittee on the environment, the Senate Subcommittee on Air and Water Pollution, was created. Shortly thereafter, Congress passed the Clean Air Act, a landmark piece of legislation that would continue to be refined up into the 1970s. In 1964 the Wilderness Act was signed into law, protecting about 9 million acres of federal land from development. Following those legislative accomplishments, Congress continued to focus on environmental protection, passing several acts in 1965 including the Water Quality Act, the Noise Control Act, and the Solid Waste Disposal Act. Perhaps most significant was the creation of the Environmental Protection Agency (EPA) in 1970, an overarching agency tasked "to consolidate in one agency a variety of federal research, monitoring, standard-setting and enforcement activities to ensure environmental protection" (US EPA n.d.).

Legacy

To this day, many credit *Silent Spring* with starting the modern environmental movement, and the book remains a source of controversy for its emotional and urgent tone, research cited, and its effects on society and commerce. Al Gore, the former vice president of the United States wrote, "*Silent Spring* came as a cry in the wilderness, a deeply felt, thoroughly researched, and brilliantly written argument that changed the course of history. Without this book, the environmental movement might have been long delayed or never have developed at all" (Gore 2002). The biologist E. O. Wilson, writing forty years after its publication, remarked, "*Silent Spring* delivered a gigantic jolt to public consciousness, and, as a result, infused the environmental movement with new substance and meaning" (Wilson 2002, 357).

Others find fault with the book's impact and legacy, citing the burden of regulation and the creation of hysteria among the public with regard to the environmental effects of chemicals and industrial activity. On the anniversary of Carson's one-hundredth birthday, one commentator wrote, "She practically invented the environmental alarmist strategy that has been so successful in pushing a radical environmental agenda" (Murray 2007) In 2005 a conservative magazine published a list entitled the "10 Most Harmful Books of the 19th and 20th Centuries," where *Silent Spring* won an honorable mention. (The winner was Karl Marx and Freidrich Engels's *The Communist Manifesto*; other honorable mentions included Charles Darwin's *The Origin of Species* and John Stuart Mill's *On Liberty*.) The author of an editorial in the magazine *Analytical Chemistry* wrote, "I believe that too many environmentalists are sadly lacking in respect and regard for human life and the economic benefits that come with the chemical control of insects" (Murray 2002).

Many critics of Carson point to DDT's effectiveness in fighting malaria, a mosquito-borne illness, and the

effects on human health from the spread of the disease due to increasing bans in the use of DDT. According to the United Nations, DDT is still produced in some parts of the world, including China, India, and North Korea, and is used in high-risk areas of Africa even though it was prohibited from use in the United States in 1972. Despite the controversy surrounding the message of the book and the methods of Carson's research, significant changes in the way chemical pesticides were regulated and applied occurred.

In the wake of *Silent Spring* and the awareness it generated, many countries placed multiple restrictions on the production and application of chemical pesticides. In an effort to organize these restrictions on an international level for the health of the entire planet, the United Nations proposed the Rotterdam Convention in 1998 and the Stockholm Convention in 2001. Both of these conventions work to account for the increasing number of chemicals or persistent organic pollutants (POPs) in the world, but they seek different outcomes. The Rotterdam Convention focuses mainly on sharing information between countries, including which substances are banned and which substances are emerging as environmental or human health concerns, as well as accurate and standard labeling and data sheet creation. The Stockholm Convention seeks to classify existing and new substances as POPs, and requires participating nations, "to take action, control their production and use and reduce or eliminate their release into the environment." The goal of the Stockholm Convention parallels the conclusion of *Silent Spring*, arguing that persistent harmful chemicals should be tested, monitored, and used judiciously, and that some should not be used at all. Most of the chemicals highlighted in *Silent Spring* are classified as POPs by the Stockholm Convention, in addition to many other agricultural and industrial chemicals. Still, the production and use of new chemicals continues to increase due to obsolete regulations, some over thirty years old, as well as the over sixty-two thousand chemicals that were exempted in the Toxic Control Substances Act of 1976 in the United States. In 2010 there were over eighty thousand chemicals on the US market used in a variety of foods and consumer goods; regulators have no information about most of these (Layton 2010).

Another offshoot of the attention *Silent Spring* garnered is use of natural methods to control pests, what Carson called "biological methods" in the final chapter of the book, "The Other Road." Biological methods as Carson describes them are "based on understanding of the living organisms they seek to control, and to the whole fabric of life to which these organisms belong" (Carson 2002, 278). This biological method developed into the practice of integrated pest management (IPM). IPM, which gained widespread acceptance in the late twentieth century, involves the "coordinated use of pest and environmental information with available pest control methods to prevent unacceptable levels of pest damage by the most economical means and with the least possible hazard to people, property, and the environment" (US EPA 2009b)

This coordinated use of information falls into four basic principles of IPM:

- Thresholds: The organism in question must first be identified as a pest and thresholds (economic, agricultural, or health related) must be established to determine at what point the organism will cause damage.
- Monitoring: The organism must be acting in a manner that would cross the established threshold. The presence of a single organism does not necessarily require intervention.
- Prevention: If an organism is deemed harmful, a preventative approach of crop rotation, replanting, or different cultivation methods can be attempted.
- Control: If preventative methods are unsuccessful, using one or more control methods may be attempted. These include biological controls with predators or parasites of the pest organism; trapping the pest; intercropping, or growing crops adjacent to one another; and cultural controls, which involve changes in planting, mulching, and harvesting, and disposing of wastes differently. The targeted application of pesticides is considered a last resort.

The principles of IPM bring to fruition Rachel Carson's message that in order for crops to flourish while maintaining the health of people and the natural world, an integrated approach to managing pests must be used, including the "sparing, selective and intelligent use of chemicals" (US EPA 2009a).

The early years of the twenty-first century still bear the legacy of *Silent Spring*. The growing awareness of chemicals in food, consumer goods, and the environment has encouraged people to ask more questions about their use and harmful effects. This awareness fuels the burgeoning organic food industry, where no chemicals are used in the production of food. The move toward producer responsibility, where the producers are held accountable for the contents of their goods and are required to support recycling efforts for their products, is another outcome. International organizations continue to strengthen regulatory environments, clean up abandoned toxic sites, regulate the production and use of new and existing chemicals, and promote alternatives to the use of chemical pesticides.

Michael D. SIMS
Independent scholar, Eugene, Oregon

See also in the *Berkshire Encyclopedia of Sustainability* Biotechnology Legislation; Chemicals Legislation and Policy; Convention on Persistent Organic

Pollutants; Endangered Species Act; Grassroots Environmental Movements; National Environmental Policy Act; Registration, Evaluation, Authorisation, and Restriction of Chemicals; Restriction of Hazardous Substances Directive

FURTHER READINGS

Carson, Rachel. (2002). *Silent spring.* New York: Mariner Books. (Original work published 1962)

Darby, William J. (1962, October 1). Silence, Miss Carson. *Chemical & Engineering News*, 62–63. Retrieved August 2, 2010, from http://www1.umn.edu/ships/pesticides/library/darby1962.htm

Gore, Albert. (2002). *Silent Spring*: An introduction by Al Gore. Retrieved August 27, 2010, from http://www.uneco.org/ssalgoreintro.html

Graham, Frank. (1970). *Since* Silent Spring. New York: Houghton Mifflin.

Layton, Lyndsey. (2010, August 2). US regulators lack health data on health risks of most chemicals. *The Washington Post.* Retrieved August 2, 2010, from http://www.washingtonpost.com/wp-dyn/content/article/2010/08/01/AR2010080103469.html

Lee, John M. (1962, July 22). *Silent Spring* is now noisy summer. *The New York Times.* Retrieved July 25, 2010, from http://www.mindfully.org/Pesticide/Rachel-Carson-Silent-Spring.htm

Leonard, Jonathon Norton. (1964, April 15). Rachel Carson dies of cancer; *Silent Spring* author was 56. *The New York Times.* Retrieved July 25, 2010, from http://www.nytimes.com/books/97/10/05/reviews/carson-obit.html

Marco, Gino; Hollingworth, Robert; & Durham, William (Eds.). (1987). Silent Spring *revisited.* Washington, DC: American Chemical Society.

Monsanto Corporation. (1962, October). The Desolate Year. *Monsanto Magazine*, 4–9.

Murray, Iain. (2007). Silent alarmism: A centennial we could do without. *National Review Online.* Retrieved August 17, 2010, from http://www.nationalreview.com/articles/221126/i-silent-i-alarmism/iain-murray

Murray, Royce. (2002). Forty years after *Silent Spring. Analytical Chemistry*, 74(19), 501A.

The President's Science Advisory Committee. (1963). *The use of pesticides.* Washington, DC: The White House.

Rotterdam Convention: Share responsibility. (n.d.). Overview. Retrieved July 20, 2010, from http://www.pic.int/home.php?type=t&id=5&sid=16

Stockholm Convention on Persistent Organic Pollutants (POPs). (2008). About the convention. Retrieved July 20, 2010, from http://chm.pops.int/Convention/tabid/54/language/en-US/Default.aspx#convtext

Stockholm Convention on Persistent Organic Pollutants. (2008). *Global status of DDT and its alternatives for use in vector control to prevent disease.* Geneva: UNEP Stockholm Convention.

The ten most harmful books of the 19th and 20th centuries. (2005). *Human Events.* Retrieved November 9, 2010, from http://www.humanevents.com/article.php?id=7591

US Environmental Protection Agency (EPA). (n.d.). History webpage. Retrieved November 14, 2010, from http://www.epa.gov/history/

US Environmental Protection Agency (EPA). (2009a). Integrated pest management (IPM) principles. Retrieved July 20, 2010, from http://www.epa.gov/pesticides/factsheets/ipm.htm

US Environmental Protection Agency (EPA). (2009b). Pesticides and food: What "integrated pest management" means. Retrieved November 16, 2010, from http://www.epa.gov/pesticides/food/ipm.htm

van Emden, Helmut, & Peakall, David. (1996). *Beyond* Silent Spring: *Integrated pest management and chemical safety.* London: Chapman & Hall.

White-Stevens, Robert. (1972). A perspective on pesticides. Retrieved August 21, 2010, from http://turf.lib.msu.edu/1970s/1972/720717.pdf

Wilson, Edward. (2002). Afterword. In Rachel Carson, *Silent Spring* (pp. 357–363). New York: Mariner Books.

Tort Law

Torts are civil wrongs that occur when one person harms another in a way that the law prohibits. The first environmental laws were torts, and torts remain an important legal vehicle for redressing environmental harms. Tort law continues to evolve to address environmental challenges, particularly those that involve multiple countries.

The term *tort* is derived from the Latin word *tortus*, meaning "a wrong." A tort is a civil wrong—a harm done by a private party to a private party—and is typically distinguished from crimes and from breach of contract. Someone who is harmed by a private party may bring a suit (i.e., act as a plaintiff) in tort to collect damages from the *tortfeasor* (i.e., the defendant).

To successfully sue in tort, the plaintiff must establish all of the elements of the tort in a court of law. Typically, this means that the plaintiff must show that he/she was injured by the defendant's actions in a way that violates some "duty of care" that the defendant owed the plaintiff.

Development of Tort Law

The concept of the tort was developed in English common law—that is, law developed by judges rather than legislatures—by the fourteenth century. Subsequent centuries saw the development of various types of tort, each of which was designed to deal with a particular kind of wrongful activity. Today, many policy analysts think of torts as providing an antiquated approach to environmental problems, an approach that has been largely replaced by administrative regulation. Nevertheless, the area of environmental torts—and particularly of toxic torts, which occur when people are harmed by chemical exposure—remains lively, and tort law remains a viable vehicle for (and against) the promotion of sustainability.

Important Types of Environmental Torts

This article addresses five types of torts that have emerging or established uses in environmental contexts: nuisance, trespass, negligence, products liability, and strict liability torts.

Nuisance

Some of the earliest environmental laws had a form very similar to modern nuisance law, where a cause of action is given to parties who are substantially affected by another party's unreasonable land use. Early uses of this tort, which date back to the Middle Ages in Europe, often concerned the disposal of waste. Modern uses of nuisance law often operate around complex structures of land-use planning, which may include zoning restrictions or other environmental regulations that overrule potential nuisance claims.

Nuisance law can be divided into two main branches: private nuisance and public nuisance. Private nuisance actions are brought by private parties, typically property owners whose enjoyment of their property has been substantially and unreasonably infringed upon. Examples of private nuisance include a factory polluting the river that runs through your property, causing fish to die; or a neighbor keeping animals that create noxious smells. An action for public nuisance, in contrast, is typically brought by public officials in response to activities that substantially and unreasonably infringe upon the rights of the public. Noise and light pollution are often held to be public nuisances. More recently, several courts of appeals in the United States have ruled that fossil fuel–based power companies may be sued in nuisance for injuries from global warming.

Trespass

Trespass exists at the intersection of tort law and property law, and is generally defined as the intentional interference with the property interest of a property owner. Like nuisance, trespass has deeply historical roots. Early English law distinguished between three types of trespass: trespass to person, trespass to chattels, and trespass to land. Throughout the first few centuries of its use, trespass law was primarily used as a vehicle for civil liability for physical interferences, including assaulting a person, destroying personal property, and walking across someone's land without permission. Because trespass was seen as fundamentally affecting property owners' "right to exclude" others from their property, common law courts were traditionally quite aggressive, often awarding at least nominal damages even for trifling trespasses. More recently, trespass law has enjoyed something of a renaissance in environmental law, as courts grapple with the possibility of subsurface and chemical trespass, including trespass at the molecular level. This area of the law continues to evolve; for now, different jurisdictions have handled these issues differently, some imposing liability for the trespass of pollutants only when the plaintiff demonstrates actual and foreseeable injury, others requiring that the emitter of the pollutant know with certainty that the pollutant will migrate to neighboring property.

Negligence

The tort of negligence arises where a tortfeasor fails to satisfy a standard of reasonable care while performing acts that foreseeably harm other people. This tort is often established by showing that there was an "untaken precaution" that the defendant could reasonably have taken to prevent the harm. A factory that polluted the local groundwater might well be sued under a negligence theory. To recover damages, the plaintiff in such a case would have to show that (1) the factory had a duty to the public not to pollute the groundwater; (2) the factory failed to take reasonable care to prevent the pollution from occurring, most likely by failing to take a reasonable precaution; (3) the plaintiff experienced actual harm; and (4) the harm was caused by the pollution. Such a case would be an example of a "toxic tort." Successful toxic tort suits have been brought as a result of many kinds of toxic exposures, including lead paint, asbestos, and pesticides, as well as polluted air and water.

Products Liability

Product liability torts arise when someone manufactures and/or distributes a product that causes harm to a person or property. In the European Union, products liability law is governed by the Products Liability Directive, which requires businesses to pay for any damage caused by defective products. In most common-law jurisdictions, the harm need not be foreseeable, and the tortfeasor's intent is irrelevant. After Hurricane Katrina, for example, thousands of people displaced by the hurricane sued the manufacturers of their emergency trailers on the grounds that their health was damaged by dangerously high levels of formaldehyde in the trailers.

Strict Liability Torts

In some tort regimes, tortfeasors are held strictly liable for hazardous activities, meaning that they must pay damages for any loss caused by their acts or omissions, even if those harms were neither foreseeable nor intended, and even if the tortfeasor took reasonable precautions against the loss taking place.

A common application of strict liability in environmental contexts is in the release of toxic chemicals. One such

strict liability tort regime is the United States' Comprehensive Environmental Response, Compensation, and Liability Act (CERCLA or Superfund). CERCLA, which was designed to address environmental damage from hazardous waste disposal sites, is based on a statute rather than common law. The elements of a CERCLA claim differ from most common law claims, in that property owners can be liable for cleanup costs even if they purchased the property after the hazardous waste was disposed on it, and even if no harm has resulted from the waste disposal.

Defenses

In most jurisdictions, defendants seeking to defend themselves against tort suits have three principal options. Two of these—that the plaintiff consented to the tortious activities or that the plaintiff was acting illegally at the time of the tort—come up rarely in environmental contexts. The third defense, contributory negligence, is more common. Under this defense, the defendant seeks to show that the plaintiff was also partially to blame for whatever harm occurred. For example, a defendant might argue that although his factory polluted local groundwater, the local people continued to use the groundwater long after they knew of the pollution. This defense is sometimes partial, meaning it requires a contribution from the plaintiff for the portion of the damage for which he was responsible. At other times, it is a full defense, in which case showing that the plaintiff was even 1 percent responsible for the harm means that he cannot recover any damages whatsoever.

Remedies

Historically the main remedy in tort was monetary damages in the amount that was required to make the plaintiff "whole," as if the tort had never occurred. Modern courts frequently provide injunctions, commanding the defendant to stop the objectionable activity, instead of or as well as monetary damages. In particularly egregious cases, courts sometimes also award punitive damages in addition to compensatory damages.

International Variation in Tort Law

As a general matter, countries with legal systems based on English common law—including England, Scotland, Ireland, the United States, Australia, New Zealand, and Canada—share similar approaches to tort law. That said, there can be significant variation even across different portions of a single country (e.g., the United States, where tort law is almost exclusively the province of the individual states),

and the technical requirements of each tort vary widely by jurisdiction.

In the European Union, tort law in member states remains significantly heterogeneous. Typical of the general legal approaches of continental European countries, however, tort law also tends to be more formally codified than in the common law countries. The trend in Europe seems to be toward increasing uniformity: the European Court of Justice (ECJ) has made recent steps to promote harmonization across member states.

In 2010, China enacted a set of tort laws that allow its citizens to sue, among other things, in products liability and for environmental harm. These laws include punitive damage provisions for harms that were caused intentionally, and may eventually provide significant incentives for sustainable development.

There has been some effort to create more global environmental tort laws, but these efforts have been widely viewed as failures, due to difficulties in international enforcement of remedies.

Tort Law as a Vehicle for Sustainability

Tort law is an "ex-post" liability regime, in that it only takes effect after the harm occurs. It is often compared to "ex-ante" regulatory regimes, which seek to regulate behavior proactively, before the harm occurs. Tort law can therefore be understood as one end of a continuum of enforcement, focusing on responding to negative events and promoting compensation rather than preventative regulation.

This structure creates both strengths and weaknesses for tort law as a tool for sustainability. Tort law's primary strengths include the facts that it is relatively quick and cheap for a plaintiff to bring suit (rather than seek anticipatory regulation); parties who are harmed can actually be compensated; and it has the potential to deter future bad actors. It can be expected to perform particularly well where individual parties are likely to have informational advantages over regulators, as may be the case, for example, in determining the environmental impacts of an activity on a particular parcel of land.

Tort law faces many challenges in the context of sustainability as well. Chief among these are the mechanisms within tort law for establishing causation, which can be particularly problematic when complex scientific evidence must be interpreted by judges and juries; the fact that tort liability only takes effect after the harm is caused; and the fact that the impact of potential liability is limited by the chance that defendants may be insolvent, or where they can escape on other legal grounds (as where a statute of limitations has expired). In that sense, tort law is poorly matched to environmental contexts that have long latency periods (where evidence may age and statutes of limitations expire), involve complex causal chains, or have potentially catastrophic outcomes that might exceed the capacity of a defendant to pay damages.

In sum, tort law remains a viable vehicle for redressing many environmental harms once they have occurred. New applications of tort law continue to develop as more is learned about the nature of environmental harm and as countries continue to struggle with the difficulties of addressing environmental issues that span man-made borders.

Arden ROWELL

University of Illinois College of Law

See also in the *Berkshire Encyclopedia of Sustainability* Dark Sky Initiatives; Enforcement; Environmental Law (several articles: China; Europe; United States and Canada); Nuisance Law; Real Property Law

FURTHER READINGS

Boomer v. Atlantic Cement Co., 26 N.Y. 2d 219 (1970).

Brennan, Troyen. (1993). Environmental torts. *Vanderbilt Law Review*, *46*(1), 1–74.

Epstein, Richard. (1999). *Torts*. New York: Aspen.

Farber, Daniel A. (1999). *Eco-pragmatism: Making sensible environmental decisions in an uncertain world*. Chicago: University of Chicago Press.

Madden, M. Stuart. (Ed.). (2005). *Exploring tort law*. New York: Cambridge University Press.

Menell, Peter S. (1991). The limitations of legal institutions for addressing environmental risks. *Journal of Economic Perspectives*, *5*(3), 93–113.

Miller, Jeffrey A. (1989). *Private enforcement of hazardous waste laws and its effect on tort law and practice*. C427 ALI-ABA 929.

Sachs, Noah. (2008). Beyond the liability wall: Strengthening tort remedies in international environmental law. *UCLA Law Review*, *55*, 837–907.

Shavell, Steven. (1984). Liability for harm versus regulation of safety. *Journal of Legal Studies*, *13*(2), 357-374.

Symposium: Common Law Environmental Protection. (2008, Spring). *Case Western Law Review*, *58*(3)..

Van Gerven, Walter. (2004). Harmonization of private law: Do we need it? *Common Market Law Review*, *41*, 505–532.

Waldmeier, Patti. (2010, June 30). China tort law set to trigger surge in claims. *Financial Times: Asia-Pacific*. Subscription information retrieved November 10, 2010, from http://www.ft.com

Transboundary Water Law

Freshwater resources cross national boundaries around the globe, leaving sovereign states to compete for their use. The legal rules that govern the management of transboundary waters contribute to the fundamental tenets of law—peace, security, and human rights. International laws concerning transboundary waters also aid in the peaceful management of the world's water resources.

Approximately 300 major watercourses and some 270 groundwater basins stretch across the political boundaries of two or more nation states, with about nineteen of these shared by five or more riparian (adjacent) sovereign states. Close to 70 percent of the world's population depends upon water resources that cross international borders, which account for approximately 60 percent of the global water supply. A recent study by the National Center for Atmospheric Research evaluating the current flows of 923 rivers around the world concludes that several large transboundary watercourses, including the Columbia River (Canada, United States), the Ganges (Bangladesh, Nepal, India), and the Colorado River (Mexico, United States), are already experiencing diminished flows that will threaten future water and food security (Dai, Qian, Trenberth, and Milliman 2009). International law provides a framework for sustainably managing freshwaters that traverse sovereign nations. In the context of water and the environment, sustainable development instructs people and societies to relate to and utilize the natural environment, especially freshwater resources, in ways that do not compromise the potential benefits for future generations (UNEP 2010). The rules of international law governing transboundary waters, including customary international law and treaty law, have evolved over time. The 1997 UN Convention on the Law of the Non-Navigational Uses of International Watercourses (UN Watercourses Convention [UNWC]),

is the most authoritative text regarding the law governing transboundary waters. International water law serves to facilitate regional cooperation, guide international negotiations, and prevent conflict between riparian countries, thus helping to achieve a water-secure world.

International Water Law

Rules of international water law determine the rights and duties of international transboundary watercourse states related to the development and management of their shared freshwater resources. These rules govern situations where transboundary watercourse states disagree over their respective uses of shared water resources or pollute the resource in ways that adversely affect their riparian neighbors. The term *watercourse* was adopted by the UN International Law Commission (ILC) to mean "a system of surface and groundwaters constituting by virtue of their physical relationship a unitary whole and normally flowing into a common terminus." This definition, adopted in the final text of the UNWC, does not cover shared aquifers. This matter is currently under study by the ILC, which has produced a set of draft articles on the Law of Transboundary Aquifers, considered by the UN General Assembly at its sixty-third session in 2008.

Evolution of International Water Law

International watercourse law is an integral part of public international law, and as such it is infused with those ideals contained in the UN Charter: maintaining international peace and security, enhancing regional cooperation, preventing threats to peace, and advancing the fundamental freedoms of all (Wouters and Hendry 2009). International water law has evolved on the basis of state practice, national and international judicial decisions, and the codification and progressive development efforts undertaken by the United Nations, nongovernmental organizations, and private institutions. Interest in this area of law grew in parallel with the Industrial Revolution, which resulted in increased demands on shared water resources for economic development. The rules of international law are now an identifiable corpus of substantive and procedural norms; from a legal perspective, transboundary watercourse regimes can best be understood using five elements for analysis: (1) scope (what water resources / parties are covered?), (2) substantive rules (what rules determine the lawfulness of use?), (3) procedural rules (what process is to be followed for new or changed uses?), (4) institutional mechanisms (what organ / governance structure is in place to implement the agreement?), and (5) dispute settlement (what procedures apply where disputes arise?) (Wouters, Vinogradov, Allan, Jones, and Rieu-Clarke 2005). This analytical framework is a powerful tool for the overall assessment of transboundary watercourse regimes, identifying the important legal issues to be addressed in any particular case.

Customary Law (State Practice)

States, as sovereign entities, invoke three theories in support of their right to use the waters of an international watercourse crossing their territory. These theories include absolute territorial sovereignty, meaning that a state can use the water within its territory without regard to other watercourse states; absolute territorial integrity, entitling a state to the undiminished and unaltered natural flows into its territory; and limited territorial sovereignty, when a state's entitlement to use the waters of an international watercourse is limited by the same rights and obligations of co-riparian states. Most states that have entered into agreements relating to international watercourses have embraced limited territorial sovereignty as the basis for their cooperation (Wouters 1997). From this theory, the principle of equitable utilization has emerged as the governing rule for transboundary water law, directing that each watercourse state is entitled and obliged to utilize an international watercourse in an equitable and reasonable way.

Codification of International Water Law

Over 3,500 treaties have been concluded on transboundary water bodies since 800 CE, with many of these initially concerning navigational uses. One of the first efforts to codify the rules of international law governing transboundary waters for purposes other than navigation was made by the Institut de Droit international (IDI) in its Declaration of Madrid (1911). Separately, the International Law Association (ILA) developed and adopted the Helsinki Rules

on the Uses of the Waters of International Rivers (1966), the first systematic and comprehensive document to codify the relevant rules in this area. Member states of the United Nations called for more study on the topic, primarily as a result of a series of regional disputes related to the development of transboundary watercourses, debated in the UN General Assembly. This led to the request in 1971 by the General Assembly to the UN International Law Commission to undertake a study on the law of the nonnavigational uses of international watercourses, with a view to its progressive development and codification. A consolidated draft document containing some thirty-seven provisions was produced by the ILC after almost three decades of study and debate. This formed the foundation for the only framework treaty on the topic, the UN Convention on the Law of the Non-Navigational Uses of International Watercourses (UNWC), which was adopted by UN resolution on 23 May 1997. The convention was supported in the General Assembly by 104 states and requires the ratification of 35 states for it to enter into force. As of October 2010, 20 states have ratified the UNWC (Finland, Germany, Guinea-Bissau, Hungary, Iraq, Jordan, Lebanon, Libya, Namibia, Netherlands, Norway, Nigeria, Portugal, Qatar, South Africa, Spain, Sweden, Syria, Tunisia, and Uzbekistan) and an additional five are signatories (Cote d'Ivore, Luxembourg, Paraguay, Venezuela, and Yemen). Thus, at present, the UNWC requires 15 more states to ratify, before it enters into force (i.e., has full legal force for the states party to the UNWC). The UNWC is now the subject of an international campaign launched by the World Wildlife Fund, which is promoting it as a global instrument that would enhance the cooperative and peaceful development of the world's international watercourses, with support especially for the weakest watercourse states. As a result, several states have moved forward with their efforts, including most recently Nigeria.

Why haven't all states signed up for the UNWC? There are a range of reasons, none of which challenge substantively the integrity of the convention. While some states raised issues during the initial negotiation of the convention, such as the relationship between the convention and existing watercourse agreements, whether the principle of equitable and reasonable utilization should take precedence over the rule of no significant harm, and if certain dispute settlement mechanisms should be compulsory—none of these concerns are paramount today. In fact, the real obstacle appears to be more about "treaty congestion" (i.e., too many global treaties for national governments to consider and process) and a widespread lack of local capacity, especially in developing countries. A study reveals a basic misunderstanding of the current status and potential positive contribution of the UNWC (Rieu-Clarke and Loures 2009). From a legal point of view, there are compelling reasons for the entry into force of the UNWC as a global instrument that would promote the peaceful management of the world's shared freshwater, in line with the law of nations.

The UNWC defines the basic international norms governing international watercourses (Wouters 1999). The main objective of the convention is to "ensure the utilization, development, conservation, management and protection of international watercourses and the promotion of the optimal and sustainable utilization thereof for present and future generations . . . taking into account the special situation and needs of developing countries" (UNWC 1997, Preamble).

The primary role of international water law is to determine a state's "entitlement" to the use of an international watercourse (substantive rules) and to establish certain requirements for states' behavior while developing the resource (procedural rules) (Wouters, Vinogradov, Allan, Jones, and Rieu-Clarke 2005). The most important substantive rule, the principle of reasonable and equitable use, is codified in Article 5 of the UNWC. Article 6 of the convention provides an indicative list of relevant factors to be considered and sets forth the methodology for determining an equitable and reasonable use—all relevant factors are to be considered together, and a "conclusion reached on the basis of the whole."

The second fundamental substantive rule of the convention is the principle of no significant harm. Article 7 adopts a due-diligence approach and requires states to "take all appropriate measures to prevent the causing of significant harm to other watercourse states." The origins of the no-harm rule have been traced to the Roman law maxim *sic utere tuo ut alienum laedas* (so use your own property as not to injure your neighbor). Three prominent cases are cited in support of the no-significant-harm rule, including the Trail Smelter arbitration, the Corfu Channel case, and the Lac Lanoux arbitration. The no-significant-harm rule must be read within the context of the overarching rule of equitable and reasonable utilization, which permits some measure of harm, provided that the use is considered to be equitable and reasonable.

As a bridge to the substantive rules, Article 8 of the UNWC introduces the general obligation to cooperate (on the basis of sovereign equality, territorial integrity, mutual benefit, and good faith) in order to attain optimal utilization and adequate protection of an international watercourse.

Article 9 provides for the regular exchange of data and information, which is supported further by the package of procedural rules contained in Part III ("Planned Measures") of the UNWC. Part III sets forth a framework of actions to be followed in the event of proposed new uses, including specific provisions requiring prior notification and exchange of data as well as information, consultations, and negotiations. This collection of procedural rules is one of the most important contributions of the UNWC, providing clear directions to watercourse states where planned measures are proposed, paving the way for transparent exchanges, and enhancing the opportunity for cooperative engagement and decision making. The procedural rules are supplemented by the dispute settlement mechanisms in Article 33 of the convention, which contains a menu of options available to states for the resolution of any differences that might arise. The provision introduces several innovations, including fact finding, and approaches conciliation in its application.

A recent case that explores substantive and procedural rules of international water law is the judgment concerning Pulp Mills on the River Uruguay (*Argentina v. Uruguay* 2010). In that case, the International Court of Justice (ICJ) held that Uruguay had breached its procedural obligations to cooperate with Argentina during the development of plans for the pulp mills. Notably, the court decided that Uruguay, in authorizing the construction and commissioning of the Orion Mill, had not breached its substantive obligations related to environmental protections as set forth in the Statute of the River Uruguay.

The relevance of the UNWC was recognized by the ICJ in the Gabčíkovo–Nagymaros case involving Hungary and Czechoslovakia, where the court referred to it as the most authoritative statement of the fundamental principles of international water law. Broad support for the UNWC can be seen in extensive state practice, with numerous treaties from around the world following its provisions, often to the letter, in basin-specific agreements. The case of the Mekong River basin is one such example. A survey of international state practice reveals that there is universal endorsement of the importance of cooperative management of the world's transboundary waters. Such cooperation was acknowledged as necessary to promote the sustainable

management of water at the basin level by the UN Secretary-General Advisory Panel on Water and Sanitation in 2009. The United Nations supports the continued endorsement of the UNWC as an important element as part of its forward-looking strategy for the peaceful management of the world's transboundary water resources.

The Mekong River

The Mekong River is the twelfth longest river in the world (4,173 km), and ranks tenth in terms of total volume. The basin covers 795,000 square kilometers and encompasses six countries, serving a burgeoning population in one of the most poverty-stricken regions of the world (Radosevich and Olson 1999.) The Mekong begins on the Tibetan plateau and runs from China through Myanmar, Laos, Thailand, Cambodia, and Vietnam. In April 1995, the four national governments of the lower Mekong River basin—Cambodia, Laos, Thailand, and Vietnam—signed the Agreement on the Cooperation for the Sustainable Development of the Mekong River Basin. The agreement established the Mekong River Commission (MRC) as the main institutional mechanism and created a set of substantive and procedural rules for the reasonable and equitable use of the basin's water resources. Principles of international water law, including the UNWC draft provisions, provided the backbone for both the negotiation process and the final text of the Mekong Agreement. The substantive rules included the principle of reasonable and equitable utilization where "parties undertook to utilize the waters of the Mekong river system in a *reasonable and equitable manner* . . . pursuant to all relevant factors and circumstances" (Article 5, Mekong Agreement). The procedural rules and mechanisms include provisions related to data and information exchange and sharing, and preliminary procedures for notification, prior consultation, and agreement. The Mekong regime evolved over fifty years with assistance from the United Nations and external donors, and it continues to develop. The Mekong Agreement is aligned with the key provisions of the UNWC and provides an operational platform for the development and ongoing management of the Mekong. Although the upstream states, China and Myanmar, for political and geographical reasons, have chosen not to be party to the agreement, they participate as observers to the MRC. Current challenges on the Mekong include the development of hydroelectric power (upstream), the protection of the fishery in the Great Lake (Tonle Sap), and saltwater intrusion in Vietnam.

The Nile

International river basins cover more than 60 percent of the African continent (UNEP 2010). The Nile, the longest river in the world, is shared by ten riparian states and drains close to 10 percent of all of Africa. The river basin exceeds 3 million square kilometers, and its waters are vital for the livelihood of over 180 million people (Hilhorst, Schütte, and Thuo 2008). In 1999, the Nile River Basin Initiative (NBI) was established as a transitional arrangement between all Nile riparians (with the exception of Eritea) to facilitate cooperation over the waters. Despite considerable time and resources invested in the process, a basin-wide agreement on the cooperative development and management of the Nile water resources has been difficult to achieve. In 1996, in parallel to the transitional arrangement of the NBI, a Panel of Experts was established to review international water law, assess the applicability of the substantive and procedural provisions of the UNWC to the Nile river basin and draft the Nile River Basin Framework Agreement (CFA). The CFA would also formalize the transformation of the NBI into a permanent Nile River Basin Commission and facilitate its legal recognition in the member countries as well as regional and international organizations. In May 2010 Ethiopia, Rwanda, Tanzania, Kenya, and Uganda signed the CFA (Abseno 2009). The agreement requires six ratifications to enter into force, and as of September 2010, no state had ratified the CFA. Egypt and Sudan resist signing the CFA, arguing that the prior appropriation agreed in the 1959 bilateral agreement between them should be recognized. The Nile basin states are divided in their views on the validity of colonial-era agreements and existing water-use sharing arrangements. The CFA includes the fundamental principles of the UNWC, most notably the substantive principles of "reasonable and equitable utilization" and "no significant harm." Regardless of whether the CFA is signed by the Nile basin states, the governing rule of equitable and reasonable use should apply to the development and management of the shared freshwaters of the Nile, and the UNWC provides a helpful framework for the ongoing negotiations across the basin and throughout Africa.

Future Challenges

International water law is essential to achieving the sustainable management of transboundary watercourses and has an integral role to play in the current and future challenges in this field. Despite the emergence of a number of watercourse treaties and the existence of a clear body of customary rules, 60 percent of the world's transboundary waters are not covered by agreements. Many agreements that do exist are bilateral and do not include all riparian states (Loures, Rieu-Clarke, and Vercambre 2008). This bilateral approach runs contrary to the generally accepted notion that the entire watercourse should be the unit of management and results in piecemeal and sometimes inconsistent development along the stretch of the watercourse.

The current world order, complicated by increasingly complex water-related resource scarcity challenges, requires innovative responses. Within this context, the peaceful development and management of the world's shared freshwater resources offers a platform to address some of these challenges, consistent with ideals of maintaining international peace and security and promoting human rights. The UNWC, coupled with the United Nations' continued work on the issue of the management of transboundary waters (including the recently adopted Resolution on the Human Right to Water and Sanitation) contributes directly to these objectives. Achieving a "water-secure world" (GWP 2010) and delivering on the universally endorsed Millennium Development Goals concerning water, require a concerted, coherent, and comprehensive effort. International water law must be part of this endeavor. The challenge for the international community is to increase local capacity, both human and financial, to address the complex issues related to the development and management of the world's shared water resources.

Patricia WOUTERS and Ruby MOYNIHAN
University of Dundee

See also in the *Berkshire Encyclopedia of Sustainability* Clean Water Act; Convention to Combat Desertification; Enforcement; Gabčíkovo–Nagymaros Dam Case (*Hungary v. Slovakia*); International Court of Justice; International Law; Ocean Zoning; Real Property Law; Tort Law; Water Act (France); Water Security

FURTHER READINGS

Abseno, Musa. (2009). The concepts of equitable utilization, no significant harm and benefit sharing under the Nile River Basin Cooperative Framework Agreement: Some highlights on theory and practice. *Journal of Water Law, 20*(2/3), 86–95.

Dai, Aiguo; Qian, Taotao; Trenberth, Kevin E.; & Milliman, John D. (2009). Changes in continental freshwater discharge from 1948 to 2004. *Journal of Climate, 22*(10), 2773–2792.

Global Water Partnership (GWP). (2010). *Water security for development: Insights from African Partnerships in Action.* Stockholm: GWP.

Hilhorst, Bart; Schütte, Peter; & Thuo, Simon. (2008). *Supporting the Nile basin shared vision with "Food for Thought": Jointly discovering the contours of common ground.* Entebbe, Uganda: Global Water Partnership.

Loures, Flavia Rocha; Rieu-Clarke, Alistair; & Vercambre, Marie-Laure. (2008). *Everything you need to know about the UN Watercourses Convention.* Gland, Switzerland: WWF International.

Radosevich, George E., & Olson, Douglas C. (1999). *Existing and emerging basin arrangements in Asia.* Third Workshop on River Basin Institution Development (24 June 1999). Washington, DC: The World Bank.

Rieu-Clarke, Alistair. (2007, December). Entry into force of the 1997 UN Watercourses Convention: Barriers, benefits and prospects. *Water, 21*, 12–16.

Rieu-Clarke, Alistair, & Loures, Flavia Rocha. (2009). Still not in force: Should states support the 1997 UN Watercourses Convention? *Review of European Community & International Environmental Law, 18*(2), 185–197.

Tanzi, Atilla, & Arcari, Maurizio. (2001). *The United Nations Convention on the Law of International Watercourse.* London: Kluwer Law International.

United Nations. (1945). Charter of the United Nations. Retrieved September 21, 2010, from http://www.unhcr.org/refworld/docid/3ae6b3930.html

UN Environmental Programme (UNEP). (2010). *The greening of water law: Managing freshwater resources for people and the environment.* Nairobi, Kenya: UNEP.

UN Secretary-General's Advisory Board (UNSGAB) on Water and Sanitation. (2010). *Hashimoto Action Plan II: Strategy and objectives through 2012.* New York: UNSGAB.

University of Dundee and United Nations Educational, Scientific and Cultural Organization (UNESCO). (2010). IHP-HELP centre for water law, policy and science. Retrieved September 27, 2010, from http://www.dundee.ac.uk/water/

Wouters, Patricia. (1997). *International water law: Selected writings of Professor Charles B. Bourne.* London: Kluwer Law International.

Wouters, Patricia. (1999). The legal response to international water conflicts: The UN Watercourses Convention and beyond. *German Yearbook of International Law, 42*, 293–336.

Wouters, Patricia. (2003). Universal and regional approaches to resolving international water disputes: What lessons learned from state practice? In International Bureau of the Permanent Court of Arbitration (Ed.), *Resolution of international water disputes: Papers emanating from the Sixth PCA International Law Seminar* (pp. 111–154). The Hague, The Netherlands: Kluwer Law International.

Wouters, Patricia. (forthcoming 2011). *Rivers of the world: Water law, state practice and current issues.* London: International Waters Association.

Wouters, Patricia, & Hendry, Sarah. (2009). Promoting water (law) for all: Addressing the world's water problems—A focus on international and national water law and the challenges of an integrated approach. *Journal of Water Law, 20*(2–3), 45–52.

Wouters, Patricia; Vinogradov, Sergei; Allan, Andrew; Jones, Patricia; & Rieu-Clarke, Alistair. (2005). *Sharing transboundary waters: An integrated assessment of equitable entitlement—The legal assessment model.* Paris: United Nations Educational, Scientific and Cultural Organization.

Wouters, Patricia; Vinogradov, Sergei; & Magsig, Bjørn-Oliver. (2009). Water security, hydrosolidarity and international law: A river runs through it. *Yearbook of International Environmental Law, 19*, 97–134.

Wouters, Patricia, & Ziganshina, Dinara. (2011). Tackling the global water crisis: Unlocking international law as fundamental to the peaceful management of the world's shared transboundary waters—Introducing the H2O paradigm. In R. Quentin Grafton & Karen Hussey (Eds.), *Water resources planning and management* (pp. 175–229). Cambridge, UK: Cambridge University Press.

TREATIES / RESOLUTIONS / COURT CASES

Agreement on the Cooperation for the Sustainable Development of the Mekong River Basin (5 April 1995). Retrieved November 15, 2010, from http://www.mrcmekong.org/agreement_95/agreement_95.htm

Gabčíkovo–Nagymaros Project (*Hungary v. Slovakia*), Judgment, I.C.J. Reports 1997, p. 7.

Pulp Mills on the River Uruguay (*Argentina v. Uruguay*), Judgment, I.C.J. Reports 2010, General List no. 135.

UN Convention on the Law of Non-Navigational Uses of International Watercourse [UNWC], UN Doc. A/Res/51/869, 36 ILM 700 (21 May 1997).

United Nations—Overview of Conventions and Agreements

The United Nations has addressed sustainability through conventions, agreements, and protocols. Environmental issues such as climate change, air pollution, and biodiversity are global, regardless of the origin of the initial harm. As an international body, the United Nations provides a forum for multilateral agreements, helping countries work together toward sustainability. Together with its member states, the United Nations has the power to affect great change.

The United Nations (UN) is a major international organization and the key player with regard to multilateral environmental agreements (MEAs) addressing international environmental law. The UN will continue to have an important role in addressing the sustainable use of our planet, but its role is limited; member states must agree to the terms of the MEAs and their subsequent protocols.

History

In the 1970s, the need to protect and preserve the environment and its natural resources for both present and future generations began to gain global recognition. In 1972 the UN organized the United Nations Conference on the Human Environment in Stockholm, noting "the need for a common outlook and for common principles to inspire and guide the peoples of the world in the preservation and enhancement of the human environment" (UNEP 1972). Although the Stockholm Conference itself did not establish any legally binding obligations, it increased the impetus to adopt binding MEAs. Moreover, it led to the establishment of the United Nations Environment Programme (UNEP). UNEP's mission is "to provide leadership and encourage partnership in caring for the environment by inspiring, informing, and enabling nations and peoples to improve their quality of life without compromising that of future generations" (UNEP 2010). UNEP also promotes the progressive development and implementation of international environmental law through MEAs.

In 1992 the UN convened a global forum in Rio de Janeiro, Brazil. The United Nations Conference on Environment and Development (UNCED) focused on the integration of environmental considerations into the use of natural resources for development. The scope and accomplishments of UNCED were significant. The legally non-binding principles adopted, known as Agenda 21, served as a blueprint with regard to sustainable development and emphasized the need to develop and codify environmental law at the international level. This led to the adoption of the 1992 United Nations Framework Convention on Climate Change, the 1992 United Nations Convention on Biological Diversity, and the 1994 United Nations Convention to Combat Desertification.

In 2002 the UN World Summit on Sustainable Development (WSSD) in Johannesburg, South Africa, sought to reinvigorate the Rio process, placing special emphasis on the implementation of sustainable development in a globalized world. Unlike the Rio process, the 2002 WSSD did not lead to any binding MEAs, but rather provided political commitments to sustainable development—specifically, the 2002 Johannesburg Declaration on Sustainable Development.

The UN has addressed many environmental issues through the use of MEAs. The subjects of these agreements include the atmosphere, biodiversity, desertification, deforestation, the transport of waste, and the marine environment.

Protection of the Atmosphere

As is true with most other natural resources, the air around us makes life on Earth possible. Pollution, ozone depletion,

194

and climate change threaten the security of our planet. These problems must be addressed on an international level, as they are not confined to one country or region.

Long-Range Transboundary Air Pollution

The growing concern over the transboundary effects of air pollution resulted in the 1979 Convention on Long Range Transboundary Air Pollution (LRTAP). The LRTAP was adopted on 13 November 1979 within the forum of the United Nations Economic Commission for Europe (UNECE), a regional UN organization including eastern and western European countries, the United States, and Canada. The LRTAP addressed the issues of acidification and acid rain caused by the sulphur and nitrogen emissions, which might travel thousands of kilometers through the atmosphere (Wettstone and Rosencranz 1984, 89). The LRTAP serves as an institutional framework that, instead of offering precise rules, requires nonspecific international cooperation to eliminate and prevent the adverse effects of long-range transboundary air pollution. It is supported by the Cooperative Programme for the Monitoring and Evaluation of Long Range Transmission in Europe (EMEP). The general commitments of the LRTAP have been specified by eight subsequent protocols concerning the financing of EMEP and the reduction of sulphur and nitrogen oxides emissions, volatile organic compounds, heavy metals, persistent organic pollutants, and ammonia. This approach served as a precedent for subsequent treaties in other fields of environmental law, such as ozone depletion and climate change.

Ozone Depletion

Prompted by scientific evidence that emerged in the mid-1970s linking emissions of chlorofluorocarbons (CFC) and other chlorine-based substances with the depletion of the ozone layer (Molina and Rowland 1974; Stolarski and Cicerone 1974), international environmental efforts started to focus on threats to the global atmosphere. Therefore, in 1977 UNEP established the Coordinating Committee of the Ozone Layer to periodically assess ozone depletion.

International negotiations aimed at adopting a convention on the issue of ozone depletion started in 1981, which led to the adoption of the Vienna Convention for the Protection of the Ozone Layer in March 1985. The Vienna Convention established an institutional framework lacking any substantive commitments.

Firm targets to reduce the production and consumption of CFCs have been agreed upon by a subsequent protocol to the Vienna Convention, the 1987 Montreal Protocol on Substances that Deplete the Ozone Layer. These targets were based on the principle of common but differentiated responsibility, according to which the major

industrialized countries—the greatest contributors to ozone depletion—were obligated to eliminate the production and consumption of CFCs by no later than 2000, whereas the developing countries had a ten-year grace period, eliminating CFCs by 2010.

Climate Change

Another issue involving the protection of the world's atmosphere, which gained global recognition in the late 1980s, is the global warming caused by carbon dioxide emissions—the so-called greenhouse effect. In addressing this issue, the international community chose the same approach applied to the protection of the ozone layer, namely, to adopt a framework convention, specified by subsequent protocols. The first advance in the attempt to stop global warming was the adoption of the United Nations Framework Convention on Climate Change (UNFCCC) at the 1992 UNCED in Rio de Janeiro. In addition to the general commitment of the UNFCCC to stabilize the concentration of greenhouse gases at a level that would prevent dangerous interference with the climate system, some significant principles prompted by the principle of common but differentiated responsibility were negotiated. In this regard, the contracting parties agreed that the division of the financial burden would be based on the respective capabilities, and that developing countries would promote the transfer of environmentally sound technologies.

The move from the framework stage to a binding protocol was subject to highly controversial negotiations. At the third Conference of the Parties to the UNFCCC, the parties finally agreed to adopt the Kyoto Protocol, which required the major industrialized nations to reduce greenhouse gas emissions by at least 5 percent in the period from 2008 to 2012. Developing nations, however, rejected any new commitments.

There remains conflict between developed and developing countries concerning the implementation of binding protocols for the reduction of greenhouse gas emissions. Developed countries argue that developing countries should agree on binding emission targets. Developing countries argue that developed countries still have to bear the major burden with regard to the reduction of greenhouse gas emissions. This debate was one of the main reasons why the 2009 Conference of the Parties to the UNFCCC did not led to a new internationally binding convention. Thus, it will be left to future climate conferences to agree on binding emission targets for the years after 2012.

Biodiversity

Supporting biodiversity means protecting the various species of wildlife, both plant and animal, around the world.

Economic factors, from poaching to industrialization, cause the destruction of flora and fauna. Thus, specific MEAs have been created to protect global biodiversity while allowing for economic development.

Convention on International Trade in Endangered Species

The text of the Convention on International Trade in Endangered Species (CITES) was agreed upon in Washington, D.C., on 3 March 1973. It does not directly protect endangered species but seeks to control or prevent their international commercial trade. The international commercial trade of endangered species is regulated under CITES by means of an international permit system to control and monitor trade so that it does not lead to species extinction or decline. The permit system strictly forbids the import or export of species threatened with extinction and requires that import/export licenses must be secured for species suffering declines. Many environmentalists, however, have argued that CITES does not go far enough. CITES only pertains to certain species—those that have a market value. Further, it addresses international trade, but does not limit hunting or killing at the domestic level.

Convention on Biological Diversity

At the 1992 UNCED, agreement was reached on the conservation and sustainable use of the world's biodiversity through the adoption of the UN Convention on Biological Diversity (UNCBD). The UNCBD contains numerous progressive provisions on environmental law, such as the obligation to "regulate or manage biological resources important for the conservation of biological diversity whether within or outside protected areas, with a view to ensuring their conservation and sustainable use" (Article 8(c)); to "promote the protection of ecosystems, natural habitats and the maintenance of viable populations of species in natural surroundings" (Article 8(d)); and to "adopt measures relating to the use of biological resources to avoid or minimize adverse impacts on biological diversity" (Article 9(b)). These provisions are balanced against the sovereign right of each state to use its natural resources. Thus, countries may adopt only those protection standards that meet their economic needs and priorities.

In April 2002 the parties to the UNCBD committed to achieving a significant reduction of the current rate of biodiversity loss by 2010 as a contribution to poverty alleviation and to benefit all life on Earth. This target was subsequently endorsed by the 2002 World Summit on Sustainable Development in Johannesburg, South Africa, and the United Nations General Assembly, and was incorporated as a new target under the UN Millennium Development Goals.

Desertification and Deforestation

Land degradation is a result of human exploitation of the land. Both desertification and deforestation have harmful effects, not only on the land, but on humankind as well. These types of land degradation contribute to global problems such as poverty, hunger, and climate change.

United Nations Convention to Combat Desertification

Deforestation is one of the greatest contemporary environmental problems, considering that 10–20 percent of the global drylands are already degraded (Millennium Ecosystem Assessment 2005, 1–8). The primary objective of the UN Convention to Combat Desertification (UNCCD) is "to combat desertification and mitigate the effects of drought . . . particularly in Africa" (Article 36). Thereby, the UNCCD calls for "an integrated approach addressing the physical, biological and socio-economic aspects of the processes of desertification and drought" (Article 4). In addition to these general commitments, the UNCCD sets down several specific obligations for both developed and developing countries. Specifically, developing countries affected by drought are to combat desertification by creating new policies for sustainable development, promoting public awareness and participation, and establishing and enforcing desertification legislation. Developed countries are under specific obligations to support the efforts of affected developing countries financially and technologically.

The UNCCD gives special priority to combating desertification in Africa. Nevertheless, regional implementation strategies for Asia, Latin America and the Caribbean, the northern Mediterranean, and central and eastern Europe are codified in its annexes.

Deforestation

The issue of deforestation has been of concern for many years, and its implications seem to become greater with time. The loss of animal habitats and the effects on global warming are serious concerns associated with deforestation. Several MEAs have been designed to address this problem.

International Tropical Timber Agreements

In 1983, under the auspices of the UN Conference on Trade and Development, agreement was reached to regulate the $7.5 billion industry of tropical timber. This was achieved through the adoption of the 1983 International Tropical Timber Agreement (ITTA) and supplemented by the 1994 ITTA.

The aim of the ITTA was to establish a framework for cooperation and consultation between producer and consumer countries. The 1983 and 1994 ITTAs were primarily commodity agreements lacking any objective standards for sustainable forestry. Therefore, a new international agreement to govern trade in tropical timber—the 2006 ITTA—was adopted on 27 January 2006 in Geneva, Switzerland, under the aegis of the UN Conference on Trade and Development to promote the expansion and diversification of international trade in tropical timber from sustainably managed and legally logged forests. The agreement proposes setting up a partnership fund, whereby timber-importing countries would assist the producing nations to finance necessary investment in sustainable and ecologically sound forestry management practices. As of late 2010, the 2006 ITTA has not entered into force.

UNREDD Programme

The issue of deforestation has gained global recognition with regard to the reduction of emissions from deforestation and forest degradation (REDD). As estimated by the Fourth Assessment Report of the Intergovernmental Panel on Climate Change, deforestation accounts for approximately 17 percent of the global greenhouse gas emissions. Consequently, the 2007 Bali Action Plan of the UNFCCC mandates that any forthcoming policy instrument addressing the issue of climate change needs to include incentives for REDD strategies in developing countries.

To promote REDD strategies in forested developing countries, in September 2008 the UN launched the UNREDD Programme under the expertise of the Food and Agriculture Organization (FAO), the United Nations Development Programme (UNDP), and UNEP. These strategies include, among others, the transfer of the flow of resources; the assessment of payment structures and capacity support to create incentives for emission reductions; the engagement of indigenous peoples, civil society, and other stakeholders; and low-carbon sector transformation.

The UNREDD currently supports REDD strategies in nine pilot countries, namely, Bolivia, Democratic Republic of Congo (DRC), Indonesia, Panama, Papua New Guinea, Paraguay, United Republic of Tanzania, Vietnam, and Zambia, of which four have already begun to implement national REDD strategies.

Transport of Waste

The export of environmental harm by developed countries through the transport and disposal of hazardous waste led to the adoption of the 1989 Convention on the Control of Transboundary Movements of Hazardous Wastes and Their Disposal, commonly known as the Basel Convention. The Basel Convention does not prohibit the transboundary movement of hazardous waste, but rather regulates it in a way that encourages wastes to be disposed of in the state of origin. Therefore, under the Basel Convention the import or export of wastes is only permissible if the state of origin does not have the capacity for disposal or if the importing state requires them as raw materials and will manage them in an environmentally sound manner. Moreover, under the Basel Convention any transboundary movement of hazardous waste requires prior informed consent of the state of transit and import. The parties have, in general, the right to ban the entry of hazardous waste into their territory and are even under the obligation to prohibit its import or export to states not party to the convention.

Hazardous wastes, in terms of the Basel Convention, include, among others, metal carbonyls, organic cyanides, and asbestos (dust and fibers). Many of the Basel Convention's provisions also apply to other wastes, such as household wastes. Radioactive wastes and wastes deriving from the normal operations of a ship, however, are not under the scope of the Basel Convention, as long as they are regulated by another international instrument.

Marine Environment

The 1982 United Nations Convention on the Law of the Sea (UNCLOS) is the first universally comprehensive legal regime governing the law of the sea. Although economic considerations largely influenced drafting negotiations, the protection of the marine environment left its mark. As stated in its preamble, one of UNCLOS's main objectives is to "promote the peaceful uses of the seas and oceans, the equitable and efficient utilization of their resources, the conservation of their living resources, and the study, protection and preservation of the marine environment."

Considering that under UNCLOS, the sea is divided in several maritime zones—the territorial sea, up to 12 nautical miles; the exclusive economic zone, up to 200 nautical miles; the high seas beyond 200 nautical miles, and the continental shelf constituting the natural prolongation of the landmass of the coastal state—environmental protection under UNCLOS is governed by several different regimes. UNCLOS, however, also stipulates a comprehensive legal framework to protect and preserve the marine environment and its resources in all maritime zones (Beyerlin 1995, 553). Part XII of UNCLOS sets down the following general commitments: (1) to "protect and preserve the marine environment" (Article 192); (2) to "take, individual or jointly as appropriate, all measures that are necessary to prevent, reduce and control pollution of the marine environment from any source, using for this purpose the best practical means at their disposal and in accordance with their capabilities" (Article 194(1)); and (3) to "take all measures necessary to ensure that activities under their jurisdiction and control are so conducted [as] not to [harm] other states" (Article 194(2)).

Taking into account the different needs and capabilities of several regions with regard to the protection of the marine environment, UNEP established a regional seas program in 1974. It encourages states to ensure the sustainable use of the marine environment through the adoption of MEAs at the regional level. As of 2010, 140 states take part in 13 regional sea programs under the auspices of UNEP.

The United Nations and Sustainability

The UN comprehensively addressed all fields of environmental law to ensure the sustainable use of the world's natural resources. It fulfills key roles in the creation of MEAs, from the establishment of nonbinding political commitments to negotiations and implementation. The role of the UN in the promotion of sustainable development should not be overestimated, however. True progress is dictated by the consent of each sovereign state to be bound by the commitments concerning sustainable development. Therefore, the UN is a forum that establishes an institutional framework; its member states must commit to the sustainable use of our planet to fully achieve the UN objectives.

Erik PELLANDER
University of Cologne

See also in the *Berkshire Encyclopedia of Sustainability* Convention on Long Range Transboundary Air Pollution; Convention to Combat Desertification; Customary International Law; Development, Sustainable—Overview of Laws and Commissions; Environmental Law, Soft vs. Hard; International Law; Law of the Sea; Montreal Protocol on Substances That Deplete the Ozone Layer; Waste Shipment Law; World Constitutionalism

FURTHER READINGS

Beyerlin, Ulrich. (1995). New developments in the protection of the marine environment: Potential effects of the Rio process. *ZAÖRV*, 55, 544–579.

Bodansky, Daniel M. (1993). The United Nations Framework Convention on Climate Change: A commentary. *Yale Journal of International Law*, 18(2), 451–558.

Burns, William C. (1995). The International Convention to Combat Desertification: Drawing a line in the sand? *Michigan Journal of International Law*, 16(3), 831–882.

Caron, David D. (1991). Protection of the stratospheric ozone layer and the structure of international environmental lawmaking. *Hastings International Law & Comparative Law Review*, 14(4), 755–780.

Chandler, Melinda. (1993). The Biodiversity Convention: Selected issues of interest to the international lawyer. *Colorado Journal of International Environmental Law and Policy*, 4(1), 141–1756.

Charney, Jonathan I. (1994). The marine environment and the 1982 United Nations Convention on the Law of the Sea. *International Lawyer*, 28(4), 879–901.

Franckx, Erik. (1998). Regional marine environment protection regimes in the context of UNCLOS. *International Journal of Marine and Coastal Law*, 13(3), 307–324.

French, Duncan. (1998). 1997 Kyoto Protocol to the 1992 UN Framework Convention on Climate Change. *Journal of Environmental Law*, 10(2), 227–239.

Hackett, David P. (1990). An assessment of the Basel Convention on the control of transboundary movements of hazardous wastes and their disposal. *American University Journal of International Law and Policy*, 5, 291–323.

Hill, Kevin D. (1990). The Convention on International Trade in Endangered Species: Fifteen years later. *Loyola of Los Angeles International and Comparative Law Journal*, 13(2), 231–278.

Millennium Ecosystem Assessment. (2005). *Ecosystems and human well-being: Desertification synthesis*. Washington, DC: World Resources Institute.

Mitchell, Roland B. (2003). International environmental agreements: A survey of their features, formation, and effects. *Annual Review of Environment and Resources*, 28, 429–461.

Molina, Mario J., & Rowland, F. S. (1974). Stratospheric sink for chlorofluoromethanes: Chlorine atom-catalyzed destruction of ozone. *Nature*, 249, 810–812.

Potvin, Catherine, & Bovarnik, Andrew. (2008). Reducing emissions from deforestation and forest degradation in developing countries:

Key actors, negotiations and actions. *The Carbon & Climate Law Review, 2*(3), 264–272.

Stolarski, R. S., & Cicerone, R. J. (1974). Stratospheric chlorine: A possible sink for ozone. *Canadian Journal of Chemistry, 52*, 1610–1615.

Tarasofsky, Richard G. (1996). The global regime for the conservation and sustainable use of forests: An assessment of progress to date. *Zeitschrift für ausländisches öffentliches Recht und Völkerrecht, 56*(3), 668–684.

United Nations Environment Programme (UNEP). (1972). Declaration of the United Nations Conference on the Human Environment. Retrieved December 2, 2010, from http://www.unep.org/Documents.Multilingual/Default.asp?documentid=97&articleid=1503

United Nations Environment Programme (UNEP). (2010). About UNEP: The organization. Retrieved December 2, 2010, from http://www.unep.org/Documents.Multilingual/Default.asp?DocumentID=43

Wettstone, Gregory, & Rosencranz, Armin. (1984). Transboundary air pollution: The search for an international response. *Harvard Environmental Law Review, 8*, 89–138.

CONVENTIONS

Convention on International Trade in Endangered Species of Wild Fauna and Flora. 3 March 1973, 993 UNTS 243.

Convention on Long Range Transboundary Air Pollution. 13 November 1979, 1302 UNTS 217.

United Nations Convention on the Law of the Sea. 10 December 1982, 1833 UNTS 3.

1983 International Tropical Timber Agreement. 18 November 1983, 1393 UNTS 671.

Vienna Convention for the Protection of the Ozone Layer. 22 March 1985, 1513 UNTS 293.

Montreal Protocol on Substances that Deplete the Ozone Layer. 16 September 1987, 1552 UNTS 3.

Convention on the Control of Transboundary Movements of Hazardous Wastes and Their Disposal. 22 March 1989, 1673 UNTS 57.

United Nations Framework Convention on Climate Change. 9 May 1992, 1771 UNTS 107.

United Nations Convention on Biological Diversity. 5 June 1992, 1760 UNTS 79.

1994 International Tropical Timber Agreement. 26 January 1994, 1955 UNTS 81.

Convention to Combat Desertification in Those Countries Experiencing Serious Drought and/or Desertification, Particularly in Africa. 14 October 1994, 1954 UNTS 3.

Kyoto Protocol to the UNFCC. 11 December 1997, 2303 UNTS 148.

2006 International Tropical Timber Agreement. 27 January 2006. Retrieved December 6, 2010, from http://www.itto.int/itta/

Utilities Regulation

The traditional system of public utility regulation in the United States and other nations has transformed dramatically since the 1970s. New laws and policies to encourage renewables, conservation, and energy efficiency programs have changed the electric industry from its traditional focus on increasing production to incorporating more environmental values. Much more is still necessary for electric utilities to become environmentally friendly and demand responsive.

Until recently, regulation of electricity production in the United States and elsewhere did not reflect its full social costs for two fundamental reasons. First, pollution caused by electric utilities was unregulated, allowing utilities to avoid the costs of controlling it. Since the 1970s, the system of air pollution regulation, beginning in the United States with the 1970 Clean Air Act Amendments and adopted elsewhere, has changed this substantially. Second, under traditional utility regulation in the United States, utilities had no incentive to adopt energy efficiency and demand response (DR) programs, such as time-based pricing, to reduce consumption. Under traditional regulation, utilities have a strong incentive to increase sales, because their costs are largely fixed. Increased sales mean increased profits, thus there is no incentive to reduce sales and profits. DR and energy efficiency programs reduce utilities' sales, and utilities resisted them as restaurants would shun diet plans. Yet these programs have enormous potential. Energy efficiency and DR saved utilities 32,741 megawatt hours in 2008 (US Department of Energy 2010), and much more is possible.

Traditional regulation did not give utilities any incentive to purchase power generated by solar, wind, and other renewable energy facilities. As monopolies, utilities were the only potential buyers for this power (Eisen 2010b), and

they refused to deal with companies they saw as potential competitors. They viewed renewable power as more expensive than electricity generated from fossil fuels; however, the cost of electricity made from coal, oil, and natural gas did not reflect its full environmental costs (Herzog, Lipman, Edwards, and Kammen 2001). Utilities also pointed to other purported disadvantages of renewables (e.g., wind power's intermittent nature) as reasons to avoid purchasing it (Eisen 2010b).

The relationship between environmental values and utility regulation has changed dramatically since the 1970s, as regulatory changes have attempted to internalize the full costs of generating and transmitting electricity by promoting energy efficiency, DR, and renewables. Unfortunately, the "restructuring" of the 1990s and early 2000s, a general term for deregulatory initiatives that modified or eliminated traditional regulation systems, had a profoundly negative impact on utilities' environmental programs. Today, a wide variety of state and federal initiatives promote conservation, efficiency, and renewables.

Shortcomings of Traditional Utility Regulation

Public utilities such as electric and gas companies provide essential services to the public. Economists describe these companies as having natural monopoly positions, because the large amount of capital required to build infrastructure creates formidable barriers for new companies to compete with existing utilities. If left unregulated, utilities could exercise their monopoly positions to set above-market prices. The electric utility regulatory system is complex; electricity is often produced in one state and distributed in another through the transmission grid. Generally speaking, state public utility commissions (PUCs) regulate local utility operations, including rate setting, and the Federal Energy Regulatory Commission (FERC) regulates interstate wholesale of electricity and interstate transmission grid operations.

The first decades of utility regulation focused on curbing utilities' monopolistic tendencies through price regulation. In this system, state PUCs granted utilities valuable franchises, giving them sole rights to serve all customers in a specific territory. In return, utilities accepted state regulation of rates, known as cost of service (COS) regulation because it was based on calculating the utilities' costs of providing service, plus a fair rate of return. Understanding this process is critical to understanding how environmental values were traditionally disregarded. Regulators begin by setting the revenue the utility must recoup to meet its costs. PUCs make judgments about power plant, fuel, capital, and operating costs based on hearings in which utilities and other interested parties present testimony. Rates are typically fixed for several years until the next rate case, but utilities can recover intermediate cost increases with fuel adjustment clauses. Once required revenue is established, the PUC sets rates; for example, it might set the price per kilowatt hour (kWh) as revenue divided by kWh sold.

COS regulation does not give utilities any incentive to minimize costs. They have what economists call the "throughput incentive": all the costs they incur are passed through to consumers and recovered from them. In a famous paper, the economists Harvey Averch and Leland Johnson demonstrated that this gives utilities incentives to increase capital expenditures and other costs without limit, making them inefficient (Averch and Johnson 1962). Under COS regulation, utilities have every incentive to sell as much electricity as they can. Their costs are largely fixed, so the more they sell, the more revenue they generate. Political scientists argued that over time, regulators failed to reverse these incentives and force utilities to cut costs because utilities gained excessive influence over regulators, "capturing" them (Estache and Martimort 1999).

Until the 1970s, utilities expanded virtually without limit. The industry's mascot, Reddy Kilowatt, boasted that "things work better electrically" and promoted consumption to millions of Americans. New products using electricity were designed and marketed, such as the "all electric kitchen." Increasing demand led to the construction of new power plants, and PUCs aided in this expansion process by keeping electric rates low.

Rate Regulation Evolves

In the 1970s, electricity rates began to increase, and consumers started to object to utilities' unchecked growth. A primary driver of rate increases was rapid cost escalation in construction of new nuclear power plants, which coincided with antinuclear opposition from environmental groups. When crises in the Middle East threatened the supply of imported petroleum, consumers pressured utilities to consider conservation techniques. President Jimmy Carter pushed for a national energy policy, setting an example by keeping the heat low and wearing a sweater in the White House, and telling Americans that conserving energy and weaning the nation off foreign oil was the "moral equivalent of war."

Responding to these societal forces, the utility rate-setting process began to evolve. The Public Utility Regulatory Policies Act of 1978 (PURPA) was one of the laws that responded to the 1970s energy crises. PURPA revised rate-making structures and directed states to provide incentives encouraging electric utilities to establish conservation programs. Over time, these changes had a strong influence on utilities. In 2000, 962 American electric utilities had one or more efficiency and DR programs, and the 516 largest utilities saved 53.7 million kWh of electricity (US Department of Energy 2002).

To promote conservation by utilities themselves, states enacted statutes requiring utilities to consider various options to meet increasing demand in a planning process called integrated resource planning (IRP), which originated in the 1970s in California. A utility implementing IRP forecasts a range of future demand possibilities and considers all alternatives to meet that demand, including conservation and renewables (Cavanagh 1986). IRP is different from traditional utility planning, in which utilities sought to meet demand with the construction of new power plants and gave little consideration to conservation or renewables. The Energy Policy Act of 1992 directed states to consider IRP, and many did so.

PURPA's Avoided-Cost Mandate

In the 1970s, traditional electric utilities provided virtually all new generating capacity, incorporating little generation from renewables. They generally refused to purchase power from nonutility companies. Changing the standards of business, PURPA required utilities to purchase power from cogenerators and other small power producers. Rates were set at utilities' avoided cost—the cost of generating power, had the utilities not purchased it elsewhere. This statutory provision and the regulations implementing it had a revolutionary impact on small power production, especially in states such as California that set relatively high avoided-cost rates. At the same time, technologies matured, and renewable resources, such as solar and wind power, experienced dramatic growth.

The avoided-cost mandate had an important side effect. Until the 1990s, investor-owned utilities that were vertically integrated, performing all functions of generating, transmitting, and distributing electricity in their service territories, generated two-thirds of the United States' electric power. PURPA led to the rise of an entire class of non-utility generators (NUGs), merchant firms that generate electricity and compete with existing utilities but are not utilities themselves (e.g., they do not own transmission and distribution facilities).

Restructuring Transforms the Industry

The introduction of competition through PURPA was one of many trends that led to calls for utility deregulation in the early 1990s. Free market economists had achieved deregulation of the airline industry in 1978, and other industries were transforming as well. Many believed the largely successful restructuring already underway in the natural gas industry could serve as a model for deregulating electric utilities and providing electricity to consumers at a lower cost (US Department of Energy 2002). The FERC spurred restructuring with a series of orders that called for open access to the nation's transmission grid as well as regional transmission organizations to control the transmission grid, transforming the industry by operating new wholesale electricity marketplaces. The FERC required that utilities separate their transmission divisions from their generation and distribution divisions. In response, utilities began to break up into separate businesses.

In addition, about twenty-five states introduced retail choice, giving consumers the ability to choose their own electric suppliers. This choice, however, turned out to be largely illusory. In California, retail choice was a spectacular failure for numerous reasons, including market manipulation by Enron and others. The failure of restructuring in California made other states cautious, and few states experienced much, if any, retail competition between new companies and incumbent utilities. There were many reasons for this, including state statutes that kept electricity rates low, making market entry difficult. Today, competition in the retail market is largely discredited, and many states have abandoned restructuring and returned to traditional regulation. FERC continues to regulate wholesale electricity sales with regulations that address excess market power.

Impact on Environmental Programs

A central debate during utility restructuring was the idea of "stranded costs." Utilities had spent money, planning to recoup it over the following decades. They argued that states were forcing them to compete immediately with new generators who did not have to incur the same costs. In response, states allowed existing utilities to recover these costs from customers, and to discontinue programs that made it uneconomical for them to compete with new generators. This policy choice had major negative impacts on existing environmental programs, which utilities thought of as burdensome in a competitive environment (Black and Pierce 1993). During the transition to competition, these were among the first programs to be cut, and utilities' budgets for conservation and DR programs fell by over 50 percent nationwide (Brown and Sedano 2003). IRP also became less common, because state PUCs had less control over utilities' supply planning decisions in a competitive environment (DSIRE 1998).

Many also advocated repeal of the avoided-cost mandate. Ironically, PURPA's success helped bolster this position. There were far more NUGs in the mid-1990s than in 1978, and many believed that in a more competitive industry, NUGs should compete equally with other electricity suppliers (Black and Pierce 1993). Specific industry conditions exacerbated the problem. Utilities were obligated to continue purchasing power under long-term contracts with small power producers, even though generation costs had dropped. This, they argued, was a form of stranded costs that kept electricity rates high. In 2005, Congress responded by discontinuing the avoided-cost requirement in areas of the United States served by wholesale electricity markets.

System Benefits Charges

As efficiency and DR programs were being discontinued, a number of states stepped into the gap and established statewide charges, imposing a small fee on all customers' electric bills. While the fee imposed is typically small, the funds raised can amount to millions of dollars. States use these system benefit charges for purposes perceived to benefit the entire public, such as efficiency and DR programs, or rebates on renewable energy systems. The programs vary considerably from state to state, and are not a substitute for more comprehensive action to promote conservation, DR, and renewables.

Renewable Electricity Standards

To promote renewables, states have established renewable portfolio standards or renewable electricity standards (RES); the terms are interchangeable. A RES typically requires a utility to obtain a specified percentage of the power it sells from renewable sources, or to compensate by purchasing tradable credits from suppliers that have excess production. The RES is meant to encourage renewable energy deployment, stimulate industry growth, and make renewable power more competitive in price. In 2010, thirty-five states had RES mandates, voluntary goals for renewable power generation, or other RES-like programs (Pew Center on Global Climate Change 2010).

The American Clean Energy and Security Act climate bill, passed by the US House of Representatives in 2009, would have established a national RES, including both energy efficiency and electricity produced from renewables. Some believe that replacing state standards with a single, national RES and credit marketplace would provide more support for renewables (Davies 2010). While many in Congress support a national RES, others have blocked progress, citing potential for higher consumer costs and unequal regional impacts.

Other nations have had success with national targets for renewables. In 2008, the EU Renewable Energy Directive established a binding target of a 20 percent share of renewable energy sources in energy consumption by 2020. All twenty-seven European nations have some form of regulatory mandate or financial incentive designed to meet their individual national targets for renewables (Commission of the European Communities 2008). China has also made considerable progress in increasing use of renewable energy systems. While 80 percent of the nation's electricity is still generated from coal (Eisen 2010a), China has a strong Renewable Energy Law and aggressive national targets.

Feed-In Tariffs

One frequent objection to RES is that they require building more renewable energy facilities. To critics, this forecloses any possibility that other policies can do the same job at a lower cost. A different idea for promoting renewables currently gaining attention is the feed-in tariff (FIT). Under the FIT, renewable energy project owners are paid an above-market rate. The rate is locked in for a specific term of years, and is either a fixed amount defined in advance, or a premium over the wholesale price of electricity. This is in contrast to a RES because it focuses on the generator's cost and profit, not the utility's supply procurement process. The direct payment aims to generate a reasonable profit and make project financing easier; many support it because they believe it will lead to more deployment of renewables (Rickerson, Bennhold, and Bradbury 2008). Others, however, view paying above-market rates to renewable energy producers as anticompetitive (Eisen 2010b).

The FIT is based on successful European programs. The German FIT caused explosive growth in solar and wind power, and enabled Germany to more than double its supply of electricity produced from renewables between 2000 and 2007 (Rickerson, Bennhold, and Bradbury 2008). Other EU countries and the Canadian province of Ontario have adopted FITs. A number of US states have considered FITs, but by 2009, only three states and some localities had adopted them.

There is an overlap between a FIT and net metering initiatives underway in many states. Net metering rewards a customer for installing a renewable energy system that sometimes provides more than enough electricity to meet the customer's needs, and the customer sells power to the grid. FITs, by comparison, can pay anyone for electricity generated from renewables, regardless of a specific customer's needs. States need to design FITs carefully so that they work with net metering programs.

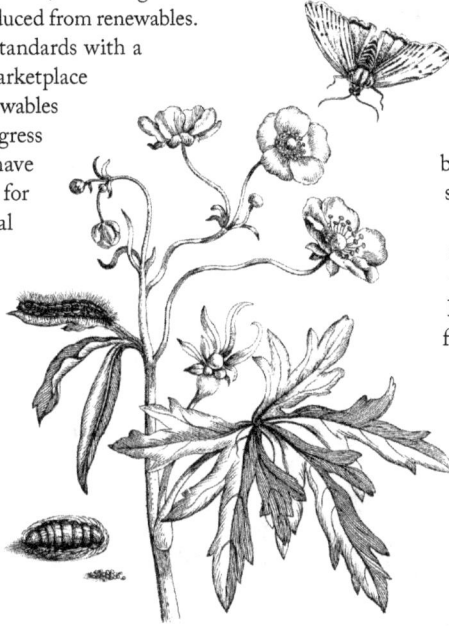

Real-Time Pricing and Green Pricing

Some believe that programs for real-time pricing (RTP) of electricity for residential utility customers have enormous promise to help reduce the demand for electricity and yield billions of dollars in savings for consumers. In 2008, however, only 1.1 percent of all US customers were enrolled in these programs (US Department of Energy 2009). In its simplest form, RTP involves providing price signals to consumers in real time, allowing them to adjust their behavior by cutting back on demand when prices are high. This would require wide adoption of a form of technology that is uncommon today. The standard electric meter gives no information to consumers about the price of electricity, thus more advanced meters are necessary for RTP be successful.

Green pricing programs also promote electricity sources that do not rely on fossil fuels. More than five hundred utilities offer these voluntary programs, which allow customers to purchase electricity based on its fuel source and emissions profile. These programs are limited in effectiveness for two primary reasons. First, they often require consumers to pay a price premium for renewable energy, which many consumers are unwilling to do. Second, because these programs are voluntary, they do not have large numbers of consumers enrolled. Therefore, green pricing is not likely to be as successful as specific, targeted mandates in encouraging the development of renewables.

Increased Deployment of Renewables

Increased deployment of renewables will require substantial improvements to the United States' transmission grid, as there has been chronic underinvestment in the electricity transmission and distribution system. Hundreds of thousands of high-voltage transmission lines cross the nation, but only 668 additional miles have been added since 2000 (US Department of Energy 2008). Many potential wind energy projects cannot connect to the grid, due to a lack of transmission lines in remote locations, where the wind tends to blow more strongly. Inadequate transmission capacity is also a problem in nations such as China, where solar and wind projects are located far from eastern urban centers. China expects to build many new ultra-high-voltage transmission lines in the next decade.

The current system in the United States for approving new transmission lines has contributed to the slow pace in overhauling the grid, although it is in desperate need of modernization. State and local regulators determine whether new transmission lines are needed, and focus on benefits to in-state ratepayers. Some states take into consideration renewables and other climate goals during transmission planning and siting decisions, but most states do not address these concerns. A project can fail if states argue that their ratepayers will pay for a project primarily benefiting customers in other states, as is the case with renewables projects connected to a grid that crosses state lines.

FERC traditionally had no jurisdiction over transmission siting, which was left entirely to the states. In 2005, a new Federal Power Act section expanded FERC's limited powers, allowing it to designate "national interest electric transmission corridors" and exercise "backstop" authority. This empowers FERC to preempt a state and issue a permit for the siting, construction, or modification of a proposed transmission line in a designated corridor if a state has withheld approval for more than a year. Federal courts, however, have rejected a number of FERC's attempts to overcome state resistance to transmission projects.

The American Clean Energy and Security Act climate bill, passed by the US House of Representatives in 2009, endorsed regional planning for new transmission lines and would have empowered FERC to review regional transmission plans. Among other goals, FERC would have been directed to approve transmission plans that "facilitate the deployment of renewable and other zero-carbon and low-carbon energy sources for generating electricity to reduce greenhouse gas emissions." With climate bills stalled, however, transmission siting remains largely an issue of state and local regulation.

Another significant barrier facing new transmission lines is deciding who will pay for them. Typically, ratepayers in the area of the project pay for new transmission lines through rate increases. This makes it uneconomical for utilities to invest in transmission projects that will benefit customers in other parts of the nation. A difficult issue is how the costs of future investments in the transmission grid will be shared differently, reflecting environmental and economic benefits that transcend the territorial boundaries of individual utilities.

Smart Grid Programs

Upgrading transmission lines is one component of the effort underway in the United States to develop a smart grid.

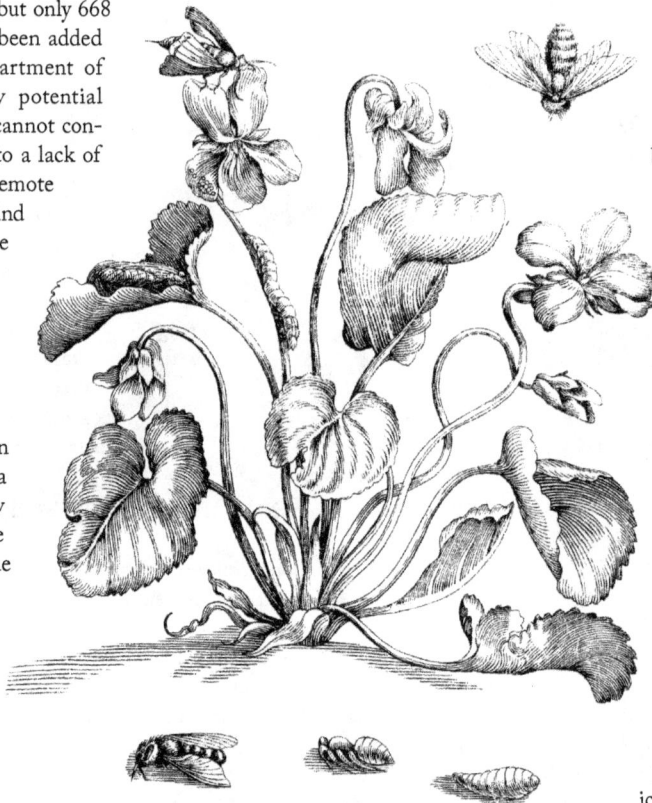

The current electricity transmission grid does a good job of what it was designed to do: one-way delivery of a product (electricity) that cannot be stored and must be consumed as soon as it is made. Despite occasional high-profile outages and blackouts, the system is generally strong and reliable. The term *smart grid* refers to a next-generation electricity transmission and distribution network that would provide many more capabilities through real-time two-way communication between consumers and utilities. A smart grid could drive much wider adoption of renewables and demand reduction, as well as improve reliability, operating efficiency, and grid resiliency to terrorist threats.

A smart grid would require many new ideas and technologies to achieve these disparate objectives. For example, it would rely on advanced meters that provide real time data between the customer and utility. When customers can tell how much electricity they are using and what it costs, they might be more inclined to buy "smart" devices like thermostats, clothes washers and dryers, microwaves, hot water heaters, and refrigerators that can interact with the smart grid. A Department of Energy study has found that these devices can reduce demand and energy costs (US Department of Energy 2009). Advanced meters could enable real-time pricing programs as well.

A major focus of the smart grid would be managing the two-way flow of electricity, enabling customers to generate or store electricity and sell it back to the grid during peak periods, when prices are highest. This would be a major incentive for deployment of small-scale solar, wind, and other renewable energy systems. Consumers could also store electric energy during the day in plug-in hybrid electric vehicles, and provide it back to the grid in off-hours. Managing the reverse flow of electricity will require sophisticated smart grid technology to overcome possible safety and reliability issues.

Developing a smart grid in the United States will entail massive improvements to the system currently in place and billions of dollars in funding. The federal stimulus package of 2009 allocated $3.4 billion for smart grid projects, but this is only a portion of the amount necessary. Development efforts are underway at both prominent American companies, such as IBM and Google, and grid technology startups, which have moved to create smart grid technologies (The Cleantech Group 2010). Simply establishing the rules by which a smart grid will operate is a daunting task, and a wide variety of technical standards for the smart grid are being developed in an effort led by a governing board at the US National Institute of Standards and Technology. In China, the State Grid Corporation's "Strengthened Smart Grid" plan calls for a similar effort oriented toward the construction of new transmission lines and the development of standards for a smart grid as well as the technologies needed for operation and control. A cooperative effort with the United States to foster development of these technologies is also underway.

Decoupling

An important regulatory mechanism to promote utilities' environmental programs is decoupling, breaking the link between sales and profits. Decoupling gives utilities incentives to adopt programs that encourage consumers to use less electricity. Rate cases continue as before, but price adjustments between cases allow utilities to recover revenue totals that are redefined as consumers use less electricity. As of 2009, seventeen states have decoupling mechanisms for individual utilities. Adjusted rates are still set as per-unit charges that give customers an incentive to reduce energy consumption, while enabling the utility to recover costs and revenue.

More frequent adoption of decoupling may facilitate progress toward reducing greenhouse gas emissions. Some call energy efficiency and DR programs the least expensive means for reducing electricity consumption and carbon emissions (United Nations Foundation 2007). Decoupling is itself not a means to address climate change. It does, however, allow a utility to recover its fixed costs even if consumption declines, and thus it may help implement the wide variety of carbon reduction policies being developed by states, regions, and the federal government.

Joel Barry EISEN
University of Richmond School of Law

See also in the *Berkshire Encyclopedia of Sustainability* Climate Change Disclosure—Legal Framework; Energy Conservation Incentives; Energy Subsidies; Environmental Law—China; Environmental Law—United States and Canada; Free Trade; Green Taxes; Investment Law, Energy

FURTHER READINGS

Averch, Harvey, & Johnson, Leland L. (1962). Behavior of the firm under regulatory constraint. *American Economic Review, 52*(5), 1052–1069.

Black, Bernard S., & Pierce, Richard J., Jr. (1993). The choice between markets and central planning in regulating the US electricity industry. *Columbia Law Review, 93*, 1339.

Brown, Matthew H., & Sedano, Richard P. (2003). A comprehensive view of US electric restructuring with policy options for the future (Electric Industry Restructuring Series, National Council on Electricity Policy). Retrieved September 15, 2010, from http://www.hks.harvard.edu/hepg/Papers/BrownSedano.pdf

Cavanagh, Ralph C. (1986). Least-cost planning imperatives for electric utilities and their regulators. *Harvard Environmental Law Review, 10*(2), 299–344.

Ceres. (2010). The 21st century electric utility: Positioning for a low-carbon future. Retrieved September 13, 2010, from http://www.ceres.org/Page.aspx?pid=1263

Chen, Cliff; Wiser, Ryan; & Bolinger, Mark. (2007). Weighing the costs and benefits of state renewables portfolio standards: A comparative analysis of state-level policy impact projections. Retrieved September 27, 2010, from http://eetd.lbl.gov/ea/ems/re-pubs.html

The Cleantech Group LLC. (2010). 2010 US smart grid vendor ecosystem: Report on the companies and market dynamics shaping the current US smart grid landscape. Retrieved September 27, 2010, from www.energy.gov/news/documents/Smart-Grid-Vendor.pdf

Commission of the European Communities. (2008). The support of electricity from renewable energy sources. Retrieved September 27, 2010, from http://ec.europa.eu/energy/climate_actions/doc/2008_res_working_document_en.pdf

Database of State Incentives for Renewables and Efficiency (DSIRE). (1998). State programs and regulatory policies report. Retrieved September 20, 2010, from http://www.dsireusa.org

Davies, Lincoln L. (2010). Power forward: The argument for a national RPS. *Connecticut Law Review, 42*(5), 1339.

Eisen, Joel B. (2010a). China's renewable energy law: A platform for green leadership? *William and Mary Environmental Law and Policy Review, 35,* 1.

Eisen, Joel B. (2010b). Can urban solar become a "disruptive" technology?: The case for solar utilities. *Notre Dame Journal of Law, Ethics & Public Policy, 24,* 53.

Estache, Antonio, & Martimort, David. (1999). Politics, transaction costs, and the design of regulatory institutions (World Bank Policy Research Working Paper No. 2073). Retrieved October 25, 2010, from http://papers.ssrn.com/sol3/papers.cfm?abstract_id=620512

Hendricks, Bracken. (2009, February). Wired for progress: Building a national clean-energy smart grid. *Center for American Progress.* Retrieved September 27, 2010, from http://www.americanprogress.org/issues/2009/02/wired_for_progress.html

Herzog, Antonia V.; Lipman, Timothy E.; Edwards, Jennifer L.; & Kammen, Daniel M. (2001). Renewable energy: a viable choice. *Environment, 43*(10), 8–20.

Lesh, Pamela G. (2009). Rate impacts and key design elements of gas and electric utility decoupling: A comprehensive review. Retrieved September 13, 2010, from www.raponline.org/Pubs/Lesh-CompReviewDecouplingInfoElecandGas-30June09.pdf

Pew Center on Global Climate Change. (2010). Homepage. Retrieved September 30, 2010, from http://www.pewclimate.org/

The Public Utility Regulatory Policies Act of 1978, Pub. L. No. 95–617, 92 Stat. 3117 (codified in scattered sections).

Rickerson, Wilson; Bennhold, Florian; & Bradbury, James. (2008). Feed-in tariffs and renewable energy in the USA—A policy update. Retrieved September 27, 2010, from www.wind-works.org/FeedLaws/USA/Feed-in_Tariffs_and_Renewable_Energy_in_the_USA_-_a_Policy_Update.pdf

Rossi, Jim. (2009). The political economy of energy and its implications for climate change legislation. *Tulane Law Review, 84,* 379–428.

Rossi, Jim, & Brown, Ashley C. (2010). Siting transmission lines in a changed milieu: Evolving notions of the "public interest" in balancing state and regional considerations. *University of Colorado Law Review, 81,* 705.

Shapiro, Sidney A., & Tomain, Joseph P. (2005). Rethinking reform of electricity markets. *Wake Forest Law Review, 40,* 497–543.

Shirley, Wayne. (2010). Mechanics & application of decoupling. Retrieved September 13, 2010, from http://www.raponline.org/docs/RAP_Shirley_PennsylvaniaDecoupling_2010_04_28.pdf

Stigler, George J., & Friedland, Claire. (1962). What can regulators regulate? The case of electricity. *Journal of Law and Economics, 5,* 1–16.

United Nations Foundation. (2007). *Realizing the potential of energy efficiency: Targets, policies, and measures for G8 countries.* Retrieved October 25, 2010, from http://www.globalproblems-globalsolutions-files.org/unf_website/PDF/realizing_potential_energy_efficiency.pdf

US Department of Energy (DOE). (2002). A primer on electric utilities, deregulation, and restructuring of US electricity markets. Retrieved October 25, 2010, from http://www1.eere.energy.gov/femp/pdfs/primer.pdf

US Department of Energy (DOE). (2006). Benefits of demand response in electricity markets and recommendations for achieving them. Retrieved September 13, 2010, from http://eetd.lbl.gov/ea/EMP/reports/congress-1252d.pdf

US Department of Energy (DOE). (2008). The smart grid: An introduction. Retrieved September 27, 2010, from http://www.oe.energy.gov/DocumentsandMedia/DOE_SG_Book_Single_Pages.pdf

US Department of Energy (DOE). (2009). Smart grid system report. Retrieved September 27, 2010, from http://www.oe.energy.gov/DocumentsandMedia/SGSRMain_090707_lowres.pdf

US Department of Energy (DOE). (2010). Demand-side management actual peak load reductions by program category. Retrieved October 25, 2010, from http://www.eia.gov/cneaf/electricity/epa/epat9p1.html

US Department of Energy (DOE) & Energy Information Administration (EIA). (2000). The restructuring of the electric power industry: A capsule of issues and events. Retrieved September 13, 2010, from http://tonto.eia.doe.gov/FTPROOT/other/x037.pdf

US Department of Energy (DOE) & Energy Information Administration (EIA). (2002). US electric utility demand side management (DSM) data 2000. Retrieved September 15, 2010, from http://www.eia.doe.gov/cneaf/electricity/page/eia861dsm.html

US Environmental Protection Agency (EPA). (2008). National action plan vision for 2025: A framework for change. Retrieved September 13, 2010, from http://www.epa.gov/cleanenergy/energy-programs/suca/resources.html

Waste Shipment Law

Since the 1980s, rules at global, regional, and national levels regulate the transboundary movement of hazardous and other problematic wastes. Their main purpose is to prevent the uncontrolled dumping of such waste in poorer countries where it would damage the environment and human health. Key instruments to achieve these goals are export and import bans and the requirement of prior notification and consent of all countries concerned.

Since the mid-1970s, growing environmental awareness, new legislation, and rising technical standards have led to a sharp increase in the costs of waste disposal in Europe and North America. Combined with a steady increase in the quantity of waste and the globalization of shipping, this made the export of waste—notably hazardous industrial waste—to less-developed countries financially attractive. This action is often due to low wages and lack of adequate enforcement of legislation (when it exists), good governance, financial means, trade union and neighbor rights, and a culture of environmental and health protection in less-developed countries. The lack of controls on waste movements became apparent particularly in the 1980s with several scandals involving the remains of industrial accidents (e.g., Seveso) or ships (e.g., *Khian Sea, Karin B, Radhost*) that sought to unload toxic wastes from the United States or Europe in ports or on the shores of third world countries.

As part of the 1981 Montevideo Programme (a long-term, strategic plan for the field of international environmental law), senior governmental experts concluded that guidelines, principles, or agreements should be developed regarding, among other things, the transport, handling, and disposal of toxic and dangerous wastes. As a result of further negotiations, the Cairo Guidelines for the environmentally sound management of hazardous wastes

were adopted in 1985, which paved the way for the Basel Convention.

At a regional level, the uncontrolled disappearance and resurfacing of drums of chemical waste from the Seveso disaster site several years later in a French storehouse prompted the European Economic Community in 1984 to issue a directive (No. 84/631) establishing the first transnationally binding and comprehensive system for the supervision and control of hazardous waste shipments.

Basel Convention

After two years of negotiation under the auspices of the United Nations Environment Programme (UNEP), the Convention on the Control of Transboundary Movements of Hazardous Wastes and Their Disposal was adopted by the conference of plenipotentaries in Basel, Switzerland, on 22 March 1989 and signed by the representatives of fifty-three governments and the European Economic Community. The so-called Basel Convention entered into force on 5 May 1992; as of 20 September 2010, 174 countries and the European Union (EU) have become parties to it. Three countries—Afghanistan, Haiti, and the United States of America—signed the convention but did not ratify it.

Scope and Definitions

The geographic scope of the Basel Convention (BC) is global; its overall objective is to protect human health and the environment against the adverse effects that may result from the generation, transboundary movement, and management of hazardous wastes.

Hazardous wastes, as defined by Article 1 of the BC are (a) wastes that belong to any category contained in Annex I, unless they do not possess any of the hazard characteristics listed in Annex III, and (b) wastes that are not covered by this definition but are considered to be hazardous by the domestic legislation of the parties of export, import, or transit. In addition, the BC applies also to the shipment of certain "other wastes" specified in Annex II, namely mixed wastes collected from households and residues arising from the incineration of household wastes. Annexes VIII and IX contain lists of wastes, in the form of codes with a letter (*A* or *B*) and four digits, that are typically considered as hazardous or nonhazardous.

Excluded from the scope of the BC are radioactive materials and wastes deriving from the normal operation of a ship, insofar as these wastes are covered by other, more specific international instruments.

Wastes are defined for the purposes of the convention in Article 2.1 as substances or objects that are disposed of, intended to be disposed of, or required to be disposed of by the provisions of national law. "Disposal" in this sense has a wide meaning, covering operations like landfilling or incineration (cf. Annex IV.A) as well as operations that may lead to resource recovery, recycling, or reuse (Annex IV.B).

Obligations and Instruments

Article 4 of the BC lays down general obligations on the parties, notably not to permit the export of hazardous wastes to other parties that have prohibited the import of such wastes and have duly notified this, and to take appropriate measures to ensure that the generation and the transboundary movement of hazardous wastes is reduced to a minimum consistent with the environmentally sound and efficient management of such wastes. BC parties should also ensure the availability of adequate environmentally sound disposal facilities, if possible within their borders; prevent the export and import of hazardous and other wastes if they have reason to believe that those wastes will not be managed in an environmentally sound manner; and take appropriate action for enforcement, including measures to punish illegal traffic.

Apart from export and import bans and the principle of environmentally sound management, the main control instrument of the BC is the system of prior notification and consent (cf. Article 6; also called "prior informed consent," or PIC), whereby the competent authorities of the

countries of export, import, and transit have to be notified in writing and give their consent before a hazardous waste shipment takes place. The BC provides for a standardized procedure with notification and movement forms, requirements for information and documentation, as well as timelines for the communication between the notifier and the authorities concerned. If a waste movement cannot be completed, or in the case of illegal traffic, the state of export is primarily under a duty to ensure the reimport of the waste (cf. Articles 8 and 9).

While a party shall in principle not permit hazardous wastes to be exported to or imported from a non-party (Article 4.5), Article 11 allows for the conclusion of bilateral, multilateral, or regional agreements or arrangements regarding transboundary waste movement also with non-parties, provided that such agreements or arrangements do not derogate from the environmentally sound management required by the convention. Bilateral agreements play a significant role in some parts of the world, for example, in relation to waste exports from Japan to neighboring Asian countries. Standards concerning the environmentally sound management of certain waste streams have been specified over the years in various nonbinding technical guidelines.

Institutions

The governing body of the Basel Convention, as with other UNEP conventions, is the Conference of the Parties (COP), which holds meetings every two or three years. Halfway between these sessions the Open-ended Working Group (OEWG) meets to follow up on decisions and prepare future meetings of the COP. To assist these bodies, a permanent secretariat was established; based in Geneva, it also transmits information and maintains an extensive website (www.basel.int). Other subsidiary bodies of the convention are the Expanded Bureau, which provides directions to the secretariat between COP meetings, and a Compliance Committee. A network of fourteen Basel Regional and Coordinating Centres (BCRCs) has been set up, primarily in Asia, Africa, and Latin America, to promote implementation.

Implementing the convention is essentially a matter for the parties, which are obliged to cooperate with each other, to designate one or more competent authorities and one focal point for contact, and to report annually on their activities.

Other International Agreements

Several international agreements regarding waste shipments exist in addition to the Basel Convention. Some apply only to specific types of waste or to a specific world region and have grown out of dissatisfaction with perceived gaps and weaknesses of the Basel Convention.

OECD Decision

The Organisation for Economic Co-operation and Development (OECD), which currently consists of thirty-three industrial countries (all parties to the Basel Convention, apart from the United States), has established a special framework for its members to control transboundary movements of wastes destined for recovery. OECD Council Decision C(2001)107/FINAL applies to shipments of hazardous as well as nonhazardous waste, and distinguishes between a "green" and "amber" control procedure. A "green" procedure means the set of customs controls that applies in normal commercial transactions and is used also for nonhazardous wastes. The "amber" procedure follows the Basel Convention's system of prior notification and consent, but with certain modifications in order to facilitate the shipment of wastes for recycling and energy recovery within the OECD. This 2001 decision in particular requires only tacit consent (instead of an explicit written permission) for waste shipments to go ahead, and envisages a list of preconsented recovery facilities where a competent authority has declared for a certain number of years not to raise objections against imports to such a facility within its jurisdiction.

Bamako Convention

The Bamako Convention on the Ban on the Import into Africa and the Control of Transboundary Movement and Management of Hazardous Wastes within Africa was elaborated under the auspices of the Organisation of African Unity (OAU) and adopted in Bamako (Mali) on 30 January 1991. It entered into force on 22 April 1998 but, as of February 2010, had been ratified only by twenty-four of fifty-three African states. Provoked by dissatisfaction with the agreed text of the Basel Convention, which was regarded as not giving enough protection against waste shipments from industrial states, it contains a wider definition of hazardous wastes (including radioactive materials and deregistered hazardous substances) and generally prohibits the import of such wastes into Africa from noncontracting parties.

Waigani Convention

The Convention to Ban the Importation into Forum Island Countries of Hazardous and Radioactive Wastes and to Control the Transboundary Movement and Management of Hazardous Wastes within the South Pacific Region opened for signature in Waigani (Papua New Guinea) in 1995 and entered into force in 2001. As of June 2008, thirteen member countries of the Pacific Island Forum have become parties to the convention, including Australia and New Zealand. France, the United Kingdom, and the United States are eligible to join but have not done so. The Waigani Convention is based on the text of the Basel Convention but also covers radioactive wastes and extends beyond the territorial sea to the economic exclusion zone of the parties.

Mediterranean Hazardous Waste Protocol

A number of other regional and multilateral environmental agreements also concern the control of transboundary waste shipments (Basel Convention n.d.a). They include notably the Protocol on the Prevention of Pollution of the Mediterranean Sea by Transboundary Movements of Hazardous Wastes and their Disposal of 1996, which is in force since December 2007. Like the Bamako Convention, the protocol also applies to deregistered hazardous substances and contains an obligation to ban the export and transit of hazardous wastes to developing countries and, in so far as parties are not member states of the EU, to prohibit the import of such wastes.

Rules on Radioactive and Ship-Generated Waste

Specifically for radioactive waste, the International Atomic Energy Agency developed a Joint Convention on the Safety of Spent Fuel Management and on the Safety of Radioactive Waste Management, which was adopted in 1997 and entered into force in June 2001. The Joint Convention, as of August 2010, has been ratified or otherwise joined by fifty-six countries and by the European Atomic Energy Community (EURATOM). It applies to spent fuel and radioactive waste from civilian nuclear facilities and requires the prior notification and consent of the state of destination before transboundary movements of such waste may take place. States of destination may give their consent only if they have the administrative and technical capacity and the regulatory structure needed to manage the waste in a manner consistent with the convention.

The management of ship-generated waste, including its transport on board the ship until discharge at a port reception facility, is regulated by various annexes of the

International Convention for the Prevention of Pollution from Ships of 1973, as amended by the Protocol of 1978 (informally known as MARPOL 73/78). Notably, Annex V prohibits the disposal of garbage into the sea and obliges ships to use port reception facilities. Annexes I, II, and IV deal with the prevention of pollution by oil, chemicals, and wastewater respectively, and thereby cover the sea transport of such wastes until they are off-loaded in port. All these annexes have entered into force between 1983 and 2003 and have been so far ratified by 125–150 member countries of the International Maritime Organization (IMO).

EU Waste Shipment Regulation and National Laws

In addition to being subject to the Basel Convention and other international agreements, waste shipments are also regulated at the national (and, in the case of the European Union, supranational) level.

European Union

The EU, which became a party to the Basel Convention as a Regional Economic Integration Organization (REIO), transposed the convention originally by its Council Regulation (EEC) No. 259/93 of 1 February 1993 on the supervision and control of shipments of waste within, into, and out of the European Community. This was replaced in July 2007 by Regulation (EC) No. 1013/2006 of the European Parliament and of the Council of 14 June 2006 on shipments of waste. The regulation has directly binding effect throughout the EU and is supplemented by some secondary rules, in particular Commission Regulation (EC) No. 1418/2007 as of 2010, which concerns the export of so-called green-listed (non-hazardous) wastes for recovery to non-OECD countries. The EU law basically implements the rules of the Basel Convention and of the above-mentioned 2001 OECD decision but also provides for a range of additional measures. Most notably, it transposed the Basel Ban Amendment of 1995 (as explained below) and thus prohibited the export of all wastes for disposal to non-European countries and all hazardous wastes for recovery to non-OECD countries as of 1998. In addition, the regulation also requires shipments of green-listed waste to be accompanied by an information document, and the EU Commission systematically requests non-OECD countries to inform about their import rules for green-listed waste, in order to prevent unwanted exports from the EU.

United States

Though it did not become a party to the Basel Convention, the United States introduced a prior informed consent procedure for the export of hazardous waste in 1986, with an amendment to the Resource Conservation and Recovery Act (RCRA). Its definition of hazardous waste differs in terminology from that of the Basel Convention in that it covers "discarded material" that is either listed as hazardous or exhibits certain hazard characteristics. Besides, US law contains more exceptions from the PIC principle, such as for the export of used lead acid batteries and certain other recyclable materials. There are other major differences to the Basel system: (a) in US law there is no requirement for environmentally sound management of the waste in the country of destination, and (b) the exporter is not obliged to reimport wastes that cannot be handled in accordance with the shipment contract. The great majority of hazardous waste exports from the United States are destined for Mexico and Canada and subject to bilateral agreements with these countries.

China

China was among the first countries to ratify the Basel Convention (in December 1991) and also transposed the Ban Amendment in May 2001. Under the Law on the Prevention and Control of Environmental Pollution by Solid Waste of 1995, it is forbidden to import solid waste that cannot be used in an environment-friendly way or as raw material. The State Environmental Protection Administration (SEPA) decides on the wastes that are allowed for import as raw materials, which then have to conform to national environmental protection standards. This means in practice also that some materials, such as end-of-life ships that are imported for recycling, are not considered as waste in Chinese law.

A special feature of China's shipment control system is the requirement for importers and foreign exporters to hold an import license issued by SEPA or be registered with the General Administration of Quality Supervision,

Inspection and Quarantine (AQSIQ), respectively. In addition, China has established a system of preshipment inspections that are carried out in the ports of export by independent inspectors recognized by AQSIQ.

India

India ratified the Basel Convention in March 1992 but has refrained from signing the Ban Amendment, although since 2000 a ban on the import of hazardous wastes and their export for dumping or disposal has existed in national law. The Hazardous Wastes (Management and Handling) Rules of 1989, as last amended in July 2009, define such wastes on the basis of their hazard characteristics and by including them in certain schedules. A significant exception, however, is made for import and export of hazardous wastes as raw material for recycling or reuse, the term *raw material* not being defined in the 1989 rules. From this it again follows in practice that the import of end-of-life ships—for which India is a leading recycling country worldwide—is not subject to waste shipment controls even when the ships are contaminated with hazardous materials.

Special rules exist also for the management and shipment of electronic wastes, batteries, and municipal waste. Like China, India requires in principle a preshipment inspection of wastes and a corresponding certificate from an inspection agency in the exporting country.

The Basel Ban Amendment

The Conference of the Parties of the Basel Convention, at its third meeting in 1995, adopted Decision (III/1), amending the Basel Convention by inserting an Article 4A that prohibits the transboundary movement of hazardous waste from countries listed in a new Annex VII to countries not listed there. The countries mentioned in Annex VII are parties and other states that are members of OECD or the European Community (EC) as well as Liechtenstein. The so-called Ban Amendment essentially forbids the export of hazardous waste from OECD countries to non-OECD countries in order to protect the latter against environmental and health risks that they at present cannot manage properly.

The Basel Ban has not entered into force in international law as of 2010, due to an insufficient number of ratifications and a dispute over exactly how many signatures are needed. As of 20 September 2010, sixty-nine parties have ratified the Ban Amendment, including the EU (which does not count in addition to its member states), but only forty-seven of these countries were present in 1995 and so constitute far less than the sixty-two needed under the "fixed time approach," which requires ratification by three-fourths of

the eighty-two parties that were present when the amendment was adopted. The reluctance of most industrial states outside Europe and even of many non-OECD countries, which nowadays regard some hazardous wastes as valuable raw materials, make it seem unlikely that the Basel Ban will enter into force in the foreseeable future. To break this deadlock, in 2008 Switzerland and Indonesia started a country-led initiative (CLI) that should explore "in an informal, dynamic, and non-dogmatic manner" ways to reach the objective of the Ban with alternative means.

Relevant Court Cases and Important Events

There is as yet no jurisprudence of the International Court of Justice (ICJ) on the Basel Convention or directly on matters of waste shipment. The Panel and the Appellate Body of the World Trade Organization (WTO) have given their opinion on a case where Brazil restricted the import of retreaded tires for environmental reasons. The Appellate Body essentially upheld this trade restriction if applied in a nondiscriminatory fashion against all such tire imports (WTO 2007).

Other relevant case law up to now has accrued mainly in national courts and in the European Court of Justice (ECJ). The ECJ in particular pronounced on the distinction between shipments for recovery and for disposal (e.g., cases C-203/96 *Dusseldorp*, C-228/00 *Commission v. Germany*, C-458/00 *Commission v. Luxembourg*) and on the application of the notification procedure to certain types of waste or mixtures of waste (e.g., cases C-176/05 *KVZ retec GmbH v. Austria* and C-259/05 *Omni Metal Service*) (EC 2010a).

Widely published decisions of national courts have questioned whether the Basel Convention applies to end-of-life ships and have answered in the affirmative: for example, judgments of the Dutch Council of State in the *Sandrien* and *Otapan* cases; of the French Council of State in the *Clemenceau* case; and of the Administrative Court of Izmir, Turkey, in the *Sea Beirut* case (Basel Convention n.d.b).

The *Probo Koala* Incident

In August 2006, the *Probo Koala*, a bulk/oil tanker belonging to a Greek owner but registered in Panama and chartered by the Swiss-, Dutch-, and UK-based trading company Trafigura, off-loaded a toxic mixture of oil and sulfur compounds in the former capital of Côte d'Ivoire, Abidjan, where it was then dumped by a local company on various places on the outskirts of the city. The dumping reportedly caused the death of seventeen people; injured thirty thousand; and poisoned food, water, and soil on a large scale. Previously, the charterer had tried to off-load the toxic mixture as "regular slops" (typically only a mixture of water, oil, and cleansing agents leftover from ship cleaning) at the port reception facility of Amsterdam but had stopped the process on account of the high disposal costs. In the aftermath of the disaster, two managers of Trafigura who visited Côte d'Ivoire were arrested and released only several months later when the company had agreed to pay £100 million in compensation to the government. Various criminal investigations and civil lawsuits were initiated, some of which are ongoing. In July 2010, a Dutch district court imposed a fine of €1 million on Trafigura for illegally exporting hazardous waste to western Africa.

The incident caused worldwide uproar and dominated the Conference of the Parties (COP) 8 of the Basel Convention in Nairobi, Kenya, in November 2006. Under legal aspects, a controversy ensued as to whether the transfer of the liquid mixture, which appears to have been the result of a failed oil-blending operation, from Europe to Africa was governed by the Basel Convention or the rules of MARPOL 73/78 on ship-generated waste. The main argument for the application of waste shipment rules in this case was that the off-loading in Amsterdam had already begun, and part of the hazardous mixture was then pumped back to the ship. As a consequence, the IMO and the Basel Convention COP agreed to intensify their cooperation in order to close gaps of implementation and enforcement. Pending the outcome of criminal proceedings, however, the incident has not yet led to any changes of international law.

Current Issues

The COP 9 meeting of the Basel Convention in June 2008 produced a Bali Declaration on Waste Management for Human Health and Livelihood, which calls for raising awareness of the links between waste management and health issues, and improved cooperation between national authorities and stakeholders in these sectors. The initiative has been taken up by the World Health Organization (WHO), which, in a May 2010 resolution, urged its member states to apply the health impact assessment as a key tool in dealing with the health aspects of waste management.

Another issue is waste from electric and electronic equipment, which is the fastest growing waste stream worldwide. Even in African countries the amount of e-waste from personal computers (PCs) is estimated to increase more than threefold within the next decade (Schluep et al. 2009). A high proportion of end-of-life computers, TV sets, and refrigerators from Europe and North America end up in west Africa and Asia, often being shipped there as "used products." This e-waste is mostly treated with primitive methods, such as burning of cables and plastic casings, which creates health risks for both workers and neighbors,

pollutes the environment, and achieves only a low rate of resource recovery. Apart from attempts to fix criteria for the distinction between products and waste, and to improve collaboration between waste shipment authorities, customs, and police, the Basel Convention parties try to tackle the problem through partnerships with industry on the recycling of mobile phones and computing equipment.

Like other UNEP structures, the institutions of the Basel Convention suffer from chronic underfunding, which considerably reduces their effectiveness. In an effort to optimize working capacity, the Conferences of the Parties to the Basel, Rotterdam, and Stockholm conventions agreed in 2008 to set up interim joint services. For the time being, this means a partial merger of the three secretariats in Geneva and the appointment of a joint executive secretary.

Future Role of Waste Shipment Law

The waste shipment law as developed over the last twenty-five years has largely succeeded in stopping the export of hazardous production wastes from Europe and North America to developing countries. But the Basel Convention has not reached its declared aim to minimize the generation and transboundary movement of hazardous and other wastes in general. The convention has failed to work for certain waste streams, such as end-of-life ships, which in spite of their contamination with hazardous substances offer high economic benefits to operators in the countries of destination. Moreover, no global standards for environmentally sound management are effectively in place. In the next decades, waste shipment law will face a huge challenge, particularly with the rising flow of e-waste from rich to poor nations.

The prior informed consent system of the Basel Convention is likely to remain the basic framework of international shipment controls in the future also. But at a time when the bulk of industrial activity itself shifts increasingly from the OECD to emerging economies like China, the indiscriminate Basel Ban of the 1990s looks more and more outdated. While export and import bans may still serve a function to protect the poorest countries from hazard transfers, the inexorable globalization of industry and waste recycling will require more flexible instruments. A future waste shipment law might instead focus on a worldwide network of environmentally sound waste management facilities that are properly audited and certified by independent bodies, and whose authorizations and certificates are transparent to waste shipment authorities, potential customers, and the general public.

Thomas ORMOND
Regional government of South Hesse, Germany

See also in the *Berkshire Encyclopedia of Sustainability*
Brent Spar; Convention for the Prevention of Pollution From Ships; Convention for the Safe and Environmentally Sound Recycling of Ships; Convention for the Safety of Life at Sea; Environmental Law (several articles: Africa, Saharan; Africa; Sub-Saharan; China; Europe; India and Pakistan; Southeast Asia; United States and Canada); MOX Plant Case (*Ireland v. United Kingdom*); Restriction of Hazardous Substances Directive; United Nations—Overview of Conventions and Agreements

FURTHER READINGS

Asante-Duah, D. Kofi, & Nagy, Imre V. (1998). *International trade in hazardous wastes*. London: E. & F. N. Spon.

Basel Action Network (2010). *About the Basel Ban: A chronology of the Basel Ban*. Retrieved Sept. 9, 2010, from http://www.ban.org/about_basel_ban/chronology.html

Basel Convention. (n.d.a). Bilateral, multilateral and regional agreements and arrangements. Retrieved October 11, 2010, from http://www.basel.int/article11/multi.html

Basel Convention. (n.d.b). Dismantling of ships—relevant caselaw. Retrieved October 9, 2010, from http://www.basel.int/ships/relev-caselaw.html

Belenky, Lisa T. (1999). Cradle to border: US hazardous waste export regulations and international law. *Berkeley Journal of International Law, 17*, 95–137.

Clapp, Jennifer. (2001). *Toxic exports: The transfer of hazardous wastes from rich to poor countries*. Ithaca, NY: Cornell University Press.

Dieckmann, Martin. (2007). The revised EC regulation on shipments of waste. *Journal of European Environmental & Planning Law (JEEPL), 4*(1), 37–46.

European Commission / Environment (EC). (2010a). Case law of the European Court of Justice with particular relevance to waste shipments. Retrieved October 10, 2010, from http://ec.europa.eu/environment/waste/shipments/case_law.htm

European Commission / Environment (EC). (2010b). Frequently asked questions (FAQs) on Regulation (EC) 1013/2006 on shipments of waste. Retrieved Sept. 7, 2010, from http://ec.europa.eu/environment/waste/shipments/pdf/faq.pdf

European Environment Agency. (2009). Waste without borders in the EU? Transboundary shipments of waste. Retrieved Sept. 7, 2010, from http://www.eea.europa.eu/publications/waste-without-borders-in-the-eu-transboundary-shipments-of-waste

Fagbohun, Olanrewaju A. (2007). The regulation of transboundary shipments of hazardous waste: A case study of the dumping of toxic waste in Abidjan, Cote d'Ivoire. *Hong Kong Law Journal, 37*, 831–858.

Giampetro-Meyer, Andrea. (2009). Captain Planet takes on hazard transfer: Combining the forces of market, legal and ethical decisionmaking to reduce toxic exports. *UCLA Journal of Environmental Law & Policy (JELP), 27*(1), 71–92.

Greenpeace. (2008). Poisoning the poor: Electronic waste in Ghana. Retrieved September 7, 2010, from http://www.greenpeace.org/raw/content/international/press/reports/poisoning-the-poor-electonic.pdf

Kummer, Katharina. (Ed.) (1995). *International management of hazardous wastes: The Basel Convention and related legal rules*. Oxford, UK: Oxford University Press.

Langlet, David. (2009). *Prior informed consent and hazardous trade: Regulating trade in hazardous goods at the intersection of sovereignty, free trade and environmental protection*. Alphen aan den Rijn, The Netherlands: Wolters Kluwer.

Sander, Knut, & Schilling, Stephanie. (2010). *Transboundary shipment of waste electrical and electronic equipment / electronic scrap: Optimization of material flows and control*. Retrieved September 7, 2010, from http://www.umweltdaten.de/publikationen/fpdf-l/3933.pdf

Schluep, Mathias; Hageluekenb, Christian; Kuehrc, Ruediger; Magalinic, Federico; Maurerc, Claudia; Meskersb, Christina; et al. (2009). *Recycling—from e-waste to resources*. Retrieved November 16, 2010, from http://www.unep.org/pdf/Recycling_From_e-waste_to_resources.pdf

Scovazzi, Tullio. (2001). The transboundary movement of hazardous waste in the Mediterranean regional context. *UCLA Journal of Environmental Law & Policy, 19*, 231–245.

Vander Beken, Tom. (Ed.). (2007). *The European waste industry and crime vulnerabilities*. Antwerp, Belgium /Apeldoorn, The Netherlands: Maklu Publishers.

Van Hoogstraten, David, & Lawrence, Peter. (1998). Protecting the South Pacific from hazardous and nuclear waste dumping: The Waigani Convention. *Review of European Community and International Environmental Law (RECIEL), 7*, 268–273.

Widawsky, Lisa. (2008). In my backyard: How enabling hazardous waste trade to developing nations can improve the Basel Convention's ability to achieve environmental justice. *Environmental Law, 38*, 577–625.

Wirth, David A. (2007). Hazardous substances and activities. In Daniel Bodansky, Jutta Brunnée, & Ellen Hey (Eds.), *The Oxford handbook of international environmental law* (pp. 394–422). Oxford, UK: Oxford University Press.

World Trade Organization (WTO). (2007, December 3). Brazil—measures affecting imports of retreaded tyres (WT/DS332/AB/R, Appellate Body Report). DSR 2007:IV, 1527.

Water Use and Rights

United Nations treaties guarantee the human right to water. Although states must fulfill this human right and businesses must respect the state's obligation, approximately 900 million people around the world do not have access to safe drinking water. Despite growing awareness of the need for sustainable water use by companies, increasing global population and inequitable access to water will create controversy and lead to conflict.

All human beings are born with equal and inalienable rights and duties. The right to water is an implicit part of the right to an adequate standard of living and the right to the highest attainable standard of physical and mental health, both of which are protected by the International Covenant on Economic, Social and Cultural Rights, adopted by the United Nations in 1966. The human right to water is explicit in two United Nations human rights treaties: the Convention on the Elimination of All Forms of Discrimination against Women (1979) and the Convention on the Rights of the Child (1989). The Geneva Conventions (1949, 1977) guarantee the protection of this right during armed conflict.

The United Nations Committee on Economic, Social and Cultural Rights (CESCR) monitors the implementation of the International Covenant on Economic, Social and Cultural Rights, and in its General Comment 15 on the right to water in 2002, CESCR stated that "the water supply for each person must be sufficient and continuous for personal and domestic uses."

About thirty governments (including South Africa, Uruguay, and Ecuador) have explicitly recognized the right to water in their constitutions or national laws. These states have three types of obligations (World Water Council 2005):

- Respect: Government must refrain from unfairly interfering with people's access to water (for example, disconnecting their water supply).

- Protect: Government must protect people's access to water from interference by others and provide an effective remedy for those who are denied this right (for example, when third parties set unaffordable prices for access to water).

- Fulfill: Government must take all possible steps with available resources to realize people's right to water (for example, passing legislation and implementing programs to increase access to water and monitor progress toward achieving this right).

As such, this explicit recognition aims to ensure water for all and gives the poorest and most excluded consumers a voice to hold governments accountable for their obligations. In 2006, 93 percent of the population in South Africa had access to safe drinking water, according to the World Health Organization (WHO) and United Nations Children's Fund (UNICEF) Joint Monitoring Programme (JMP) for Water Supply and Sanitation (2008). Nevertheless, around the world approximately 900 million people currently do not have access to this right to water for drinking, personal sanitation, washing of clothes, food preparation, or personal and household hygiene (WHO and UNICEF JMP 2008).

The Role of Business

Those states that have recognized the right to water have a duty to ensure that everyone enjoys access without discrimination. While states have overall responsibility for ensuring that the right to water is realized, each individual state determines the manner in which services are provided, managed, or regulated to meet its obligations. The right does not prescribe the particular model for service delivery, the role of public and private sectors, or the role of civil society.

An emerging area of debate relates to whether water as a right is at odds with the view of water as profit: who guarantees the right when government confers water provision to a private company? When rights are in place and prioritized, are governments equipped to adequately regulate them? The Dublin Principles recognize that water has an economic value in all its competing uses and should be recognized as an economic good (International Conference on Water and the Environment 1992). A WHO and UNICEF cost-benefit analysis showed that every dollar invested in improved drinking water and sanitation services could yield economic benefits of four to thirty-four dollars (2005, 4). Managing water as an economic good is claimed to be an important way of achieving efficient and equitable use, and of encouraging conservation and protection of water resources.

CESCR's General Comment 15 makes clear that having a right to water does not mean having a right to free water, but the water must be:

- safe (of adequate quality)
- accessible (within safe physical reach and affordable)
- sufficient (adequate, continuous, water supply for personal/domestic uses)

Some private water providers, including Suez Environment, have explicitly recognized the right to water: "We see progress towards universal access to water and sanitation as one of the raisons d'être of a private water operator" (Suez Environment 2007, 1). In addition, PepsiCo adopted a human-right-to-water policy for its domestic and overseas operations in 2009. The announcement committed PepsiCo to respecting the right to sufficient clean water, as well as individuals' rights to be involved in the development of processes that extract water from their communities (PepsiCo Inc. 2009). Such recognition is not just altruistic; it is also driven by the enlightened self-interest of a company that intends to operate over the long term. Consideration of water uses and water rights can decrease the costs of operations in water-scarce areas, increase profit margins, mitigate risks to operations (including social, economic, regulatory, and reputational risks), and ensure that communities give companies the social license to operate (Morikawa, Morrison, and Gleick 2007).

Thus, companies have legal and moral obligations to operate in ways that do not undermine the state's obligation to respect, protect, and fulfill human rights. John Ruggie, the United Nations special representative on the issue of human rights and transnational corporations and other business enterprises, has developed a framework that outlines the state's general duty to protect human rights and the responsibility of business to respect human rights (Ruggie 2008; Morikawa, Morrison, and Gleick 2007).

Raising Awareness of Unsustainable Practices

Concepts such as *virtual water*, *water footprints*, and *water offsetting* have been developed to discuss how domestic, industrial, environmental, and agricultural uses of water contribute to water stress or environmental impacts.

Virtual water (or embodied water) is a measure of the total water used in production of a good or service. For instance, one cup of coffee requires 140 liters of water to grow, produce, package, and ship the beans. That is roughly the same amount of water that an average person in England uses daily for drinking and household needs. Proponents of this concept believe that consumption will be cut, and sustainability will improve, if consumers are aware of how much water is used to produce everyday items.

Companies are using the *water footprint*—an indicator of the total volume of fresh water that is used to produce the goods and services consumed by an individual or community or produced by the business—to better understand water sustainability issues in their operations and supply chain. For instance, the water footprint of SABMiller's beers in South Africa and the Czech Republic has been measured as equivalent to 155 liters of water for every liter of beer (SABMiller and WWF 2009).

The *water-neutral* or *water-offset* concept (similar to that of carbon-neutral or carbon-offset) requires that individuals and corporations undertaking water-consuming activities make their activity "water neutral" by investing in water-saving technology, water-conservation or environmental-protection measures, wastewater treatment, and clean water supply to the poor. Such enlightened self-interest will contribute to the company operating over the long term. For instance, PepsiCo India is working to achieve a positive water balance by reducing water use in manufacturing plants, saving water through reuse and recycling initiatives, constructing rainwater-harvesting structures on manufacturing facilities, and implementing projects like the direct seeding of paddy fields in Punjab, Rajasthan, Tamilnadu, and Karnataka.

Concepts like virtual water, water footprints, and water neutrality or water offsetting might be useful for raising awareness—informing consumers of how much water is used in products and services—but conclusions drawn from such measurements often need clarification. It is necessary to assess products both for how much water they use and the impact on the country where they are produced. For example, a high-water-content item imported from a dry country should be rated worse than one from a place where water is abundantly available. If labeling products to inform consumers of the amount of water used in their production leads to boycotting, negative consequences for economic growth and poverty reduction could result. It remains to be seen whether these tools are attempts at corporate "bluewashing" (equivalent of greenwashing for the water and sanitation sector)—or whether concern for sustainable water use will remain a long-term business concern.

One potential mechanism to assist companies—both directly and through supply chains—in the development, implementation, and disclosure of water sustainability and sanitation policies and practices is the CEO Water Mandate. This public-private initiative was launched in July 2007 by the United Nations Global Compact, the government of Sweden, and a group of companies. As of 11 November 2009, it had fifty-eight signatories. The CEO Water Mandate expects industrial water users to make a commitment to water stewardship and to ensure that their activities have a favorable impact on the right of access to water (for example, undertaking a human rights impact assessment before setting up a facility; ensuring access to information and community participation; abiding by relevant laws, regulations, and policies; ensuring that wastewater and industrial byproducts are treated to minimize their impact on communities, aquatic systems, and water sources).

Controversies

Globally, roughly 10 percent of all water is used for domestic purposes, 20 percent is used for industrial uses, and 70 percent is used for agriculture. Changing certainty of water resource availability affects all water-using sectors—agriculture, hydropower, water supply and sanitation, and the environment.

Water Scarcity

While the global population is expected to rise significantly, accessible freshwater supplies are not. Inequitable access to water (both supply services and the natural resource) results in unmet water needs and causes economic, social, and environmental problems. In addition, it is expected to trigger conflict in and between countries. For example, as water scarcity becomes more apparent, instances of violence and conflict over water availability will increase at the global level and down—for example, in the Middle East region (Zeitoun 2008), in the country of Darfur (Tearfund 2007), and at the local level in the Sanjay Nagar slum in Bhopal, where family members who drilled

a hole in a water pipe to collect water during a drought were murdered by angry neighbors who accused them of stealing water (Chamberlain 2009).

Sub-Saharan Africa is more at risk from water scarcity and water stress than other regions. In 2006, only 58 percent of the population of sub-Saharan Africa had clean drinking water (JMP 2008). And the United Nations Environment Programme (UNEP) estimates that by 2025, up to twenty-five African nations—roughly half the continent's countries—will suffer from a greater combination of increased water scarcity and water stress. Experts recommend that countries at the greatest risk of climate variability require significant investment in rainwater harvesting and water storage: yet Ethiopia has only 43 cubic meters of storage capacity per capita (World Bank 2009), less than 1 percent of the 5,000 cubic meters of storage capacity per capita of the United States and Australia (World Bank 2009). In Kenya, flooding in 1997 and 1998 cost the country 11 percent of its gross domestic product (GDP), while the drought in 1999 and 2000 cost the country 16 percent of its GDP. Better water storage could have prevented that drought from significantly affecting Kenya's economy (Malkiewicz 2008).

Industrial and Agricultural Uses

Without sufficient water, agriculture and industry are impossible. Agricultural development has the potential to increase economic growth, yet just 3.7 percent of arable land in sub-Saharan Africa is irrigated (compared with 26 percent in Asia) (UNECA 2003, 2). The Commission for Africa recommends a doubling of this area by 2015 to help poor farmers cope with rainfall variability and increase their productivity (2005).

In relation to soil, water, and agriculture, commentators refer to *blue water*, the water in rivers and streams, and *green water*—which accounts for two-thirds of water supply—the water that is in the soil and available to plants. Thus water access and water rights are often linked to land distribution. Yet this is a source of great inequity in many societies. Nine out of ten poor people in rural areas are smallholder farmers who depend on plots of less than two hectares for their food. And while women perform the majority of the world's agricultural work, they often do not have secure land tenure since customary laws often prevent women from inheriting land. The right to property, land reform, and small-scale agricultural improvements (such as drip irrigation) offer a solution to

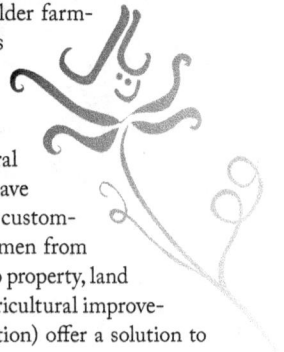

water stress and could play an important role in ensuring access to a dependable food supply.

Along with concern about developed countries using the water resources of some of the world's driest countries (manifest in measurement tools such as water footprints), more recently alarm has been raised about agri-colonialism—the acquisition of arable land and water by water-and-resource-scarce countries (for instance, those in the Middle East) in other more water-abundant countries (for example, Madagascar or Sudan) to ensure their own food security.

Similarly, beverage companies have been criticized for exacerbating water shortages in regions that suffer from water scarcity (Girard 2005). Extraction of groundwater for soft-drink and bottled-water production can compete with smallholder farmers' dependence on water for their livelihoods, in some cases leaving them unable to irrigate their lands and exposing poor households to the risk of losing their livelihoods. Complaints have also been made that these companies have contaminated groundwater, which further depletes the quantity of available usable water.

Traditional or Customary Users of Water

Customary law and customary water rights, particularly in rural areas and those countries where customary law constitutes a legitimate source of law, can also have a significant role in water resource management. Where water is scarce, the impact of inequitable distribution of water use and rights can be a cause of stress in communities. For instance, conflict may arise where official mechanisms for regulating the extraction and use of water resources through government permits or licenses conflict with customary practices. Moreover, conflict may result where access to safe drinking water for personal and domestic uses is prioritized over agricultural uses or where there are tensions between sedentary and nomadic pastoralists competing for water and grazing land.

Water is central to the well-being and survival of livestock, a key asset and often a source of income in many communities for providing traction power, manure for crop growing, and milk and meat for nutrition. In the case of a drought, nomadic and sedentary herders lose their livestock and their livelihoods, leaving them with no financial resources to acquire food.

Water, Food, and Energy Nexus

Almost 70 per cent of all available freshwater is used for agriculture. According to the United Nations Environmental

Programme (UNEP), approximately 20 percent of worldwide water use is industrial (UNEP 2002). Increasing population will need more food and more electricity, meaning that two of the largest water users (water for agriculture and storage for hydropower generation—19 percent of the total electricity product, according to Walter Hauenstein [2005]) are in potential competition for a predictable supply. Investment in hydropower and irrigation has a clear role to play in fostering economic development. Yet economic development, industrialization, population growth, and rapid urbanization can, in turn, increase pressure on the quantity of available water and create tensions about how water is assigned to new urban and industrial development.

Sociocultural Activities

Water plays a role in many religious and cultural ceremonies or beliefs (for instance, the ceremony of baptism for Christians, the cleansing ritual of *abhisheka* for Hindus, and ablutions like *ghusl* and *wudu* for Muslims). Some cultures believe in water animism—that river water, lakes, and springs are living and possess souls. But there is still very limited understanding of how the use of water for cultural and religious activities fits within a rights-based approach (Zenani and Mistri 2005).

Transboundary Water

Conflicts over water in regions where water resources are shared between countries, such as those in the Nile Basin, have economic and political implications for food and water security in those river basins. Increasing cooperation and investment in the fair allocation of water resources will help reduce water scarcity and conflict and promote economic development. Yet questions remain about how to regulate, govern, and implement treaties aimed at managing cross-boundary resources.

Outlook for the Next Decade

The realization and implementation of the human right to water has yet to be evaluated for the improvements it has made to drinking-water supply in developing countries. Research is required to establish what the right means, the difference it makes to access, and the impact of context on the realization and implementation of the right. For instance, Article 25 of the UN's Universal Declaration of Human Rights (adopted in 1948) acknowledged the following: "Everyone has the right to a standard of living adequate for the health and well-being of himself and his family, including food." Yet the 2008 Global Hunger Index stated that thirty-three countries, mostly in Africa, face a "grave" threat of hunger. Altogether the number of people chronically hungry worldwide rose from 848 million in 2007 to 923 million people in 2008—about one-sixth of the world's population (von Grebmer et al. 2008).

Right to Sanitation

One of the targets of the United Nations Millennium Development Goals (MDGs) is to halve the proportion of people without access to basic sanitation by 2015—that is, sanitation that prevents human contact with human waste. Yet in 2006, 2.5 billion people around the world did not have access to a basic toilet (WHO and UNICEF JMP 2008, 2). At the current rate of progress in sub-Saharan Africa, this target will not be met for another century. Lack of sanitation has implications for health, dignity, education, and economic growth.

Access to sanitation benefits the economy: studies have shown that for every dollar invested in sanitation, the economic return is nine dollars (WHO and UNICEF 2005). Lack of sanitation also has direct consequences for individual businesses: companies that do not provide accessible, sufficient, suitable, and separate sanitation facilities for men and women prevent employees from performing their jobs effectively and interfere with the employees' right to work in healthy and safe working conditions. Women are particularly affected by a lack of sanitation, especially during menstruation and pregnancy.

Water Use and Climate Change

The impacts of climate change for water use and water rights must also be considered. The Stern Review on the Economics of Climate Change (HM Treasury 2006) and the fourth Intergovernmental Panel on Climate Change (IPCC 2009) Assessment Report, published in 2007, both noted that the majority of the impacts resulting from climate change would be experienced through the impact on water. By 2025, it is estimated that 3 billion people will live in water-stressed countries—75 to 250 million in Africa alone (UNDP 2006). The Intergovernmental Panel on Climate Change estimates that by 2080 an extra 1.8 billion people—a quarter of the world's current population—could be living and dying without enough water. In just twenty-five years the glaciers in the Himalayas,

which provide water for three-quarters of a billion people, could disappear entirely. And although not clearly attributable to climate change, El Niño events have become more common in recent decades, bringing droughts and heavy rain that result in flooding. Such water shortages, droughts, and floods result in damage to crops, livestock, infrastructure, and homes; increased drylands; lost biodiversity; declining water quality; changing patterns of pests and disease; and reduced economic growth.

Lower and more erratic rainfall together with water shortages will increase the difficulty of accessing safe drinking water and basic sanitation, especially for the poorest and most vulnerable people. This has serious implications for MDG targets to halve the proportion of people without sustainable access to safe drinking water and basic sanitation by 2015. And its consequences for water use and water rights require further investigation.

Sue CAVILL and M. SOHAIL
*WEDC (Water, Engineering and Development Centre),
Loughborough University*

See also in the *Berkshire Encyclopedia of Sustainability* Agriculture; Climate Change Disclosure; Ecolabeling; Ecosystem Services; Energy Industries—Hydroelectric; Energy Industries—Wave and Tidal; Health, Public and Environmental; Human Rights; Public–Private Partnerships; United Nations Global Compact

FURTHER READING

Chamberlain, Gethin. (2009, July 12). India prays for rain as water wars break out. Retrieved October 30, 2009, from http://www.guardian.co.uk/world/2009/jul/12/india-water-supply-bhopal

Commission for Africa. (2005). *Our common interest: Report of the Commission for Africa.* Retrieved October 30, 2009, from http://allafrica.com/sustainable/resources/view/00010595.pdf

Food and Agriculture Organization of the United Nations (FAO). (2009, June 19). 1.02 billion people hungry: One-sixth of humanity undernourished—more than ever before. Retrieved October 30, 2009, from http://www.fao.org/news/story/en/item/20568/icode

Girard, Richard. (2005). *Corporate profile: Coca-Cola Company—inside the real thing.* Retrieved October 30, 2009, from http://www.polarisinstitute.org/files/Coke%20profile%20August%2018.pdf

Hauenstein, Walter. (2005, November). Hydropower and climate change—A reciprocal relation. *Mountain Research and Development,* 25(4), 321–325. Retrieved January 5, 2010, from http://www.bioone.org/doi/pdf/10.1659/0276-4741(2005)025%5B0321:HACCRR%5D2.0.CO%3B2?

HM Treasury. (2006). Stern review final report. Retrieved October 30, 2009 from http://www.hm-treasury.gov.uk/sternreview_index.htm

Intergovernmental Panel on Climate Change (IPCC). (2009). The IPCC assessment reports. Retrieved October 30, 2009, from http://www.ipcc.ch/

International Conference on Water and the Environment (ICWE). (1992).The Dublin statement on water and sustainable development. Retrieved October 30, 2009, from http://www.un-documents.net/h2o-dub.htm

Malkiewicz, Tadeusz. (2008). Capacity building in developing countries as the aftermath of natural disasters: South-south support initiative. Retrieved October 30, 2009, from http://www.worldwatercongress2008.org/resource/authors/abs90_article.pdf

Morikawa, Mari; Morrison, Jason; & Gleick, Peter. (2007). Corporate reporting on water: A review of eleven global industries. Retrieved October 30, 2009, from http://www.pacinst.org/reports/water_reporting/corporate_reporting_on_water.pdf

PepsiCo Inc. (2009). Water. Retrieved October 30, 2009, from http://www.pepsico.com/Purpose/Environment/Water.html

Ruggie, John. (2008). Protect, respect and remedy: A framework for business and human rights. Retrieved October 30, 2009, from http://www.reports-and-materials.org/Ruggie-report-7-Apr-2008.pdf

SABMiller, & World Wildlife Fund (WWF). (2009). Water footprinting: Identifying & addressing water risks in the value chain. Retrieved October 30, 2009, from http://www.sabmiller.com/files/reports/water_footprinting_report.pdf

Suez Environment. (2007). *Human rights and access to drinking water and sanitation.* Retrieved October 30, 2009, from http://www2.ohchr.org/english/issues/water/contributions/PrivateSector/Suez.pdf

Tearfund. (2007). Darfur: Relief in a vulnerable environment. Retrieved October 30, 2009, from http://workplan.unsudanig.org/mande/assessments/docs/Relief%20in%20a%20vulnerable%20envirionment%20final.pdf

United Nations. (2009). The universal declaration of human rights. Retrieved October 30, 2009, from http://www.un.org/en/documents/udhr/

United Nations Committee on Economic, Social and Cultural Rights (CESCR). (2002). Substantive issues arising in the implementation of the international covenant on economic, social and cultural rights. General Comment No. 15 (2002) The right to water (arts. 11 and 12 of the International Covenant on Economic, Social and Cultural Rights). Retrieved October 30, 2009, from http://www.unhchr.ch/tbs/doc.nsf/0/a5458d1d1bbd/13fe1256cc400389e94/$FILE/G0340229.pdf

United Nations Development Programme (UNDP). (2006). Human development report 2006: Beyond scarcity: Power, poverty and the global water crisis. Retrieved October 30, 2009, from http://hdr.undp.org/en/reports/global/hdr2006

United Nations Economic Commission for Africa (UNECA). (2003, September 17). The state of food security in Africa progress report 2003. Retrieved January 12, 2010, from http://www.uneca.org/csd/CSDIII_The%20State%20of%20Food%20Security%20in%20Africa%202003%20as%20sent%20for%20approval.doc

United Nations Environment Programme (UNEP). (2002). Vital water graphics. Retrieved January 5, 2010, from http://www.unep.org/dewa/assessments/ecosystems/water/vitalwater/15.htm

United Nations Global Compact. (n.d.). The CEO water mandate. Retrieved October 30, 2009, from http://www.unglobalcompact.org/Issues/Environment/CEO_Water_Mandate/

Von Grebmer, Klaus; Fritschel, Heidi; Nestorova, Bella; Olofinbiyi, Tolulope; Pandya-Lorch, Rajul; & Yohannes, Yisehac. (2008). *Global hunger index: The challenge of hunger 2008.* Retrieved October 30, 2009, from http://www.ifpri.org/sites/default/files/publications/ghi08.pdf

The World Bank. (2009). Shoring up water infrastructure: Water-stressed India needs to shore up its water infrastructure. Retrieved October 30, 2009, from http://go.worldbank.org/I7M6HR9BP0

World Health Organization (WHO) & United Nations Children's Fund (UNICEF). (2005). *Water for life: Making it happen.* Retrieved October 30, 2009, from http://www.who.int/water_sanitation_health/waterforlife.pdf

World Health Organization (WHO) & United Nations Children's Fund (UNICEF) Joint Monitoring Programme for Water Supply and Sanitation (JMP). (2008). *Progress on drinking water and sanitation: Special focus on sanitation.* Retrieved October 30, 2009, from http://www.wssinfo.org/en/40_MDG2008.html

World Water Council. (2005). Frequently asked questions: Which obligations for state parties? Retrieved October 30, 2009, from http://www.worldwatercouncil.org/index.php?id=1764&L=0target%253D_blank%22%20onfocus%3D%22blurLink%28this%29%3B

Zeitoun, Mark. (2008). *Power and water in the Middle East—The hidden politics of the Palestinian-Israeli water conflict.* London: I.B. Tauris.

Zenani, Vuyisile, & Mistri, Asha. (2005). *A desktop study on the cultural and religious uses of water: Using regional case studies from South Africa.* Retrieved October 30, 2009, from http://www.dwaf.gov.za/Documents/Other/RMP/SAADFCulturalWaterUseJun05.pdf

World Constitutionalism

World constitutionalism has its roots in international documents such as the UN Charter. Its advocates seek to establish a holistic and coherent global constitution that sets out fundamental norms and values by which all nations and jurisdictions can abide. This concept has also been explored in the international environmental law regime to assess the scope for an international environmental constitution.

The twenty-first century is witnessing a growing interest by legal and other scholars in the concept of world or global constitutionalism. World constitutionalism advocates for the application of constitutionalist principles in the international legal sphere with a basic view to improving the fairness and effectiveness of the international law regime. In essence it entails the integration of constitutionalist features in international law. This would essentially require the existence of an international community, an international value system, and some structures for enforcement (de Wet 2007, 3). The concept draws on the global trend toward more coherence in constitution making on a national level.

Origins and Development

Traditionally, the term *constitution* resides in the domestic realm. While it has been said that Cicero (106–43 BCE) was the first true constitutionalist, the notion of a constitution really emerged much later, during the eighteenth and nineteenth centuries, often in response to social or political revolutions. In essence, a constitution is an instrument through which a community creates some form of fundamental legal order that sets out the governance model in a given state and regulates the relationship between the state and its citizens. Some constitutions are written as a

single codified document, and some, such as the British constitution, are not. But all constitutions contain a number of substantive and procedural (rule of law) elements such as a bill of rights, separation among the powers of the organs of state, onerous amendment procedures, and judicial review of the actions of the legislative and executive arms of the state. It is clear that some of these elements, such as the bill of rights, serve to protect citizens from the threat of tyrannical states. Constitutions thus seek to limit public power but may, in fact, serve a dual function, both constituting and constraining power (Bodansky 2009, 572) in that they set out *constitutive* rules defining the basic values, institutions, and decision-making processes of a political community.

World constitutionalism is, however, constitutionalization: the emergence, creation, and identification of constitution-like elements beyond the state (Milewicz 2009, 420). The idea of constitutionalism beyond the state is not altogether alien, as illustrated by the constitutionalization process within the European Union (EU) that resulted in the Treaty Establishing a Constitution for Europe. This treaty has already taken the process of constitutional architecture beyond the classic conditions of a constitution, "namely the inherent association of a constitution and constitutional law with state- and peoplehood Instead, the European constitutional order envisages competing (national) polities within a larger polity order in the form of shared values and political organization" (de Wet 2007, 4).

Scholars have argued that precedents for a global constitution already exist. Some, such as Bardo Fassbender, a professor of international law, believe that the United Nations Charter (the Charter), which was adopted as an international treaty in the post–World War II era, operates to articulate the fundamental rules of the global order and incorporates core elements akin to a constitution. These elements include the governance structures, a duty upon members to fulfill obligations under the Charter, the prohibition of the use of force, and the obligation to promote and respect human rights. Fassbender argues that as a "visible document," the Charter is an authoritative statement of both the fundamental rights and responsibilities of the members of the international community and the values to which this community is committed. The Charter created a "constitutional moment" at a time when nations, responding to the aftermath of two world wars, sought to move away from continual international aggression. Another such moment now exists to create an impetus for a world constitution (Slaughter and Burke-White 2002). This current constitutional moment stems from the so-called war against terror and the resulting international fear and insecurities. Some scholars make a case that the current constitutional moment is based on universal threats to the environment and to sustainability, including climate change and loss of biodiversity. These conditions set the scene for a discussion on the existence of an international environmental constitution.

An International Environmental Constitution

There is no longer one international legal regime, and recent years have, in fact, seen a growth in the existence of sectoral international regimes. Some authors, as a result, question whether it is still possible to talk of one international community and one international value system (de Wet 2007, 4). Instead, these authors "see the emergence of a variety of functional constitutional regimes or 'networks' . . . characterized by the absence of hierarchy between their respective normative systems, which would determine the outcome of any inter-regime conflicts" (de Wet 2007, 6). One such sector is the multilateral trade regime epitomized by the World Trade Organization (WTO). The WTO, because of its model of treaty making through negotiation rounds and its effective dispute settlement system, is arguably one international institution that has achieved substantial success in terms of adherence to international agreements. The WTO, therefore, provides some scope for world constitutionalism in its sphere, safeguarding trade interests and not environmental interests.

An international environmental constitution does not exist, however, and multilateral environmental agreements are not necessarily designed to act as constitutions; while they establish ongoing systems of governance to address specific issues that involve the creation of institutions, rules, and procedures, they still require the consensus of the participating governments with regard to any decision making and are, in fact, state-driven (Bodansky 2009, 574–577).

The general principles of international environmental law—such as the all-important principle of sustainability, the duty to prevent cross-border harm, the "polluter pays" principle, the precautionary principle, and the principle of common but differentiated responsibility—may represent the core value system that is required for an international environmental constitution (Bodansky 2009, 580). These principles currently seem not only weak but also vague, and although they serve to structure international discourse on environmental problems, they have so many different meanings that they hardly exercise real constraint on the behavior of states or international institutions. International environmental law also lacks the procedural and governance systems required for constitutionalism.

The Earth Charter, a declaration of fundamental ethical principles for establishing a sustainable global society that has been endorsed by various civil society organizations, provides at a minimum a guide not only for an international environmental constitution, but for world constitutionalism. Ecological integrity is one of the major themes, but "the Earth Charter also recognizes that the goals of ecological protection, the eradication of poverty, equitable economic development, and respect for human rights, democracy, and peace are interdependent and indivisible. It provides, therefore, a new inclusive, integrated ethical framework to guide the transition to a sustainable future" (Earth Charter Initiative n.d.) as it reflects the concept of sustainable development with its three pillars of environmental, social, and economic equity.

Resistance to World Constitutionalism

Scholars, international lawmakers, and social activists don't always agree on the need for or the suitability of a world constitution. World constitutionalism is sometimes perceived to be threatening for jurisprudential, ethical, cultural, social, and political reasons (Johnston 2005, 19–20). Jurisprudential resistance stems from the belief that constitutions should ideally operate at a national level at which governments can be held directly accountable to the people they serve. There are also ethical concerns about the unrepresentative status of international judges who are called upon to adjudicate international disputes.

Cultural concerns stem from the theory of cultural relativism—the notion that an individual's beliefs and cultural practices should be understood by others from the perspective of that individual's own culture and not from the perspective of the dominant (often Western) culture. The fear is that a global constitution would somehow reflect a certain set of ideals. Social activists similarly oppose the idea of a world constitution, viewing it as a way of granting more power to states. Finally political objections are reflected in the reluctance of states to give up their sovereign powers.

Scholars do agree that a need exists for a global constitution founded on the principles of sound governance, a respect for human rights, and sustainability. This would provide normative powers to existing regimes, such as the international human rights regime and the international environmental law regime. Whether independent nations will ultimately agree to renounce some of their sovereign powers in favor of a world constitution remains to be seen.

Loretta Annelise FERIS
University of Cape Town

See also in the *Berkshire Encyclopedia of Sustainability* Common Heritage of Mankind Principle; Customary International Law; Environmental Law, Soft vs. Hard; Intergenerational Equity; International Law; Precautionary Principle; Polluter Pays Principle; Principle-Based Regulation; Transboundary Water Law; United Nations—Overview of Conventions and Agreements; Weak vs. Strong Sustainability Debate

FURTHER READINGS

Besson, Samantha. (2009). Whose constitution(s)? International law, constitutionalism, and democracy. In Jeffery L. Dunoff & Joel P. Trachtman (Eds.), *Ruling the world?* (pp. 376–380). New York: Cambridge University Press.

Bodansky, Daniel. (2009). Is there an international environmental constitution? *Indiana Journal of Global Legal Studies, 16*, 569–570.

Charter of the United Nations. (2010). Retrieved October 30, 2010, from www.un.org/en/documents/charter/index.shtml

de Wet, E. (2007). The emerging international constitutional order: The implications of hierarchy in international law for the coherence and legitimacy of international decision-making. *PER, 2*, 1–27. Retrieved November 27, 2010, from http://ajol.info/index.php/pelj/article/viewFile/43435/26971

Earth Charter Initiative. (n.d.). What is the Earth Charter? Retrieved November 28, 2010, at http://www.earthcharterinaction.org/content/pages/What-is-the-Earth-Charter%3F.html

Fassbender, Bardo. (2008). The United Nations Charter as constitution of the international community. *Columbia Journal of Transnational Law, 38*, 530–619.

Johnston, Douglas M. (2005). World constitutionalism in the theory of international law. In Ronald St. John Macdonald & Douglas M. Johnston (Eds.), *Towards world constitutionalism* (pp. 19–20). Leiden, The Netherlands: Martinus Nijhoff Publishers.

Kennedy, David. (2009). The mystery of global governance. In Jeffery L. Dunoff & Joel P. Trachtman (Eds.), *Ruling the world?* (pp. 37–68). New York: Cambridge University Press.

Milewicz, Karolina. (2009). Emerging patterns of global constitutionalization: Toward a conceptual framework. *Indiana Journal of Global Legal Studies, 16*(2), 413–436.

Paulus, Andreas L. (2009). The international legal system as a constitution. In Jeffery L. Dunoff & Joel P. Trachtman (Eds.), *Ruling the world?* (pp. 69–109). New York: Cambridge University Press.

Peters, Anne. (2006). Compensatory constitutionalism: The function and potential of fundamental international norms and structures. *Leiden Journal of International Law, 19*(3), 579–610.

Peters, Anne. (2009). The merits of global constitutionalism. *Indiana Journal of Global Legal Studies, 16*(2), 397–411.

Slaughter, Anne-Marie, & Burke-White, William. (2002). An international constitutional moment. *Harvard International Law Journal, 43*, 1–20.

Glossary of Terms

Although we have defined legal terms as they appear throughout the articles in this book, we have also included a glossary of basic terms used across broad legal fields.

ad hoc: Ad hoc refers to something (such as a committee or a law) formed to address a specific purpose. Ad hoc laws might include those of limited jurisdiction that are created one at a time to form a corpus of laws on a subject, as opposed to one comprehensive law covering all applicable areas. Ad hoc can also refer to committees in organizations or governments that are created, often temporarily, to handle situations not covered by any existing groups.

civil law: Civil law is a system inspired by laws codified in the sixth century under the Byzantine Roman emperor Justinian and further codified under Napoleon Bonaparte in the nineteenth century. Nations and states establish self-regulatory civil laws pertaining to ordinary matters (as opposed to criminal or military law) and which follow predetermined rules that are not subject to interpretation by judges. Civil law is most important in Europe, Central and South America, and parts of Asia and Africa, and is the basis for most international law.

common law: Common law is based on court rulings rather than on legislation enacted by legislative bodies. Under common law judges are obliged to rule in accordance with precedents set by similar cases.

Common law is practiced in Britain and its former possessions—the United States, Canada, Australia, New Zealand, South Africa, India, and Pakistan, among others.

contract law: Contract law is a body of law that regulates and enforces promises and exchanges, for either immediate or future performance, between two or more consenting parties; it guarantees a form of legal remedy if one or more of the parties break an agreement. It is rooted in the premise that promises made are to be kept.

convention: In international law a convention is an agreement, compact, or treaty entered into by two or more parties, usually nations, to address a specific subject or problem. International law largely comprises the provisions of international conventions.

criminal law: Also known as penal law, criminal law involves a societal wrong—a crime against the social order. Although it may only affect one person, criminal law is distinguished from other types of law by the prosecutor, which is always the government rather than another party (as in tort or contract law).

customary law: Customary, or general, international law is based on the customs or practices that have become widely accepted by a society. In international law, if the initial act of one state becomes the practice of "many," then it can be recognized, usually by international courts or tribunals or in the foreign policies of states, as a positive rule of customary international law. The law only applies, though, to those states that consent to recognize it as law (opinio juris).

"hard" law: "Hard" law is the body of international law that is legally binding and as such bears consequences for noncompliance that involve legal response. "Hard law" generally covers treaties, customary international law, and United Nations Security Council resolutions. It is used most often to contrast "soft" law.

intellectual property law: Intellectual property law endeavors to protect the rights of people who have generated and lay claim to (often intangible) creations such as music, software, business techniques, or inventions. It includes patent, copyright, trademark, and trade secret law.

international law: International law provides a structure for dealings among international and transnational governments. It is generally considered a body of law since most countries follow international law most of the time, and because those countries that violate its norms do frequently suffer consequences. Existing international law generally lacks the capacity to enact laws binding on all nations, enforce existing laws, and arbitrate through judicial tribunals that have broad jurisdiction or the power to issue binding and enforceable decrees.

natural law: Natural law is composed of rights that are determined to be universal to everyone and are drawn from human nature and/or religious creed. The right to life is primary among standards recognized as natural law. It is often contrasted with positive law.

normative: Normative, as it is regarded in law, is used to describe how something should exist based on a particular value or norm. It describes principles, laws, and statements that are prescriptive (how it ought to be), rather than descriptive (how it is). The term also implies the capacity of law, especially a so-called soft law, to directly or indirectly shape the conduct of the persons or agencies it addresses.

nuisance law: Nuisance, as a legal concept or principle, refers to an activity or person that causes harm, particularly harm that violates rights. Nuisance law especially provides a legal remedy for owners and users of land who are disrupted in their use and enjoyment of it. Nuisance law also instructs landowners to use their property in ways that cause no legal harm to other landowners or the public.

positive law: Positive law refers to statutes that people have come up with (or posited), as opposed to those determined to be inherent to all people (natural law). Positive law covers the vast majority of laws that have been created, with the exclusion of those that are widely accepted as universal rights (such as the right to live).

property law: Property law is the body of law that provides regulations and guidance to reinforce the concept that property exists and can be claimed by parties. Property law includes real property, intellectual property, and private property.

protocol: In international law, a protocol is typically a type of international agreement that provides direction on how a situation should be conducted or how a problem should be solved. Protocols often supplement existing treaties or international agreements by adding amendments or provisions that are ratified by signatories. This especially occurs in cases where the original treaty does not provide a specific course of action for ratifying nations.

real property law: Real property law refers to laws created by the government to protect certain interests in land or certain resources such as trees, water, oil, or minerals that are relatively immovable. When a person or group has a legally recognized interest under real property law, they have the exclusive right to possess, use, and transfer land or resources.

soft law: Soft law refers to agreements made by parties internationally that are not legally binding, which can include United Nations General Assembly resolutions, action plans, or declarations. The reaction to breaches of soft law norms is sociopolitical rather than legal in nature (in contrast to hard law, which can be legally enforced). Soft law gains its strength, however, from an international political-moral order.

tort law: Tort law involves a civil wrong—a harm done by a private party to a private party—and is typically distinguished from criminal law and contract law. Someone who is harmed by a private party may bring a suit (i.e., act as a "plaintiff") in tort to collect damages from the tortfeasor (or "defendant"). The defendant is only responsible for compensating the plaintiff if it is established that the defendant breached a legal duty to the plaintiff, which resulted in damages. Tort law often covers traffic accidents, negligence, false imprisonment, and some environmental pollution.

Index

Bold entries and page numbers denote article titles in this book.

Bold entries and page numbers denote article titles in this book.

J

Jamaica
    environmental agencies in, *70*
    environmental law in, 75
Japan, 48, 59
    Environmental Agency *(kankyocho)*, 81
    Kyoto Protocol, 82
Jeddah Convention, 31
Joint Convention on the Safety of Spent Fuel
        Management, 209
Jordan, 190
judge-made common law, in Canada, 125
jus cogens, 29

K

Kazakhstan
    air quality management and protection, 109
    energy and environment, 109, 110
    land management and protection, 108
Kennedy, John F., 182
Kenya, 192
Kilowatt, Reddy, 201
Kyoto Protocol, 2–3, 52, 53, 82, 85, 137, 171, 195
    Article, 6
Kyrgyzstan
    energy and errivonment, 109, 110
    land management and protection, 108
    water management and protection, 108, 109

L

land degradation, 196
landownership, 152–154
land tenure laws, 177–179
land use
    natural resources law, 154–155
Land Use Act of 1978 (Nigeria), 178
land use rights, 178
Laos, 192
Law of the Sea, 147–150
    fisheries conventions, 148–149
    marine environment, contemporary threats to, 150
    regional seas conventions, 149
    shipping and marine pollution, regulation of, 149
    1982 UN Law of the Sea Convention, 147–148
Law of the Sea Convention, 137
Law on Air Protection 1999 (Russia), 106
Law on Desert Prevention and Transformation 2002
    (China), 86

Law on Energy Conservation 2008 (China), 86
Law on Environmental Impact Assessments 2003
    (China), 86
Law on Environmental Protection 2002 (Russia), 106
Law on Handling of Wastes 1998 (Russia), 106
Law on Hydrometeorology 1998 (Russia), 106
Law on Mineral Resources 1986 (China), 86
Law on Minerals (Russia), 106
Law on Prevention and Control of Atmospheric
    Pollution 2000 (China), 86
Law on Prevention and Control of Environmental
    Pollution by Solid Waste 1996 (China), 86
Law on Prevention and Control of Pollution from
    Environmental Noise (China), 86
Law on Prevention and Control of Radioactive Pollution
    2003 (China), 86
Law on Prevention and Control of Water Pollution 1984
    (China), 86
Law on Promoting Circulation Economy 2009 (China), 86
Law on Promotion Cleaner Production 2003 (China), 86
Law on Specially Protected Areas 1995 (Russia), 106
Law on the Prevention and Control of Environmental
    Pollution by Solid Waste of 1995, 210
Law on the Protection of Wildlife 1989 (China), 86
Law on Water and Soil Conservation 1982 (China), 86
Law on Wildlife 1995 (Russia), 106
Laws of armed conflict, 135
Laws on Commercial Secrets 2004 (Russia), 106
Laws on State Secrets 1993 (Russia), 106
Lebanon, 190
legislation by reference, 148
Libya, 190
    framework environmental laws, 33
    General Agreement Between Libya and Tunisia on
        Marine Fishing, 32
lifecycle analysis (LCA), 19
limited territorial sovereignty, 190
Lisbon Treaty (2007), 89, 91
Local Government Act of 1974 (New Zealand), 67
Local Government Act of 2002 (LGA), 67
London Convention (1972), 149–150
Long-Range Transboundary Air Pollution
    (LRTAP), 195
Luxembourg, 190

M

Maastricht Treaty, 89, 173
Madrid Protocol, 48, 49, 50
Maltese proposal (1967), 22, 24
marine environment, 198
    contemporary threats to, 150
Marine Environment Protection Law of 1982 (China), 86

Bold entries and page numbers denote article titles in this book.

Bold entries and page numbers denote article titles in this book.

Image Credits

The illustrations used in this book come from many sources. There are photographs provided by Berkshire Publishing's staff and friends, by authors, and from archival sources. All known sources and copyright holders have been credited.

Bottom front cover photo is of fireflies (*Pyractomena borealis*) on an Iowa prairie, by Carl Kurtz.

Engraving illustrations of plants and insects by Maria Sibylla Merian (1647–1717).

Insect illustrations on pages 3 and 4 by Lydia Umney. Other illustrations courtesy of the Library of Congress and the New York Public Library.

Cover and page design by Anna Myers.

Front cover images, left-to-right:

1. *Dappled leaf, the Botanic Gardens at Smith College, Northampton, Massachusetts, USA.* Photo by Amy Siever.
2. *Salps in water near Cordell Bank, California, USA.* Photo courtesy of the Gulf of the Farallones National Marine Sanctuary.
3. *Rocks off Sheep Point Cove, Newport, Rhode Island, USA.* Photo by Amy Fredsall.

Back cover images, left-to-right:

1. *Prickly pear cacti and flowers, Red Rocks State Park, Sedona, Arizona, USA.* Photo by Amy Siever.
2. *Autumn view from Big Crow Mountain, Keene, New York, USA.* Photo by Amy Fredsall.
3. *Travertine terraces, Yellowstone National Park, Wyoming, USA.* Photo by Amy Siever.

Pages viii & 223, *Water lilies.* Photo by Carl Kurtz.

Page 1, *Bindweed.* Photo by Carl Kurtz.

Page 5, *Farm in the Connecticut River Valley, Hadley, Massachusetts, USA.* Photo by Bill Siever.

Page 10, *Pink sedum.* Photo by Anna Myers.

Pages 15, 21, 27, & 147, *Sunset, Hawaii, USA.* Photo by Zhang Xiaojin.

Pages 31, 36, 45, 52, 57, 63, 69, 77, 81, 89, 94, 99, 105, 112, 117, & 123, *Minnows in Jordan's Pond, Acadia National Park, Maine, USA.* Photo by Amy Siever.

Page 130, 134, 137, & 142, *Prickly pear cacti and flowers, Red Rocks State Park, Sedona, Arizona, USA.* Photo by Amy Siever.

Pages 151, 159, & 163, *Dappled leaf, the Botanic Gardens at Smith College, Northampton, Massachusetts, USA.* Photo by Amy Siever.

Pages 168 & 173, *Waterfall, Kent Falls State Park, Kent, Connecticut, USA.* Photo by Amy Fredsall.

Pages 176, *Autumn maple, Pound Ridge Reservation, Pound Ridge, New York, USA.* Photo by Bill Siever.

Page 180, *Air bubbles in ice, Bartholomew's Cobble, Sheffield, Massachusetts, USA.* Photo by Amy Siever.

Pages 184 & 189, *Flowers and vines growing on trunk, Innisfree Garden, Millbrook, New York, USA.* Photo by Karyn Samuelson.

Pages 194 & 200, *Spring view of Bath, Somerset, UK.* Photo by Amy Siever.

Page 207, *Terraces covering the hills of eastern Gansu Province, China.* Photo by Tom Christensen.

Page 214, *Buddhist cairns along Qinghai Lake, China.* Photo by Thomas Christensen.

Author Credits

Introduction—Environmental Law and Sustainability
by **Jonathan Z. CANNON**
University of Virginia School of Law

Biotechnology Legislation
by **Catherine RHODES**
University of Manchester (United Kingdom)

Cap-and-Trade Legislation
by **John C. DERNBACH**
Widener University Law School

Chemicals Legislation and Policy
by **Georg KARLAGANIS**
United Nations Institute for Training and Research (UNITAR)
and **Franz Xaver PERREZ**
Ambassador, Federal Office for the Environment, Switzerland

Common Heritage of Mankind Principle
by **Prue TAYLOR**
University of Auckland (New Zealand)

Customary International Law
by **John Martin GILLROY**
Lehigh University

Environmental Law—Africa, Saharan
by **Lisa GOLDMAN**
Environmental Law Institute

Environmental Law—Africa, Sub-Saharan
by **Louis J. KOTZÉ** and **Werner SCHOLTZ**
North West University (South Africa)

Environmental Law—Antarctica
by **Alan D. HEMMINGS**
University of Canterbury (New Zealand)

Environmental Law—Arab Region
by **Tarek MAJZOUB**
Beirut Arab University (Lebanon)
and **Fabienne Quilleré-MAJZOUB**
University of Rennes 1 (France)

Environmental Law—The Arctic
by **Timo Koivurova**
University of Lapland (Finland)

Environmental Law—Australia and New Zealand
by **Susan SHEARING**
University of Sydney (Australia)
and **Vernon TAVA**
University of Auckland (New Zealand)

Environmental Law—Central America and the Caribbean
by **José Juan GONZÁLEZ MÁRQUEZ**
Metropolitan Autonomous University (Mexico)

Environmental Law—China
by **Jingjing LIU** and **Adam MOSER**
Vermont Law School

Environmental Law—East Asia
by **Jeffrey BROADBENT** and **Yu-Ju CHIEN**
University of Minnesota

Koichi HASEGAWA
University of Tohoku (Japan)
Dowan KU
Environment and Society Research Institute (South Korea)
Taehyun PARK
Kangwon University (South Korea)
and **Jun JIN**
Tsinghua University (China)

Environmental Law—Europe
by **Thilo MARAUHN** and **Ayse Martina BOEHRINGER**
University of Giessen (Germany)

Environmental Law—India and Pakistan
by **Armin ROSENCRANZ**
Stanford University
and **Dominic J. Nardi, Jr.**
University of Michigan

Environmental Law—Pacific Island Region
by **Justin Gregory ROSE**
University of the South Pacific (Fiji)

Environmental Law—Russia and Central Asia
by **Irina KRASNOVA**
Moscow State Academy of Law (Russia)
Dinara ZIGANSHINA
University of Dundee (United Kingdom)
and **Bakhtiyor R. MUKHAMMADIEV**
United States Embassy, Tashkent (Uzbekistan)

Environmental Law—South America
by **Renata Campetti AMARAL, Alejandra BUGNA, Gustavo BORUCHOWICZ, Alessandro De Franceschi DA CRUZ, Antonio ORTUZAR, Jr., María Eugenia REYES, María Victoria ROMERO,** and **Cristina RUEDA**

Baker & McKenzie, branches in various cities (São Paolo, Buenos Aires, and Porto Allegre, Brazil; Santiago, Chile; Caracas, Venezuela; and Bogotá, Colombia)

Environmental Law—Southeast Asia
by **Dominic J. Nardi Jr.**
University of Michigan
Sansanee DHANASARNSOMBAT
ENHESA Inc. (United States)
James KHO
Ateneo de Manila University School of Government (The Philippines)
KOH Kheng-Lian and **LYE Lin Heng**
National University of Singapore
Chit Chit MYINT
SEEgreen (Myanmar)
and **Deny SIDHARTA**
Soemadipradja & Taher (Indonesia)

Environmental Law—United States and Canada
by **John Martin GILLROY**
Lehigh University
and **Rebecca M. BRATSPIES**
City University of New York School of Law

Intergenerational Equity
by **Bryan G. NORTON**
Georgia Institute of Technology

International Law
by **Jon M. VAN DYKE**
University of Hawaii

Investment Law, Energy
by **Peter CAMERON** and **Abba KOLO**
University of Dundee (United Kingdom)

Investment Law, Foreign
by **Kate MILES**
University of Sydney (Australia)

Law of the Sea
by **David FREESTONE**
The George Washington University Law School

Natural Resources Law
by **Eric T. FREYFOGLE**
University of Illinois College of Law

Nanotechnology Legislation
by **David AZOULAY**
Center for International Environmental Law

Nuisance Law
by **Eric T. FREYFOGLE**
University of Illinois College of Law

Polluter Pays Principle
by **Gerhard ROLLER**
University of Applied Sciences (Germany)

Precautionary Principle
by **A. Karim AHMED**
National Council for Science and the Environment

Real Property Law
by **Anastasia TELESETSKY**
University of Idaho College of Law

Silent Spring
by **Michael D. SIMS**
Independent scholar, Eugene, Oregon

Tort Law
by **Arden ROWELL**
University of Illinois College of Law

Transboundary Water Law
by **Patricia WOUTERS** and **Ruby MOYNIHAN**
University of Dundee (United Kingdom)

United Nations—Overview of Conventions and Agreements
by **Erik PELLANDER**
University of Cologne (Germany)

Utilities Regulation
by **Joel Barry EISEN**
University of Richmond School of Law

Waste Shipment Law
by **Thomas ORMOND**
Regional government of South Hesse (Germany)

Water Use and Rights
by **Sue CAVILL** and **M. SOHAIL**
Loughborough University (United Kingdom)

World Constitutionalism
by **Loretta Annelise FERIS**
University of Cape Town (South Africa)

This **BERKSHIRE** *Essentials* book was distilled from the

Berkshire Encyclopedia of Sustainability VOLUMES 1–10

Knowledge to Transform Our Common Future

In the 10-volume *Berkshire Encyclopedia of Sustainability*, experts around the world provide authoritative coverage of the growing body of knowledge about ways to restore the planet. Focused on solutions, this interdisciplinary print and online publication draws from the natural, physical, and social sciences—geophysics, engineering, and resource management, to name a few—and from philosophy and religion. The result is a unified, organized, and peer-reviewed resource on sustainability that connects academic research to real world challenges and provides a balanced, trustworthy perspective on global environmental challenges in the 21st century.

Ray C. Anderson

General Editor

Sara G. Beavis, Klaus Bosselmann, Robin Kundis Craig, Michael L. Dougherty, Daniel S. Fogel, Sarah E. Fredericks, Tirso Gonzales, Willis Jenkins, Louis Kotzé, Chris Laszlo, Jingjing Liu, Stephen Morse, John Copeland Nagle, Bruce Pardy, Sony Pellissery, J.B. Ruhl, Oswald J. Schmitz, Lei Shen, William K. Smith, Ian Spellerberg, Shirley Thompson, Daniel E. Vasey, Gernot Wagner, Peter J. Whitehouse

Editors

10 VOLUMES • 978-1-933782-01-0
Price: US$1500 • 6,084 pages • 8½ × 11"

"This is undoubtedly the most important and readable reference on sustainability of our time"

—Jim MacNeill, Secretary-General of the Brundtland Commission and chief architect and lead author of *Our Common Future* (1984–1987)

"The call we made in *Our Common Future*, back in 1987, is even more relevant today. Having a coherent resource like the *Encyclopedia of Sustainability*, written by experts yet addressed to students and general readers, is a vital step, because it will support education, enable productive debate, and encourage informed public participation as we join, again and again, the effort to transform our common future

—Gro Harlem Brundtland, chair of the World Commission on Environment and Development and three-time prime minister of Norway

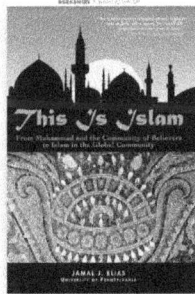

www.ingramcontent.com/pod-product-compliance
Lightning Source LLC
Chambersburg PA
CBHW080526220326
41599CB00032B/6214